Vergil's *Aeneid* and the Roman Self

🙶 🙶 🙶

Vergil's *Aeneid*

AND THE

Roman Self

ʊ̄ʂ ʊ̄ʂ ʊ̄ʂ

Subject and Nation in Literary Discourse

Yasmin Syed

THE UNIVERSITY OF MICHIGAN PRESS

ANN ARBOR

First paperback edition 2022
Copyright © 2005 by the University of Michigan
All rights reserved

For questions or permissions, please contact um.press.perms@umich.edu

Published in the United States of America by the
University of Michigan Press
Printed and bound by CPI Group (UK) Ltd, Croydon, CR0 4YY

A CIP catalog record for this book is available from the British Library.

Library of Congress Cataloging-in-Publication data has been applied for.

First published November 2022
Syed, Yasmin, 1964–
 Vergil's Aeneid and the Roman self : subject and nation in literary
discourse / Yasmin Syed.
   p. cm.
 Based on the author's thesis (Ph.D.—University of California).
 Includes bibliographic references (p.) and index.
 ISBN 0-472-11432-8 (alk. paper)
 1. Virgin. Aeneis. 2. Epic poetry, Latin—Latin—History and criticism.
3. Aeneas (Legendary
 character) in literature. 4. Identity (Psychology) in literature. 5. National
characteristics,
 Roman. 6. Literature and society—Rome. 7. Group identity in
literature. 8. Ethnic groups
 in literature. 9. Authors and readers—Rome. 10. Sex role in literature.
11. Self in literature.
 I. Title.
 PA6825.S94 2005
 873'.01—dc22   2004058002

ISBN: 978-0-472-11432-0 (Hardcover : alk paper)
ISBN: 978-0-472-02569-5 (ebook)
ISBN: 978-0-472-03916-6 (pbk : alk. paper)

Coniugi carissimo
parentibusque carissimis

Acknowledgments

This book began as a PhD dissertation at the University of California, Berkeley. I owe a debt of gratitude to many people who have generously devoted their time to reading parts of the manuscript in its various stages and giving many suggestions for improvement. All remaining flaws are all my own. I would like to thank my original dissertation committee, Shadi Bartsch, Mark Griffith, and Erich Gruen, for their constant support, stimulating insights, and diligent supervision of the dissertation. The Andrew W. Mellon Foundation provided me with financial support while I was at Berkeley. I would also like to thank Stanford University for a year of academic leave I was granted in 2001–2, which allowed me to work intensively on the manuscript. My sincere thanks also go to Alessandro Barchiesi, Maurizio Bettini, Gian Biagio Conte, Denis Feeney, Laura Gibbs, Kate Gilhuly, Sander Goldberg, Ralph Hexter, Stephen Hinds, Leslie Kurke, Kathleen McCarthy, Susan Stephens, Haley Way, and Michael Wigodsky, who read and commented on portions of the manuscript at various points. I am especially grateful to Tom Habinek, Stephen Harrison, John Henderson, and three anonymous readers at The University of Michigan Press, who read the whole manuscript and to whom I owe many substantial improvements. Finally, I owe my greatest debt to Trevor Murphy, who read the manuscript at every stage, and without whose support I could not have written it in the first place.

Contents

Abbreviations

All journal abbreviations used in the notes and bibliography follow the conventions of *L'Année Philologique.*

ANRW   Haase, W., and H. Temporini, eds. *Aufstieg und Niedergang der römischen Welt.* Berlin 1972–99.

Enc. Virg.   *Enciclopedia Virgiliana.* Rome 1984–91.

LIMC   *Lexicon Iconographicum Mythologiae Classicae.* Zurich 1981–99.

Lewis & Short   Lewis, C., and C. Short. 1879. *A New Latin Dictionary.* New York.

OLD   *Oxford Latin Dictionary.* 1968–82.

RE   Wissowa, G., and W. Kroll, K. Mittelhaus, K. Ziegler, K. Witte, W. John, eds. 1893–1980. *Paulys Real-Encyclopädie der classischen Altertums wissenschaft,* Neue Bearbeitung. Munich.

Introduction to the Second Edition

Several Egyptian papyri from the late first to early second centuries AD give us insight into a curious aspect of acculturation in the Roman Empire. These papyri contain what appear to be school exercises in language acquisition: lines from a famous Latin poem, glossed with Greek translations in facing columns.[1] This evidence of language acquisition of Latin suggests that—although the language of administration in the Greek East of the Roman Empire was Greek—some people in the Greek-speaking East seem to have found it desirable to acquire a facility in Latin. It may not come as a surprise to many of my readers that among the texts most commonly glossed and used in such contexts is Vergil's *Aeneid*. The very fact that this is not surprising speaks to the extent to which we already know that reading Vergil's *Aeneid* was for many people in the Roman Empire synonymous with inhabiting a sense of identity as a Roman.

But however obvious this fact may seem to us, it does nevertheless bear thinking about. Why should it be this particular poem that played this role in this cultural context? Homer's poems—which played the same role for ancient Greek culture—stand at the beginning of Greek literature and continued to perform the same role throughout antiquity. The Romans, on the other hand, abandoned Ennius's *Annales* as the text central to school education, the poem every literate person would know, and adopted the *Aeneid* instead. Education being a strictly private business in antiquity, no emperor could have forced any teacher to adopt a new text for this purpose, however pleasing the subject matter of the poem must have been to

---

1. Dickey (2015), Scappaticcio (2010).

Augustus. The shift from Ennius to Vergil was therefore voluntary. It was also fairly swift and ultimately unanimous.[2]

Nor is the adoption of Vergil's poem as a main go-to text for learning Latin obvious from a modern utilitarian perspective. Nowadays the teaching of modern Spanish, for instance, is not based on reading Cervantes. It is not even based on any other one specific, more contemporary author. Despite the logistical disadvantages of the ancient world in achieving such cultural consensus when compared with our modern world with its technological connectedness, Vergil was everywhere, from the frontiers of the Roman Empire in Britain to its provinces in the much more ancient cultures of the empire's East. It was not, then, utilitarian factors or ease of access that drove the centrality of the *Aeneid* in the educational canon of antiquity for speakers of Latin as well as Greek. Apart from its obvious literary merit, the *Aeneid* must have held a compelling appeal to both readers and teachers, such that it became central in the popular imagination, powerfully associated with Roman cultural identity. As Homer's poems embodied and defined a cultural identity for Greek readers throughout antiquity, so Vergil's *Aeneid* performed the cultural work of creating Roman cultural identity. The present study is an exploration of the poem from the perspective of this cultural context. As such, I approach the poem at least partly from an anthropological perspective.

When I started writing this book I wanted to understand more fully how the poem's Roman readers thought about themselves as Romans and how this poem affected their conceptions of Roman identity. My interest lay in the processes of acculturation that made the *Aeneid* a leading factor in creating a sense of common identity for the empire's inhabitants, as well as in the poem's textual strategies for forging this identity. The proem of the *Aeneid* tells us that we are to hear about the origin story of Rome, and about the toils and sufferings involved in "founding the Roman people" (*tantae molis erat Romanam condere gentem*). The proem also juxtaposes Rome with the city of Carthage, which is set up as Rome's rival from the very beginning. These two themes show that Roman identity is indeed among the explicitly

---

2. Although direct evidence of Vergil's role in school curricula of the late first century BC and the early first century AD throughout the empire is hard to come by, Gwynne (1926, 153–57) and especially Suerbaum (2012) marshal a rich array of references suggesting that even during that period Vergil was swiftly replacing earlier authors. The transition from Ennius to Vergil was probably slower in the outer regions of the empire than it was in Rome itself; Vergeest (1950, 33ff). By the time for which we do have ample evidence Vergil had already become canonical.

stated themes of the poem, and that this identity will emerge from Rome's relationship with Carthage, that Carthage will play a major role in establishing Roman identity in this poem. Since the entire action of the plot is set in a time before Rome even existed, and no exemplary Roman is set up here as a guide for what it means to be Roman, representations of different ethnicities in the poem are vital to the poem's construction of Roman identity. The poem's constellation of characters with different ethnicities, and their complex juxtapositions allowed ancient readers to forge their own versions of Roman identity within the poem's ethnic parameters. The love story of Dido and Aeneas draws the issue of gender into the poem's construction of identity. The poem's use of gender and ethnicity, therefore, are central themes of this study. I have also focused on the point of view adopted in the narrative of book 1, or to put it differently, the construction of the reader's gaze, as a foundational tool of the poet in establishing the reader's sense of identity. For instance, the way Aeneas sees Carthage for the first time is how the reader sees it, and we view the images on Juno's temple in Carthage through the eyes and with the emotions of Aeneas.

At the time of its first publication in 2005 the major themes of the present study—the poem's treatment of gender and ethnicity, and the creation of a subject position for the reader through the poem's handling of the reader's gaze—were underrepresented in Vergilian scholarship. In the forty years previous, much of American scholarship on Vergil's *Aeneid* had concentrated on the question of Vergil's attitude to Augustus and to Roman imperialism. In the wake of critiques of modern American imperialism in the context of the Vietnam War, many American Vergil scholars argued that Vergil spoke with two voices in the *Aeneid*, one overtly positive and Augustan, and the other, underlying it, pessimistic and critical of Augustanism. This focus was necessarily trained on the poet's intentions as the source of meaning of the poem. My focus on the poem's role in the formation of Roman identity among its readers was not a mainstream issue in Vergilian scholarship in 2005. In the sixteen years since the book's first publication, however, Vergilian studies have undergone a major shift. Whereas the focus of my book needed justification in 2005, the issues addressed here have since been picked up in numerous more recent studies of the *Aeneid*. This preface to the second edition gives me the opportunity to briefly mention a few monographs published in the interim that pertain specifically to themes addressed in this book.[3]

---

3. The following discussion of recent scholarship on themes addressed in this book cannot by any means do justice to the rich and complex discussions currently taking place among

　　Among the books published after 2005 and concerned with similar top-
ics is Reed (2007). Reed's study, like mine, deals with issues of gender,
ethnicity, and the gaze in the *Aeneid*; the main difference between it and
the present study lies in Reed's focus, acknowledged in the book title *Vir-
gil's Gaze*, on the poet's intentions as a source of meaning. As such, his
study remained in the more traditional orbit of Vergilian scholarship in
that it did not escape the question of Vergil's attitude toward Augustus or
toward Roman imperialism that had animated Vergilian scholarship in the
forty years previous. In contrast, my interest lies not so much in Vergil's
intentions, that is, what Vergil wanted or did not want to say, or in what
he thought about Augustus, but in what the poem may have meant to its
readers, and how it may have shaped their sense of identity as Romans.
This distinction is not trivial. It shifts the focus from the personal (Vergil
and Augustus) to the cultural (Roman readers of the *Aeneid* as a society of
Romans "learning" how to be Roman). Ancient Roman readers derived
a sense of cultural identity—and therefore actively generated meaning—
from the poem for a long time after the deaths of both Vergil and Augus-
tus. It also means that I did not assume that Vergil's attitude to Augustus or
Augustus's intentions for the *Aeneid* can be deduced from the poem itself,
any more safely than ancient readers' receptions of the poem, which are the
focus of my discussion.

　　More closely aligned with my goals in this book, but coming from the
cultural context of performative Roman religion, is Florence Dupont's
2011 book on Roman identity, which incorporates the *Aeneid* in its argu-
ment. Despite the difference in focus with regard to the poem's cultural
context—religion as opposed to education—I share with her the out-
look of taking seriously aspects of the poem's cultural context other than
its political bent vis-à-vis Augustanism. Like Dupont, I treat the *Aeneid*
as a "complex anthropological object, like every other cultural practice,"
rather than plumbing its depths of meaning as a literary masterpiece.[4]
The first part of the present study lays out my focus on the *Aeneid* as a
cultural agent acting upon ancient audiences, and its role in establishing
a sense of identity for its readers. My argument in this part of the book
is based on ancient theories of rhetoric, concerning the power of poetry
over the minds of its audiences, as well as the sociocultural contexts of

---

scholars, and should be taken only as a sampling of some recent additions to these debates.
For issues pertaining to Vergilian studies, I would refer readers to the Vergil bibliography
published every year in the journal *Vergilius*.

　　4. Dupont (2011, 17).

reading the *Aeneid* in antiquity. This argument can now be supplemented by reference to Suerbaum (2012), an article on the processes of the canonization of Vergil in antiquity; and to Wiseman (2015), whose argument about Roman performance culture suggests that Roman literature—far from being an elite activity performed primarily before small upper class audiences—actually reached wide audiences by means of public readings of literary works.

My argument in this book about the *Aeneid's* construction of Roman identity is, among other things, a contribution to exploring processes of acculturation in the Roman Empire. Ancient historians have long been interested in such processes. An important recent treatment of the topic of Roman identity from the perspective of cultural history is Dench (2005), published in the same year as the first edition of the present book. In older scholarship, historians used to conceive of the concept of a shared identity in the Roman Empire in terms of *Romanization*, assuming that Rome's subject nations assimilated to Roman identity as something foreign and imposed. More recently scholars have taken into account general theories of state formation, arguing, for instance, that social cohesion and ideological integration of subject nations and their conquerors can be achieved by generating "consensus grounded in trust."[5] For Vanacker and Zuiderhoek (2017), the formation of Roman identity consisted, at least partly, in achieving a sense of belonging to the culture and polity of the Roman Empire. As I argue in the present study, the prominence of the *Aeneid* in education shows that the poem was an important vehicle of acculturation. Knowledge of the *Aeneid* was one of the means by which inhabitants of the Roman Empire achieved a sense of belonging. With respect to ethnic identities, for instance, the poem's representations of a multiplicity of ethnic groups signaled to its ancient readers—consisting of a multiethnic mix of the empire's inhabitants—that envisaging a common Roman identity was possible.

One important underlying assumption in this book is that notions of self, other, and the emotions are not universal but culturally constructed. Recent books about the ancient self more generally include Bartsch (2006) and Sorabji (2006); both, like Foucault (1986), are without reference to Vergil. An important recent general study of modes of alterity in antiquity is Gruen (2010). In the context of the theme of self and other in ancient thinking it is worth mentioning two general studies on the unconscious

---

5. Padilla Peralta (2020, 8).

in antiquity and the relationship of psychoanalysis to classical studies by Oliensis (2009) and Keenan (2019). A more general study of the gaze in ancient epic is Lovatt (2013), who also coedited a collection of articles on the same topic in the same year.[6] Smith's study of visuality in the *Aeneid* was published, like mine, in 2005. Polleichtner (2009) and Fletcher (2014) are two recent studies on the topic of the emotions in the *Aeneid*, both paying attention to the emotions of Aeneas. Fletcher's discussion of Aeneas's emotions pertains to the hero's love of Italy, intertwining the theme of the emotions in literary discourse with that of colonization and city foundation. Fratantuono (2007) examines the connection between madness and Roman identity as it manifests itself in the *Aeneid*. Hardie (2016) is a collection of essays by several scholars on the irrational in Augustan poetry. Cairns and Nelis (2017) is a collection of articles on discourses of the emotions in antiquity.

On the topic of gender in Roman epic there is now Pyy (2021). McAuley (2016) is a discussion of motherhood in Vergil and a few other Roman poets. James and Dillon (2012) have a section on women in the Augustan period, including a discussion of Vergil's Dido. Among other recent volumes on gender in antiquity are Lateiner et al. (2013) and Skinner (2014). On the topic of ethnicity, Giusti (2018) is a study of Carthage in the *Aeneid*. There is also an interesting volume on the role of Carthage as the ethnic other in the Roman popular imagination more generally in *Classical Philology*,[7] which has an introduction by Denis Feeney and contains both historical and literary perspectives.[8] Among other titles on Roman identity Rantala (2019) and Alston and Spentzou (2011) are collections of articles, some of which specifically pertain to notions of gender or subjectivity in antiquity.

Because of its concern with gender, ethnicity, and questions of identity in the context of Roman imperialism, the present study has sometimes been seen in the context of postcolonial studies.[9] I would, however, alert the reader that my approach to literary theory has been consciously eclectic. Theoretical frameworks such as structuralism, deconstruction, reader response theory, postcolonial theory, gender theory, film theory, and psychoanalytic theory have influenced my thinking pertaining to this project, but I have steered clear of theoretical purity as a goal.

---

6. Lovatt & Vout (2013).

7. 112, n.3 (2017).

8. See also my chapter on literary depictions of the ethnic other in Harrison (2004).

9. Perkell 2013. See also my entry on postcolonialism and the *Aeneid* in Thomas & Ziolkowski (2013).

BIBLIOGRAPHY

Alston, R. and E. Spentzou. eds. 2011. *Reflections of Romanity: Discourses of Subjectivity in Imperial Rome*. Columbus, OH.

Bartsch, S. 2006. *The Mirror of the Self: Sexuality, Self-Knowledge, and the Gaze in the Early Roman Empire*. Chicago.

Becker, E.-M. and S. Scholz. eds. 2012. *Kanon in Construktion und Dekonstruktion: Kanonisierungsprozesse religiöser Texte von der Antike bis zur Gegenwart. Ein Handbuch*. Berlin.

Cairns, D. and D. Nelis. eds. 2017. *Emotions in the Classical World: Methods, Approaches, and Directions*. Stuttgart.

Dench, E. 2005. *Romulus' Asylum: Roman Identities from the Age of Alexander to the Age of Hadrian*. Oxford.

Dickey, E. 2015. "Columnar Translation: An Ancient Interpretive Tool the Romans Gave the Greeks." *CQ*, n.s., 65(2): 807–21.

Dupont, F. 2011. *Rome, la Ville Sans Origine. L'Énéide: Un Grand Récit du Métissage?* Paris.

Fletcher, K. F. B. 2014. *Finding Italy: Travel, Nation and Colonization in Vergil's* Aeneid. Ann Arbor.

Fratantuono, L. 2007. *Madness Unchained: A Reading of Virgil's* Aeneid. Lanham, MD.

Giusti, E. 2018. *Carthage in Virgil's* Aeneid: *Staging the Enemy under Augustus*. Cambridge.

Gruen, E. 2010. *Rethinking the Other in Antiquity*. Princeton.

Gwynn, A. 1926. *Roman Education from Cicero to Quintilian*. Oxford.

Hardie, P. R. 2016. *Augustan Poetry and the Irrational*. Oxford.

Harrison, S. J. ed. 2004. *Blackwell Companion to Latin Literature*. Oxford.

James, S. and S. Dillon. eds. 2012. *A Companion to Women in the Ancient World*. Blackwell Companions to the Ancient World. Chichester.

Keenan, V. L. 2019. *The Ancient Unconscious: Psychoanalysis and the Ancient Text*. Oxford.

Lateiner, D., B. K. Gold, and J. Perkins. eds. 2013. *Roman Literature, Gender and Its Reception: Domina Illustris*. New York.

Lovatt, H. 2013. *The Epic Gaze: Vision, Gender and Narrative in Ancient Epic*. Cambridge.

Lovatt, H. and C. Vout. eds. 2013. *Epic Visions: Visuality in Greek and Latin Epic and Its Reception*. Cambridge.

McAuley, M. 2016. *Reproducing Rome: Motherhood in Virgil, Ovid, Seneca and Statius*. Oxford.

Oliensis, E. 2009. *Freud's Rome: Psychoanalysis and Latin Poetry*. Roman Literature and Its Contexts. Cambridge.

Padilla Peralta, D. 2020. *Divine Institutions: Religions and Community in the Middle Roman Republic*. Princeton.

Perkell, C. 2013. "Critical Theory." In Thomas and Ziolkowski.

Polleichtner, W. 2009. *Emotional Questions: Vergil, the Emotions, and the Transformation of Epic Poetry. An Analysis of Select Scenes*. Bochumer altertumswissenschaftliches Colloquium 82. Trier.

Pyy, E. 2021. *Women and War in Roman Epic. The Language of Classical Literature.* vol. 33. Leiden.

Rantala, J. ed. 2019. *Gender, Memory, and Identity in the Roman World.* Amsterdam.

Reed, J. D. 2007. *Virgil's Gaze: Nation and Poetry in the* Aeneid. Princeton.

Scappaticcio, M. C. 2010. "Tra Ecdotica e Performance: per un *Corpus Papyrorum Vergilianarum*," *APF* 56(1): 130–48.

Skinner, M. B. 2014. *Sexuality in Greek and Roman Culture.* 2nd ed. Malden, MA.

Smith, R. A. 2005. *The Primacy of Vision in Vergil's* Aeneid. Austin.

Sorabji, R. 2006. *Self: Ancient and Modern Insights About Individuality, Life, and Death.* Chicago.

Suerbaum, W. 2012. "Der Anfangsprozess der 'Kanonisierung' Vergils." In ed. by Becker and Scholz, 171–221.

Syed, Y. 2004. "Romans and Others." In ed. by Harrison, 360–71.

Syed. 2013. "Postcolonialism." In ed. by Thomas and Ziolkowski.

Thomas, R. F., and J. Ziolkowski. eds. 2013. *The Virgil Encyclopedia.* 3 vols. Malden, MA.

Vanacker, W. and A. Zuiderhoek. eds. 2017. *Imperial Identities in the Roman World.* Abingdon, Oxon.

Vergeest, A. 1950. *Poetarum Enarratio: Leraren en Schoolauteurs te Rome van Cicero tot Quintilianus.* Diss. Nijmegen.

Wiseman, T. P. 2015. *The Roman Audience: Classical Literature as Social History.* Oxford.

Introduction

If there is any literary work that embodied and defined a cultural identity for the readers of its time, it is Vergil's *Aeneid*. When I started writing this book I wanted to understand more fully how the poem's Roman readers thought about themselves as Romans and how this poem affected their conceptions of Roman identity. The time was ripe for an analysis of this kind. Recent classical scholarship has shown an increasing interest in ancient conceptions of identity, subjectivity, and the self. Scholars have approached these issues from a variety of contexts and with a number of theoretical frameworks. Studies of gender and ethnicity in the ancient world are as much a part of an exploration of ancient conceptions of identity as are studies concerned with the construction of the self in literary texts. Much work has been done, for instance, on ancient conceptualizations of sexuality and gender.[1] In the area of Roman literature there are numerous studies concerned with gender and sexuality.[2] There is also an increased interest in questions of ethnic identity in antiquity.[3] This renewed interest in the ancient self is the result of modern concerns such as contemporary interest in the issues of gender, ethnicity, and identity in general, as well as modern theories of the self, such as psychoanalysis.

For several reasons, Vergil's *Aeneid* is an important text for the study of the history of the ancient self. The self-consciously new national epic of the Roman Empire, written at perhaps the most significant political turning point in Rome's development from republic to autocracy, the poem stands at a historical and cultural watershed. Culturally, the Augustan Age is an interesting time in the history of the ancient self because it is situated at the end of the Hellenistic period in which ancient conceptions of the self underwent a gradual transformation from a more socially determined model relevant for the *polis* culture of Classical Greece to one determined more by internal experience in the Roman imperial period.

What is interesting about the *Aeneid* is that it fuses an interest in the inner workings of the self with an articulation of the individual's place within the social structure. Like a Janus-headed hybrid in the history of the ancient self, the *Aeneid* looks both backward and forward in time: back to earlier conceptualizations of the self within the structures of *polis* and *res publica,* and forward to the later rising interest in the interiority of the self, as we see it, for instance, in Augustine. Both modes of conceptualization of the self are important to the *Aeneid,* and both are analyzed in this book.

An analysis of the *Aeneid* adds to our understanding of the history of the ancient self in two significant ways. First, since the *Aeneid* belongs to a period of transition in the history of the ancient self, it allows us to observe more closely how this shift took place. Secondly, as a work that speaks to the imagination, the *Aeneid* provides an important supplement to discussions based on philosophical and other theoretical texts, which discuss the ancient self more explicitly than literary texts.

The disadvantage of focusing exclusively on ancient philosophical texts is that they are interested primarily in a prescriptive definition of the ancient subject, that is, in the question of how one should govern oneself. But poetry and mythology should form a vital part of the study of ancient subjectivity, because mythology was omnipresent even to the illiterate, and because some works of poetry (such as the Homeric epics and the *Aeneid*) were so central a part of ancient education that knowledge of them was almost equivalent to literacy. Looking at mythology and epic poetry, therefore, provides us access to the stories that formed a sense of self for large sections of the population of the ancient world. An analysis of how such stories influenced the Romans' sense of self adds to more theoretical and therefore more prescriptive definitions of the subject a more descriptive one, less determined by precepts and more focused on the imagination.

The present study of Vergil's *Aeneid* is a contribution to the study of the Roman self as it is articulated in this influential poem. I argue that the *Aeneid* had a significant impact on its Roman readers' sense of self as Romans and that the poem articulated Roman identity for them through the reader's identification with and differentiation from its fictional characters. The identity articulated in the poem for the reader is conceived both as a personal and a collective identity, that is, the poem constructs its version of the reader's individual self from the constituent elements of the self and further defines this individual self in terms of collective determinants such as gender and ethnicity.

In analyzing how the poem constructs Roman identity, I focus on these two levels of identity: the individual and the collective. That is, I deal with both the level of the subject and the level of ethnicity and gender. This double focus proceeds from the textual strategies of the *Aeneid* itself: the poem intertwines collective determinants of identity with determinants of identity on the level of the subject, for instance, when a character's emotional life is linked to his/her gender and/or ethnicity. Dido and Aeneas are good examples for this linkage of the individual and the collective levels of identity. I argue that the emotional lives of both figures are linked to and motivated by their gender and ethnic identities.

The study is divided into three parts. Part 1 explores why the *Aeneid* should be seen as having had a profound influence on its Roman readers' conceptions of Roman identity. In this section I consider the power ascribed to the *Aeneid* over its audiences by ancient rhetorical and philosophical theories. Part 2 argues that the reader finds his[4] identity by sharing the gaze of some fictional characters on the events of the poem—which facilitates identification with them—and by differentiating himself from other characters who are conceived as spectacles for this gaze. In part 3 I analyze several of these figures of identification and differentiation in terms of their gender and ethnic identities to understand how these fictional figures collectively contribute to the reader's sense of identity as a Roman.

To clarify what I mean by "identity" here, let me define the terms *subject position* and *subjectivity* I will use in my analysis: every fictional text constructs a subject position for its readers, a vantage point or perspective from which to encounter the fictional world of the narrative. This subject position emerges from the way the text constructs its fictional characters, inviting readers to enter into the vantage points or emotional lives of some characters while separating them from those of others through various textual strategies. The readers' perspective on the fictional world of the *Aeneid* and their emotional response to it is shaped by their relationship to the perspectives and emotional lives of the poem's characters. An example may best illustrate this point: readers have strong emotional responses to the Dido narrative, and their reactions to that narrative are shaped by the way the text depicts Dido's emotional life. A reader's emotional reactions to Dido's story contribute to what may be called his or her subject position.

While the subject position is constructed by the text for the reader to occupy, I use the term *subjectivity*, by contrast, to denote both the reader's subject position and the way the fictional characters are constructed in the narrative, a construction that can have a powerful impact on the reader's subject position. So the term *subjectivity* is used in this book to express the relationship between the reader's sense of self and the characters of the narrative. Unlike other Vergil scholars I do not use the term *subjectivity* to discuss the poet's sympathies with his fictional characters or his outlook on the world. Instead I draw on various overlapping theoretical frameworks such as semiotics and psychoanalysis to arrive at a definition of the subject that suits the discussion of fictional characters and the impact they have on the reader's sense of self.

In my analysis of the fictional characters' subjectivities I focus on three constituent elements of the subject that are particularly important to the way the poem constructs the fictional characters, as well as the reader, as subjects. These are a character's (and reader's) gaze, emotions, and voice. Through the characters' gazes, emotions, and voices, the reader's subject position emerges as the reader's gaze on the poem's fictional world and his emotional reactions to the events of the narrative. I focus on vision or the gaze as an integral constituent element of the readers' and the characters' subjectivities, because ancient theories of poetry and the self ascribed to the visuality of poetry a special power over its audiences. Another constituent element of subjectivity I concentrate on is emotion. The emotions of some fictional characters are central to their construction as subjects. Correspondingly, the reader's emotional responses to poetry were central to ancient discussions of the effects of poetry on the self. A third constituent element of subjectivity I consider here, although not in as much detail as the other two, is the voice. Many characters of the poem are constructed primarily through their voices, rather than their gazes or emotions. It was precisely the acquisition of a voice, that is, of correct Latinity and the ability to speak publicly, which was the goal of the rhetorical education that often formed the context of the study of the powers of poetry.

I deliberately chose the term *gaze* in this study because the space the poem creates for its readers is more than a "point of view." We will see that the *Aeneid* was regarded as having the power to shape its reader's voice and emotions, through *phantasia* and the gaze, through its language, and through moral precepts. By shaping the reader's gaze, his voice, and his emotions, the poem was seen as influencing those elements of the reader's self that ancient thinking considered as central and important parts of the self, its constituent elements. But my choice of terminology in this study also shows that the questions I ask here are shaped by modern discourses and modern concerns, such as theories of the self and of identity in general.

In the following two chapters I use terms such as *gaze, desire,* and *the subject* because my modern frame of reference for inquiries into the self in literature takes many of its central concepts from psychoanalytic theory and postmodern literary criticism. These modern theories of identity are concerned with the subject, its entry into language, its gaze, and the birth of desire. In psychoanalytic theories, language and desire are associated with the emergence of the self. A baby's voice, its use of language for communication, can emerge only at the point at which it can distinguish between the self and the outside world. This same moment of recognition is also associated in psychoanalysis with the birth of desire. Hence, the emotions are again a defining element of the self.[5]

The gaze is seen as a constituent element of subjectivity in the context of psychoanalysis and film theory. For film criticism, the gaze is the defining component of the audience's subject position, because the audience takes in the visual cinematic narrative through their gazes.[6] As we see below, ancient theories of the self also consider vision or the gaze as having an important influence on the emotions and hence on the self. Ancient and modern literary theories of the gaze thus converge in assigning to the gaze a defining force for the self. This striking convergence of ancient and modern theories of the self encourages an analysis of the poem's visuality and of the fictional characters' gazes as a means of better understanding the ancient self. But it is not as a validating gesture that I make the observation of the convergence between ancient and modern theories of the self. I also do not see any continuity between ancient and modern articulations of the gaze. The ancient discourse on *phantasia* comes from a completely different milieu (rhetoric and education) than the modern discourse of psychoanalysis (science and medicine). The purposes to which the two discourses are put are completely different. Nevertheless, their convergence in assigning to the gaze a formative force for the self is striking, and it motivates the central importance of the gaze for this book's study of the self in the *Aeneid*'s characters and readers.

My interest in subjectivity in Vergil's *Aeneid* is a well-established line of inquiry in Vergilian scholarship. Critics have concerned themselves intensively with various aspects of the question of how subjectivity is expressed in the poem. Discussions have often focused, however, on the poet's voice and his sympathies with particular characters of the poem. Ever since the publication of Adam Parry's famous article, "The Two Voices of Vergil's *Aeneid*" in 1963, the voice of the poet has become a hotly debated issue.[7] Another line of inquiry into the subjectivity expressed in the poem was represented by Heinze (1928) and Otis (1964), who used the terms *Subjektivität* and *Empfindung*, or *subjective style*, to talk about the poet's voice. Otis, for instance, distinguished between the poet's empathy with his characters and his sympathy for them.[8] Conte (1986) used very similar terminology— *sympatheia* and *empatheia*—to connect this debate with the pessimist interpretation of Vergil that flourished mainly after the publication of Otis's book. Conte argued that while Vergil's *empatheia* allows multiple voices to be heard within the poem, his *sympatheia* operates as a counterforce, pulling together with a unifying voice the multiplicity of other voices and integrating them rather than allowing them to clash with each other.[9]

My focus on the gaze, the voice, and the emotions in the *Aeneid* is by no means unprecedented. Vergilian scholarship has long been interested in the poem's voices, whether critics interpreted them as expressions of the poet's intentions, as has been the tendency in much work commonly labeled Two-Voices scholarship, or as multiple and divergent perspectives on the events of the poem, as Conte has understood them in his seminal work on the *Aeneid*. Work on the poem's voices has also often been concerned with the emotions expressed in the poem by various characters and by the narrator, discussing the poet's ability to empathize with his characters and the sympathies and subjective statements he occasionally expresses.

More recently Vergil scholars have become more interested in the poem's gazes as well. Much work has been done on the ecphrastic passages of the *Aeneid*, which are among the most obvious parts of the poem in which the reader's imaginary gaze is engaged.[10] From the theoretical framework of narratology, the poem's gazes have become an object of study in Don Fowler's work, who has formulated his interest in the question "who sees" (as opposed to "who speaks") in the narratological concept of focalization.[11] Fowler's narratological approach to the poem's voices and gazes has much in common with what follows, but I will not use the terminology of narratology, because my interest in the poem's voices and gazes is psychologically and culturally motivated. Terms such as *gaze, voice, desire,* and *subjectivity* can be applied equally to the psychological makeup of fictional characters and to the elements that constitute the reader's self. Hence, they allow me to explore the relationship between the characters and their readers more easily than does the terminology of narratology. The terminology I do use, however, is not unprecedented in Vergilian scholarship, either.

Alison Keith's recent study on women in Roman epic considers the deaths of women in the *Aeneid* as an object of the reader's gaze.[12] There are other Latin authors who have recently been approached by scholars with a similar theoretical framework. Spectacle and the gaze are a central concern of Andrew Feldherr's recent study of Livy.[13] The element of spectacle and the imaginary gaze is also a topic in Ann Vasaly's work on Cicero.[14]

Interest in the *Aeneid*'s readers as producers of the poem's meaning has also been on the rise recently. On both sides of the debate about the pro- or anti-Augustan tendencies of the *Aeneid,* scholars have been interested in ancient readers' potential attitudes to the events described and the sentiments expressed in the poem. Scholars opposing the pessimist interpretation of the *Aeneid,* which has become the mainstream interpretation of Vergil in Anglophone scholarship, have often invoked the ancient reader as having sensibilities different from modern critics.[15] On the other side of the debate, scholars have increasingly turned to theoretical frameworks that empower the reader as a source of meaning. Scholars whose interest lies in the uncovering of multiple and contradictory meanings have on occasion used the theoretical framework of reader response criticism as a response to those interpretations of the poem that would limit and fix its meaning by appealing to the poet's intention as the sole source of meaning.[16] While the theoretical framework of reader response criticism gives weight particularly to the modern reader and her response to the poem as a source of meaning, Vergil scholars working within this framework have also paid meticulous attention to reconstructing, as far as possible, the possible responses of ancient readers.[17]

My own interest in the ancient readers of the *Aeneid* and the poem's effect on their sense of self as Romans stems from a desire to understand more fully, in which ways ancient Roman culture was different from our own, or to put it somewhat differently, to get to know that ancient reader more intimately in all his foreignness and idiosyncrasies in comparison to ourselves today. This project must be largely conjectural, as it cannot primarily be based on ancient evidence of readers' reactions to reading the *Aeneid.* Instead, I suggest how the *Aeneid* shaped Roman identity based first on ancient theories of the power of poetry over its readers' selves (part 1), and secondly on my analysis of the construction of the reader's identity in the *Aeneid* (parts 2 and 3).

My study proceeds from the assumption that the *Aeneid* shaped the reader's sense of self by various textual strategies that establish a relationship between the reader and the fictional characters. It is therefore necessary to make some remarks about the way I treat character as a critical category in this study. Contemporary criticism of the modern novel has two ways of looking at the concept of character in narrative. A more conventional way of conceiving of the characters of a novel is to treat them as entities that could have an existence prior to and independent of the text. The concern of such criticism is primarily whether the novelist accomplishes a rounded portrait of a person that could exist in the real world. Bound up as this approach is with the realism of the European novel, it has come under attack by postmodern critics who emphasize that what is called a character in a narrative is indeed no more than the sum total of those passages of the narrative that are concerned with that figure, that to treat the text as if it were reflecting a figure that could exist outside the text is to buy into the fiction of classic realism.[18]

When we approach the texts of the ancient world with this theoretical framework, we must take into account the differences between those ancient texts and the modern novel for which these theories of character have been developed. One difference between the modern novel and the *Aeneid* that seems to me important is that, unlike Jane Austen's Emma Woodhouse or Tolstoy's Anna Karenina, the figures we encounter in this poem do have an existence outside the poem, in the literary and historical texts of other ancient writers, and in the mythological imaginations of ancient readers. As mythological figures associated with the early history of Rome, the characters of the *Aeneid* were to ancient readers more historical and therefore more "real" than they can be to us today.

This is not to deny the fictionality of the poem, but it does mean that the portrait that emerges from the *Aeneid* of any given character must be seen in the context of other depictions of this character in Greek and Roman literature and of other uses a mythological figure was put to in ancient culture, such as its depiction in art or its use in religious and political contexts, such as coinage. Many of the mythological figures of the *Aeneid* were, in the eyes of ancient readers, familiar symbols with a life of their own, a history, and even a historical reality. This is an important point for my argument, because the kind of identification I imagine ancient readers experienced when reading the *Aeneid* was embedded in a well-established cultural practice of identifying with such mythological figures in contexts far removed from literary pursuits. When Alexander the Great or Pyrrhus of Epirus identified with Achilles, they did so because of their familiarity with the *Iliad,* but such identification went beyond the fancy of a literary connoisseur; it had personal and political meaning. It is this personal and political dimension of identification with mythological figures that makes the following study of *Aeneid* characters and their relationship to the reader's sense of self of significance for Roman culture more generally.

PART I

THE *AENEID*

AND

ROMAN IDENTITY

છક છક છક

CHAPTER I

Vergil's *Aeneid* in
Roman Imperial Culture

ஃ THE INFLUENCE OF THE *AENEID* ON THE ANCIENT SELF

Chapters 3 to 8 of this book attempt to show how Vergil's *Aeneid* constructs a subject position for its readers within the poem and articulates a Roman identity for them. The first two chapters argue that this poem's construction of the reader and its articulation of Roman identity was of particular relevance to the Romans' sense of self generally, and to their understanding of what it meant to be Roman. Hence, any insights we gain from the subsequent literary analysis of the *Aeneid*'s construction of the reader and of Roman identity must be seen in the context of the arguments of the first two chapters. In other words, the *Aeneid*'s articulation of Roman identity is not just a literary issue, but has an impact on the Romans' cultural identity. How large this impact was, that is, how relevant the poem was to Roman cultural identity, is suggested in the following pages.

The pervasive presence of Vergil's *Aeneid* in Roman culture from its publication to the end of antiquity is well known and can be documented in several contexts. Even during his lifetime Vergil was taught in school by Q. Caecilius Epirota.[1] The impact of the *Aeneid* on subsequent poetry was immediate and so pervasive that an account of it would fill several books. Already for Ovid the poem was among the most important works of Roman literature.[2] Vergil's impact in rhetorical circles only one generation after his death is documented by Seneca the Elder, who reports several declaimers who imitated Vergilian lines in their speeches and discusses such imitations for instructional purposes.[3]

Lines from Vergil are quoted in graffiti from Pompeii and elsewhere.[4] The ability of graffiti writers to reproduce lines from the *Aeneid* is often used by scholars to make conjectures about the levels of literacy in different social strata of Roman imperial society; they are taken as evidence of a widespread firsthand experience of the text itself, among the literate at least.[5] In another instance, scholars even conjecture that the presence of *Aeneid* graffiti in a certain location indicates the presence of a school there.[6] For these reasons scholars suggest that literacy and knowledge of the *Aeneid* may have gone hand in hand for many inhabitants of the Roman Empire, at least in the non-Greek-speaking provinces.[7]

Even in the Greek-speaking provinces conceptions of Roman identity were tied to Vergil's epic. The evidence of the corpus of Latin papyri from Egypt suggests that reading *Aeneid* passages formed part of instruction in the Latin language there. Many texts in this corpus are quotes of passages from the *Aeneid,* some of them bilingual, in the form of word-for-word text and translation.[8] Other epigraphic evidence for knowledge of the *Aeneid* comes primarily from tombstones. Vergil is the most popular author to be adapted on epitaphs. Indeed, of all Latin authors Vergil is most often quoted as well as most often adapted in verse in epigraphic documents.[9]

Knowledge of the *Aeneid* could extend to the uneducated, too.[10] Public recitations of the *Aeneid* were common even in late antiquity. *Aeneid* stories, such as that of Dido, were frequently performed in the theater and were among the most popular subjects in art.[11] Lines from Vergil's poetry had entered everyday language in the form of proverbs.[12] Among the well educated, recitals of epic could form part of dinner entertainment or command an audience in their own right. The proper manner of reciting epic was taught to boys in school as a preparation for proper comportment in their later oratorical activities.[13]

Reciting the *Aeneid* was a central and often repeated experience in a Roman boy's education. It was therefore not uncommon to know Vergil's works by heart in their entirety. It is in the climate of such knowledge of the poems that we encounter the genre of Vergilian centos, poems composed entirely of lines and half-lines from Vergilian poetry, but treating topics ranging from the religious to the obscene.[14] Most centos are from late antiquity, but they show the kind of familiarity with classical authors like Vergil that was the goal of instruction in the Roman school throughout the imperial period. Indeed, many authors of centos were grammarians, the teachers of the standard first stage of Roman education outside the home.[15]

The existence of commentaries on Vergil's poetry, such as that of Servius, also illustrate how important his works were at this stage of Roman education. Such commentaries were concerned with issues that were likely to be helpful to the *grammaticus* in teaching. They provide the exposition or exegesis that forms part of the grammarian's instruction: explanations of facts, rhetorical figures, and issues of scansion. They also discuss issues of correct language usage, which was among the most important goals of the grammarian's instruction.[16] Other works written by grammarians quote Vergil frequently, as do some rhetorical works. Use of Vergil in rhetorical works reflects his importance in rhetorical education, the next stage of education after the school of the *grammaticus*.[17]

Vergil's works were not only seen as a standard for correct Latinity, but were also thought to contain all wisdom, much like the Homeric poems.[18] This belief gave rise to a cultural practice that may well have brought people from lower social strata in contact with Vergil's poems. From the second century AD onward Vergil's works were used as oracles for predicting the future. This practice is known as the *Sortes Vergilianae*. Use as an oracle puts Vergil's works on a par with the Sibylline Books, Homer, and the Bible, all of which were put to similar purposes. Either because of their sacred nature or because of the wisdom that was ascribed to them, these were the most venerated books of antiquity.[19]

This survey of different forms of Vergil's impact on Roman culture is not meant to be exhaustive. It merely serves to show some of the different modes in which Romans in different geographical locations and at different time periods were likely to have encountered the *Aeneid*. It is not possible to measure with any precision the extent of some of these areas of Vergilian influence on Roman culture. When it comes to defining the ancient readership of the *Aeneid*, it is beyond doubt that the poem was read by many different readers in varying forms and with different purposes. We may imagine that the boy who encountered the poem in school read and understood the poem in ways that would differ from the reading experience of his *grammaticus*, just as the grammarian's experience may have differed from that of a poet or other member of the literary elite.

We must, therefore, avoid eliding different types of readers or the different modes of reading in which different readers engage. In an important article on ancient reading practices, Johnson (2000) suggests that different texts require different approaches to understanding their ancient audiences.

He uses the terms *reading communities* and *reading cultures* to delineate the different social and cultural contexts in which reading of texts occurred. In the case of Vergil it is evident that there was more than one reading culture for the *Aeneid*. But many of the individual instances of Vergilian influence on Roman culture discussed above point to Roman education as a particularly important reading culture that strongly affected Vergil's importance in other cultural contexts. The poem's centrality in Roman education is therefore perhaps the most important factor in gauging the impact of the *Aeneid* on Roman cultural identity more generally, and the following discussion focuses more specifically on this reading context.[20]

For centuries the *Aeneid* was among the most important literary works read in Roman schools throughout the empire. It became ever more important as the list of authors read in schools narrowed further and further with time.[21] The geographical spread of the poem's dissemination through education was considerable, because the contents and modes of teaching in Roman schools were fairly homogeneous, whether the school in question was in Rome, in Italy, or in the provinces. Kaster writes of the Roman school taught by the *grammaticus* as providing the governing classes of the empire with "the one thing that approached a common experience."[22]

Because much of the grammarian's mode of instruction consisted in repeated recitation (by teacher and pupils) of the canonical texts, Vergil's poetry was indelibly impressed upon the minds of the literate classes.[23] Augustine described the effects of this type of schooling as it was still conducted in the early fifth century AD. He tells us that in his time schoolboys had to memorize the *Aeneid* to such an extent as to make it impossible to erase it from their memories again later:

> *\<Vergilium\> parvuli legunt ut videlicet poeta magnus omniumque praeclarissimus atque optimus teneris ebibitus animis non facile oblivione possit aboleri. (Civ. Dei 1.3)*
>
> [As little boys they read Vergil so that, absorbed into their delicate minds, the great, most famous and best of all poets cannot easily be erased from memory by oblivion.]

His contemporary Orosius reports that he, too, had the *Aeneid* "burned into his memory" in his early school days, when he attended a *ludus litterarius*. The *ludi litterarii* were schools of low status and provided the basics of literacy, directing their services to the broader masses. They may not regularly have taught the *Aeneid,* but the fact that some of them did suggests a readership for the *Aeneid* that reaches far beyond the literary elite of Rome or even the urban centers of the empire.[24] Pupils learned the rudiments of reading and writing from the *Aeneid* and continued to read the poem throughout the rest of their schooling.

Various scholars have suggested that in the provinces the Roman educational system served the Roman state not only by supplying it with educated administrators, but also by bestowing on its pupils a sense of Roman identity, a sense of belonging to the social, political, and cultural elite of the Roman Empire. Such an effect of teaching the Latin language and Roman values to provincials would then be a powerful tool in stabilizing the empire by inviting provincial elites to share both the power and the identity of their imperial masters.[25] If the *Aeneid* was central to such an educational system, then a large part of this sense of Roman cultural identity was derived from the student's experience of the *Aeneid* in this educational context.[26]

We must, of course, be careful not to overestimate either the power of any educational system to bestow such a sense of cultural identity to its students or the actual extent of the dissemination of this education and, with it, of knowledge of the *Aeneid.* Farrell alerts us to the danger of buying into the Romans' own fictions about the power of Latin culture to prevail over other cultures, or the Roman poets' claims that their poetry would be read throughout the world. He points out that it is especially the *Aeneid* that represents Latin culture in terms of such potency and universal extension.[27] We need only think of Jupiter's promise to Juno that the Latins, even when united with the Trojans, will retain their name, language, and customs, or his promise to Venus that he has already granted to the Romans "an empire without end" (*Aen.* 1.279: *imperium sine fine*). With this caveat in mind, I still think that much can be learned about Roman identity by looking at the articulation of this identity in the poem most educated Romans and provincials were likely to know in common.

I have shown that Vergil held a central position in the Roman educational canon. My claim about the *Aeneid*'s determining influence on Roman cultural identity rests not only on this bare fact; it is supported by a set of ancient beliefs about education, language, epic poetry, and the functioning of the human mind, as well as consideration of the specific reading practices of the ancient school. I will set out below how these collude to suggest that the *Aeneid* had a special power over its readers.

As a starting point, let me turn to Quintilian. Although he believed that the reading of the poets in school primarily served the purpose of forming a sense for style preparatory to oratorical training, he also acknowledged that style alone cannot have been the sole object of students' attention at the early age when they first encountered the poem. Notice the reasons he gives for recommending the practice of reading Homer and Vergil as first authors in school:

> *Ideoque optime institutum est, ut ab Homero atque Vergilio lectio inciperet quamquam ad intellegendas eorum virtutes firmiore iudicio opus est; sed huic rei superest tempus, neque enim semel legentur. Interim et sublimitate heroi carminis animus adsurgat et ex magnitudine rerum spiritum ducat et optimis imbuatur.*   (Quint. 1.8.5)

> [Therefore it has been established well that reading starts off with Homer and Vergil, although an understanding of their qualities requires a more mature judgment; but there is time enough for this later, for they will not be read only once. In the meantime let the mind soar through the sublimity of epic, and let it derive inspiration from the greatness of the subject matter, and let it be instructed in the best values.]

Even though these boys did not have the ability to appreciate the stylistic sophistication of the great poets, Quintilian saw a purpose in letting them read Homer and Vergil at an early age, and not only as a basis for their future training.[28] Rather, it was the content of heroic poetry, its sublimity, and the ethical values it incorporated and bestowed on its readers that Quintilian saw as a valuable educational goal in itself. He characterizes these beneficial qualities of the poems as *sublimitas* and *magnitudo rerum.* Although these words may seem like tired clichés to the modern reader, they describe for Quintilian the poems' power over young minds. We should therefore pay closer attention to them and try to discover their implications for the ancient reading experience. I understand these terms as important gestures toward certain psychological qualities of the text that I will discuss further on. For now, it is important to take note that Quintilian expected the poems to work on the emotions of their young readers. By influencing the readers' emotions, epic poetry was perceived as having the power to act on people's sense of morality. Thus, the emotive power of heroic poetry and its influence on a person's ethical framework was the acknowledged object of early exposure to the *Aeneid*. For many Romans who did not go on to rhetorical training, this was presumably the main impression the poem made on them.

Quintilian's words suggest that epic poetry had a considerable influence on the formation of the ancient self. At an early age, students committed the poems to memory by constant rereading; as Augustine and Orosius say about the *Aeneid*, they could not be erased from memory later. The heroic stories they contained were seen as planting the seeds of morality in people's minds at an early, impressionable age. Moreover, this moral foundation was laid not by philosophical reasoning, but by force of emotion. It is here that we begin to see most clearly the importance of the *Aeneid* for the history of ancient subjectivity. Ancient thinking about education saw the centrality of the poem in the school canon as a beneficial influence on the formation of the self.

ANCIENT MODES OF READING THE *AENEID*

In the following I want to look more closely at Quintilian's observations on the beneficial effect of *Aeneid* reading. Here I am particularly interested in the psychological effects the poem is held to have on individual readers, and in how these psychological effects on readers were conceptualized. I am also interested in the modes of reading that formed the context in which these psychological effects were expected to take place. From the evidence we have, it is not possible to say much about the actual psychological effects the poem may have had on actual ancient readers, because few readers of the poem apart from Augustine tell us much about their experiences of reading it. So this section is not concerned with social realities or historical data on the ancient reading experience.[29] Instead it considers how the ancients thought about the experience of reading the *Aeneid*, how they represented that experience to themselves and others.

We have already seen one example of such a representation. In the passage cited above from the beginning of his *Institutio Oratoria*, Quintilian reports that instruction in reading began with Vergil and Homer. He commends this practice because he expects their epic poems to have a very specific effect on the minds of the young.

> *Et sublimitate heroi carminis animus adsurgat et ex magnitudine rerum*
> *spiritum ducat et optimis imbuatur*   (Quint. 1.8.5)

[Let the mind soar through the sublimity of epic, and let it derive in-
spiration from the greatness of the subject matter, and let it be in-
structed in the best values.]

In this context the epics are valued by Quintilian because their tone and
subject matter are characterized by sublimity and grandeur. The effect
Quintilian expects them to have on young boys is one of elevation, inspi-
ration, and moral instruction. In other words, he expects a very specific
emotional effect of the poems to lead to the establishment of an ethical
framework.

What interests me here is the notion that Quintilian can predict a par-
ticular emotional response to a poem. Surely we would expect that read-
ing the *Aeneid* can lead to many differing emotional responses. Since he is
talking about young boys, he is perhaps more justified in our eyes for ig-
noring more complex responses. But his attitude here is in fact consistent
with other ancient discussions of reading, elsewhere in Quintilian and in
other writers. Ancient rhetorical theory builds on the assumption that the
emotional responses of audiences and readers are predictable and can be
produced by the proper application of rhetorical devices.[30] In such theo-
retical discussions reading was implicitly elided with listening to a live per-
formance, as Ruth Webb has observed:

> When describing his responses to texts, [Quintilian] does so in terms
> of their direct impact on him, as if he were a member of a live audi-
> ence, and not a distanced reader reflecting on a text. The common
> practice of reading aloud would, in itself, have helped to preserve the
> oral nature of the text for the reader. Thus, the act of reading was as-
> similated to that of listening to a live performance in which the
> speaker communicated directly with the audience; and this re-
> mained the model of reception assumed by the rhetoricians in their
> discussion of written texts. For Quintilian, the power of language to
> arouse *pathos* is vital to this immediate, even intimate, communica-
> tion between speaker and listener.[31]

Webb distinguishes two kinds of readers here, one who experiences the
text as if it were a live performance, and another whose experience is more
distanced and reflective. She argues that in ancient discussions of reading,
the latter model of a reader was of no interest. Modern literary critics
would, of course, identify more with the model of the reflective reader, but

Quintilian seems to talk about an entirely different reading experience. Indeed, when he speaks of Vergil as the first poet to be read in school, what he has in mind is learning to read out loud, perfecting the delivery of the poetry read, as preparation for rhetorical training. This type of reading necessarily affects the type of reaction we can expect readers to have to the poem. There will be more attention paid to the actual words, their sound, the rhythm of the meter, and the reader's skill in delivery. There will also be less time to reflect on all the implications of the words. Above all, in a situation where reading a poem means having it read to you by a performer or slave, the lack of an actual physical book or scroll prevents the "reader" from poring over the text, leafing through it, going back and forth and comparing lines, expressions, words. The ancient reader himself, the one performing the reading, will have his attention engaged in the delivery in addition to any reflection he may have about the poem while reading it.

Such a reading experience is much closer to the experience of performer and audience in a context of declamation than it is to that of modern readers. Indeed, one of the grammarian's educational goals was to perfect his students' delivery. For this purpose the teaching of the *grammaticus* was sometimes supplemented by actors' instruction in delivery.[32] The goal of reading instruction was therefore performative and directed at developing the reader's ability to engage his audience by inhabiting the personae of the performed text. This aspect of performative reading, the ability to inhabit the personae of the text, will become important later on in my argument, when I discuss the issue of reader's identification with fictional characters in the *Aeneid* as a bridge between the identity created for the reader within the poem and his sense of self as a Roman.

Much more than in the modern model of reading, in the ancient model the audience's emotions are swayed by the power of the poetry, enhanced by the skill and force of the performer. This does not mean that ancient readers of the *Aeneid* necessarily had the emotional responses expected by Quintilian or intended by Vergil. But it does mean that the idea of the "distanced reader reflecting on a text" is not a model of reading that interested those writers in antiquity who were most interested in the act of reading. In this, the ancient reading experience should be seen as culturally specific to antiquity and therefore not elided with modern ideas about reading. Consequently, the types of emotions aroused by that ancient reading experience cannot be uncritically elided with modern responses to the poem.

There are examples of different kinds of reading the poem, less con-
cerned with its delivery and the *pathos* aroused by it, and more with its
content. In Augustine we find a more reflective, indeed a resistant, reader
of the *Aeneid*. His example will prove quite instructive for a better under-
standing of the differences between ancient reading experiences and our
own. In a famous passage from the *Confessions* Augustine relates to us his
early delight in reading the *Aeneid* and his subsequent rejection of this ear-
lier attachment to the poem.[33]

*Quid autem erat causae, cur graecas litteras oderam, quibus puerulus
imbuebar, ne nunc quidem mihi satis exploratum est. adamaveram
enim latinas, non quas primi magistri, sed quas docent qui grammatici
vocantur. nam illas primas, ubi legere et scribere et numerare discitur,
non minus onerosas poenalesque habebam quam omnes graecas. unde
tamen et hoc nisi de peccato et vanitate vitae, qua caro eram et spiritus
ambulans et non revertens? nam utique meliores, quia certiores, erant
primae illae litterae, quibus fiebat in me et factum est et habeo illud,
ut et legam, si quid scriptum invenio, et scribam ipse, si quid volo,
quam illae, quibus tenere cogebar Aeneae nescio cuius errores, oblitus
errorum meorum, et plorare Didonem mortuam, quia se occidit ab
amore, cum interea me ipsum in his a te morientem, deus, vita mea,
siccis oculis ferrem miserrimus.*

*Quid enim miserius misero non miserante se ipsum et flente Didonis
mortem, quae fiebat amando Aenean, non flente autem mortem suam,
quae fiebat non amando te, deus, lumen cordis mei . . . amicitia mundi
huius fornicatio est abs te . . . et haec non flebam, et flebam Didonem
extinctam ferroque extrema secutam, sequens ipse extrema condita tua
relicto te . . .* (Aug. *Conf.* 1.13)

[Not even now have I sufficiently explored why I hated Greek let-
ters, in which I was instructed as a boy. For I loved Latin, not what
the first teachers teach, but what those named *grammatici* teach. For
I considered the first part, where reading and writing and counting
is learned, to be as onerous and tedious as Greek. What else is this
but sin and vanity of life, as I was only flesh and spirit wandering,
but not returning? For those first letters were better to use, because
safer (with which was formed the skill I have now, namely, to read if
I find something written and to write something myself, if I want)
than those where I was forced to memorize the wanderings of some

Aeneas, oblivious to my own, and to bewail dead Dido, because she killed herself for love, while in the meantime I, most wretched with tearless eyes, carried my dying self in these employments away from you, God, my life.

For what is more wretched than a wretch who does not pity himself, but bewails Dido's death which was caused by loving Aeneas, a wretch who doesn't bewail his own death which is caused by not loving you, God, light of my life . . . Love of this world is fornication against you . . . but I didn't bewail this and bewailed only dead Dido who pursued death with the sword, while I myself pursued the lowest things of your creation, forsaking you.]

Augustine here argues that he must reject his love for the *Aeneid,* the emotional involvement and investment that was part of his reading experience, if he is to reconstitute himself as a Christian. To bewail Dido, to memorize the wanderings of Aeneas, came naturally to the young, pagan Augustine, but it would not do for a Christian. He contrasts the wanderings (*errores*) of Aeneas with his own waywardness (*errores*), his pity for Dido's death with his lack of pity for his own dying self, and Dido's love of Aeneas with his lack of love for God.

Even if we make allowances for the rhetorical purpose these statements serve in Augustine's main argument here, the passage gives us a pervasive sense of the intimate connection Augustine feels between his own former sense of self and the stories and characters of the *Aeneid.*[34] What Augustine attests to here is the exact counterpart to the sense of identity that Greeks throughout antiquity derived from the Homeric epics. We need only think of Socrates who in Plato's *Apology* (28b9ff.) implicitly compares himself to Achilles, or of Alexander the Great, or Pyrrhus of Epirus who more explicitly did the same. Epic poetry played a powerful role in the shaping of cultural identity in the ancient world. Much as the *Iliad* was for the Greeks, the *Aeneid* was for Augustine, even in his Christian writings, a central point of reference, the embodiment of ideals cherished and fostered in the educational context of which he writes. As in the *Confessions* passage, so in the *City of God* Augustine again uses the *Aeneid* as a starting point. The story of the vanquished *Penates* of Troy that Aeneas brings to Italy with him serves as a springboard for Augustine to prove the superiority of the Christian god. To be sure, the *City of God* does not solely depend on the *Aeneid* as a pagan backdrop for its Christian arguments. Figures of Roman history and legend are also used to define non-Christian views and ethics, but it is significant that Augustine begins from the *Aeneid* and returns to it throughout the work. In their effort to define Christian identity, the church fathers often used the *Aeneid* as a target of criticism, assigning it the role of embodiment of pagan identity.[35]

This function of classical literature as bestowing a sense of identity on a community has been expressed very well by Wendy Doniger, who defines classics and myths as cultural icons embodying the values of a community:

> Myths are a species of the more general genus (or genre) of classics. For we might define a classic in a rather broad sense as a work of art (particularly but not necessarily a work of literature) that comes from the past and is accepted by a tradition over a great period of time as *embodying what is good and important.* In addition to this criterion of content, a classic is usually regarded as a paradigm of form: it is beautifully expressed.
>   . . . Myths and classics resemble one another primarily in the way they are transmitted and received. One reason for the historical endurance of classics (as for the remembrance of myths) is that the theme(s) on which they are based may be redefined as *models for the interpretation of experience.* The connection between the myth and the classic is therefore hermeneutic; what they share is a way of interpreting things that turns out to have applicability to widely different historical and existential situations.[36]

Doniger captures very well the cultural dimensions of classical literature. But there is perhaps one addition to be made to her definition of the classic, and that is the function it can serve as a unifying cultural icon for culturally diverse audiences. Unlike orally transmitted myths, literary classics function to give a sense of identity to far larger audiences, bridging both geographical and temporal distances. Literary classics thus performed in antiquity a function that can be compared to the mass media today. For us shared cultural identity bridges geographical distance easily, but this is possible only through modern technology and mass media, which obviously were not available to the ancient Romans. Yet the Romans did accomplish a tremendous degree of cultural unity within the boundaries of their vast empire. Only a shared language and literature as well as shared cultural icons like the *Aeneid* could sustain such cultural unity as existed in the Roman Empire. As I have observed above, an education in Latin language and literature provided a common ground for people of different geographical and cultural origins.

That Augustine felt compelled to reject his love for the *Aeneid* suggests all the more strongly the influence the poem must have had on the shaping of Roman pagan identity. The values conveyed in Roman education and embodied in the *Aeneid* constituted an integral part of Augustine's old pagan Roman self, much as it did for Romans generally. The ancients constructed an identity for themselves around the stories of their national epics, and for the Romans of the imperial period this national epic was clearly the *Aeneid*.

But we might object to all this that modern readers are moved by these narratives just like Augustine, that their appeal is universal and that, far from forming part of pagan identity, the *Aeneid* simply moves many readers in the same way regardless of time, place, and nationality. For instance, it is not surprising that Aeneas and Dido would figure most largely in Augustine's imagination. After all, modern readers have very similar reactions. Furthermore, evidence from graffiti—mainly first lines of the first two books—suggests that the first half of the poem with its protagonists Aeneas and Dido figured most prominently in the recollection of ancient readers as well.[37] Augustine, it could be argued, merely intimates in this passage from the *Confessions* that—much like modern readers—ancient readers identified with Aeneas and were strongly moved by the fate of Dido.

But there is one thing that separates Augustine from modern readers, namely, the sense of obligation Augustine feels as a Christian to reject his earlier sentiments. This is an important point, because it highlights the intimate link Augustine perceives between his emotionally involved reading of the *Aeneid* and his pagan Roman identity, a connection modern readers certainly cannot have and do not in general reflect on. It is easy to read the *Aeneid* and be moved in the way Augustine was and to think that there is no substantial difference between his reading experience and ours. However, the passage quoted above illustrates that it is worth considering the temporal and cultural gap between ourselves and the writing of the *Aeneid*. Augustine's reading experience is bound up with the cultural shift that is taking place at the end of antiquity from a culture still based on pagan Roman determinants to one determined by Christianity. By drawing attention to the different views of the *Aeneid* engendered by his own change from pagan to Christian, Augustine alerts us to the cultural specificity of reading experiences, to the way in which our own cultural context shapes our reading.

৵ *PHANTASIA* AND THE AROUSAL OF EMOTIONS

A closer look at the ancient reading experiences represented by Quintilian and Augustine will allow us further insight into ancient conceptualizations of the self. In the passage discussed above, Quintilian implies that reading the *Aeneid* calls forth certain emotions in young boys. Augustine, too, tells us that reading the *Aeneid* had a particular emotional impact on him. He loved Latin, he says, because he learned about the stories of the *Aeneid*. Later on in this passage he uses an interesting phrase to describe the delight he took in the poem:

> *Dulcissimum* spectaculum *vanitatis equus ligneus plenus armatis, et Troiae incendium, atque ipsius umbra Creusae.* (*Conf.* 1.13)
>
> [The wooden horse full of armed men, and the burning of Troy, and the ghost of Creusa, was a most delightful *spectacle* of vanity.]

It was the visuality of the *Aeneid* that attracted Augustine, the spectacle of images invoked in his imagination. And indeed, it is this aspect of fictionality, of images living in our minds without referents in the outside world, that troubled Augustine later and led him to condemn his preference for poetry over arithmetic and spelling, as we can read in the same passage from the *Confessions*.

Such visuality is prized by Quintilian, too. In his instructions for forensic oratory he makes the point that the most important task for the forensic orator is to arouse the emotions of the judges and to mold them to his purpose:

> *Quare adhuc opus superest, cum ad obtinenda quae volumus potissimum, tum supradictis multo difficilius, movendi iudicum animos atque in eum quem volumus habitum formandi et velut transfigurandi.* (Quint. 6.ii.1)
>
> [Therefore we still have to discuss a task which is the most powerful in obtaining what we want and at the same time much more difficult than what I have discussed before, namely, how to arouse the emotions of the judges and bend and change them into the attitude we wish for.]

The way to achieve this is by appealing to the imagination of his listeners:

Quas φαντασίας Graeci vocant, nos sane visiones appellemus, per quas imagines rerum absentium ita repraesentantur animo, ut eas cernere oculis ac praesentes habere videamur. Has quisquis bene conceperit, is erit in adfectibus potentissimus.   (Quint. 6.ii.29–30)

[Let us call "visions" what the Greeks call φαντασίαι. By means of these, images of absent things are represented to the mind in such a way that we seem to see them with our eyes and to have them present. Whoever expresses these well will be the most powerful over the emotions.]

The author he quotes to illustrate how an orator can successfully conjure up images in the minds of his listeners and thereby arouse their emotions is none other than Vergil.[38] He adduces as examples four passages from the *Aeneid* in which an image is vividly evoked to great effect: the spindle Euryalus' mother dropped when she heard of her son's death (9.476: *excussi manibus radii, revolutaque pensa*), dead Pallas' gaping wound as Aeneas sees it upon entering the death chamber (11.40: *levique patens in pectore vulnus*), the weeping horse at Pallas' funeral, its trappings laid aside in mourning (11.89: *positis insignibus*), and a dying warrior's last imaginary glimpse of his native Argos (10.782: *et dulces moriens reminiscitur Argos*). All these are moments of high *pathos* in the poem, and Quintilian points out how Vergil arouses his readers' emotions by painting a vivid picture in their imagination.

In effect, Quintilian is saying here that one of the most powerful tools of rhetoric, a tool that gives the speaker power over his listeners, is something we can learn from the *Aeneid*. That tool is the ability to create images in the minds of an audience. Macrobius, too, treats Vergil as a master of φαντασία. In a discussion of Vergil's mastery of the techniques of rhetoric one of the interlocutors in the *Saturnalia* (probably Symmachus) lists passages from the *Aeneid* where Vergil uses descriptions of outward appearance to express and arouse emotion (Macrob. *Sat.* 4.1).[39]

What does all this mean for ancient conceptualizations of the self? As we have seen, Quintilian sees the ability to conjure up images in the mind's eye as conferring on the orator a certain power over his audience, and it seems that this power can be learned from Vergil. What we see described in Quintilian, Macrobius, and Augustine is the power the *Aeneid* was held to have had over the imagination of its readers. It is the power of Vergil's *spectacula* that Augustine sees as dangerous to his new identity as a Christian.

If such power is ascribed to Vergil's ability to stir the imagination, if this power is seen as dangerous to one's identity as a Christian, then it is worth looking at this technique in greater detail. Ancient literary critics and theorists of rhetoric used a variety of expressions to convey the notion that poets and orators invoke in their audiences images of the things they describe: φαντασία, εἰδωλοποιία, διατύπωσις, ἐναργεία, *sub oculos subiectio, evidentia*—all these are used by various literary and rhetorical scholars to denote the concept of visualization of poetry or oratorical discourse.[40] The arousal of the imagination was a topic that was interesting not only to teachers and students of rhetoric. Ancient critics of the canonical literary works often observed and commented on the poets' visuality. As we have seen, Macrobius is one example of this in the field of ancient Vergilian criticism. In the Homeric scholia, too, we find this interest in the poet's arousal of the imagination. See, for instance, this comment about a list of places Homer gives to describe Hera's path from Olympus to Lemnos:

τῇ γὰρ ὀνομασίᾳ τῶν τόπων συμπαραθέουσα ἡ διάνοια τῶν ἐντυγχανόντων ἐν <u>φαντασίᾳ καὶ ὄψει</u> τῶν τόπων γίνεται.   (bT Scholion on *Il.* 14.226–27)

[for, rushing along with the naming of the places, the understanding of the readers is accomplished in their <u>imagination and vision</u> of the places].

This passage presents only one of many instances of the ancient critics' interest in the visual quality of epic.[41]

The importance of epic's visuality lies in the notion that by influencing the reader's imagination, the poet can also influence the reader's emotional responses to the poem. It is on the basis of this assumption that Quintilian instructs orators to use *phantasia* in their speeches: it is the orator's aim to win his case by influencing the emotions of the judges, who are his audience. What we see at work in Quintilian's discussion of *phantasia* is an implicit theory of the workings of the human mind and the emotions. To ancient critics and rhetoricians alike, oratory and poetry were instruments that exerted an influence over the human mind and allowed the speaker to exert an influence over his audience. Augustine, Quintilian, and ancient theorists of rhetoric in general shared the assumption that the imagination was so closely bound up with the emotions that having influence over the one meant also having influence over the other.

⳵ SUBLIME POETRY

The visuality of epic, then, was one of two major qualities that in ancient estimation gave to epic a formative power over the self. The other quality was what Quintilian called *sublimitas,* that is, epic poetry was held to have power over the emotions of its readers because of its elevated style. We have seen that Quintilian referred to the sublime style of epic poetry as particularly suited to establish a sense of morality in children. Quintilian was not alone in regarding Vergil's *Aeneid* in this light. Vergil and Homer were the epic poets par excellence of the sublime style. The ancient concept of the sublime is important for understanding how the ancients thought about the effects of certain types of language on the minds of an audience. But connotations the term *sublimity* has acquired in postclassical times are likely to mislead us, if we are not careful to distinguish them from the ancient concept.

In the eighteenth century, Ps.-Longinus' treatise *On the Sublime* exerted a powerful influence over literary critics and thinkers whose fascination with this concept, as they understood it, elevated it to what might be called a regular cult of the sublime.[42] In antiquity, on the other hand, the concept of the sublime played a far less central role in literary criticism. The modern tendency to connect the sublime with associations such as religious awe and the vastness of nature will not be helpful in understanding the concept in its ancient context. Instead, the ancient concept is intimately linked to notions of the power of poetry over its audience, as will emerge from an analysis of the usage of the term *sublimitas* and its Greek equivalent ὕψος. We will see that the sublime quality of epic was regarded as having power over the minds of its audience by expressing emotions itself and as stirring very specific emotions in readers. The intellect, on the other hand, seems to play a negligible role in the influence of the sublime over its audience.

The application to authors and literary works of the terms *sublimitas, sublimis,* ὕψος and ὑψηλός starts in the first century BC. Dionysius of Halicarnassus uses the term ὑψηλός to describe the high style of oratory in contrast to that of Lysias, in a passage worth looking at in greater detail because it describes the properties of the sublime:

ὑψηλὴ δὲ καὶ μεγαλοπρεπὴς οὐκ ἔστιν ἡ Λυσίου λέξις οὐδὲ καταπληκτικὴ μὰ Δία καὶ θαυμαστὴ οὐδὲ τὸ πικρὸν ἢ τὸ δεινὸν ἢ τὸ φοβερὸν ἐπιφαίνουσα οὐδὲ ἁφὰς ἔχει καὶ τόνους ἰσχυροὺς οὐδὲ θυμοῦ καὶ πνεύματός ἐστι μεστὴ οὐδ᾽, ὥσπερ ἐν τοῖς ἤθεσίν ἐστι πιθανή, οὕτως <u>ἐν τοῖς πάθεσιν ἰσχυρὰ</u> οὐδ᾽ ὡς ἡδῦναι καὶ πεῖσαι καὶ χαριεντίσασθαι δύναται, οὕτω <u>βιάσασθαί τε καὶ προσαναγκάσαι.</u>   (Dion. Hal., *Lys.* 13)

[Lysias' style is not, however, <u>lofty or grandiose</u>, nor does it <u>stir us or inspire us with awe</u>, nor convey bitterness, <u>forcefulness or fear</u>, nor does it operate by touching us or using intensity; it is not full of spirit and liveliness, nor is it as <u>strong in its passion</u> as it is morally persuasive, nor can it <u>exert power and influence</u> as it can please, persuade, and be graceful.]

In drawing a contrast between Lysias' style and the sublime style, Dionysius defines the sublime style as one that causes marvel and portrays fear, that is "strong in emotions," and, most importantly, as one that exerts force and compulsion over its audience, a striking formulation of the power of the sublime. He explicitly contrasts the sublime style with one that persuades and pleases, qualities engaging the intellect more than the emotions. Notice also that Dionysius couples the term ὑψηλὴ with μεγαλοπρεπὴς ("grandiose"), which reminds us of Quintilian's expression *magnitudo rerum* ("grandiosity of subject matter"), the second quality he ascribes to epic along with *sublimitas.*

This is the earliest extant passage in which ὑψηλός is used to express the power of language.[43] All other instances of this usage of ὑψηλός, *sublimis,* and their relatives belong to later periods,[44] but nevertheless we know that even in this period scholars were interested enough in the concept of the sublime that one of them devoted a monograph to it. Caecilius of Caleacte, a critic of the first century BC, is the author of a treatise *On the Sublime* to which the extant *On the Sublime* of Ps.-Longinus presents itself as a response and expansion. From Ps.-Longinus we know that Caecilius limited his inquiry to defining the sublime rather than showing how it can be produced.

Our best source for understanding the ancient concept of the sublime is the treatise *On the Sublime,* wrongly attributed to the third-century AD critic Cassius Longinus, and probably belonging to the first century AD.[45] *On the Sublime* describes the sublime as that which produces ecstasy, amazement, and wonder and exerts invincible power over the hearer (Ps.-Long. 1.4). Later on the author says that real sublimity is impossible to resist:

δύσκολος δέ, μᾶλλον δ' ἀδύνατος ἡ κατεξανάστασις, ἰσχυρὰ δὲ
ἡ μνήμη καὶ δυσεξάλειπτος.   (Ps.-Long. 7.3)

[Struggle against it is difficult, indeed impossible, memory of it is
strong and hard to wipe out.]

This again suggests the power of the sublime in terms of physical strength.
He also says of the sublime that it exhibits the orator's power (Ps.-Long.
1.4: τὴν τοῦ ῥήτορος εὐθὺς ἀθρόαν ἐνεδείξατο δύναμιν). He argues that
emotion is both a source of the sublime (one of its ingredients: Ps.-Long.
8.1: δεύτερον δὲ τὸ σφοδρὸν καὶ ἐνθουσιαστικὸν πάθος) and one of its
effects (Ps.-Long. 15.2). Ps.-Longinus sees the sublime as existing both in
poetry and in oratory.

The elements of the sublime just outlined for Ps.-Longinus are in agree-
ment with the picture that emerges of the sublime from other sources. The
younger Pliny uses the term to describe a speaking style that compels even
the unwilling (1.10: *repugnantes quoque ducat, impellat*). Apart from Ps.-
Longinus, Quintilian is the most frequent user of the term. At one point
he describes the effects of Cicero's sublime oratory on an audience: they
were swayed not because they judged his arguments to be compelling, but
because his sublimity captured them against their will, without their
knowing where they were (Quint. 8.3.3.: *mente captos et quo essent in loco
ignaros*). Thus the notion of power over the audience is part of every dis-
cussion of the sublime. With respect to poetry sublimity is ascribed to epic
(Quint. 1.8.5, Juv. 7.28) and to other serious works such as that of Lu-
cretius (Ov. *Am.* 1.15.23) and to tragedy (Quint. 10.1.66; Ov. *Am.* 3.1.39).

All the terms and metaphors of physical strength, violence, and com-
pulsion used in the passages discussed here show that power is an impor-
tant component in the ancient concept of the sublime. This means that
when Quintilian ascribes *sublimitas* to the *Aeneid,* we must keep in mind
the association in ancient literary criticism between the sublime and pow-
erful, even violent, control over the audience's emotions. All the texts ad-
duced support Quintilian's notion that epic has a formative effect on the
minds of its audience because of its sublimity.

Regarding the effect of the sublime style of epic on the self, Quintilian
expected that children's early reading of the *Aeneid* lets "the mind soar"
(*animus adsurgat*) and "derive inspiration" (*spiritum ducat*).[46] Ps.-Longinus
adds to this picture in similar terms in his description of the effects of the
sublime in general:

Φύσει γάρ πως ὑπὸ τἀληθοῦς ὕψους ἐπαίρεταί τε ἡμῶν ἡ ψυχὴ
καὶ γαῦρόν τι ἀνάστημα λαμβάνουσα πληροῦται χαρᾶς καὶ
μεγαλαυχίας, ὡς αὐτὴ γεννήσασα ὅπερ ἤκουσεν.   (Ps.-Long. 7.2)

[For by its very nature our soul is uplifted by true sublimity, and
gaining a certain exultant majesty it is filled with joy and pride, as
though we have created what we have only heard.]

The notion of uplifting, which is already inherent in the terms *sublimis*
and ὑψηλός, here again forms part of the definition of the sublime, as it
had in Quintilian. And like Quintilian, who had seen epic as giving
courage or inspiration (*spiritus*) to its readers, Ps.-Longinus sees the sub-
lime as filling its audience with joy and confidence. What is even more in-
teresting about this passage from Ps.-Longinus is his idea that audiences
are disposed by nature to be affected by the sublime in this particular way.
This brings us back to our earlier observation that in ancient thinking
about the reading experience, the author expects to achieve a very specific
effect in his audience.

     Another comment in Ps.-Longinus is similarly revealing. When he dis-
cusses the shortcomings of Caecilius' monograph, the author implies that
it is not necessary to describe the sublime, because we all know what it is
(Ps.-Long. 1.1). This is maddening to outsiders of ancient culture such as
ourselves, who don't know what the ancient sublime is. But it does show
us that the term was so firmly established in ancient critical thinking that
Ps.-Longinus did not expect disagreement about its nature. Thus, not only
are his remarks about the effects of the sublime in agreement with those
of other authors discussed here and with those of Quintilian about the ef-
fects of the epic reading experience, but they can be seen as representative
of ancient thinking about the sublime. In chapter 3 we will see that at
times Aeneas' emotional reactions to spectacles one might call sublime
closely conform to typical effects of the sublime as outlined above. And as
we will see shortly, it is the emotive power of the sublime that makes it
powerful in the eyes of ancient critics, rhetoricians, and philosophers.

CHAPTER 2

Poetry, Power,
and the Emotions

In the last chapter I discussed two qualities of epic poetry that in ancient consideration gave this genre a formative influence over the self: its visuality and its sublime style. It was primarily the rhetoricians who were interested in holding such influence over the minds of their audiences, and it was their classifications of styles and rhetorical figures and tropes in language that led them to identify the qualities of epic that they considered to be most effective in gaining such influence. What rhetoricians were really interested in was to understand the workings of the power of poetry and to harness it for their own ends. We have seen that they identified poetic visuality and the sublime style as major elements of this power and argued that these qualities influence the audience by stirring their emotions.

The crucial quality of both poetic visuality and the sublime style is that they stir the emotions rather than the intellect, and that they can even stir the emotions against the better judgment of the intellect. The notion of compulsion against one's will formed part of several of the descriptions of the sublime style surveyed above. The concept of *phantasia,* too, was primarily prized because it was considered to be the most powerful means of appealing to the emotions, and because in rhetoric such appeals to the emotions were thought to give the orator the greatest influence over the minds of his audience, greater than appeals to logical reasoning. It was the power of Vergil's images that Quintilian held up as examples of rhetorical effectiveness in exerting influence, and it was the power of the *Aeneid*'s spectacles that Augustine had felt he had been ensnared by as a boy.

Epic poetry, then, was seen as holding power over a reader's emotions, and this power over the emotions was seen as a way of exerting influence without appeal to the intellect. In subsequent chapters I explore examples of the visuality of the *Aeneid* and of the various ways in which it appeals to the readers' emotions. I do so with the idea in mind that the visuality of crucial scenes of the poem and the emotions represented in these scenes are carefully constructed to have certain emotional effects on the readers, effects that would have been expected by those trained in the art of rhetoric.

I do not imply that it was Vergil's intention for these particular scenes to have only these particular effects, or that they could not be read in a different way. We must expect Vergil to have been familiar with contemporaneous philosophical doctrines like the Stoic belief that appeals to the emotions are detrimental to the soul, and with Alexandrian aesthetic views such as the one expressed by Eratosthenes, that poets aim to entertain, not to teach and hence exert influence (Strabo 1.1.10). Much Vergilian scholarship has explored the ways in which Vergil's *Aeneid* reflects such views, and I do not argue that Vergil was not influenced by these intellectual currents. But I argue in subsequent chapters that observing the visual scenarios of certain narrative sequences and the emotions represented in them can lead us to some interesting questions about the rhetorical effects they were meant to have on readers.

Even if I am right and Vergil's use of *phantasia* in these instances is a deliberate rhetorical means of invoking certain emotional effects in readers, this does not mean that all ancient readers would inevitably have been affected in this way. We will see below that some philosophers argued that the power of poetry over one's emotions could be rendered entirely inconsequential. It was the quest of more than one major Hellenistic philosophical school to gain control over the emotions. Learned readers and readers with a special philosophical interest in controlling their emotions would have been careful with poetry intended to appeal to the emotions.

But these were sophisticated readers. The Epicureans, for instance, argued that philosophy could teach what is true and untrue in poetry and thereby help the reader avoid being ensnared by appeals to the emotions. They thought of poetry as inconsequential and mere entertainment only in this way, as we will see below. Only in this way could poetry have no power over the soul for the Epicureans. In other words, according to the

Epicureans, only the Epicurean philosopher could enjoy poetry as entertainment without being subject to its powerful influence on the soul.

But the *Aeneid* does not exclusively or even primarily address itself to philosophers. And it is for that reason that it is necessary to consider the theories of the rhetoricians mentioned above. Whatever Vergil's personal wishes with regard to his intended audience for the poem may have been, the poem addresses itself to a general audience, on occasion even to a "Roman." As we have seen above, it was the most widely read Latin poem in the Roman Empire. It tells the story of the origins of the Roman people to the Roman people. How did such a poem speak to this wider, in general less sophisticated audience, an audience that could not be expected to be trained in philosophy before being exposed to the powerful influence of this epic?

My argument in this book is that the *Aeneid* used its visuality and its sublime style to appeal to the readers' emotions, and that it created a fictional space for an internal reader within the poem for whom the poem could articulate an identity by creating various fictional characters as figures of identification. By thus involving its readers emotionally and articulating a Roman identity, the *Aeneid* was expected and considered to exert a formative influence on its readers, profoundly shaping their sense of self as Romans. This argument may be troubling to modern critics. The idea that poetry could have such an influence certainly was very troubling to ancient critics, not only critics of literature, but also philosophers. Indeed, a brief recapitulation of ancient views of the power of poetry over the self will show just how much was at stake for ancient thinkers in this question, who were almost unanimous in considering certain kinds of poetry to have power over the self. Before I proceed to analyze the poem itself, therefore, I want to separate out the competing strands of thought on this subject that may have been present in the intellectual background of the poem's composition, and in the minds of its earliest elite readers. This review will demonstrate how deeply rooted and widespread was the assumption that poetry could exercise great power over the emotions and hence over the soul.

POETRY AND MORALITY

From its beginning, the power of poetry for good or bad was a central concern of ancient literary criticism. The earliest issue in literary criticism was Homer's depiction of the gods, which some critics saw as immoral.[1] And the moral influence of poetry on its readers was a particular concern to literary critics and philosophers because Greek and Roman education was based on instruction in poetry. There was a general assumption, contested by philosophers and asserted by the practitioners of school education later on, that early instruction in poetry was beneficial to children and to the city because poetry was a sort of proto-philosophy that could teach students about life, encourage good behavior with heroic tales, and deter from bad behavior with frightening stories.[2]

Implicit in this view was a widespread, long-established belief in the consequentiality of poetry, its power to influence the mind, an attitude evident not only in regard to children and school education. The importance of this belief is hard to overstate. In Athens, tragedy was considered to have similar powers over its audience. Aristophanes, for instance, seems to take its power for granted when in the *Frogs* he has Dionysus decide on the relative merits of Aeschylus and Euripides on the basis of their moral influence over their Athenian audiences.

Gorgias made the same assumption in his *Encomium of Helen,* a rhetorical showpiece that proposed to prove Helen's innocence in her abduction by Paris by arguing that the power of Paris' rhetoric was invincible. Gorgias claimed that poetry had an irresistible influence over the emotions. His claim shows that he expected the audience to share his view without the need for argument. On the basis of this he claimed that rhetoric had the same power. He argued that rhetoric could overpower the emotions to such a degree that a listener such as Helen could be deemed not responsible for her actions. Aristophanes and Gorgias shared the assumption that poetry can overpower the emotions and influence the morals of a person. But while Aristophanes focuses on the beneficial effects of poetry's influence on the moral fiber of its audience, Gorgias highlighted the danger that its influence might work in the cause of moral corruption.

As is well known, Plato reacted vehemently to the traditional view of poetry as beneficial for the individual and the city. His concern was about the effect poetry had on the soul of the viewer of tragedy. In the *Republic* he had Socrates argue that seeing the suffering of a heroic figure enacted on stage caused the audience to experience vicariously the character's sorrow. This would allow the viewer to feed his appetite for indulging without restraint in emotions that in real life he should strive to control. Such indulgence of the emotions weakened the rational part of the soul that could govern the emotions. The viewer of tragedy ran the risk that his soul would be governed by passions rather than reason.[3] So Plato decided that the influence of poetry over the emotions was so strong and dangerous that poetry must be banned from his ideal city. But like Gorgias, he did not deny that poetry had such power over the minds of its audience.

Aristotle, while not denying the consequentiality of poetry, held a more favorable view of its moral value. He restored poetry to the role it had occupied for Aristophanes, as a power beneficial to the city. In the *Poetics* he discussed how the representation in tragedy of heroic figures in situations of conflict and suffering arouses the viewer's piety and fear. But Aristotle saw this experience as cathartic. In other words, Aristotle acknowledged Plato's point in the *Republic* that poetry arouses the emotions, but while Plato concluded that therefore poetry is harmful to the city and must be banned, Aristotle countered that poetry provides a safe outlet for emotions. More specifically, the right kind of tragedy, Aristotle argued, produces a very particular emotional response, the arousal of pity and fear. By feeling these particular emotions in response to the tragic performance, the audience has the beneficial experience of *catharsis,* literally a cleansing of the soul.[4] As we shall see later on in this chapter, Aristotle's view of this emotional response is important to the experience of reading the *Aeneid.*

After Aristotle there was continuing disagreement about the moral benefits of poetry for the individual and the city. But another disagreement was added to the debate about the power of poetry: for the first time, some denied that it had such power. Some voices were raised to the effect that poetry was not meant to be instructional but merely for entertainment, that it was inconsequential, or should be rendered so. Explicit statements of the position that poetry was inconsequential are less common, less fully articulated, and more elusive than statements of the position that it should be rendered inconsequential. I will discuss a few of them below. But those who argued that poetry should and could be rendered inconsequential were also convinced that poetry was potentially harmful to the soul, which means that they continued to believe in the power of poetry over the self. I have already mentioned the Epicureans, who were the most important proponents of this view.

Their views are of some importance to our question because of the Epicurean philosophers and poets Lucretius and Philodemus, whose connections to Vergil through personal friendship or literary debt are significant enough—not to think that they turned Vergil into an Epicurean—but to acknowledge that Epicurean ideas were an important component of the intellectual climate in which the *Aeneid* was written.[5] This means that we should consider the possibility that Epicurean ideas about poetry may be present in the *Aeneid*—either in an Epicurean spirit, as they are in Lucretius, creating an Epicurean poetics, or, alternatively, that they are absent, or present in a negating way, in that the poem articulates a poetics that responds to and dismisses the Epicurean rejection of poetic appeals to the emotions. In light of the various ways in which the *Aeneid* appeals to the readers' emotions, the latter case is more plausible.

The Epicureans are generally associated with the belief that poetry is harmful.[6] Sextus Empiricus recounts their views in his book *Against the Grammarians,* where he uses their position on poetry to argue against the representatives of the teaching profession who believe in the beneficial powers of poetry (*Adv. Math.* 1.270). The Epicurean position according to Sextus' account considers poetry as harmful for several reasons. First, it contains more harmful than useful statements, and without guidance, the audience is apt to take in only what is harmful (*Adv. Math.* 1.279–80). Secondly, poets aim to move the soul (*psychagogia*), and it is easier to move the soul with falsehood than with the truth (ibid. 1.296–97). Lastly, poetry is a stronghold of the passions and inflames anger, a desire for sex or drink, and other passions in its audiences (ibid. 1.298).

Similar views are attested for the Epicurean philosopher and poet Philodemus. For him, too, poetry was potentially harmful. He saw little or no use in poetry, while agreeing with Sextus' Epicureans that poetry intensifies the passions.[7] And like the earliest literary critics of Homer, he considered the poets' beliefs about the gods impious and therefore harmful to humans ethically.[8] But being a poet himself, Philodemus seems to have been able to reconcile this Epicurean position with his own artistic activities by sticking to light and inconsequential genres such as epigrams. Presumably he granted poetry a role in life as entertainment.

This is precisely the role Sextus' Epicureans envisaged for poetry, to render it harmless. Instruction in philosophy, they said, can help the student distinguish between the good and bad in poetry, and with this knowledge in mind it is possible to enjoy just the enchantment of poetry.[9] This is also the view of the Epicurean Torquatus in Cicero's *De Finibus,* who held that poetry is not useful for him but only gives a childish delight (*puerilis delectatio*) to its audience (*De Fin.* 1.71–72). For the Epicureans, then, poetry could at best serve only to entertain, on the condition that it was rendered harmless by proper instruction. Another proponent of the view that poetry was entertainment rather than instructional was the Alexandrian polymath Eratosthenes. In his *Geography* Strabo recorded Eratosthenes' view that poets did not aim to instruct their audiences, but merely to entertain them (*psychagogein*), and that therefore Homer's representation of geographical places served no useful or instructional purpose (Strabo 1.2.3).

But while Eratosthenes' statement harmonized well with the aesthetic principles articulated and followed by the Alexandrian poets and later also by the Neoterics, not all Hellenistic critics agreed that poetry was meant only to entertain. Neoptolemus of Parium emphasized that poetry must both entertain and benefit the audience.[10] In this view he agreed with Aristotle in general terms, insofar as Aristotle, too, had seen a benefit to the audience in the cathartic effect of their vicarious experience of emotions enacted on the tragic stage, although Neoptolemus' statement lacks the sophistication and complexity of Aristotle's model. In the Augustan period Horace articulated the same doctrine in his *Ars Poetica,* that poets want to entertain or to instruct or both (Hor. *AP* 333–34), as did Strabo in similar terms, as we will see shortly. While the proposition that poets entertain and instruct may be a simple one that reflected mainstream Greek beliefs, in the face of Platonic, Epicurean, and other criticism of poetry it also articulated a philosophical position of allegiance with the Aristotelian view of the benefits of poetry, a position the Stoics shared as well.[11]

Despite the dissenting voices of the philosophers who called poetry harmful or inconsequential, the general tacit assumption continued to be what we have seen in Quintilian, that early education in heroic poetry was morally beneficial. In Sextus Empiricus' *Against the Grammarians* the practitioners of education based their arguments for the usefulness of their discipline on poetry's beneficial power. The grammarians defended the usefulness of grammar and school education based on poetry by saying that poetry contains starting points for wisdom and happiness, but that these starting points had to be explained by the grammarians to be useful to the student (Sext. Emp., *Adv. Math.* 1.270–73). As long as this was done, they maintained, poetry was useful and even necessary to cities (1.275–76). This was the position the Epicureans attacked later on in the dialogue, set up as a traditional viewpoint. We might also see it as a response to Plato's ban against poetry, and as an articulation of allegiance with Aristotle's restoration of poetry to a position of usefulness to the soul of the individual and the health of the community. And although their position was not a philosophical one, in the form it takes in Sextus it can be seen as a response to the issues raised by Stoicism and Epicureanism about poetry's power and its usefulness for the morals of its readers.

Sextus shows us that traditional Greek education based on poetry continued to be considered beneficial to the individual and the community by those who practiced it, and, despite Plato's verdict, this tradition kept going strong and unchanged. Strabo's views on Homer in education are interesting here, because he discusses the beneficial effects of poetry in education with particular reference to its impact on the emotions. Against Eratosthenes' view that Homer's geographic descriptions are fictional and serve no useful purpose, Strabo argues in favor of poetry's traditional benefits. Strabo proclaims himself a Stoic, but his value as a source for Stoic views on poetry and education is doubtful, since he does not claim to engage in writing philosophy. It is perhaps best to regard his remarks as the views of an intellectual with Stoic convictions who was also a contemporary of Vergil.[12]

Like Horace and Neoptolemus, Strabo saw poetry as both enjoyable and instructive. He therefore approved of the Greeks' use of poetry in school education. In his view this custom was derived from the ancients' belief that poetry was a sort of proto-philosophy that was meant to instruct children and benefit them morally (1.2.3). He saw poetry's enchantment as a necessary enticement for learning, especially for children. But he extended the usefulness of poetry for this purpose even to adults. Insofar as they were more likely to benefit from moral instruction hidden in poetry than they are from philosophical instruction, the uneducated, the half-educated, women, and common people must be regarded as children, too. Strabo also explains why poetry could be used to instruct those who are not receptive to philosophy. Those who do not respond to appeals to their reasoning faculty can be instructed by appealing to their emotions. Mythical stories about heroic deeds give pleasure and encourage the audience to good behavior; frightening ones stir fear and deter them from bad deeds. And it is the mythical element, the miraculous that does not correspond to everyday life, that is particularly suited to stir the emotions (1.2.8).

Strabo's views on poetry and the emotions in education fit in well with the grammarians' arguments Sextus Empiricus quotes about the usefulness of instruction in poetry. Both Strabo and the grammarians took for granted that poetry has power to influence the mind. And like the grammarians, Strabo, too, acknowledged that there was both true and untrue material in Homer, and that further guidance, such as his own in the *Geography*, was necessary to make poetry useful. In terms of Stoic views on poetry, Strabo's account is somewhat problematic, because appeals to pleasure and fear would seem out of place in a philosophical system in which emotions were generally shunned. But with regard to uneducated audiences the Stoics generally agreed with Strabo's views of the benefits of poetry. Although the educated person should be addressed with rational means, Stoics saw the practical efficacy of appealing to the emotions of the uneducated with heroic poetry.[13] If the result of such appeals was positive, then the emotions called forth by poetry were a necessary bait for the moral instruction of those unable to be reached by rational discourse.

Other writers in Vergil's time expressed the view that poetry has a beneficial power over a person's morality. In a poetic essay on themes of literary criticism, Horace characterized the poet's role in society as a teacher of the young, instructing them in the correct use of language and depicting heroic deeds as paradigms of moral excellence (Hor. *Epist.* 2.1.126–31). Cicero had expressed a similar view in his defense speech for the poet Archias, where he described historical epic as useful to the Roman state because by depicting the heroic deeds of the Romans it provided not only historical records and a vehicle for praise, but also patterns of excellence to be followed by its readers (Cic. *Arch.* 14; 19–22; 31).

It is commonly believed that Cicero's views in this speech were old-fashioned in his own time and that many of the leading poets of the day saw poetry as having no such moral responsibilities. Catullus and his fellow Neoteric poets could refer to their poetry as trifles (*nugae* Cat. 1.4), and Catullus' corpus certainly contains more poems likely to stir passions than inspire heroic or morally upright behavior.[14] In the esthetics of much Alexandrian poetry moral instruction does not play a role, and many genres in Hellenistic poetry as well as Roman poetry of the late republic and early empire would have been unsuitable for moral instruction of children.

But this may be as much an issue of genre and content as it is of the changing times. Whenever poetry is spoken of as morally beneficial, the genre concerned is one of high status, such as epic or didactic. The poems of Archias to which Cicero referred in his defense speech as useful to its readers and to the Roman state were historical epics. And the passage of Horace cited above explicitly said that the poet who is so useful to the state is one who depicts heroic deeds as paradigms of moral excellence (Hor. *Epist.* 2.1.128–31). While Horace's description of this poetic content is open enough to include some of his own lyric poetry, it gestures more obviously to epic and perhaps also tragedy.[15] As I have discussed, Quintilian recommends Homer and Vergil as the best authors for reading by young boys because he ascribes a morally beneficial effect to epic's elevated subject matter and genre. In the same passage he also recommends tragedy, calling it useful (*utiles*), and some lyric, provided that the subject matter of the lyric poetry is suitable (Quint. 1.8.6).

So, although Cicero's views on poetry in *Pro Archia* differ from those that emerge from the Catullan corpus, and although they are more traditional than the attitude Catullus adopts in his opening poem, where he defines his poetry as personal, playful, and highly refined, we should not see this as a generational shift. Rather, it was an ongoing debate about the role of poetry in society and its power over the minds of its readers. The Hellenistic aesthetic norm prized small-scale poetry that lacked pretensions to moral authority. Such a norm fit well into the Hellenistic philosophical scene, in which the question of poetry's power over the passions of its readers had come under intense scrutiny. But the poets who refused to conform to the traditional roles of poets in society and the philosophers who strove to make poetry harmless did so in the face of deeply engrained cultural patterns that granted poetry an authoritative power to shape the minds of its readers.

We have already seen that the Epicureans relegated poetry to an inconsequential role in society as harmless entertainment. We will see below that the Stoics had developed a theory of psychology that would have allowed them to argue that poetry, as a form of sense perception, could have no direct impact on the emotions, because the soul was entirely rational. The Stoics, then, did not provide a theoretical framework for the beneficial power of poetry over the emotions either. In such an intellectual climate light genres would best fit the bill. Indeed, this was an intellectual environment in which it would seem as momentous for Horace to reaffirm the role of the poet as a moral authority as it would for Vergil's *Aeneid* to attain the cultural status that soon turned the poem de facto into the supreme example of authoritative poetry.

While major political shifts such as the establishment of the Augustan principate played an undeniable role in these developments, the Hellenistic philosophical positions themselves must be seen as allowing the reaffirmation of poetry's authority. The Epicureans saw poetry as potentially dangerous, and as harmless only if rendered so by philosophical instruction. This presumes that poetry did have a quite powerful influence over the mind of its reader, albeit a negative one. In order for poetry to be inconsequential, it had to be made so, that is, poetry was not inconsequential to begin with, it was always powerful first, harmless only after arduous exertion. Thus the Epicureans implicitly acknowledged that poetry possessed power over the soul, although generally they did not see this power as beneficial and authoritative.

Lucretius is, of course, the exception to this rule, in that he used poetry as an authoritative discourse. His didactic philosophical poem *De Rerum Natura* used poetry as a medium to articulate Epicurean ideas, even framing the poem as instruction of a student of Epicureanism (Lucr. *DRN* 1.50–57). Through his choice of the didactic genre and the explicit use of the instructional relationship between author and reader, Lucretius implicitly reasserted the traditional role of some poetic genres as authoritative and instructional and showed that this traditional role of poetry could be used in the service of the dissemination of Epicurean ideas.[16]

Lucretius compared his use of poetry in his project to the "honey a physician applies to the rim of a cup of bitter medicine" (Lucr. *DRN* 4.11–13). But he used poetry not only because it made philosophical discourse more enjoyable. He would not have done this had he believed that poetry could only be detrimental to the soul, or that it was a medium whose social role was mere entertainment. His choice suggests that he believed with Strabo that poetry could reach the soul in ways that instruction based solely on logical reasoning cannot—even though he may have disagreed with much else of what Strabo would say about education—and that this power could be used for the benefit of the reader.

In this his view of poetry may have differed from most other Epicureans, but his decision to write philosophical poetry was not as contrary to Epicurean doctrine as is often assumed.[17] The belief that poetry can be harmful to the soul is only the flip side of the belief that it can be beneficial. Lucretius shared with other Epicureans the fundamental belief that poetry holds power over the minds of its readers, a belief many Stoics seem to have subscribed to tacitly as well. Some early Stoics quoted poets to support their philosophical arguments; and as the Epicurean Lucretius would do later on in a different way, so the Stoic Cleanthes had used poetry as a medium for articulating philosophical ideas in his *Hymn to Zeus*.[18]

Thus the major Hellenistic philosophical schools, despite the reservations some philosophers expressed about the detrimental powers of poetry, continued to take for granted the power poetry was traditionally held to have over its audiences. Lucretius' use of poetry as an authoritative medium for instruction in philosophy foreshadowed the claims to poetic authority so often found in Augustan poetry, especially in Horace, but also in Vergil. Together with the force of a strong tradition favoring the belief in poetry's beneficial power and authority, Lucretius' precedent paved the way for an authoritative poem in a high-status genre, such as the *Aeneid,* to emerge and claim a central cultural role in the formation of Roman identity.

ஃ VISION AND EMOTION

The previous discussions of philosophical, rhetorical, and other culturally important views of poetry's power over the self have highlighted how widespread and persistent was the belief that poetry was able to exert influence over the souls of its audiences by appealing to the emotions rather than the intellect. While Plato and other philosophers worried about poetry's ability to stir excessive and detrimental passions such as grief or sexual desire, others saw benefits to the soul in the pride, joy, and sense of elatedness bestowed on readers by heroic poetry. The benefits these people saw in the latter effect of heroic poetry on its audience are most often described, if at all, as a desire to emulate heroic behavior, an increase of courage, and an increased sense of right and wrong. As Strabo explicitly states, these effects are achieved by an appeal to the emotions and can reach readers who are unable (as yet or ever) to be reached by persuasion based on logical reasoning (Strabo 1.2.8).

In chapters 3 and 4 I analyze in selected passages how the *Aeneid* appeals to the readers' emotions by means of its visual qualities whose emotional effect on readers is conceptualized in the idea of *phantasia*. Because my subsequent readings focus on the visuality of these scenes, I want to discuss here how ancient literary critics, rhetoricians, and philosophers described the emotional impact of such mental images, and more generally of sense perceptions, on the emotions of the reader of poetry. In the course of this discussion I will suggest some theoretical frameworks in which we may see Vergil's use of *phantasia* and spectacle in various scenes.

I have said that its sublime style and visuality were two of the qualities with which, according to ancient critics and rhetoricians, the *Aeneid* appealed to the emotions and exerted its power over the self. As to the poem's sublime style, there is much that could be said about the use of particularly elevated or grandiose language. The *Aeneid* can be called sublime in the ancient sense not only because it is an epic poem. There are many passages in which the language is particularly weighty, usually in keeping with the nature of the narrative situation. Among the most obvious examples of such elevated language are Jupiter's prophecy in book 1 where his promises to Venus about Rome's future power are couched in terms so sweeping and totalizing (e.g., 279: *imperium sine fine dedi*) that even modern readers can be affected emotionally and can vicariously experience a Roman reader's sense of elation; or the pageant of heroes in book 6 (756–859) whose pathos—already of the highest register because it is a survey of future Roman heroes throughout history, viewed by the ancestor of the Roman people in the Underworld on a supernatural visit to see his dead father—is heightened to a pitch when it closes with a lament for the death of young Marcellus, a designated heir to Augustus' power (868–86).

It would by very interesting to analyze how the elevated language of such passages operates within its context and in what ways we can see it as operating on the emotions of the readers. A closer analysis of Jupiter's prophecy would be especially desirable for chapter 3, where I analyze the visual qualities of a narrative sequence following closely upon the prophecy. My working hypothesis would be that the elevated style of the prophecy is calculated to set up the reader to be affected emotionally and to be ready for more appeals to the emotions. Hence, the prophecy and the visuality of the narrative sequence following it may have been meant to correspond to each other and to reinforce and enhance their respective emotional effects on readers.

However, I have not detailed this argument in this book, because this is a book about Roman identity in the *Aeneid,* not exclusively about the rhetorically expected emotional effects of the poem. I have limited my explorations of these to the poem's visual qualities and instead expanded on these results to reach a broader analysis of the poem's definition of Roman identity, in terms that include determinants such as gender and ethnicity. Thus the focus of chapters 3 and 4 of this book is to examine the visual qualities of selected passages, observing through whose eyes the reader sees scenes, which characters are consistently represented as visual spectacles, and to look at emotions represented in the passages, considering ancient expectations about the effects of the representations of such emotions on the reader.

My readings of the poem's visual qualities proceed from the assumption in ancient thinking that mental images evoked in readers by certain types of poetic narrative and description are particularly suited to arouse certain emotions. The concept of *phantasia* is one of the terms used in rhetorical theory to describe this belief. As it is used in the passages discussed above, the idea of *phantasia* explains the power of poetry and rhetoric over the minds of their audiences through a model of how language is transformed into visual images and how these mental images affect the mind. *Phantasia* turns the issue of the power of language into an issue of the power of visual perception. The connection between poetry and vision established by the concept of *phantasia* moves the issue of the power of poetry into the conceptual framework of theories of sense perception. If visual perception stirs the emotions, then so can the mental images conjured up in the mind's eye of the reader of poetry, or the audience of a speech.

For rhetoricians there was no need to theorize why visual perception or visualization in oratorical and poetic discourse stirred the audience's emotions. They simply made the assumption that *phantasia* worked as a rhetorical tool because it was effective. It achieved the desired result. Neither was there a theory of visualization and its effects on the emotions in nonphilosophical texts of ancient literary criticism. Critics pointed out when poets used *phantasia* effectively, but they did not discuss why and how it should affect the emotions of the reader. Developing an explicit theory of perception and the emotions was the domain of philosophers. It would have been out of place in such literary critical contexts as commentaries.

But generally speaking, the rhetorical and literary concept of *phantasia* assumed that poetic visuality had a direct effect on the emotions. Thus it depended on an implicit model of the soul in which visual perception more generally had a direct impact on the emotions. Most philosophers agreed that sense perception can have a direct influence on the emotions. Plato and Aristotle had discussed the effects of poetry on the emotions as a direct result of visual and auditory perception. Both envisaged performance as the main medium for experiencing poetry. Plato's critique of poetry in the *Republic* had focused on the emotional effects of a tragic performance on its audience. Aristotle's discussion of *catharsis* in the *Poetics,* too, considered the emotions aroused in the viewer of tragedy.

Indeed, Aristotle specifically commented on the visuality of tragedy, albeit briefly. The visuality of tragedy, the vividness of its spectacle, was for Aristotle one of the reasons why he considered it the best genre, superior even to epic. He did not just consider the visuality of tragedy as dependent on seeing it performed in actuality but even said that it could also be felt in reading.[19] Although he credited epic with producing the same emotional effects as tragedy, he preferred tragedy for its superior visuality and greater effectiveness. In Aristotle's terms, if the goal of poetic performance or reading is *catharsis* through the arousal of pity and fear, then the genre that best arouses these emotions achieves *catharsis* best. If visuality is a factor in arousing these emotions, then the most visual genre best arouses them.

Aristotle mentioned the visuality of tragedy in reading as an afterthought. Like Plato, he saw performance as the primary arena for encountering poetry. Both he and Plato discussed the power of drama over the emotions with the underlying definition of poetry as *mimesis,* or imitation of action, rather than with the later concept of *phantasia.* But the idea that vision more generally has the power to stir the emotions was already present in Gorgias' *Encomium of Helen*. Although the power of vision over the emotions is here not directly linked to the power of poetry, the two are curiously juxtaposed. Gorgias' main argument in favor of Helen's innocence was the power of rhetoric, but at the end of the speech he argued that the visual perception of an external object could exert the same influence over the soul as poetry and rhetoric. He argued that Helen was equally guiltless whether she was persuaded by Paris' rhetoric or by his beauty, because visual perception of something beautiful could stir violent emotions such as love, and, as Gorgias put it, one cannot help seeing what one sees.[20]

After Aristotle, discussions about poetic visuality were concerned not so much with viewers of theatrical performances as with readers of texts or audiences of rhetorical performance. *Phantasia* became one of several terms used to describe the visuality of poetry experienced in reading. Later literary critics ascribed to epic the visuality Aristotle had ascribed to tragedy. By focusing on reading and rhetorical performance, critics showed a continuing interest in understanding how this visuality worked on the human mind and how knowledge of these processes could be exploited for rhetorical purposes.

But while rhetoricians' and literary critics' interest in *phantasia* and the visuality of poetry in the Hellenistic period suggests that educators and orators continued to believe in the power of poetry's visuality over the emotions of its audiences, Hellenistic philosophers disagreed widely in their positions on the effects of visual and auditory sense perception on the emotions. While the Epicurean model of sense perception, articulated most vividly by Lucretius (*DRN* 4), held that vision could have a direct, and devastating, impact on the soul, some Stoics claimed that it was impossible for outside forces such as reading or listening to poetry to influence the emotions directly.

Chrysippus, the main proponent of this Stoic view, believed that sense perceptions, including hearing poetry or visualizing events of a narrative, were operations of the reasoning faculty, and that the soul consisted entirely of reason, emotions being merely the result of faulty reasoning, not a natural part of the soul.[21] Chrysippus, then, would have seen emotional reactions to poetry as the result of the faulty reasoning of the soul in response to the visualization or auditory perception of a poetic narrative, curable or avoidable by rational means.

In this Stoic theory of sense perception *phantasia* was a central concept. It denoted the ability of the soul to understand and process sense perceptions. The Stoics argued that emotions are not a part of the soul, which meant that sense perceptions, such as the visuality of poetry, could not directly affect the emotions by entering the soul. For them the soul consisted entirely of reason, and all sense perception was processed by the rational soul before it could call forth any emotions. Hence, according to the Stoics *phantasia* was not a means for gaining direct access to the emotions of a rhetorical audience.

By giving the term *phantasia* a different meaning and function in their theory of sense perception from the one it had in rhetorical theory, the Stoics seemed to separate the issues of a poem's visuality and the effect of such visuality on the emotions. They developed a theory of sense perception and a model of the soul that enabled them to argue that no sense perceptions of any kind have impact on the emotions directly. But even within the Stoa, there was disagreement with this model of *phantasia* and the emotions. The Stoic Posidonius rejected the model of the purely rational soul. He returned to Plato's model of the tripartite soul, in which the emotions formed a natural part. In his view emotions could be cured by appealing to the irrational part of the soul and by operating with irrational means. Posidonius speaks of music in particular, but poetry would be just such an irrational cure for emotions. Posidonius' position on the power of poetry over the emotions is comparable to that of Aristotle, who saw the benefits of tragedy as providing an outlet for the emotions and thereby cleansing the soul of them.[22]

Other Stoics who discussed the effects of music, art, and poetry on their respective audiences also observed their emotional effects. Although they were more interested in drawing connections between the emotions stirred by the art and the rational benefit of the art to the soul, they seem to have acknowledged that art had the power to stir the emotions directly through sense perception without mediation of logical reasoning.[23] The Stoic position on the effects of poetry on the emotions, then, was not clear-cut. While Chrysippus' model would seem to preclude a direct emotional impact of poetry on the reader, other Stoics acknowledged that poetry did have such an effect. Unfortunately, we do not have an extant work of Stoic poetics that would give full articulation to this position. As sense perception was an important context for Stoic discussions of poetry, such a work might have explained how it fitted with Chrysippus' theory of sense perception.

The Epicurean model of sense perception was quite different from that of the Stoics. They believed that the process of seeing something involves a thin film image separating from the seen object, flying through the air, and physically entering the mind through the eye. Their materialism was probably not shared by many people outside their own school. Their view that sense perceptions can cause disturbances in the soul that can lead to passion was diametrically opposed to Chrysippus' Stoic theory of sense perception. But Lucretius' account that both vision and mental images can induce strong emotions corresponds exactly to the underlying assumption in rhetorical theory that *phantasia* or visualization in poetry and oratory causes certain emotions in the audience.

Lucretius laid out the Epicurean model of sense perception in the fourth book of *De rerum natura,* focusing on vision as the exemplary case of sense perception. At the end of the book Lucretius explained the phenomena of dreams and the imagination in the same materialistic framework as he had used throughout his theory of perception (*DRN* 4.722–1036). He described the effects on the soul of visual perceptions, including images in the mind's eye, arguing that once an image has entered the mind through the eyes, it can act upon it and cause emotional disturbances. His example is the passion of love, which—like Gorgias—he explained as the result of the visual perception of someone beautiful (1037ff.). For Lucretius, then, visual perception had a direct impact on the passions in the soul, and his explanation of the phenomenon of visual images before the mind's eye would have allowed him to argue that poetry could have a detrimental effect on the soul, as well.

It is against this philosophical background that we must see Vergil's use of visuality in the *Aeneid.* With the exception of the Stoics, philosophers agreed with rhetoricians and literary critics in regarding poetic visuality as a means of gaining direct access to the emotions of an audience. And even the Stoics agreed that poetry was the bait that could lure the uneducated to moral instruction because it appealed to the emotions, not to the intellect. My discussion of Hellenistic theories of sense perception has shown some of the anxieties arising from questions about the connection between poetry, its perception by the reader, the effect of its perception on the emotions, and the degree of control the rational part of the soul has over them. Because anxieties over emotions and control over them were central concerns of Hellenistic philosophy, Hellenistic theories of sense perception and the emotions are an important background for the representation of visuality and the emotions in the *Aeneid.*

But as a theoretical framework within which to read Vergil's visuality Aristotle's theory of *catharsis* in tragedy is one of the most helpful. The tragic elements of the *Aeneid*—for instance, the tragic form of the Dido story, especially in book 4—have long been recognized.[24] When Augustine talked about Vergil's *spectacula,* he spoke figuratively of spectacles before his mind's eye, but we will see shortly that Vergil's visuality does not solely lie in such brief and poignant images as Quintilian quotes as rhetorical examples of *phantasia.* In chapter 3 we will see that the *Aeneid* narrative leads the reader through a series of visual spectacles, some of which are very theatrical. Dido's story is a tragedy not just because it is a sad story or because her character can (or cannot) be shown to conform to Aristotelian norms of the heroic character in tragedy. Dido's story is also a tragedy in the sense of a visual spectacle before the mind's eye of the reader.

But there is more. In the narrative sequences I analyze below, the *Aeneid* stages tragic spectacles that represent not only the characters of the tragic action, but also an intratextual audience. The reader often sees the scenes of the narrative through the eyes of one character (mostly Aeneas), while other characters are consistently cast as spectacles. This distinction suggests that the epic narrative of the *Aeneid* uses its visual qualities to invoke the experience of tragic performance and its greater narrative flexibility to represent both the action of the tragedy and an audience reaction to it.

We will see how this functions in more detail in chapters 3 and 4. The point I wish to make here is that Aristotle's theory of *catharsis* can fruitfully be applied to the patterns of visuality I observe in several narrative sequences. By aligning the reader with an intratextual observer of a visual spectacle the *Aeneid* identifies the reader more closely with this observer, while the character represented as a tragic spectacle becomes a figure whose suffering is experienced in a more transitory way and at a greater distance. We identify with the tragic hero or heroine on the stage, we suffer with him or her, but the function of our suffering is the experience of *catharsis,* an experience beneficial to our souls because it releases us from the emotions experienced together with the tragic figure. In its visuality and its appeals to the readers' emotions, the *Aeneid* bestows on its readers both the sense of elation Quintilian and Ps.-Longinus discussed as effects of the sublime and the vicarious experience of the tragic hero's suffering, followed by the *catharsis* promised by Aristotle.

PART 2

THE READER'S
SUBJECT POSITION

୫ଏ ୫ଏ ୫ଏ

CHAPTER 3

The Gaze

In this chapter I argue that the *Aeneid* articulates an identity for the reader by creating a subject position for him or her within its narrative. In the proem the narrator creates a fictional persona for the reader by representing himself and the reader as performer and audience of an oral performance. The visuality of this and the following scenarios turns this fictional listener into a spectator as well, as the narrator conjures up the images of the narrative in the mind's eye of the reader. As we have seen in the previous chapters, ancient thinking about the self held that influence over a person's mental images brought with it influence over his/her emotions as well. We have also seen that both poetry and oratory were held to exert such power over an audience, and that epic poetry such as Homer's and Vergil's in particular was seen as having power to instill moral values in the young. It is therefore of interest to the student of the ancient self how the *Aeneid* exerted this influence over its readers.

In representing its reader within the text as a spectator of images, the poem allows us to draw conclusions about this influence from the relationships established between this represented reader and other fictional characters of the poem, including the narrator. I will show that the reader is guided by the narrator whenever his voice manifests itself in the narrative in exclamations, judgments, and apostrophes. I will then go on to look at the reader's relationship to characters of the narrative and argue that the reader's gaze at the fictional scenarios is often shared with one of the fictional characters, but that the reader is not always invited to share the fictional character's emotional response to the spectacle. For instance, we will see that the reader is sharply separated from Juno's emotional response to her glimpse of the Trojan ships en route to Italy in the poem's first fictional scenario.[1]

In Aeneas the reader then finds a figure whose gaze he or she often shares and whose emotional responses to spectacles he or she is invited to share as well. Juno's persecution of Aeneas at the beginning of the narrative, Aeneas' despair during the sea storm, his dejection upon landing in foreign territory, and the deception by his mother make it easy for the reader to empathize with him. The reader is thus invited to share Aeneas' gaze, to share his responses to events, and to empathize with him, factors that in their combination encourage the reader's identification with Aeneas.

This identification with Aeneas is significant for our conception of the reader's sense of self and thus also for our inquiry into the ancient self in general. Looking at Aeneas' emotional responses to spectacles in book 1, we find that he responds to them in the same way as Quintilian expects young readers of Homer and Vergil to respond to their reading: his spirits are lifted, and he draws strength from what he sees (Quint. 1.8.5: *sublimitate heroi carminis animus adsurgat et ex magnitudine rerum spiritum ducat*). Quintilian's assessment of the epic reading experience suggests that Aeneas can be read as a model audience in his own story. This role of model audience is represented in the poem even more forcefully when, later in book 1, Aeneas becomes an invisible spectator, surrounded by a cloud cast around him by his mother for protection. For a few scenes, Aeneas, like the reader, is removed from the stage of events: he sees without being seen, he witnesses, responds to, and interprets events and images, but he does not participate in the action of the narrative.

THE READER'S GAZE

The first image that the poet creates in the first line of the *Aeneid* is one that is of great importance to the poem's conceptualization of the reader vis-à-vis the poet. In light of my earlier discussion, it is interesting to see that the opening lines of the *Aeneid* mirror in some form the performance situation I have described as being characteristic of ancient reading experiences. In the first line of the epic the narrator uses the verb *cano* to address his audience with an exposition of his subject matter. This opening statement—a convention of the epic genre—recalls the first line of the *Iliad* (Μῆνιν ἄειδε, θεά . . .), but it also invokes the world of oral poetry and performance. This does not mean that Vergil's world is identical to the world he invokes. Even though it is likely that ancient readers of the *Aeneid* encountered the poem in some sort of reading performance, the kind of performance Vergil invokes here is that of the oral poet, a world belonging to an irretrievable past. Vergil's use of this image of the oral poet performing to an immediately present audience is a nostalgic fiction that obscures the medium of writing through which the *Aeneid* addresses itself to its public.[2] For a brief moment we find ourselves in the company of the poet performing his epic narrative, even though this moment can exist only in our imagination. *Cano* puts both us as audience and the poet as performer into an imagined scenario of performance, a scenario that the poet invokes and that we cannot but share with him. It is on these terms that we enter the world of this epic, as spectators of the images the poet invokes in our imagination.[3]

Thus, the relationship the poet establishes with his readers in the first lines of the poem is itself fictional and visual. All subsequent narrative is, of course, by its very nature, highly visual as well. But it is visual not only because mythic and epic narratives cannot escape being so. The *Aeneid*'s narrative itself emphasizes its visuality, as we will see shortly in greater detail. In this, the opening gesture of the poet is emblematic of the reading experience of the poem as a whole. The poet creates images and spectacles in our imagination, and we—guided by the poet's voice—conjure up the poet's scenarios in our imagination, gazing at them with our mind's eye. It is always in reference to the poet figure that readers find their own perspectives on the story, or even literally their imaginary gaze.[4]

Inherent in this relationship between poet and audience is a certain imbalance of power. The poet speaks, we listen. This power imbalance is another characteristic of the ancient reading experience, as we have seen it represented by ancient authors in my discussion above. It can be felt throughout the narrative, as the narrator almost imperceptibly guides the readers' responses to the scenarios invoked by the narrative, as I will argue below in more detail.[5] Just like the skilled orator who uses *phantasia* to sway his audience's emotions and exert his influence over them, so the poet exerts influence over his audience's emotional reactions to the narrative by means of the images he uses.

As we have seen, the narrator manifests his presence in the opening section of the poem by creating an image of oral performance. His presence is felt throughout this passage in various ways. He addresses the Muse— another epic convention—thereby creating another fictional image, this time of the poet in the presence of the goddess, a scenario described

vividly by Hesiod in the *Theogony*. His presence is felt most strongly in the
apostrophe he addresses to the Muse in which he asks for an explanation
for the sufferings of Aeneas and poses his famous rhetorical question: "Is
the anger of the gods really as great as this?" (*Aen.* 1.11: *tantaene animis cae-
lestibus irae?*). After this question, the narrator begins the narrative proper
with an image of Carthage and Juno, her desires and resentments. The nar-
rator's presence phases out and seems to vanish. But our gaze at Carthage
and Juno is, of course, still guided by the narrator. Most of the time, the
narrator's presence is inconspicuous, but occasionally it manifests itself in
apostrophes and judgments about the narrated events. These moments in
the poem remind us of our initial fictional relationship with the poet as he
has established it in the proem. By invoking the image of the fictional oral
poet performing to us as a live audience, they contribute to the sense we
get as readers that we are inside the imaginary scenario of performance cre-
ated in the beginning. They strengthen the readers' sense of themselves as
spectators of the images conjured up in their mind's eye. They help estab-
lish the readers' gaze.[6]

Since the narrator's presence is felt only in brief moments, I will not
pursue these instances here in greater detail. Instead, I will consider a se-
quence of scenes subsequent to the proem that establish paradigmatic re-
lationships between the reader's gaze and that of the fictional characters.
The first of these scenes is that of Juno's anger at the Trojans in *Aen.* 1.15ff.
The relationship of the reader's gaze to that of Juno in this scene is dis-
cussed in chapter 4, where we will see that Juno's gaze and her emotional
responses to what she sees are sharply differentiated from those of the
reader, who is designated specifically as a Roman reader in this scene. After
the scene of Juno's anger, the narrative moves through a number of scenes
in which the reader's gaze is not consistently focused through any one fic-
tional character but occupies a position more akin to that of the omnis-
cient narrator. I have referred to one of these scenes above in chapter 2,
Jupiter's prophecy to Venus. Although much could be said about the vi-
sual functions of these scenes, I will not consider these passages further.
Instead, I will pick up the discussion of the narrative at the point where
Aeneas meets his disguised mother Venus, because it is at this point that a
sequence of events and images starts that is filtered through the gaze of Ae-
neas. Because Aeneas' gaze will turn out to have special relevance to the
formation of the reader's gaze, his emotional reactions to the spectacles in
this sequence are worth studying in our attempt to understand the impact
of the poem on the ancient reader's subjectivity.

ᴗᔆ THE GAZE OF AENEAS

Aeneas is set up as a spectator of events in the *Aeneid* more often than any other character.[7] The impression many modern readers have of Aeneas as passive and unheroic might very well be accounted for by this feature.[8] On the other hand, it is this role of Aeneas as spectator in his own poem that renders him supremely apt as a figure of identification for the reader, since the reader, too, is a spectator of the narrated events, and often the reader's view is filtered through the gaze of Aeneas.[9] If we think of the three great ecphrastic centerpieces of the poem, the pictures of Juno's temple in book 1, the doors of the temple at Cumae in book 6, and the shield of Aeneas in book 8, we find that in each case it is Aeneas who serves as an intratextual spectator of the images presented to the reader. Similarly, speeches that narrate events or convey information not immediately connected with the plot are often addressed to Aeneas, for example, Venus' narrative of Dido in book 1, Helenus' prophecy in book 3, Anchises' two speeches in the Underworld in book 6, and Evander's story of Hercules and Cacus in book 8.[10] This narrative function of Aeneas as spectator or audience suggests that he is assimilated to the reader.

In the following I will look more closely at some instances of Aeneas as spectator and investigate how the construction of his gaze and subject position influence the reading experience of the *Aeneid*. The first book of the *Aeneid* sets up its protagonist as a spectator or audience in a sequence of several scenes.[11] I will limit the present discussion of Aeneas as spectator to this sequence for two reasons. First, this set of scenes establishes Aeneas as a model audience in the beginning of the poem and thereby sets up a pattern followed later. Second, it is in this sequence that we encounter an image supremely apt to assimilate the intratextual spectator Aeneas with the extratextual reader: the image of the cloud shrouding Aeneas at his entrance into Carthage.

The sequence begins with Aeneas' encounter with Venus in the disguise of a huntress. The scene is visually rich, and it is here that Aeneas is turned into a reader of images whose interpretations can guide the reader's reactions to the poem. Thus the passage is pivotal for the reader's gaze, whose formation can be understood more fully by analyzing the anatomy of Aeneas' gaze. The reader has knowledge superior to Aeneas' in this scene, because he knows that Aeneas is meeting Venus, while Aeneas does not know this. Indeed, Venus has gone to great lengths in her effort to disguise herself, and the narrator is equally elaborate in representing her disguise. The difference of knowledge between Aeneas and the reader has the effect of showing the reader how good a reader of images Aeneas is. He turns out to be a very shrewd one, and it is this quality that recommends him to the reader as a trustworthy guide in his journey through the poem.

✥ READING THE DISGUISE OF VENUS

When Venus meets her son, she is described in great detail. The richness of this description is necessary, because Venus has disguised herself as a huntress, an image that runs exactly counter to anyone's idea of the goddess of love:

> *Cui mater media sese tulit obvia silva*
> *virginis os habitumque gerens et virginis arma*
> *Spartanae, vel qualis equos Threissa fatigat*
> *Harpalyce volucremque fuga praevertitur Hebrum.*
> *namque umeris de more habilem suspenderat arcum*
> *venatrix dederatque comam diffundere ventis,*
> *nuda genu nodoque sinus collecta fluentis.*
>
> (*Aen.* 1.314–20)

[His mother met him in the midst of a forest, having the face, carriage, and weapons of a Spartan maiden, or one like Thracian Harpalyce when she tires out her horses and surpasses fast-flowing Hebrus in her flight. For being a huntress, she had a bow hanging from her shoulders, her hair was allowed to flow in the wind, and she was naked up to her knees, her flowing dress being hitched up with a knot.]

Rather than appearing in her accustomed form as the goddess of love, Venus comes to Aeneas in a disguise. The description the narrator gives of her is overdetermined, perhaps for the very reason that her appearance is deceptive. Because the reader knows Venus' true identity, it is necessary to represent to the reader the image of a maiden huntress that Aeneas sees. Two images are used to describe this disguise, that of a Spartan maiden and that of Harpalyce, a Thracian princess who had devoted her life to the wild and whose life story resembles Vergil's Camilla.[12] The connotations of these images are manifold, but among other things Venus is endowed here with the simplicity and virtue of the Spartans of old,[13] while association with Thrace invokes a life in wild, untamed nature, far from civilization, since Thrace is usually seen in myth as on the edge of the civilized world.[14] The following description of Venus' appearance reinforces these associations by suggesting the classical iconography of Diana, the archetypal maiden huntress: a bow is hanging from her shoulder, her hair is flowing in the wind, and her dress is hitched up above the knee. By invoking these images the narrator accomplishes a convergence of what Aeneas sees with what the reader imagines. Thus, the reader gets to share Aeneas' gaze here.

The amount of description and simile used here indicates that a serious deception is under way. Because the reader is aware that the huntress is really Venus, the narrator overlays the reader's preconceived image of Venus as the goddess of love with an array of competing images that represent her disguise. The very effort invested in doing so suggests that Venus' disguise is contrary to her real identity. Hence, the narrator's effort to describe Venus' disguise ensures that the reader is aware of the gravity of Venus' deception of her son.

Aeneas' reaction to this image is more perceptive than one would expect to be possible: as we have seen, Venus has taken great pains to disguise herself as a huntress, and the narrator has taken equally great pains to represent that disguised appearance. Nevertheless, Aeneas sees some of the truth right away: he tells her that she must be a goddess, because she does not look or sound like a mortal (*Aen.* 1.327–28). In this reaction Aeneas reminds us of another perceptive reader of a disguised Venus: in the *Homeric Hymn to Aphrodite* Aeneas' father, Anchises, is visited by Aphrodite in the guise of a mortal maiden; Anchises, too, sees right away that the woman in front of him must be a goddess (*Hom.h.Aphr.* 93–99). Thus, Aeneas' astute interpretation of the image before him has a precedent in his own father's experience. An ancient reader of the scene would probably have picked up on Vergil's allusion to the story of Aphrodite's deception of Anchises. The function of the allusion here is to establish that Aeneas is not only a shrewd reader on his own account, but that as a son of his father he can be expected to be such a shrewd reader. It thereby reinforces the reader's impression of Aeneas as a trustworthy interpreter of images.

Venus lies to Aeneas, as she did to his father, and assures him that she is mortal. This assurance is again supported by the invocation of an image, as Venus tells Aeneas that it is customary for Tyrian maidens to wear a quiver and purple hunting boots tied high on the calves (*Aen.* 1.336–37). The detail of color and attire in this image is quite unnecessary to make the simple point that Venus claims to be mortal, but it reinforces the image previously created for the reader and enhances it with yet more detail. It also reminds the reader again of Venus' deception of Aeneas and thus prepares us for the sympathy we inevitably feel for Aeneas' anguish when he himself makes the discovery.

Before I turn to Aeneas' interpretation of this scene, I want to draw attention to one detail of Venus' attire that adds another dimension to the visuality of this scene. The term Venus uses to describe her hunting boots is *coturnus,* the technical term for the shoes of tragic actors. This has led one scholar to argue that Venus' encounter with Aeneas can be understood as a tragic prologue to the Dido story, which many critics have long regarded as a kind of tragedy.[15] E. L. Harrison argues that Venus' role here should be compared to that of divinities in tragedies such as Euripides' *Hippolytus* or *Bacchae,* where the divinity appears in the prologue and gives an exposition of the events leading up to the action of the drama.[16] According to Harrison, when Venus tells Aeneas the story of Dido's escape from Tyre and the foundation of Carthage (1.338–68), she in effect gives Aeneas and the reader an exposition of the personal history of a tragic heroine. This role of Venus as the prologue goddess of a tragedy is here indicated by the detail of her hunting attire.[17]

Harrison's article has important implications both for the visuality of the scene and for the interpretation of the Dido episode as a tragedy, because he draws attention to the visual aspects of its tragic setup. It is a visual aspect, Venus' boots, that introduces the notion of tragedy into the epic. This notion of tragedy, in turn, reinforces the visuality of the narrative and the reader's visual relationship to the text, as a spectator of an imaginary spectacle. What is most important about this tragic element of the scene for our current purposes is that it leads us to understand Aeneas as a spectator of the tragic performance of Venus. By implication this suggests that Aeneas is also merely a spectator of the tragedy that is about to unfold, namely the Dido episode as a whole. This is, of course, not strictly true, because it is Aeneas' presence at Carthage and his interactions with Dido that cause the tragic events of book 4. But it may in some degree account for the relatively minor role Aeneas actually plays in those events, his absence from most of the scenes of book 4, and the relative paucity of his speeches, especially in comparison with Dido. If we take the present scene as setting a tone for the Dido episode as a whole in terms of spectators and spectacles, then Dido is alone on the tragic stage of book 4, while Aeneas is another spectator who witnesses her monologues and lonely suffering, along with the reader.[18]

Let me now return to Aeneas' interpretation of the image before him. After Venus has told Aeneas about Dido's fate and cheered his failing spirits with an omen for a more promising future, she leaves him. At that moment Aeneas recognizes his mother and accuses her of deceiving him:

> *Quid natum totiens, crudelis tu quoque, falsis*
> *ludis imaginibus? cur dextrae iungere dextram*
> *non datur ac veras audire et reddere voces?*
>
> (Aen. 1.407–9)

[Even you are cruel! Why do you deceive your son so often with false images? Why do you not grant me to shake hands and hear and speak true words?]

In calling Venus' disguise a "false image," Aeneas reads the image before him correctly once again. His emotional response to his mother's deception is anguished. He wishes for the consolation and reassurance his divine mother's undisguised presence would presumably convey. He feels cheated and considers the encounter as inauthentic: she has not granted him an exchange of "true" words. What he does not know is that right before this encounter Venus pleaded with Jupiter on the Trojans' behalf and was reassured of their ultimate success. He also does not know that right after she leaves him, she will cast a protective cloud around him to prevent anyone from seeing or interfering with him (1.411–14).

"LET THE MIND SOAR"

Still, one cannot help wondering why Venus inflicts this seemingly unnecessary disappointment on her son, whose fate has, after all, been trying enough up until this point. A partial answer to this question lies in the function Aeneas serves in this story as a figure of identification for the reader, whose emotional responses to events and images provide a model for the reader's own responses to the text. Aeneas reacts dejectedly in this scene for the last time in this book. Beginning in the next scene, Aeneas' responses to the spectacles before him are positive, sometimes even more positive than the situation seems to justify. The fact that he achieves this transformation without the supernatural support of Venus, that he achieves it in fact despite her deception of him, renders Aeneas' positive responses to the world a viable model for the reader's own responses to the story.

Aeneas' anguish in this scene is the last in a series of despondent reactions to the events of the book so far. The first time we encounter him is during the sea storm. Believing that he is about to die, he despairs and wishes he had died in Troy (1.94–101). Later on, after the Trojans have been shipwrecked and landed at the shores of Africa, Aeneas cheers his comrades, reminding them of dangers they mastered in the past and of the goal they are promised to reach in the future (1.197–209). But while he puts on a brave face before his companions, Aeneas' own spirits are depressed. It is in this troubled state of mind that Aeneas encounters his disguised mother.

It is hard to imagine a more desperate situation than Aeneas' at this moment: homeless and without hope of returning to Troy, he has been chasing after the mirage of a promised new home that keeps receding into the distance, as supernatural forces beyond his control throw obstacles in his path to prevent his arrival there. Although he had almost reached Italy, a storm has left him and his crew decimated, shipwrecked, and friendless on a foreign shore whose potential dangers are unknown to them. Dejection seems natural, and Venus' deception of her son reminds us that this is so. It is all the more remarkable, then, that in the following scenes Aeneas derives comfort and even hope and confidence from spectacles that might otherwise cause suspicion, envy, or concern.

But this is exactly the kind of response that Quintilian expects the reader of epic to have, as well. Seeing Aeneas represented as dejected, readers have an easier time identifying with him than if his heroic status shielded him completely from the frustrations of human experience. This is what draws us into Aeneas' emotional world and later on helps him guide the reader to experience the sublimity of epic that "lets the mind soar" by modeling positive reactions to the world. We cannot help but sympathize with him in this scene, because there is no obvious explanation for Venus' deception. Such sympathy makes it easy for the reader to identify with Aeneas, as the reader shares Aeneas' gaze, he or she sees what Aeneas sees and is then led to feel the same indignation Aeneas feels at Venus' deception.

It is at this juncture in the text that an image is introduced that turns Aeneas into an intratextual model reader. Venus casts around Aeneas a protective cloud that enables him to see his surroundings without being seen, to watch the interactions of others without interacting with them. In effect, Aeneas' protective cloud renders him an invisible observer of the events that unfold in the story, in short, an intratextual double for the reader. In the following scenes Aeneas' gaze coincides with that of the reader, and like the reader, Aeneas cannot influence the plot, because he is invisible to the agents of the plot. Aeneas' protective cloud may be understood as a metaphor for the reading experience itself. Just as Aeneas moves unseen through a part of his own story, so the reader enters the fictional world of the poem shrouded in his or her own protective cloud, the cloud of reading, the medium that separates the reader from the story by an unbridgeable gap.

This convergence of Aeneas' situation with that of the reader in this sequence of scenes, and the coincidence of their gazes renders Aeneas a model for the reader in his reactions to and interpretations of the scenes as well. As we have seen in our discussion of the power of images, it is the emotional impact of an image that the ancients were interested in influencing. When Aeneas reproaches his mother for disguising herself at their meeting, we cannot help feeling his anguish. Having entered into this relationship of identification and empathy with the titular hero of the poem, the reader occupies a position or vantage point that is particularly conducive to adopting Aeneas' emotional responses, as we have experienced just now in the case of Aeneas' anguish at his mother's deception. Aeneas can fulfill this function of guiding the reader's response, because the reader shares his gaze as well as empathizes with him. Both components are necessary to effect his influence on the reader. We will see later on that the reader does not identify in the same way with characters whose gaze he or she does not share.

❧ GAZING AT CARTHAGE

The scene of Venus as huntress is only the first in a whole sequence of scenes that put Aeneas in the role of a spectator whose gaze filters that of the reader. When Aeneas sees Carthage for the first time from a distance, he marvels at the spectacle of the foundation of a city:[19]

> *miratur molem Aeneas, magalia quondam,*
> *miratur portas strepitumque et strata viarum.*
> *instant ardentes Tyrii: pars ducere muros*
> *molirique arcem et manibus subvolvere saxa,*
> *pars optare locum tecto et concludere sulco;*
> *iura magistratusque legunt sanctumque senatum.*
> *hic portus alii effodiunt; hic alta theatris*

fundamenta locant alii, immanisque columnas
rupibus excidunt, scaenis decora apta futuris.

(*Aen.* 1.421–29)

[Aeneas marvels at the massive buildings, once only huts, he marvels at the gates and the bustle, and the pavements of the roads. The busy Tyrians are hard at work: some build the walls, fortify a citadel, and roll rocks with their hands, others choose a place for their home and surround it with a boundary; they choose laws and officials and an inviolable senate. Others dig a harbor here; there yet others lay deep foundations for theaters and cut immense columns from rocks, ornaments suitable to a future stage.]

Much of what is described here cannot be understood as a realistic or naturalistic description of what a person would see when looking at a city from a distance. Rather, the passage supplies the reader with an interpretation of what is seen. When we read that Aeneas sees the Tyrians choose laws and magistrates and a senate, we can assume that this is how Aeneas interprets the spectacle before him. The scene is completed with an exclamation Aeneas utters at the sight of the city:

o fortunati quorum iam moenia surgunt!

(437)

[O fortunate ones whose walls are already rising!]

Thus the reader sees Carthage not only through Aeneas' eyes and with his interpretation of the spectacle before him, but also with Aeneas' emotional response to it.[20] It is Aeneas' longing for a new home that manifests itself in this scene through his interpretation of the sights he sees. Between the description of the city and Aeneas' exclamation the narrator inserts a simile that compares the spectacle of the foundation of the city to the busy dealings of a bee colony:

qualis apes aestate nova per florea rura
exercet sub sole labor, cum gentis adultos
educunt fetus, aut cum liquentia mella
stipant et dulci distendunt nectare cellas,
aut onera accipiunt venientum, aut agmine facto

ignavum fucos pecus a praesepibus arcent;
fervet opus redolentque thymo fraglantia mella.

(430–36)

[as bees are busy with their toil in the sunshine at the beginning of
summer across the flowering countryside, when they lead out the
grown-up offspring of their race, or when they stuff in the liquid
honey and stretch out their cells with sweet nectar, or receive the loads
of the incoming bees, or in battle formation ward off the drones, that
lazy herd, from their hive; they work fervently, and the fragrant honey
is scented with thyme.]

It is not entirely clear whether it is the narrator or Aeneas who compares
the spectacle of the foundation of Carthage with a bee colony. But our in-
ability to decide this question only underlines a much more important
point: with this comparison narrator and main character fuse in their re-
sponse to the spectacle. It is quite obvious that both see an idyllic, happy
quality to the foundation of a city.[21] The bucolic image of the bee colony
in the countryside is filled with sunlight, flowers, honey, nectar, and fra-
grant thyme, while the well-ordered state of bees resembles the idealized
society of Italian farmers found in the *Georgics*. In fact, our *Aeneid* simile
here is a pastiche of quotes from *Georgics* 4,[22] where the society of bees is
described as an ideal community with a special relationship to the divine.[23]
In choosing this simile as a transition from Aeneas' longing gaze to his
openly pronounced envy of the Carthaginians, the narrator takes utmost
care to bring the reader's response to the spectacle in line with that of Ae-
neas. When the reader imagines the foundation of Carthage, it must be as
a spectacle that fills the beholder with a longing for the bucolic perfection
of the bee colony.

Aeneas' entry into Carthage is equally designed to portray Aeneas as a
spectator. His mother has now supplied him with a protective cloud that
renders him invisible to the people around him, while allowing him to see
his surroundings:

infert se saeptus nebula (mirabile dictu)
per medios, miscetque viris neque cernitur ulli.

(439f.)

[He enters their midst wrapt in a cloud (a marvel to say) and mingles
with the people, but is not seen by anyone.]

Upon entering the city Aeneas comes to the temple of Juno, which is dec-
orated with images of the Trojan War. In a lengthy *ecphrasis* the various
images are described (1.456–93). Again it is the gaze of Aeneas that filters
the reader's view of the spectacle, and again Aeneas' interpretation is im-
posed upon the images:[24] thus, we see a savage Achilles, a Diomedes
bloody with murders, an unhappy Troilus, and an unjust Minerva.[25]

Because the images depict scenes from the Trojan War, it has been ob-
served that this *ecphrasis* is in itself a reference to other epic poems, to the
Iliad and the Epic Cycle. Indeed, if we read Vergil's narrative of Aeneas'
entry into Carthage against Odysseus' stay among the Phaeacians in the
Odyssey, Vergil's *ecphrasis* corresponds structurally to the performance of a
song about the Trojan War.[26] Before Odysseus tells the Phaeacians about his
wanderings, Demodocus performs a song about this subject (*Od.* 8.72– 82).
Vergil's *ecphrasis* of scenes from the Trojan War is embedded in a narrative
abounding with conscious allusions to Odysseus' arrival among the Phaea-
cians. Aeneas meets his patron deity, Venus, who dons a disguise, just as
Odysseus had met his patron, Athena, in a similar disguise (*Od.* 7.18–78 and
Aen. 1.314–410). In both narratives the arrival of the hero among strangers
is celebrated with a banquet (*Od.* 8.55–95 and *Aen.* 1.695– 756); both ban-
quets provide an occasion for the hero to tell his guests reluctantly about the
sack of Troy and his subsequent wanderings (*Od.* 9–12 and *Aen.* 2–3).[27]

It is, then, significant that Vergil transforms Demodocus' song into an
ecphrasis. Embedded narrative has become explicitly visual. Not only does
this emphasize the visuality of the *Aeneid,* but it also self-consciously re-
flects on it. The shift from song to picture articulates a shift in emphasis
from one source of meaning to another, from singer to spectator, from au-
thor to audience. In the *Odyssey* we meet Demodocus, who performs the
song; his presence gives to his poem an origin, a source whose agency
shapes the story. In the *Aeneid,* on the other hand, the author as a source
of meaning has been removed from view. We don't find out who painted
the images on Juno's temple, who selected the scenes to be depicted. We
don't even know whether we are given an accurate description of the temple
images, because all we have is Aeneas' perception of them. Hence, the shift
from song to picture has the effect of turning the reader's attention away
from the meaning the images have for their creator, and toward the mean-
ing they have for their intratextual spectator, Aeneas. It is the effect the im-
ages have on Aeneas, the model reader, that is of interest here.

As in the previous scene, Aeneas again provides us with an emotional
response. He addresses his companion, Achates, in the following words:[28]

sunt hic etiam sua praemia laudi,
sunt lacrimae rerum et mentem mortalia tangunt.
solve metus; feret haec aliquam tibi fama salutem.

(461–63)

[Here, too, merit has its rewards, there are tears for adversity and the affairs of mortals touch the heart. Give over your fears; this fame will bring you some deliverance.]

Then the narrator comments on Aeneas' interpretation of the pictures, with the following words:

sic ait atque animum pictura pascit inani
multa gemens.

(464f.)

[Thus he spoke, and, grieving much, he fed his soul with empty images.]

By using visuality, the *Aeneid* lays explicit emphasis on the reception of its images, its stories by the reader as a source of meaning, as opposed to their creation by the artist. In this sense the present scene has much in common with the previous one. But there is a crucial difference. While in the previous scene the narrator accomplished a convergence of the reader's point of view with that of Aeneas through the bee simile, here the narrator comments directly on Aeneas' emotional response to the spectacle. When we gazed at Carthage together with Aeneas, our response was guided almost imperceptibly, but here the reader is made aware of Aeneas' response, thereby presenting two vantage points, that of the narrator and that of Aeneas, and leaving the reader to find his or her own. What is the purpose of this shift in narrative technique? Since this question is of great consequence for our understanding of the reader's gaze and its relationship to the gaze of Aeneas, it is worth considering in greater detail.

The meaning of *inani* here has been much discussed. It has been suggested that the narrator implies a misinterpretation of the temple images on Aeneas' part, because the depiction of Trojan defeat on the temple of the divine enemy of the Trojans should be a victory monument to Juno, not an expression of compassion for or praise of the Trojans.[29] W. R. Johnson reads these lines as a melancholy reflection on Aeneas' self-deception; he translates *inanis* as "deceptive" and "illusory."[30] But *inanis* can also be taken in its basic meaning and translated as "empty." If we translate in this way, an equally powerful point emerges: What the narrator accomplishes with these words is a clear distinction between the images described in the passage, which in themselves are lifeless and empty, and the interpretation that is imposed on them by Aeneas and which in turn gives him comfort, courage, and hope. It is this ability of Aeneas to draw strength from his own interpretation of the world that emerges from this scene as powerfully as from the previous one.[31] By calling the pictures empty, the narrator draws attention to the effort involved in Aeneas' response to them. Aeneas thus gives an example to the reader, how sense can be made from chaos and disorder.

Many scholars have detected a typically Vergilian melancholy in the words of the narrator here. The reading I suggest here has a different tendency. The defining characteristic of the two scenes discussed is the way the narrator guides and defines the reader's point of view by conflating it with that of Aeneas. When we ask the question some critics have asked, namely, what Aeneas is so happy about in this scene,[32] we must distance ourselves from the gaze constructed in the poem. Only when we resist the narrator's efforts to draw us into Aeneas' gaze and emotional response can we step back to review the *ecphrasis* and question the appropriateness of Aeneas' reaction to the images. If the reader remains in the space created for him/her by the poem, he/she experiences something very positive, namely, the transformation of grief and tragedy into hope and faith.[33] This transformation is modeled by Aeneas, and it accords with ancient cultural expectations of the effects of reading the sublime, as we have seen in Quintilian and others.

Up to this point in the narrative Aeneas has been set up as a spectator in a sequence of three scenes, the tragic prologue of Venus as huntress, the view of Carthage, and the images of the temple of Juno. The next scene presents the reader with yet another vivid spectacle: while Aeneas is still in Juno's temple and still concealed by a cloud, Dido approaches the same temple and proceeds to engage in her business as queen, when suddenly Aeneas' missing companions enter and approach.[34] Ilioneus addresses a lengthy speech to Dido, requesting hospitable treatment from the Carthaginians, which is followed by a generous reply from the queen.[35] The whole scene is imbued with a theatrical quality, which manifests itself not only in the dialogue between the two major characters but also in the set-up of the scene in general. The narrative introduces the temple of Juno like a stage that is entered by Dido and Ilioneus with their respective companions, as if they were actors with accompanying choruses. The dialogue narrates previous events, thus imitating messenger speeches well known in tragedy, as well as introducing potential conflict, tension, and ultimate resolution. Although Aeneas witnesses this spectacle from close by, he is invisible to those involved in it, because Venus' cloud still conceals him from view. Thus he views the action like the member of a theatrical audience, which again gives him the role of model reader of the narrative.

READING LIKE AENEAS

For book 1 the sequence of episodes constructing Aeneas as spectator is concluded with this scene, which ends with the lifting of the cloud that concealed Aeneas from view. While removing the cloud, Venus also sheds beauty on Aeneas, which succeeds in stunning Dido:

> *Obstipuit primo aspectu Sidonia Dido*
>
> (1.613)
>
> [At first sight Dido was stunned]

Aeneas now enters the scene himself and turns from invisible spectator to speaking agent, but later on in the poem there are several other instances of Aeneas in the role of spectator. There is first Aeneas' description of the scenes at the fall of Troy in book 2, which are not only images Aeneas conjures up in Dido's mind, but also events he narrates as having witnessed with his own eyes. At the beginning of book 6 Aeneas views the gates of the Apollo temple at Cumae, which contain images of the myth of the Minotaur.[36] Later on in the same book Aeneas views the Underworld. His role as spectator is especially marked when Anchises shows him the parade of unborn souls waiting to be born as Aeneas' heroic descendants.[37] Aeneas' gaze at these unborn souls is marked by a second instance of a bee simile (6.707–9), thus linking it to Aeneas' gaze at the spectacle of the foundation of Carthage in book 1. This time, the spectacle before Aeneas' eyes serves to instruct him about the nature of the universe and man's life in it, as well as being a magnificent display of Roman history. Another such spectacle of Roman history is presented to Aeneas in the description of the shield he receives from the hands of his mother.[38]

Many of the scenes in which Aeneas is a spectator follow the pattern we have observed in the sequence of book 1 discussed above. As a spectator of the pageant of heroes in the Underworld and beholder of the shield in book 8, Aeneas reacts to the spectacles by deriving joy and strength from them, as it is characteristic for him, even if he does not understand what he sees. The aspects of Roman history with which he is presented are, of course, subsequent to his own life. Nevertheless they are inextricably tied to his life: after all, it is his flight from the vanquished Troy and his journey to Italy that link the foundation of Rome to Aeneas' world of myth. When Aeneas gazes at scenes and people from the future, he may not be familiar with them, as is suggested at the end of the shield description:

> *Talia per clipeum Volcani dona parentis*
> *miratur* <u>*rerumque ignarus*</u> *imagine gaudet,*
> *attollens umero famamque et fata nepotum.*
>
> (8.729–31)

[Such were the gifts of his mother on the shield of Vulcan; he marveled at them, <u>and although he was ignorant of the things depicted</u>, he rejoiced in the image and lifted on his shoulder the glory and destiny of his descendants.]

Despite his ignorance, however, Aeneas takes heart at the spectacle of his descendants' future.[39] Not only his sense of duty toward his destined fate is responsible for Aeneas' willingness to submit to the commands of the gods; he takes an active role in controlling his emotional reactions to the spectacles he encounters. This power to control his emotional responses to the world is what makes Aeneas special in contrast with other characters. His ability to impose a positive interpretation on the spectacles of his and his people's past and future fame gives him the strength to pursue his destined course. This is the function of casting Aeneas as a spectator of the shield, or of the pageant of heroes Anchises shows him in the Underworld. As in book 1, Aeneas again proves to be an optimistic interpreter of spectacles in these cases.

The above quote makes the point that he rejoices at the image on the shield, perhaps having a vague idea that what is represented has to do with his descendants' future fame. This is not expressed here, but it is made explicit in book 6. The passages that frame Anchises' second speech with the pageant of heroes emphasize that Aeneas and Anchises are spectators of this parade of souls that Anchises talks about (6.752–55 and 886–87). Immediately following this, we find out what Aeneas' reaction to the spectacle is: his heart is burning with love of future fame (889: *incenditque animum famae venientis amore*). Aeneas' gaze is again followed by his positive

reaction to the spectacle. It is not the melancholy image of young Marcel-
lus that stays with Aeneas when he takes leave of his father, but the posi-
tive interpretation imposed on the spectacle as a whole. The high pathos
of the lament for Marcellus could even be seen as contributing to Aeneas'
reaction. The elevated tone of the passage is a supreme example of the sub-
lime style, as I have suggested in chapter 2. Aeneas' positive reaction to
such language is no different from what ancient rhetoricians expected as
an emotional response of an audience to the sublime style.

Aeneas' elation at the spectacle of the pageant of heroes in book 6 is ex-
actly comparable to his reaction to the *ecphrasis* of the Trojan scenes de-
picted on the walls of the Carthaginian temple of Juno (1.461: *Sunt hic
etiam sua praemia laudi* [Here, too, there are just rewards for virtue] and
1.463: *Feret haec aliquam tibi fama salutem.* [This fame will bring you some
salvation.]). Such is also the effect on Aeneas of watching the city of
Carthage in the process of being built, as can be seen in his exclamation:

o fortunati quorum iam moenia surgunt!

(1.437)

[Lucky ones, whose walls are already rising!]

The passages concerned with the spectacle of Roman history clearly func-
tion as motivating factors for Aeneas' quest, and they can only do so, be-
cause Aeneas imposes on them a positive interpretation.

The pageant of heroes is interesting for our discussion from another
perspective as well, for it is here that Aeneas is explicitly equated not only
with a reader of the poem, but specifically with a Roman reader. When
Anchises leads Aeneas to a hill from which they can better survey the pa-
rade of future Romans, the word used for their viewing is *legere:*

*Dixerat Anchises natumque unaque Sibyllam
conventus trahit in medios turbamque sonantem,
et tumulum capit unde omnis longo ordine posset
adversos legere et venientum discere vultus.*

(6.752–55)

[Anchises had spoken, and he led his son and the Sibyl into the
midst of the noisy crowd of assembled souls, and went to stand on
a hill from which he could scrutinize all the faces of the souls com-
ing toward them in a long procession.]

There is nothing remarkable in the choice of words here from the perspective of a native speaker of Latin, but for us the use of *legere* draws attention to the fact that viewing and reading can be expressed by the same word in Latin. The use of *legere* as meaning "to read" surely derives from the idea that in reading one sees the letters on the page, but the use of the term in this particular passage equates Aeneas with the extratextual reader of the poem in a marked way. Viewing can be expressed in Latin with many other terms, and the fact that *legere* is used here activates the reader's consciousness of his/her own act of reading. Both the reader and Aeneas are "reading" the pageant of heroes, they are united in their mode of perception at least linguistically, if not literally.

At the very end of Anchises' speech we find the famous lines addressed to the Roman reader that claim as the particular skill of the Romans the dominion over the world (851: *tu regere imperio populos, Romane, memento*). Within the narrative context of the speech, this is somewhat unexpected, since its addressee has throughout been Aeneas. He is the one Anchises is talking to, for his benefit does Anchises point out the figures from Roman history. Several times in the speech the reader is reminded of this: Anchises addresses him as "my son" (6.781: *nate*), he refers to Aeneas' son Silvius as "your son" (6.763: *tua postuma proles*) and to Lavinia as "your wife" (764–65: *quem tibi . . . Lavinia coniunx/ educet*); often he tells him to look at figures he points out, rather than to imagine them, as he would if addressing the reader (e.g., 6.760: *vides; Aen.* 6.788; 826: *cernis;* 825: *aspice*). But at the end of the speech it is the Roman reader, rather than Aeneas to whom Anchises is speaking. This transition is accomplished by emphasizing Aeneas as the addressee of the speech less and less as Anchises goes on. Before he addresses the Roman reader, he even addresses a number of heroes from the pageant (6.834–46). This gradual progress of the speech smooths over the transition from Aeneas to the Roman reader, so that in the end Anchises addresses that reader.[40] But at the very moment that Anchises does so, he has arrived at the end of his speech. The return to the narrative makes the reader aware that Anchises was addressing Aeneas all along. And yet, the double audiences Anchises invokes here draw attention to the assimilation of the reader with Aeneas, a textual strategy we have already observed in book 1. What is added in the present passage is the distinct definition of that reader as Roman. When we come to the depiction of passion in the next chapter, we will see that the passions, too, are inextricably linked to notions of ethnicity. As the reader is designated as Roman when he shares the gaze of Aeneas, so the passions of some figures discussed below will turn out to be at the same time a spectacle for the gaze of the reader and one that is linked to foreignness. Both of these textual strategies serve to distance the reader from fully identifying with the figures whose passions are depicted, as I have suggested above in chapter 2.

We have interpreted the image of the cloud that disguises Aeneas in book 1 at his entry into Carthage as a metaphor for reading. A parallel to this scenario can be found in book 2, where Aeneas again is a spectator in one scene. Here, too, a cloud is used to articulate the special type of viewing Aeneas is given, and again this image assimilates him to the reader. When Aeneas rushes through the burning Troy in an effort to defend the vanquished city, his mother appears to him and allows him to see what his fellow mortals cannot see: for Aeneas, Venus lifts the cloud that obscures the vision of mortals, preventing them from seeing how the gods interfere in the affairs of mortals. This enables Aeneas to see the gods at war in the city, all of them participating in the city's destruction, and he realizes that a defense is hopeless. In the context of Aeneas' gaze, the passage about the cloud that obscures mortal vision is of particular importance:

namque omnem, quae nunc obducta tuenti
mortalis hebetat visus tibi et umida circum
caligat, nubem eripiam.

(604–6)

[For I will remove the entire cloud which is cast over your sight and so dulls and obscures your mortal vision with its mist.]

We learn from Venus that the vision of mortals is less accurate, because there is an all-pervading mist, which can be penetrated only by the vision of the gods. Thus, Aeneas' vision at that moment is exceptional, as his divine mother grants her son a privilege not available to common mortals. But this is, in fact, the kind of vision the reader of epic always has, as the actions of the gods are depicted there along with the actions of the mortal characters. We need only think of the beginning of the *Iliad,* where Athena comes to Achilles and prevents him from killing Agamemnon, but no one sees her except Achilles himself, or of Cupid, in the *Argonautica,* who shoots an arrow at Medea to make her fall in love. Aeneas' vision is special only in comparison with that of his fellow Trojans or the Greeks, or any other mortal character of the story. Aeneas' privileged gaze in this scene is none other than that of the extratextual reader, whose knowledge is often superior to that of the characters because he shares the narrator's gaze. That Aeneas sees here what otherwise would be visible only to the reader and narrator is in line with our earlier observations of Aeneas as a model audience in his own story. The image of the cloud as a metaphor for reading is already familiar to us from book 1, although the image is employed somewhat differently there. There the cloud removes only Aeneas from the vision of other characters, and that only temporarily. In the present scene the cloud is a permanent veil that conceals the gods from the vision of mortals. But in both scenes it is the vision of other characters that is impaired, and in both scenes Aeneas gains from the cloud a kind of vision that is similar to the imaginary gaze of the reader.

In addition to this, the present scene needs Aeneas to have that kind of vision for another reason as well, for here Aeneas is himself the narrator of the scene, depicting it for Dido at her court in Carthage. By telling Dido the story of his sufferings, Aeneas here enters the role of narrator himself. Venus' intervention at Troy allows Aeneas to tell Dido the story of the battle of the gods over Troy just as the narrator would have done. This role of narrator distinguishes him from other characters in the poem. Although he is not the only character telling a story, the length of his narrative surpasses that of all others and rivals in its extent the narrative of the narrator himself, thus assimilating Aeneas with the narrator. This assimilation, as that of Aeneas with the reader, gives Aeneas a position vis-à-vis the reader that is privileged over other characters, as he is allowed to impose his perspective on the events of two entire books.

GAZING AT HELEN

We have seen that Aeneas' role in his encounter with Venus during the fall of Troy is assimilated both to that of the reader and the narrator, although he is also a character in it. All this is accomplished by the extraordinary gaze Venus grants him. How does the narrative motivate the necessity for Aeneas to attain this kind of vision? A textual problem makes it difficult for us to answer this question, because Venus' intervention immediately follows the famous Helen episode, whose authenticity is notoriously uncertain.[41] Since the status of the text is questionable at this point, it is worth looking at the textual problem if we are to understand the narrative motivation for Aeneas' special kind of gaze. In this scene Aeneas sees Helen, becomes angry at her as the cause of the destruction of Troy, and intends to kill her. This passage provides the ideal motivation for Venus' intervention, because she says she will show Aeneas the battle of the gods in order to make him understand that it is not Helen or Paris that is to blame for the destruction of Troy, but that it is the will of the gods themselves that Troy fall (*Aen.* 2.601–3). When he sees the gods at war, he returns to his earlier purpose of seeking his family.

Now, the problem with the Helen episode is that it is not contained in the best Vergil manuscripts. It is preserved by Servius Auctus, who quotes it in his commentary (*ad Aen.* 2.566) and tells us that Varius and Tucca, the editors of the *Aeneid* after Vergil's death, removed the passage according to instructions from Augustus.[42] Because of this peculiar mode of transmission of the passage, its authenticity has been disputed. Did Vergil himself write the lines, or are they the product of a later interpolator? If they are not Vergil's, what, if anything, did Vergil want to stand between lines 566 and 589?

These days, most critics assume that the passage is Vergilian, but that Vergil meant to revise it.[43] This makes good sense, since the passage is necessary to the progress of the narrative, and it also accords with the testimony of Servius, who tells us that Varius and Tucca edited the passage out. If Servius is to be trusted, then the ancients had no doubt that Vergil is the author of the passage, but their sensibilities were offended by something in it that they felt did not belong with the rest of the poem. Still, these arguments do not lay to rest the objections to Vergilian authorship that have been made by other scholars. On both sides of the question, much of the debate is dependent on evaluating the stylistic features of the language in the scene. What I would like to do here is to approach the Helen episode with attention to the gaze of Aeneas and to focus specifically on the question of what aspect of this scene was so offensive to ancient readers. This can help us understand how the episode fits into its larger narrative context in terms of its construction of the subject. Thereby we may come up with our own view of the authenticity of the scene, which can in turn help to strengthen the arguments on one side of the debate.

In the scene following the Helen episode, as we have seen, Venus grants Aeneas a supernatural gaze to cure his frenzy and grief. This frenzy is motivated in the Helen episode by Aeneas' gaze at Helen (*Aen.* 2.569: *Tyndarida aspicio*) and the effect this image has on him: his anger rises immediately upon seeing her (2.575: *exarsere ignes animo, subit ira*). We have seen that in book 1 Venus also grants Aeneas a privileged gaze, and the result of this privilege is that Aeneas is able to interpret positively and react with joy to the images he encounters. Thus, the sequence of book 1 is paralleled in book 2 to a certain extent. In both sequences Aeneas' privileged gaze positively affects his emotional reactions to events. In book 1 Aeneas goes from dejection to hope, in book 2 from frenzy to a sense of duty to his family. But the Helen episode goes beyond the sequence of book 1 by representing Aeneas' gaze as actually effecting frenzy in him. This is not paralleled in book 1. There Aeneas had been downcast previous to Venus' intervention, but he was not shown as reacting with frenzy to images he saw.

This point is important, because in chapter 2 we saw that ancient thinking about the self saw the gaze as an entryway to the soul; thus the gaze held for the ancients the danger of causing disturbances such as frenzy in the self. We have seen that Aeneas' gaze was constructed differently in book 1, because he reacted positively to the images he saw. But the *Aeneid* does contain a number of passages in which the gaze of a character causes disturbances such as frenzy in the soul. These characters, as we will see in the next chapter, are most often women: Andromache, Juno, and, most prominently, Dido. If the portrayal of such effects on the soul was seen as something primarily associated with women, then portraying Aeneas in that way would run the risk of offending ancient sensibilities. Aeneas' frenzy would then be a blot on his masculine power of self-control, so important to the ancients' ideal of manhood. This reaction of the ancients to the scene is reflected in Servius' information about the exclusion of the passage. Servius himself argues that it is unworthy for Aeneas to want to kill a woman.[44] The reasons of Varius and Tucca for excluding the passage are not given, but lack of revision cannot be the sole reason, because the poem contains numerous half-lines that were not edited out.[45]

So far, then, the construction of Aeneas' gaze in the Helen episode is different from its construction in book 1. But there is also reason to consider the passage as harmonizing with the construction of Aeneas' gaze elsewhere in the *Aeneid,* because there is something very ingenious about the Helen episode. Aeneas' gaze in this passage fits perfectly into the way Aeneas' gaze is constructed in the scenes immediately preceding and following. Before seeing Helen, Aeneas had seen the death of Priam, which had caused him to turn his thoughts to his own father and family (2.560–63: *subiit cari genitoris <u>imago</u>, / ut regem aequaevum crudeli vulnere <u>vidi</u> / vitam exhalantem . . .*). Then, when his gaze at Helen incites his frenzy, his cure is effected by another gaze, the supernatural gaze Venus grants. It is this gaze that reminds him again of his family.

Clearly, the gap between lines 566 and 589 must be filled by some scene depicting Aeneas' frenzy, since it is that which motivates Venus' intervention, as she herself says (2.594–95: *nate, quis indomitas tantus dolor excitat iras? / quid furis? aut quonam nostri tibi cura recessit?*). I think that the idea of using a gaze, Venus' supernatural gaze, as a cure for another gaze, Aeneas' frenzy-causing gaze, is so organic with the deep structure of the narrative that interpolation seems highly unlikely. The narrative from 559 to 633 is of a piece, its logic consistent within itself. But the riskiness of portraying Aeneas in this way may have caused Vergil's editors to assume that here Vergil had not put the finishing touches on the poem.

It is tempting to speculate at this point about Vergil's own intentions with regard to this passage. Did he want to make some point by portraying Aeneas early on in his story as falling prey to uncontrolled emotions? Or was he himself later on dissatisfied with the indignity this scene would cast on his hero? I believe that drawing conclusions of this sort is too speculative to be helpful in understanding the logic of the text, because by deciding between those two or any other possible scenarios, we limit our view of the poem unnecessarily. But this far I think we can go: by looking at the construction of Aeneas as a subject through his gaze, we have come to see that the Helen episode fits into the surrounding narrative organically. It is unlikely that an interpolator would have been able to fit into the gap of the Vergilian text a passage that bridges it so ingeniously by focusing the same attention on the gaze of Aeneas here as in the following scene. But the image of a frenzied Aeneas must have been problematic enough for either Vergil or his editors to consider the passage as in need of revision. Judging from these factors, it is most likely that the passage is Vergilian. Hence, our approach to the passage, in using ancient assumptions about the self and evidence about ancient sensibilities that were offended by the passage, can strengthen the arguments other scholars have brought forward to prove the authenticity of the Helen episode.

Servius and Donatus do not comment on the Helen episode, and the passage is omitted from the best Vergil manuscripts. Hence it is to be assumed that most ancient readers did not read the Helen episode. This is a pity, since together with the following scene, it would have made a powerful statement about the beneficial impact of the epic reading experience on its ancient audiences. In the Helen episode Aeneas falls prey to frenzy and is cured by a readerly view of the true causes for the fall of Troy. The identification of the reader with Aeneas that has already been established in book 1 would have allowed the reader here to experience with Aeneas both the anger at Helen and its cure by means of an epic reading experience. What better statement could there be of the ancients' belief in the benefits and moral instructiveness of reading epic?

On the other hand, an Aeneas tossed about by uncontrolled emotions is an image whose power must not be underestimated. If a reader who is swayed by an image such as this identifies with Aeneas and experiences his anger, he is left hanging with that anger. It is not counteracted by the text, because Aeneas does not in this case provide an optimistic interpretation of the situation.

Indeed, uncontrolled passions are treated in the *Aeneid* not so much as emotions to be experienced along with a figure of identification such as Aeneas, but as spectacles to be looked at from the outside, a pattern we will explore in the next chapter. A striking instance of passion as a spectacle occurs in the *ecphrasis* of the images depicted on the doors of the temple of Apollo at Cumae at the beginning of book 6. These images, which depict Pasiphae's passion for the bull, are the object of the gaze of Aeneas, who views them on his visit to the Sibyl and whose gaze the reader shares initially. The relationship of the reader with Aeneas is here the same as we have seen it in the sequence of book 1, where the reader's perspective on the images evoked in the narrative is filtered through the gaze of Aeneas.

What is different here is that Aeneas is looking at a depiction of a woman's passion and its disastrous consequences. But Pasiphae's passion is a spectacle not only because she is portrayed here in a painting. When the Sibyl refers to the pictures Aeneas is looking at, she calls them *spectacula*. This term is usually used to refer to theatrical spectacles rather than to paintings.[46] Thus, the Sibyl makes the point that this spectacle functions in a way similar to drama. The reader is to experience this spectacle as if it were a tragedy, invoking in him pity and fear, and having a cathartic effect. We will see in chapter 4 that this is also the function of other spectacles of female passion in the *Aeneid*. These spectacles of passion serve to define the reader's subjectivity, but they do so in a different way than the gaze of Aeneas. While Aeneas models the reader's subjectivity by sharing his gaze and allowing identification with him, the spectacles of female passion form the reader's subjectivity by contrast. As the function of drama is to arouse pity and fear, and hence to have a cathartic effect on the spectator, the reader of the *Aeneid* experiences the passionate female figures as a different kind of model of subjectivity, one that the reader purges himself of by the act of reading.

The danger of such spectacles is indicated in the scene from book 6 by the fact that Aeneas is not allowed to finish looking at the images. Let's see how the gaze of Aeneas operates when the spectacle before him is a spectacle of passion rather than a spectacle of Roman history.

✿ DANGEROUS IMAGES

While Aeneas is waiting to be received by the Sibyl at Cumae, he amuses himself by looking at the images on the doors of Apollo's temple. The pictures show the story of Pasiphae and the bull, the Minotaur, and the death of Minos' son Androgeos at Athens.[47] But we find out very little about the effect these images have on Aeneas, peculiarly little considering how strongly and even surprisingly Aeneas responded to the images of the Trojan War in Juno's temple at Carthage or to seeing Carthage for the first time. Yet the history of the Cumaean temple and its decoration are narrated in equally lavish detail. Just as the narrator is reluctant to reveal Aeneas' response to the images to us, so the Sibyl is eager to hurry Aeneas away from this spectacle:

> quin protinus omnia
> perlegerent oculis, ni iam praemissus Achates
> adforet atque una Phoebi Triviaeque sacerdos,
> Deiphobe Glauci, fatur quae talia regi:
> "non hoc ista sibi tempus _spectacula_ poscit:
> nunc grege de intacto septem mactare iuvencos
> praestiterit, totidem lectas de more bidentis."
>
> (Aen. 6.33–39)

[Indeed, they would have perused them all longer with their eyes, had not Achates arrived who had been sent ahead, and with him the priestess of Phoebus and Trivia, Deiphobe, daughter of Glaucus; she spoke these words to the king: "This is not a time for looking at those images; now it would be better to sacrifice seven bullocks from a herd untouched by the yoke, and as many sheep chosen according to custom."]

Of course, Aeneas immediately obeys the command of the priestess, thus leaving the reader to his/her own interpretive devices, unguided by any model reader in the text. Let us look more closely at the images that evoke such solicitude on the part of Deiphobe:

in foribus letum Androgeo; tum pendere poenas
Cecropidae iussi, miserum! septena quotannis
corpora natorum; stat ductis sortibus urna.
contra elata mari respondet Gnosia tellus:
hic crudelis amor tauri suppostaque furto
Pasiphae mixtumque genus prolesque biformis
Minotaurus inest, Veneris monumenta nefandae;
hic labor ille domus et inextricabilis error.

(Aen. 6.20–27)

[On the doors was represented the death of Androgeos; then the Athenians, bidden to pay as punishment—a dreadful sight!—seven children every year. There stands the urn after the lots have been drawn. Opposite to these scenes is represented the land of Crete, raised above the sea: here you see Pasiphaë's cruel passion for the bull, and the stratagem she used to mate with him; also represented is that hybrid creature, her double-shaped offspring, the Minotaur, a monument to her unlawful passion; and here is the famous toil of the labyrinth, the maze from which no one can escape.]

No wonder the Sibyl does not want Aeneas to contemplate this sad spectacle for too long. There is not a single heroic figure in this *ecphrasis* to lift the spirits of the beholder/reader.[48] Instead the panels depict the monstrosities of misguided passion, as well as the death of innocent children. One panel contains scenes set in Athens, the other scenes set in Crete. The Athenian panel has the death of Minos' son Androgeos and the selection of Athenian children to be sent to Crete in recompense for Androgeos' death. The Cretan panel has Pasiphae copulating with a bull, her monstrous offspring, the Minotaur, and the labyrinth he dwells in.

As we have seen in the discussion of the temple of Juno at Carthage and the shield of Aeneas, Aeneas derives motivation from seeing his and his people's past and future fame depicted in art. Even the spectacle of another city's foundation has a powerful effect on him, as we saw earlier in the discussion of Aeneas' first view of Carthage. But it is hard to imagine how Aeneas might have responded to the present scenes, had he had time to view them. The kind of fame bestowed on Athens and Crete in these pictures certainly cannot be called heroic, although the myths surrounding the Minotaur do not lack heroic figures such as Theseus and Ariadne. It is significant that they do not appear on the panels here. Compassion for the death of innocent children and condemnation of Pasiphae's monstrous passion are the reactions legitimated by the narrator,[49] reactions that are indeed modeled on those of the narrator: his exclamation *miserum!* in line 21 expresses his compassion, while he condemns Pasiphae's passion by calling the Minotaur *Veneris monumenta nefandae* in line 26. Thus we can conclude that the narrative function of this *ecphrasis* is fundamentally different from that of previously discussed *ecphraseis*.

But what is its function? Perhaps the key to answering this question lies in the narrative surrounding the *ecphrasis,* where the story of Daedalus and the circumstances of the erection of the temple are recounted:

Daedalus, ut fama est, fugiens Minoia regna
praepetibus pennis ausus se credere caelo
insuetum per iter gelidas enavit ad Arctos,
Chalcidicaque levis tandem super astitit arce.
redditus his primum terris tibi, Phoebe, sacravit
remigium alarum posuitque immania templa.

(6.14–19)

[Daedalus, as the story goes, fleeing the kingdom of Minos on swift wings, dared to entrust himself to the sky, and along an unchartered path he flew to the cold North, and finally alighted on the Chalcidian heights of Cumae. Since it was here that he had first been returned to the land, he dedicated the oarage of his wings to you, Phoebus, and built a huge temple.]

This brief narrative of the flight of Daedalus from Crete and his arrival at the shore of Cumae is reminiscent of the fate of Aeneas himself: escape from a grim situation, travels in uncharted territories, arrival at Cumae, and thanksgiving to Apollo are elements common to both stories. The parallel between the two figures is strengthened by the narrative that follows the *ecphrasis:*

magnum reginae sed enim miseratus amorem
Daedalus ipse dolos tecti ambagesque resolvit,
caeca regens filo vestigia. tu quoque magnam
partem opere in tanto, sineret dolor, Icare, haberes.
bis conatus erat casus effingere in auro,
bis patriae cecidere manus.

(28–33)

[For taking pity on the great love of queenly Ariadne, Daedalus un-
tangled the twists and turns of the building, leading Theseus' blind
steps with a thread. You, too, Icarus, would have a big share in this
great work, if grief had allowed it. Twice he attempted to depict your
fall in gold, twice did your father's hands falter.]

Both Aeneas and Daedalus are characterized by their grief, both are fathers
whose affection for their sons is a defining characteristic, and both are en-
tangled in the great love of a queen.[50] The use of the word *regina* markedly
recalls Dido in a play of allusions and reminiscences.[51] When Daedalus
aids Ariadne to disentangle the labyrinth out of compassion for her great
love, she is called *regina* not because that is the proper term for the king's
daughter, but mostly because it facilitates drawing a parallel with Dido.
But Pasiphae's story, too, recalls Dido. The passion of Pasiphae is called
cruel in a manner strongly reminiscent of Dido's passion. There is a cer-
tain amount of compassion in the narrator's view of the cruelty of love in
both sequences. The connection between Dido and Pasiphae comes up in
two other contexts as well. First, Pasiphae is one of the inhabitants of the
Lugentes Campi, a circumstance that supports my contention of an allu-
sion to Dido in the *ecphrasis* discussed above. In the *Lugentes Campi,* the
cruelty of love is again thematized. Second, there are in Dido's last speech
clear verbal reminiscences of Vergil's Pasiphae in the *Eclogues,* which we
will look at further below.[52]

If Dido lurks behind Ariadne and Pasiphae, while Aeneas' fate resembles
that of Daedalus, the images on Apollo's temple at Cumae may be more
significant than they appear initially. This in turn explains the space and
position they are given in the narrative, standing at the beginning of book
6, a book so central because of its prophecies. Marking the entry both into
this prophetic book and into the Underworld, the *ecphrasis* at Cumae pro-
vides us with a bridge into the prophetic realm we are about to enter. But
why do we need such a bridge? Since the bridge we are dealing with here is
of a visual nature and is even designated as a spectacle by the Sibyl, I pro-
pose to consider this question in terms of visuality, as a transition from one
form of spectacle to another. The spectacle the pictures lead us into is in
the Underworld. More specifically, since Aeneas' purpose is to meet his
father, we may assume that the spectacle we are being prepared for here is
that of the pageant of Roman heroes, at the end of the same book, which
Anchises shows to Aeneas as the climactic end point of his visit.

Before coming to Cumae, Aeneas had left behind him another kind of spectacle. As we have seen above, Aeneas is a spectator at Carthage, and we will explore more fully in the next chapter how Dido and her passion are narrated as spectacles in books 1 and 4, while Aeneas is not visually depicted there or elsewhere in the poem. It is this spectacle, then, the spectacle of Dido and her passion, that Aeneas has left behind when he comes to Cumae and sees the pictures of Pasiphae, prior to entering the Underworld and seeing the spectacle of the pageant of heroes. Thus, the *ecphrasis* at Cumae is a bridge between the story of Dido's passion in book 4 and the spectacle of the Underworld in book 6, a transition between two different kinds of spectacles presented to the reader, the spectacle of female desire in Dido's story and the spectacle of Roman history in the pageant of Roman heroes.[53]

It is very appropriate, then, that the transition between these two kinds of spectacle is accomplished by a visual device as well, the *ecphrasis* at Cumae. As a transition, the story told in the *ecphrasis* can be read as an allusion to Aeneas' departure from Dido. The doors of Apollo's temple encapsulate the spectacle of female passion in the paradigm of Pasiphae's passion, visible to Aeneas and described for the reader. Yet the surrounding narrative of the foundation of the temple encapsulates a response to this spectacle in the paradigm of Daedalus' flight, narrated for the reader but modeled by Aeneas earlier on in his flight from Carthage and now repeated in his hurried departure from the images.

An interesting division can be observed in the different ways in which the stories of Pasiphae and Daedalus are told. The *ecphrasis* proper depicts only Pasiphae's passion, its monstrous offspring, and the sufferings it causes the Athenians. These are the panels described on the doors of the temple of Apollo. The story of Daedalus, his involvement with "the great queen," his flight from Crete, and the love for his son frame the *ecphrasis* in the form of narrative. This division suggests that Pasiphae's passion is a spectacle to be looked at, while Daedalus' flight and suffering are not visually represented. As I have said, a similar division is operative in the story of Aeneas and Dido, as Aeneas is given the role of spectator in book 1, looking at Carthage and its queen, while Dido is cast as a spectacle.

As Daedalus departed from Pasiphae's passion, so did Aeneas depart from Dido's. But even here at Cumae, Aeneas again departs from the spectacle of female passion, as the Sibyl hurries him away from perusing the images on the doors of the temple. How important is this minor narrative detail, the Sibyl's admonition to Aeneas not to dawdle looking at pictures? I think it is important because the *ecphrasis* is one of only three extended depictions of artworks in the *Aeneid*. In the case of the other two, Aeneas is the spectator who shares the reader's gaze at the images. Why hurry him away from this one? Why even depict it, if Aeneas or anyone else in the story does not get to see it?

A comparison of this scenario with a similar scene in Achilles Tatius' novel from the time of the Second Sophistic might help us understand the Sibyl's urgency in preventing Aeneas from seeing the pictures. This later narrative contains a piece of cultural information lacking in the *Aeneid* scene, which nevertheless might explain the Sibyl's reaction to Aeneas' gaze in the earlier narrative.[54] In the novel *Leucippe and Cleitophon* a painting with scenes from the myth of Tereus and Philomela is considered a bad omen by the protagonists who see it. The scenes described in the *ecphrasis* include the rape of Philomela by Tereus, the robe Philomela weaves with images that tell Procne about the rape, and the meal the two women serve to Tereus, which consists of his infant son. The *ecphrasis* is followed by an interpretation of the pictures given by one of the protagonists of the novel:

Ἐμοὶ δοκεῖ τὴν εἰς Φάρον ὁδὸν ἐπισχεῖν. Ὁρᾷς γὰρ οὐκ ἀγαθὰ δύο σύμβολα, τό τε τοῦ ὄρνιθος καθ' ἡμῶν πτερὸν καὶ τῆς εἰκόνος τὴν ἀπειλήν. Λέγουσι δὲ οἱ τῶν συμβόλων ἐξηγηταὶ σκοπεῖν τοὺς μύθους τῶν εἰκόνων, ἂν ἐξιοῦσιν ἐπὶ πρᾶξιν ἡμῖν συντύχωσι, καὶ ἐξομοιοῦν τὸ ἀποβησόμενον τῷ τῆς ἱστορίας λόγῳ. Ὁρᾷς ὅσων γέμει κακῶν ἡ γραφὴ ἔρωτος παρανόμου, μοιχείας ἀναισχύντου, γυναικείων ἀτυχημάτων· ὅθεν ἐπισχεῖν κελεύω τὴν ἔξοδον.
(Achilles Tatius, *Leucippe and Cleitophon,* 5.4.1–2)

[I suggest we put off our trip to Pharos. You see these two unfavorable signs: the bird's aggressive wing and the threat implicit in this painting. Interpreters of signs tell us to consider the story of any painting we chance to see as we set out on business, and to plot the outcome of our action by analogy with that story's plot. Well, just look at the disasters proliferating in this scene: lawless sex, adultery without shame, women degraded! I therefore advise that we go no further.][55]

The description Menelaus gives of the images here could equally be applied to those in the *Aeneid* passage: ἔρως παράνομος, μοιχεία ἀναισχύντος, γυναικεῖα ἀτυχήματα. More specifically, these characterizations fit the Cretan panel of the Vergilian *ecphrasis* that centers around the passion of Pasiphae and her monstrous offspring. Menelaus' interpretation of the significance of seeing the painting gives us an idea why the narrative of the *Aeneid* is so eager to hurry Aeneas away from the temple doors. Appealing to the authority of interpreters of signs, he explains that the story of the pictures has an immediate bearing on the events planned by their beholder, that they might be a bad omen for the events lying in store for him. Bettini points out that this is the only explicit reference in ancient literature to the belief that painted images had a premonitory quality.[56] But he also shows that there are enough stories about images with a premonitory force to consider Menelaus' words as more than a literary invention of the author. Given the power the ancients ascribed to images over the soul, as discussed in the context of *phantasia,* we should not be surprised at the Sibyl for hurrying Aeneas away from such a spectacle as Daedalus chose as an adornment of his Apollo temple. Far better for Aeneas not to look at Pasiphae and the Minotaur. His entanglement with γυναικεῖα ἀτυχήματα lies in the past, and just as he fled from Carthage then, so he must now flee from Pasiphae in order to ensure a propitious beginning for his journey to the Underworld and his arrival in Italy. Thus the Vergilian *ecphrasis* here serves to reinforce the correctness of Aeneas' earlier choice and to reenact his flight from the spectacle of female passion.

The cultural pattern Bettini has established about ancient beliefs of the premonitory power of images thus helps us understand why Aeneas is not allowed to view the images of this temple as extensively as he viewed the images of Juno's temple in book 1. But we have not yet discussed why the reader gets to see what Aeneas does not in this scene. Clearly, the reader's gaze in this passage is more encompassing than that of Aeneas. But this is not surprising. As readers of the *Aeneid,* we have witnessed many similar spectacles of female passion before we came to this point of the narrative, and Aeneas did not always witness these spectacles with us. The first instance of such a spectacle of female passion is Juno's desire to prevent Aeneas' arrival in Italy. This spectacle is solely for the reader's gaze. Perhaps it would be too much for anyone to witness the passions of a goddess, even a hero like Aeneas, without the protective distance provided by the medium of writing, which wraps us as readers in a cloud much like the one Venus cast around Aeneas before she sent him off to Carthage. Like that cloud, the medium of writing lets us see without being seen, and it might protect us from the ominous effects of gazing at an image like that of Pasiphae or that of Tereus and Philomela. It certainly seals us off from any involvement in the story, such as Aeneas—being the titular hero of the story—can hardly avoid. When Aeneas does share our gaze at spectacles of female passion, we can sometimes glimpse the powerful impact they have on him. Dido's passion, for example, tears at Aeneas' equanimity like a storm wind blowing around a tree, as a famous simile imparts to us.[57] Andromache's grief in book 3 has a different effect on Aeneas, but one that equally stirs his own grief at the loss of Troy.[58]

So far, we have learned that the reader is often drawn into Aeneas' point of view, as when he looks at Carthage, but sometimes is also separated from it, as in the case of the images on the temple at Cumae. These different strategies serve to ally us with the protagonist while also showing us how hard it sometimes is for Aeneas to react in the positive ways that characterize his responses to the world. When the reader's perspective is set off from that of Aeneas, the reader can observe the process of Aeneas' emotional reactions at work, how his emotions are guided by effort and control. This process is best exemplified in the scene with the images on the temple of Juno. As we have seen, the control over emotional reactions to images is what makes Aeneas unique and confers on him the role of model audience in his own story. We have seen earlier that the handling of emotions is a second crucial component in the ancient conceptualization of the subject, of equal importance to the gaze and intimately linked to it. As Aeneas' gaze is integral to his subjectivity, so his control over the emotions is paradigmatic. Having observed Aeneas' control over passion, we now need to look at characters whose handling of passion is different from that of Aeneas.

In the following chapter we will turn to spectacles of female passion. Looking at the Pasiphae *ecphrasis* in *Aeneid* 6 we found that ominous spectacles of female passion such as this one could have unpropitious effects on an intratextual beholder like Aeneas. Therefore, Aeneas cannot or must not see certain things we as readers are allowed to see. Thus, there is a crucial difference between Aeneas' gaze and that of the reader: the reader's gaze is imaginary. The importance of these dangerous spectacles for the reader's gaze lies in their extraordinary power: the figures involved in them, Juno, Dido, Andromache, and Amata, are among the most vividly depicted subjects in their own right. If we assume that the fictional subjects have a formative force for the reader's subjectivity, we need to consider how these passionate female subjects affect the reader. Furthermore, as spectacles of passion presented to the reader and to Aeneas, it will be crucial to understand the impact of their passion on Aeneas as a filter for the reader's possible reactions. Interestingly, the gaze of these figures often plays a pivotal role in the emergence of their passion.

CHAPTER 4

The Spectacle
of Emotions

The previous chapter has been concerned with the gaze of Aeneas, his emotional responses to spectacles, and the reader's identification with him through sharing his gaze and empathizing with him. However, when we think of empathizing with characters of the *Aeneid*, Aeneas is probably not the first character that comes to mind. The poem is full of characters whose suffering the reader is invited to empathize with, the most obvious being Dido. In the present chapter I will turn to some of these characters and consider the relationship the text establishes between them and the reader.

Several of these figures provide instructive contrasts to the construction of Aeneas' subjectivity through his gaze. I will show that the subjectivities of Dido, Andromache, and Juno are constructed differently from Aeneas'. Although they, too, own a gaze, they are constructed as spectacles of subjectivity rather than figures of identification for the reader. Their gazes are themselves gazed at. The text constructs their subjectivities primarily through their emotions rather than through their gazes.

We have seen that the emotions and one's control over them is a central concern of ancient thinking about the self. If we consider the *Aeneid* as having a formative impact on the ancient reader's sense of self, we must consider in particular what effect the depiction of the passions has on readers. In contrast to Aeneas, whose emotions are carefully controlled, many characters in the poem give free rein to their emotions. Among them are a number of female characters. This in itself is an interesting fact.

If we focus on the nexus between gender and the emotions on a more general level, our result is predictable: unbridled emotions are often assigned to female figures. But what does this mean for the reader's perspective? In order to answer this question I will consider the relevant figures in detail and closely observe the textual strategies by which the reader's perspective is established vis-à-vis these figures.

I will argue that a number of female figures are represented as spectacles rather than as spectators of spectacles. As such, they allow the reader to see the spectacle of their passions, their genesis, their manifestations, and their outcome. When these characters do own a gaze, it has the instructive purpose of showing—rather than letting the reader experience—how a spectacle affects the figure's emotions. The ancient theory of the gaze as an entryway of the passions to the soul is put into concrete illustration in these female figures. The reader can observe from a distance how the passions entering the soul cause disturbance and turmoil. This does not mean that readers don't identify with Dido or Andromache. Dido's suffering is among the most powerful and most affecting depictions of emotions in the *Aeneid*, and inevitably we sympathize with her. Less obvious to the reader is a certain distance the text establishes in these cases. Various textual strategies such as authorial comments or casting the figure as a theatrical spectacle serve to create this distance between reader and fictional character.

The significance of these textual strategies of distancing lies in a differentiation of levels of identification the reader experiences with characters of the poem. Identification with Aeneas is qualitatively different from identification with figures such as Dido and Andromache. Because the reader shares Aeneas' gaze as well as empathizes with him, identification with him is more immediate and less perceptible. The textual strategies that assimilate the reader's gaze with that of Aeneas do not draw attention to themselves. Their imperceptibility, however, does not render them any less powerful. On the contrary, keeping the reader unaware of his assimilation of Aeneas' gaze makes identification with him more powerful than with other characters.

Figures like Dido and Andromache often invite our sympathy more overtly, by a fuller description of their emotional experiences. In the case of Dido we will see that the reader empathizes with her, but does not share her gaze most of the time. The reader in some sense experiences her feelings but does not fully identify with them. Rather, the reader experiences Dido's emotions vicariously; her suffering stirs pity and fear, it is cathartic. As we have seen in the discussion of the spectacle of Pasiphae's passion, the function of spectacle is to assimilate the experience of reading female passion to that of seeing it enacted as a drama. The quality of identification with the characters of drama is different from that of identification with Aeneas. As the effect of drama is to be cathartic, to purge oneself of the dangers represented in drama, the spectacles in the *Aeneid* form the reader's subjectivity by contrast and vicarious experience rather than by assimilation of point of view and identification.

Figures such as Dido, whose emotions are to be experienced by the reader vicariously and at a distance, are therefore represented as spectacles. This textual strategy emphasizes that the reader is to visualize these figures fully, much more fully than he or she ever can visualize Aeneas. Even the emotions of such figures attain a spectacular quality, as we will see. To begin this analysis of the spectacular quality of the emotions in female figures, I will discuss briefly two instances in which a woman's passion is encapsulated in a visible symbol on her body: Eriphyle and Amata.[1]

ꜱ EMOTIONS AS VISIBLE SYMBOLS

The story of the Italian queen Amata provides us with a particularly vivid visual representation of a character's interior life. At Juno's behest the goddess Allecto visits Latium to cause a war between the Latins and the Trojans. Amata is the first person Allecto visits on her quest.[2] The narrator tells us that Amata is already agitated and worried about the arrival of the Trojans and about the planned marriage of her daughter to Turnus, which is now in jeopardy (*Aen.* 7.344–45). Amata is therefore fertile ground for Allecto's intentions. When Allecto arrives at Amata's doorstep, she instills a frenzy in her that amplifies her already present agitation to the fullest extent. The manner in which Allecto instills this frenzy is described with a powerful image:

> *huic dea caeruleis unum de crinibus anguem*
> *conicit, inque sinum praecordia ad intima subdit,*
> *quo furibunda domum monstro permisceat omnem.*
> *ille inter vestis et levia pectora lapsus*
> *volvitur attactu nullo, fallitque furentem*
> *viperam inspirans animam; fit tortile collo*
> *aurum ingens coluber, fit longae taenia vittae*
> *innectitque comas et membris lubricus errat.*
>
> (*Aen.* 7.346–53)

[The goddess throws a snake from her dark hair at Amata and puts it
into her bosom, deep inside her heart, in order that Amata might
throw the whole house into turmoil, frenzied by this monstrous beast.
The snake glides down between her dress and her smooth breast and
slithers on without touching her. Unnoticed by Amata, it infects her
with its viperous breath and drives her mad. The huge snake becomes
a golden torque round Amata's neck, and the long ribbon of a head-
band. It weaves itself into her hair and slithers all over her limbs.)

The frenzy Allecto brings to Amata is visualized here in the image of a
snake from her own hair. Furies like Allecto were traditionally imagined
and represented as having snakes in their hair or as hair.[3] Since Furies
functioned in myth as embodiment of frenzy, snake hair by itself is used
here as an image of frenzy. Allecto uses a snake from her hair as a missile
to convey her fury to her victim. She hurls the snake into Amata's bosom,
where it works its magic, much like the arrow Cupid uses on Medea in
Apollonius Rhodius' *Argonautica.* But unlike Cupid's arrow in Apollonius,
and indeed unlike the more immaterial magic Cupid works on Dido in
the *Aeneid,* the snake of Allecto remains on Amata's body as a visible, ex-
ternal signifier of her inner emotions. Allecto's snake turns into a golden,
twisted necklace and into a headband that is twisted into Amata's hair.
We are thus invited to picture Amata as a beautifully adorned woman
(like Hesiod's Pandora), whose feminine ornaments are tokens of Al-
lecto's frenzy. Amata's beautiful appearance thus becomes a deceptive mir-
ror image of the ugly Allecto herself, whose snake hair is the looming
presence behind the picture of Amata's snake coiling around her throat
and hair in the disguise of decoration.[4]

Unlike Amata's passion, which is expressed visually by an external ob-
ject, Eriphyle's passion is visually inscribed on her body as a wound. When
we encounter Eriphyle in the *Lugentes Campi,* she is designated by the text
as one destroyed by her passion. Dwelling in the company of Dido, Phae-
dra, Procris, Euadne, Laodamia, Pasiphae, and Caeneus, she belongs to a
place in the Underworld that is reserved for those who died from love.
Upon Aeneas' arrival in this region, she shows to Aeneas and to us her
wounds (*Aen.* 6.446: *monstrantem vulnera*). This gesture is at once puz-
zling and enigmatic, because the text implies that she died of wounds in-
flicted by her son (445–46: *maestamque Eriphylen / crudelis nati monstran-
tem vulnera cernit*), not from love, as is requisite for the inhabitants of the
Lugentes Campi.

Eriphyle's presence in the *Lugentes Campi* has given scholars difficulties, because the story implied in the Vergilian narrative conflicts with other versions of the Eriphyle myth that have come down to us from antiquity.[5] Since Homer, Eriphyle, the wife of Amphiaraos, one of the Seven against Thebes, was seen as an example of greed, accepting as a bribe from Polyneices a golden necklace in return for forcing her husband to join the war.[6] Another version of the story must be implied in the Vergilian scene that would justify her presence in the *Lugentes Campi* as well as the nature of her wounds. An exact outline of this version is impossible to recover. Going on the attested versions and on the implications of Vergil's scenario, Eriphyle's story here seems to involve love, perhaps an adulterous love that leads her to send her husband off to war. Such an adulterous love may have been the motive for sending her husband off to certain death, and thus have taken the place of the greed more commonly associated with her. In this scenario Eriphyle would have died for love, with her son killing her as a result of her passion.

It is easy to imagine that Eriphyle's story could have been altered in this way on the analogy of another, more famous, mythical wife who is responsible for her husband's death. Like Eriphyle, Clytemnestra dies at the hands of her son in retribution for the murder of her husband Agamemnon. As Polyneices corrupts Eriphyle with the offer of the necklace, so Aegisthus corrupts Clytemnestra by leading her into adultery. As Eriphyle's greed leads to her husband's death, so Clytemnestra's adultery leads to the murder of Agamemnon. By introducing the element of adulterous love into the story of Eriphyle, the analogies between the two stories would be even stronger. At the same time, such a version of the Eriphyle myth would assimilate her to the other figures in the *Lugentes Campi* and to Dido, whose suicide was equally the result of her passion.

The version constructed here must be regarded as a mere guess. But it allows us to understand the significance of Eriphyle's presence in the *Lugentes Campi*. The parallels between Dido and Eriphyle are underscored in this passage by verbal cross references. Both Dido and Eriphyle are explicitly said in this passage to have wounds (6.450–51: *inter quas Phoenissa recens a vulnere Dido / errabat silva in magna*).[7] Dido's wound is mentioned only a few lines after Eriphyle's. Moreover, Eriphyle's wounds recall Dido's wounds in book 4, which I will discuss in greater detail below. But why does Eriphyle display her wounds? Dwelling, as she does, in the *Lugentes Campi,* such a display may be read in conjunction with the significance of that place. I will show below that Dido's wounds in book 4 are wounds

both of love and death. And since the significance of the *Lugentes Campi*
lies at least partly in defining the nature of Dido's love and death, Eri-
phyle's wounds, too, may be read as a visible symbol of her passion. Thus,
Eriphyle emblematizes the notion of the emotionally wounded female
subject on display: not only is she subjected to the gaze of Aeneas (and
with him to that of the reader), but she even self-consciously subjects her-
self and her emotional woundedness to the scrutiny of that gaze. The
reader's gaze is presented with a spectacle that encodes in the visible sign
of the wound the notion of Eriphyle's passion. Eriphyle's depiction un-
derscores the spectacular quality of her suffering and hence emblematizes
the relationship the text establishes between the reader and female figures
dominated by passion. In this, she provides us with an introduction to the
dynamics of the subjectivities that form the core of the next two chapters.

DIDO AS SPECTACLE

The first of these is Dido. In the following I will analyze the spectacular
qualities of the Dido narrative. We will see that Dido's subjectivity is set up
as a complement to that of Aeneas. This complement is a necessary one, as
it demonstrates to the reader what the figure of Aeneas cannot supply: in
Dido the workings of the gaze on the emotions are explored in depth and
detail. Instead of showing this in Aeneas, the *Aeneid* separates the danger-
ous effects of the gaze on the soul from the character primarily defined by
his gaze and projects this aspect of subjectivity on various figures who pre-
sent themselves as spectacles to Aeneas' (and the reader's) gaze.

Dido is the most important instance of a female figure's passion in the
Aeneid. I will show in what way the text represents Dido and her love as a
spectacle for the reader's gaze.[8] In the previous chapter we have already
seen that *Aeneid* I introduces Dido as a theatrical spectacle in various ways.
To summarize briefly, Aeneas is set up consistently as a spectator or audi-
ence in a long narrative sequence that leads up to Dido's first appearance.[9]
In this narrative sequence, the theatrical quality of Dido's story is under-
scored by the manner in which her earlier fate is recounted. In the man-
ner of a tragic prologue goddess addressing a theatrical audience, Venus
tells Aeneas of Dido's flight from Tyre and the foundation of Carthage.
When Dido first appears, Aeneas sees her from a position closely resem-
bling that of a theatrical audience vis-à-vis a dramatic stage. Shrouded in
a protective cloud, Aeneas is invisible to his surroundings but able to see
everything around him. Like a theatrical audience gazing at the actions on

a stage, Aeneas witnesses a highly dramatic encounter between Dido and a contingent of shipwrecked Trojans who had been separated from Aeneas earlier. The ensuing dialogue between Dido and the Trojan leader Ilioneus has many theatrical qualities, including the pattern of tension, conflict, and resolution often found in tragedies. The dialogue serves to characterize the principal figures through their speeches and narrates important events in the manner of the messenger speeches of tragedy.

It is after this dialogue that Venus lifts the cloud from Aeneas, rendering him visible to Dido and Ilioneus. No longer a mere spectator, Aeneas now becomes an agent in the events that ensue. But the spectacular quality of these events is not diminished. The last scene of book 1 describes the banquet to which Dido has invited her Trojan guests.[10] Gold and purple figure largely in the description of Dido's palace. When the Trojans arrive for the banquet, Dido receives them lying on a golden sofa (697–98), the Trojans take their seats at the table on purple bedspreads (700). All the details of the description of the banquet, the costly materials of Dido's furniture, the opulent quantities of food and wine, and the multitude of servants bringing bread and towels, speak of the great wealth on display at Dido's palace. No wonder, then, that the ceiling of Dido's banquet hall is made of gold. Even more extravagant are the lamps hanging from the ceiling, whose light turns night into day, as the narrator informs us (726–27).[11] If we visualize all the gold and light depicted here, we may well be blinded by the blaze surrounding Dido. Every object we hear of is gleaming with precious metals and bright colors. When Dido pours a libation, her chalice is, of course, heavy with gold and gemstones (728–30). Even the bard Iopas, who entertains the guests at the feast, has a golden lyre.[12]

The description of Dido's palace thus invites the reader to visualize Dido within a setting of ostentatiously displayed wealth. More importantly for the present argument, we see Dido herself actively setting the stage for the arrival of her guests. The narrator makes sure to let us know that Dido uses her wealth as a theatrical backdrop to offset the principal spectacle—herself—which she artfully places center stage, to be viewed by her guests in the very midst of her displayed wealth:

> *cum venit, aulaeis iam se regina superbis*
> *aurea* <u>*composuit*</u> *sponda* <u>*mediamque locavit.*</u>
>
> (697–98)

[When he arrived, the queen had already <u>placed herself center stage</u> on a golden couch beneath a splendid awning.]

Not only does this description render a vivid image of the view glimpsed by Dido's dinner guests, but it also conveys the sense that Dido self-consciously casts herself as a spectacle for her Trojan guests. Even now that Aeneas has entered the dramatic stage of the epic plot, the narrative maintains a dichotomy—established in the previous scenes—of Aeneas and Dido as spectator and spectacle.

But the visuality of the scene does not end here. Other spectators and other spectacles populate it with more or less dramatic consequences for the subsequent narrative. First, there are the gifts Aeneas brings to Dido in acknowledgment of her hospitality. These gifts, we hear, are much admired by the Tyrians (709). But another spectacle is even more admired by them, and this, too, is a spectacle brought to them by the Trojans. At the behest of his mother, Venus, Cupid had taken the form of Aeneas' son Ascanius to take his place at the banquet and work his spells on Dido.[13] When he enters the palace, the Tyrians admire his appearance, which is conveyed to the reader by an elaborate description:

> *nec non et Tyrii per limina laeta frequentes*
> *convenere; toris iussi discumbere pictis*
> *mirantur dona Aeneae, mirantur Iulum,*
> *flagrantisque dei vultus simulataque verba,*
> *pallamque et pictum croceo velamen acantho.*
>
> (707–11)

[The Tyrians, too, arrived in throngs at the gates of the festive palace. Bidden to lie down on richly decorated couches, they admired the gifts of Aeneas and marveled at Iulus, at the god's glowing features and feigned words, at the cloak and the veil adorned with saffron colored acanthus leaves.]

First and foremost among these Tyrian spectators is, of course, Dido herself. The narrator is keenly interested in the effects of these spectacles on Dido. He goes on to describe Dido's reaction in greater detail:

> *praecipue infelix, pesti devota futurae,*
> *expleri mentem nequit ardescitque tuendo*
> *Phoenissa, et pariter puero donisque movetur.*
>
> (712–14)

[Especially the unhappy Phoenician queen, already doomed to her future illness, cannot be satiated in her heart; the fire inside her blazes up as she gazes, moved equally by the boy and the gifts.]

Dido is thus both spectacle and spectator in this scene. Both here and in an earlier scene where she sees Aeneas for the first time, Dido explicitly owns a gaze. When Venus lifted the cloud from Aeneas, Dido saw him and was stunned (613).

We may now note that the subjectivity of Dido and Aeneas is constructed in a similar fashion, in that both own a gaze. But there is a crucial difference between Dido's gaze and that of Aeneas. Not only does Dido own a gaze far less frequently than Aeneas does, but both times that we see her gazing, her gaze is severely impaired or manipulated by the gods. When she sees Aeneas for the first time, Venus embellishes his appearance to make him look more handsome (588–93). Later, when Dido sees Cupid, she is tricked into thinking he is Ascanius. She also does not realize that Cupid plans to work his peculiar magic on her to make her fall in love with Aeneas. More importantly, her gaze already implicates her in the emotional upheaval planned by Cupid, for we are told that the mere act of looking at Cupid inflames Dido (713: *ardescit tuendo*). Thus, when Dido gazes, her gaze is fraught with the danger of falling in love with Aeneas.[14]

Aeneas, on the other hand, is not subject to the same impairments with respect to his gaze. Although his gaze is central to much of the narrative in *Aeneid* 1, the narrator never mentions how Aeneas is affected by seeing Dido.[15] This renders Aeneas less of a spectacle for the reader's gaze. We may see him observing his surroundings, but we assimilate his gaze with ours, while Dido is a spectacle even as she is a spectator. Equipped with the superior vision of the narrator, the reader sees Dido seeing and—unlike her—knows how her vision affects her inner life. By calling Dido *pesti devota futurae* (712) the narrator alerts us to the outcome of her passion at the very moment when she gazes at Cupid. The distance created by this imbalance of knowledge renders Dido's gaze itself an object of the reader's gaze.[16]

There is yet another dimension to Dido's objecthood here. Even grammatically, Dido often becomes an object in moments when she is an object of the reader's gaze. We will see further on that passive verbs abound when Dido becomes a spectacle, especially when we contrast her with Aeneas. Even in this passage the first signs of this trend are visible. The passives *devota* (712), *expleri* (713), and *movetur* (714) all refer to Dido. *Expleri* is particularly striking, since an active form of the verb would have been more easily understood.[17] The contrast between Dido and the other Tyrian spectators is also striking in grammatical terms. While the Tyrians are the subject of a transitive verb (1.709: *mirantur*), Dido governs an intransitive (713: *ardescit*) and a passive verb (714: *movetur*). Thus, Dido—even on the grammatical level—is a subject with impairments.

Now that we have observed the spectacular elements of the Dido narrative in *Aeneid* 1, it is time to turn to elements of spectacle in *Aeneid* 4. The dramatic qualities of book 4 have long been recognized in Vergilian scholarship.[18] Often *Aeneid* 4 is even considered to follow the formal patterns of tragedy.[19] This formal similarity in itself supports my contention that Dido is constructed as a spectacle in the narrative. Among the passages most reminiscent of tragedy are Dido's dialogues, of which there are only two. The book begins with a dialogue between Dido and her sister Anna (4.8–55). Dido confesses her love for Aeneas, and Anna encourages her to give way to her feelings. This scene is strongly reminiscent of the first dialogue between Phaedra and her nurse in Euripides' *Hippolytus*.[20] Dido's second dialogue in *Aeneid* 4 takes place after Mercury's visit to Aeneas. Dido has found out that Aeneas is making secret preparations for departure, and she confronts him, accusing him of abandoning her (4.304–91). This scene imitates the dialogue between Jason and Medea in Euripides' *Medea*.[21]

Dido's monologues, on the other hand, are more numerous than her dialogues. In some cases she addresses a mute Anna or nurse, in others she speaks the monologue in solitude. Monologues can also be considered an element imitating tragedy, but what is more important about them is that they reveal to us Dido's inner state of mind.[22] Significantly, these monologues are all crowded into the second half of the book, after her dialogue with Aeneas. She already knows of his departure, and the monologues explore her despair. What is on display here is not so much tension or conflict between several agents, as we would expect in a tragedy, but the inner life of one character alone, Dido.[23] The second half of *Aeneid* 4 is the centerpiece of the epic's spectacles of female subjectivity.

The formal similarities to tragedy that we detect in the book serve the purpose of underscoring the spectacular quality of the Dido narrative. The same effect is achieved by the direct references to tragedy that we find in a simile describing Dido's dreams. After a failed attempt to detain Aeneas in Carthage for a short time longer, Dido dreams of Aeneas, of being deserted, and of searching for her people in vain. The narrator compares her dream images with the visions of a mad Pentheus and with the fate of Orestes:

> *agit ipse furentem*
> *in somnis ferus Aeneas, semperque relinqui*
> *sola sibi, semper longam incomitata videtur*
> *ire viam et Tyrios deserta quaerere terra,*
> *Eumenidum veluti demens videt agmina Pentheus*
> *et solem geminum et duplices se ostendere Thebas,*
> *aut Agamemnonius scaenis agitatus Orestes,*
> *armatam facibus matrem et serpentibus atris*
> *cum fugit ultricesque sedent in limine Dirae.*
>
> (*Aen.* 4.465–73)

[In her sleep a savage Aeneas pursues her in her frenzy. It seems to her that she is always being abandoned and alone, that she is always walking a long road unaccompanied and seeking her Tyrians in a deserted land; just as Pentheus in his madness sees a host of Furies, a double sun, and a double Thebes appearing; or like Orestes, Agamemnon's son, driven across the stage when he flees from his mother who is armed with torches and black serpents, and the avenging Furies sit upon the threshold.)

Not only does the narrator use themes familiar from tragedy to describe Dido's state of mind, but he makes explicit reference to the context of theatrical spectacle by mentioning the *scaena* or stage (471) where Orestes is persecuted by his mother.[24] Even at a moment when it is hardest to represent Dido's state of mind visually for the reader, namely when she is asleep, the narrator accomplishes a visual representation by means of a simile that is itself taken from a context of visual representation. By comparing Dido's dream image of herself with a mad Pentheus and with Orestes, the similes interpret Dido's dream images as an indication of her madness. Her internal experience of Aeneas' impending departure is represented as the onset of Furies persecuting Pentheus or Orestes.

What distinguishes Dido from these tragic figures is that her madness is not a result of her own actions. It is therefore somewhat problematic to see *Aeneid* 4 as a tragedy, even though the narrative has many qualities that evoke drama in general and tragedy in particular. But the Dido narrative is not itself a tragedy in the strict sense, simply because there is no conflict of competing values and no disaster brought on by fateful decisions. The chain of events in this narrative is inevitable and predestined. Dido must die of love, and while she does, we may scrutinize her passion and draw our conclusions from the spectacle.

The dream passage also contains some examples of the grammatical contrast between the subjecthoods of Dido and Aeneas that I have mentioned earlier.[25] As I have observed above, the spectacular quality of the Dido narrative is often accompanied by grammatical patterns that cast Dido as a grammatical object or a subject of passive or intransitive verbs, while contrasting her with other agents who are subjects of transitive verbs. In this passage Aeneas is the subject of the transitive verb *agit* (465) of which Dido is the object (465: *furentem*). Dido governs the passives *relinqui* (466), *videtur* (467), and *deserta* (468). Again the grammatical structure reinforces Dido's status as passive and as an object of Aeneas' and others' actions. Her subjecthood is thus further limited.

We have observed that Dido's dialogues, her monologues, and the tragic similes accompanying her dreams serve the purpose of putting on display Dido's inner life. More specifically, it is her desire and its frustration that are visualized in *Aeneid* 4.[26] Like the Juno of *Aeneid* 1, the Dido of *Aeneid* 4 is a subject first and foremost through her desire, and in both cases the narrative constructs female passion as a spectacle to be gazed at from a safe distance.[27] Emblematic of this narrative pattern is Dido's suicide, which she stages with great attention to visual effect. On her funeral pyre she assembles a wax image of Aeneas, his clothes, his sword, and the bed they shared together. Like Amata's necklace, these tokens allow the reader to visualize in physical objects the cause for Dido's despair and for her resolution to die.[28] What is more, the flames of Dido's funeral pyre are visible to Aeneas, even as he is at sea, on his way to Sicily (*Aen.* 5.3–5). Aeneas—who had been set up as an intratextual audience in *Aeneid* 1—is thus again set up as an intratextual spectator, this time a spectator of the tragic and spectacular end of Dido's passion. There is yet another parallel here to the setup of the earlier sequence. As in the banquet scene, where she had arranged herself as the central visual attraction for her guests' first glimpse of the luxurious banquet hall, Dido again self-consciously stages herself as a spectacle for Aeneas' gaze. In her last words she envisages Aeneas seeing the flames of her funeral pyre at sea and carrying this image of doom with him as an omen:

> sic, sic iuvat ire sub umbras.
> *hauriat hunc oculis ignem crudelis ab alto*
> *Dardanus, et nostrae secum ferat omina mortis.*
>
>   (*Aen.* 4.660–62)

[In this manner, indeed, do I enjoy going to the shades. Let the cruel Trojan drink in this fire with his eyes from the high sea, and let him carry with him the omens of my death.]

The narrative thus returns to a dichotomy set up earlier of Aeneas as spectator and Dido as spectacle. Dido's conscious participation in this polarization of herself and Aeneas frames the story of their encounter, leaving the reader with the uncanny feeling that Dido is indeed the only spectacle in this narrative, an actress whose role is her own life, and that Aeneas has been watching her together with us all along.[29]

That Dido's passion is a spectacle can also be seen from the fact that the narrative allows us a much more concrete visual image of Dido herself in her death scene. Twice do we hear that Dido is fair-haired. Before her curse monologue, she is said to tear out her blond hair at the sight of the departing Trojan fleet (589–90: *terque quaterque manu pectus percussa decorum / flaventisque abscissa comas*). Then again, after she has stabbed herself and lies dying, the gods have to intervene and cut her blond hair in order to allow her to die, because her suicide is a premature death (698–99): *nondum illi flavum Proserpina vertice crinem / abstulerat*).[30] As Mark Griffith has pointed out, such graphic specificity as the hair color of a character is not the rule in the Vergilian narrative, although it is habitual in Homeric epic.[31] Characteristically, Vergil does not tell us about the hair color (or hair length) of Aeneas. That he chooses to give us the detail of Dido's hair color in the very moment of her greatest suffering underscores the visuality of the scene and thereby enhances the distinction made between the two protagonists of this book as spectator and spectacle, as subject of the gaze versus object of the gaze.

✒ NO GAZE AT AENEAS

The dichotomy of Aeneas and Dido as spectator and spectacle is operative to a certain degree even when Aeneas is part of the dramatic plot enacted at Carthage. There is a marked difference in the way the text allows us to visualize Dido as opposed to Aeneas in the hunting scene:[32]

> *it portis iubare exorto delecta iuventus,*
> *retia rara, plagae, lato venabula ferro,*
> *Massylique ruunt equites et odora canum vis.*

reginam thalamo cunctantem ad limina primi
Poenorum exspectant, ostroque insignis et auro
stat sonipes ac frena ferox spumantia mandit.
tandem progreditur magna stipante caterva
Sidoniam picto chlamydem circumdata limbo;
cui pharetra ex auro, crines nodantur in aurum,
aurea purpuream subnectit fibula vestem.
nec non et Phrygii comites et laetus Iulus
incedunt. ipse ante alios pulcherrimus omnis
infert se socium Aeneas atque agmina iungit.
qualis ubi hibernam Lyciam Xanthique fluenta
deserit ac Delum maternam invisit Apollo
instauratque choros, mixtique altaria circum
Cretesque Dryopesque fremunt pictique Agathyrsi;
ipse iugis Cynthi graditur mollique fluentem
fronde premit crinem fingens atque implicat auro,
tela sonant umeris: haud illo segnior ibat
Aeneas, tantum egregio decus enitet ore.

(Aen. 4.130–50)

[When the sun had risen a select group of young men left the gates of the city, bringing with them wide-meshed nets, trap-nets, and broad bladed hunting spears; Massylian horsemen rushed out with their packs of keen-scented hunting dogs. The Phoenician noblemen were waiting for the queen, who was lingering at the threshold of her bedroom. Her horse, adorned in purple and gold, was prancing impatiently and champing at the foaming bit. At last she appeared with a large entourage crowding around her, clad in a Tyrian cloak with embroidered hem; she wore a golden quiver, her hair was arranged with golden pins, and the clasp which held her purple dress was golden. The Trojan company in its turn came forth with happy Iulus. Aeneas himself, resplendent above all others, stepped forward to join the queen and united the companies. As when Apollo leaves wintery Lycia and the streams of the Xanthus and visits Delos, sacred to his mother, and starts up the dance, and a varied crowd of Cretans, Dryopians and tattooed Agathyrsians make a din around his altar; he himself strides along the ridge of mount Cynthus. Adorning his flowing hair with a soft garland he fastens it and entwines it with gold; his weapons clang on his shoulders: no less vigorously than he did Aeneas stride forth, and just as much grace radiated from his noble features.]

The text describes Dido's hunting party in lavish detail, dwelling on the costly trimmings of Dido's horse and the materials of her own attire. Needless to say, the materials with which both Dido and her horse are adorned are gold and purple (4.130–39).[33] Aeneas and the Trojan hunting party, on the other hand, are described in the vaguest of details, although an approximately equal number of lines is devoted to their description (140–150). All we find out about their appearance is that Iulus is happy (1.140: *laetus*) and that Aeneas is very handsome (1.141: *pulcherrimus*) and energetic (1.149: *haud illo segnior*). Despite his presence on the narrative stage, Aeneas escapes the scrutiny of the reader's direct gaze. In a lengthy simile comparing Aeneas to Apollo the reader is led to imagine in Aeneas everything that is dignified, while at the same time the simile avoids the graphic specificity to which Dido's appearance is subjected.[34]

The passage also differentiates between Dido and Aeneas on the level of syntax. The description of Dido's appearance in lines 133–39 starts out with Dido as the grammatical object, being awaited by her companions (4.133–34: *reginam . . . exspectant*). She is the subject of hardly a single active verb, excepting the (ironically) deponent *progreditur* in 4.136. For the most part, she is watched for (4.134: *exspectant*), surrounded (4.136: *stipante*), clothed (4.137: *circumdata*), her hair tied (4.138: *nodantur*), her brooch clasping her dress (4.139: *subnectit*). By contrast, Aeneas and Apollo to whom Aeneas is compared, are insistently active, they are the subjects of active verbs in the passage: Aeneas joins Dido (4.142: *infert se socium*) and unites his companions with hers (4.142: *agmina iungit*). In the simile, Apollo leaves Lycia (4.144: *deserit*) and comes to Delos (4.144: *invisit*). He renews dances (4.145: *instaurat*), he walks (4.147: *graditur*), he presses his locks (4.148: *premit crinem*) and braids them with gold (4.148: *implicat auro*). Just so, Aeneas, too, walks (4.149: *haud illo segnior ibat*). The grammatical differentiation between Dido and Aeneas as object and subject could not be clearer in this passage. Again the syntactic strategies of the text underscore the idea that Dido is the object of the reader's gaze.

But let us return to the issue of spectacle. Not only does Aeneas escape visualization; he also escapes the reader's scrutiny of his interior life.[35] Notice that we know Dido's feelings inside out, but we cannot tell whether or when Aeneas falls in love with her.[36] His love for Dido manifests itself only indirectly or belatedly. When he beholds Dido for the first time, there is no direct reference in the text to his emotional response to seeing her.[37] This is all the more remarkable since references to his emotional responses have been more than abundant previously when he beheld the pictures on Juno's temple or the city of Carthage. The subsequent simile that compares Dido to Diana leading a chorus of nymphs in a dance has sometimes been taken to reflect Aeneas' feelings on seeing Dido, because the simile makes reference to Diana's mother Latona rejoicing in her daughter's appearance.[38] But this suggestion is far-fetched; and even if we were to allow Latona to be an oblique reference to Aeneas, the reference would be so indirect as to leave the reader with only a vague sense of Aeneas' state of mind.

There is no reference to Aeneas' feelings about Dido until after the two make love in the cave. Even then, references are indirect, such as the rumors reaching the Libyan king, Iarbas, to the effect that Dido and Aeneas are "forgetful of their kingly rule and caught up in base passion" (4.194: *regnorum immemores turpique cupidine captos*). Later, when Mercury is sent to Carthage to remind Aeneas of his mission, Mercury calls him "a slave to his wife," perhaps implying the same charge as the rumors that had come to the ears of Iarbas (4.266: *uxorius*). That Aeneas lingers on in Carthage, even supervising the building projects (4.260), certainly suggests that he likes it there, but again direct reference to his feelings is missing. After Mercury has exhorted Aeneas to leave Carthage, we do get a small indication of Aeneas' attachment to Carthage. We are told that Aeneas "ardently wishes to flee and leave the sweet land behind" (4.281: *ardet abire fuga dulcisque relinquere terras*). But it is the land that is sweet to Aeneas, not the woman he will leave behind. When Dido confronts him about his secret preparations for departure, Aeneas shows his reluctance to follow the gods' will when he tells her that he does not seek Italy by his own choice (4.361: *"Italiam non sponte sequor"*), but he also makes it clear that his own wish would be not to stay with Dido but to have stayed behind in Troy (4.340–44). After this quarrel, Aeneas wants to comfort Dido, and he is said to be shaken in his heart by great love (4.395: *magnoque animum labefactus amore*), but it is not clear whether the great love that shakes his heart is his or hers.[39] Again, when Anna is sent to Aeneas by Dido to ask him to stay on a little longer, the mission is unsuccessful, and tears are said to flow in vain, but we cannot tell whether Aeneas is crying or Anna, or indeed Dido (4.449).[40]

Only much later, when Aeneas meets Dido's shade in the Underworld in *Aeneid* 6, do we finally get an explicit reference to Aeneas' feelings for Dido. The narrator tells us three times that Aeneas sheds tears when he speaks to Dido (6.455, 468, 476). He also tells us that Aeneas addresses Dido with sweet love (6.455: *dulci amore*). Aeneas himself tells Dido that he left Carthage against his will at the behest of the gods (6.460: *invitus, regina tuo de litore cessi*).[41] By her cold reception of his belated professions of love, Dido shows Aeneas that he really missed the right moment.[42] Considering how little we hear of Aeneas' demonstrations or sensations of love for Dido while he is actually involved with her, we may well understand Dido's exasperation with him.[43] The economy of the *Aeneid* narrative delays insight into Aeneas' feelings until it is safe for him to profess them.[44] After all, once Dido is dead, she can no longer distract Aeneas from his mission by detaining him at Carthage. Of course Aeneas must love Dido, for he would not be much of a hero if he had no feelings for the woman he got involved with. But to acknowledge this romantic involvement with Dido at the moment of his departure would be to compromise the logic he uses to justify himself to her: He is her guest (*hospes*), not her husband, and therefore free to leave. Aeneas' love for Dido was always implied by the text, but never expressed. The narrative is very skillful in presenting Aeneas as honorable, because he did not break his word to Dido. During book 4 we must remain in the dark about Aeneas' feelings, while the spotlight is on Dido. The effect of this narrative economy is to polarize the two protagonists into two different constructions of subjectivity. Dido's passion, as her whole person, is constantly on display, while Aeneas escapes (or shares) the reader's gaze during this spectacle of female desire.

We may conclude that books 1 and 4 of the *Aeneid* polarize Dido and Aeneas into opposite constructions of subjectivity. The pattern emerging from this and the following episodes is the following: female subjectivity is constructed around desire and presented as a spectacle, while male subjectivity is centered on the gaze and cast as audience of the spectacle of female desire.[45] We see Aeneas gazing at the spectacle of Dido's passion in much the same way as he later gazes at the spectacle of Andromache's grief, a passage I will turn to shortly. We will see below that Juno is also constructed as a spectacle in *Aeneid* 1. The reader gazes at the spectacle of Juno's passion in much the same way as Aeneas watches Dido and Andromache. The parallels between these instances suggest an implicit gendering of the reader's subject position, rendering the reader's vantage point male, whether or not the actual reader is a man.

ANDROMACHE AS SPECTACLE

We may further trace this pattern in some other female characters of the epic who are also constructed as spectacles of Aeneas' or the reader's gaze. Let us first consider Andromache in *Aeneid* 3.[46] During his wanderings Aeneas comes to Epirus, where Helenus, son of Priam, and Hector's widow, Andromache, reign. When Aeneas approaches their city, his first glimpse is of Andromache pouring a libation at Hector's tomb:

> *progredior portu classis et litora linquens,*
> *sollemnis cum forte dapes et tristia dona*
> *ante urbem in luco falsi Simoentis ad undam*
> *libabat cineri Andromache manisque vocabat*
> *Hectoreum ad tumulum, viridi quem caespite inanem*
> *et geminas, causam lacrimis, sacraverat aras.*
>
>   (*Aen.* 3.300–5)

[Leaving the fleet and the shore I walked forth from the harbor. At that moment it so happened that Andromache was making ritual offerings of food and gifts of mourning to Hector's ashes as she was standing before the city in a grove near the banks of a false Simois; she was invoking his shade to enter his empty tomb, which she had consecrated for him with green turf and dedicated two altars, the cause of her tears.]

Andromache clearly occupies center stage in this episode of Aeneas' adventures. The opening image of this scene introduces her in a moment that is emblematic of her persona as a tragic heroine. Although Hector lies buried in Troy and although Andromache is married to Helenus now, it is Andromache's mourning for Hector that defines her identity.[47] Her grief and her widowhood are visually captured in this passage by the representation of her in the act of pouring a libation (301: *tristia dona*) at an empty tomb erected for Hector (304: *tumulum inanem*). The tomb with its altars is called the reason for her tears (305: *causam lacrimis*), but it is really her grief that necessitates the visual image of Hector's empty tomb, for it provides both the reader and Aeneas with an external representation of Andromache's emotional life.

Andromache's grief for Hector is thus a spectacle for Aeneas' and the reader's gaze, just as Juno's anger and Dido's passion are spectacles. The theatrical quality of the scene is underscored by another stage prop: We are told that Hector's tomb is situated in front of the city, in a grove near a false Simois (302: *falsi Simoentis ad undam*).[48] By calling the river a false Simois, Aeneas gives us advance knowledge of the city Andromache lives in now. Helenus and Andromache have built their new home in the likeness of the old one, creating a little Troy, a *parva Troia,* which Aeneas describes in greater detail some lines later (3.349–51). Not only does Andromache still grieve for Hector, but she also still lives in Troy. Thus, the theatrical backdrop for the spectacle of Andromache's grief is a reproduction of the city where her sorrows originated. Even in the first glimpse Aeneas catches of her, she is seen against the background of this re-creation of Troy, with the false Simois invoking the whole scenario right from the beginning.

Like Dido, Andromache also owns a gaze in this passage, and as in the case of Dido, Andromache's gaze is itself a spectacle. After Aeneas has taken in the image of Andromache's grief, she in turn sees Aeneas. Aeneas gives a detailed description of her reaction to seeing him, dwelling both on the visible signs of her reaction (which he can see) and on her state of mind (which he infers):

> *ut me conspexit venientem et Troia circum*
> *arma amens vidit, magnis exterrita monstris*
> *deriguit visu in medio, calor ossa reliquit,*
> *labitur, et longo vix tandem tempore fatur.*
>
> (*Aen.* 3.306–9)

[When she saw me coming and perceived in a frenzy that Trojan armor was around her, she froze as she gazed, frightened by these great marvels; the warmth left her bones, she fainted, and after a long time she finally spoke with difficulty.]

The shock Andromache experiences at seeing Aeneas may be understandable, since she probably does not know that Aeneas survived the sack of Troy. But in terms of narrative technique, Andromache's reaction to the sight of the Trojans is interesting for another reason. Andromache's gaze in this scene is handled in a manner that is strongly reminiscent of Dido's gaze. Just as the reader can see Dido's gaze and understand how it implicates her in her passion, so Andromache's gaze at Aeneas reveals to us her inner life.

We can understand why it is disturbing to Andromache to be confronted with a living image from her past, since we already know from the opening image of Hector's tomb that she is obsessed with her past and re-creates it both internally and externally. Since she could not herself have re-created a living image of Aeneas, however, she may well wonder whether she is going mad. That is why Aeneas describes her as *amens* in this very moment (307). When Aeneas describes Andromache's gaze in this passage, he also gives an account of Andromache's agitated state of mind which is revealed in her gaze: doubting her sanity, frightened at what she sees, Andromache freezes and faints. A little later, when Aeneas asks her about her fate, she casts down her eyes (320: *deiecit vultum*) before recounting her tribulations, a powerfully expressive use of the gaze as spectacle to represent Andromache's sorrow and humiliation at being enslaved by the Greeks.

Since Aeneas is the narrator of the present scene, the reader sees Andromache's gaze through Aeneas' eyes and with his interpretation of what he sees. Aeneas' gaze again merges with that of the reader, as we have observed before. Andromache's gaze, then, is represented with the same narrative technique we have observed earlier on in *Aeneid* 1, the convergence of the gazes of Aeneas and the reader. These narrative strategies articulate the qualitative difference between the gazes of Aeneas and Andromache. While Aeneas' gaze is here also the gaze of the narrator and thus defines the reader's gaze, Andromache's gaze is a spectacle.

ᴒ THE VOICE OF HELENUS

The patterns of gender differentiation that we have observed in *Aeneid* 1 for the construction of subjectivity are confirmed in the Andromache episode.[49] Another element of this episode further corroborates our earlier conclusions. The characterization of Andromache's new husband, Helenus, differs significantly from that of Andromache.[50] Aeneas' and the reader's gaze do not linger on Helenus at length to describe his appearance or his reactions at seeing his compatriots. While the narrative lavishes more than forty lines on exploring Andromache's subjectivity (3.301–45), only four lines cover the ground for the description of Helenus (3.345–48). But this does not mean that Helenus is not important to the narrative, for his prophecies occupy a large part of the book and provide vital information to Aeneas. The difference between him and Andromache lies precisely in the mode in which his subjectivity is constructed by the narrative. Unlike Andromache, Helenus is not a spectacle. Although both characters have a voice, Helenus is constructed primarily through his voice. More importantly, the quality of his voice differs from that of Andromache, for while her voice serves to characterize her inner life, his voice is the voice of historical (external) truth and divine knowledge. The epithet he is given repeatedly by the narrative—*vates* (3.358, 433, 463)—thus sums up the quality of Helenus' subjectivity: Helenus is a seer, not one whose main purpose in the narrative is to be seen.

❧ THE PASSIONS OF JUNO

The pattern we have so far observed of representing female subjectivity as a spectacle of emotions is also operative in the representations of Juno. Juno, too, is constructed as a spectacle, even when she gazes. But Juno is not merely a parallel to Dido and Andromache. The construction of her subjectivity has a special relationship to the reader's gaze. In a sense she is the paradigm of female subjectivity as spectacle, the blueprint that Dido and Andromache follow. Her gaze and her emotions are differentiated not from Aeneas, but from the reader. Because this relationship between the reader and Juno is established at the very beginning, it has a defining force for the reader's gaze throughout the poem.

Juno is the first fictional character in the narrative.[51] We encounter her after a remarkable visual moment, the description of the geographical location of Carthage. Having established the narrator's relationship with his audience, the proem concludes in the famous narrator's rhetorical question: Is the anger of the gods really as great as this? (11: *tantaene animis caelestibus irae?*). Our first glance in the narrative is at Carthage—the stage of events for many books to come.

> *Urbs antiqua fuit (Tyrii tenuere coloni)*
> *Karthago, Italiam contra Tiberinaque longe*
> *ostia, dives opum studiisque asperrima belli,*
> *quam Juno fertur terris magis omnibus unam*
> *posthabita coluisse Samo. Hic illius arma,*
> *hic currus fuit; hoc regnum dea gentibus esse,*
> *si qua fata sinant, iam tum tenditque fovetque.*
>
> (*Aen.* 1.12–18)

[There was an ancient city, a Tyrian colony, called Carthage, situated opposite Italy and the mouth of the Tiber, at a great distance, rich in wealth and very fierce in the pursuits of war. They say that Juno loved this city more than any other place, even more than Samos. Here were her weapons, here her chariot. That this city was to be the capital of nations, if only the Fates should allow it, was even then the goddess' ambition and cherished desire.]

Our gaze zooms in from a broad, maplike sweep of the central Mediterranean, locating Carthage opposite Italy and the Tiber. This opposition is full of meaning, of course, and goes beyond mere geographical positioning. But it is interesting to observe how the narrative establishes Carthage visually as opposite to Rome long before it explains in what other ways the two cities are opponents. The visual image of Carthage opposite Rome immediately makes sense to the ancient reader in a symbolic way, as well, because of the importance Carthage held in the Romans' historical imagination as Rome's most important opponent on its way to world domination.[52] The next image is of Juno's sacred objects at Carthage, her weapons and her chariot (16–17). Juno is linked to Carthage right from the beginning of the narrative. But the connection between the goddess and her favorite city is going to deepen even further.

After these brief visual moments we encounter Juno herself—presumably not at Carthage, but in some location of divine residence that is not specified. And it is not really important where Juno is, for we do not really see her from the outside, but rather from the inside. It is as though we have entered into the core of her heart to witness her hopes and fears, her desires and resentments.[53] Juno is thus first and foremost introduced into the narrative as a desiring subject.[54] It is this aspect of her subjecthood that plays the most important part in the story. Her love of Carthage, we hear, leads her to desire world domination for her favorite city, if fate might only allow this to happen. But we know, and indeed are told in the following lines, that Juno's desire must remain unfulfilled.

> *progeniem sed enim Troiano a sanguine duci*
> *audierat Tyrias olim quae verteret arces;*
> *hinc populum late regem belloque superbum*
> *venturum excidio Libyae; sic volvere Parcas.*
>
> (*Aen.* 1.19–22)

[But she had heard that descendants from Trojan blood were one day to overturn the Tyrian citadels; from there a nation was to come to the destruction of Libya, a kingly people superior to them in war; thus the Parcae had ordained.]

The narrator sets up Juno as the desiring subject par excellence, because the object of her desire is eternally out of her reach. By wishing to establish Carthage as the reigning city, Juno pits herself against fate itself, which has ordained that the descendants of the Trojans will conquer Carthage and rule the world. And there is no getting around the fact that nothing will happen contrary to fate. Any reader of the *Aeneid,* ancient or modern, realizes as much, for by Vergil's time the Carthaginian empire had been crushed by the Romans for over a century.

So what does it mean for a Roman audience in the time of Augustus to be reading about Juno's desire for Carthaginian world domination? Leaving aside the religious aspects of this question,[55] I would like to draw attention to an interesting movement at work in this sequence. The connection established here between the Punic Wars and the goddess Juno[56]—who is, after all, a Roman deity—brings with it a politicization of Juno's desire as well as a personalization of the Punic Wars. In other words: Roman history has been turned into a story about female desire, the desire of Juno—and later on the desire of Dido as well.[57] This process has been effected so successfully in the narrative that we do not even question the premise it rests on, namely, that one of the greatest obstacles to Roman world domination was not so much the existence of an equally strong political and military opponent as the desire of a passionate female, whose hostility to Rome had to be overcome.[58]

But this is, of course, a narrative about the origins of Roman culture. In a way it can be taken to explain why Juno has come to be a Roman deity, because the epic's closure is effected only by appeasing Juno. And yet there is something very significant about Vergil's portrait of Juno. Not only is she made to be foreign before she becomes reconciled to Rome, but the very core of her being is defined by her thwarted desire for destroying the budding origins of Rome.

This is, then, the kind of subject we encounter in Juno: the first subject of the narrative proper is defined first and foremost by her desire, a desire, moreover, which by its very nature can only be ungratifiable. Once this premise is established, we remain inside Juno's heart to explore the nature of her resentments against the Trojans, whom she hates not only as the future opponents of Carthage, but also as her personal enemies.

> *id metuens veterisque memor Saturnia belli,*
> *prima quod ad Troiam pro caris gesserat Argis—*
> *necdum etiam causae irarum saevique dolores*
> *exciderant animo; manet alta mente repostum*
> *iudicium Paridis spretaeque iniuria formae*
> *et genus invisum et rapti Ganymedis honores:*
> *his accensa super iactatos aequore toto*

Troas, reliquias Danaum atque immitis Achilli,
arcebat longe Latio

(Aen. 1.23–31)

[Fearing this and remembering the old war, which she had been the
first to wage against Troy for her beloved Argives, the daughter of
Saturn (for not yet had she forgotten the reasons for her anger and
her fierce grief; she stored in her memory the judgment of Paris and
the offense of her spurned beauty and the hated nation and the hon-
ors of abducted Ganymede) was angered additionally by these
things; she kept the Trojans, that were left over by the Greeks and
fierce Achilles, from Latium for a long time.]

The Trojan War, we are reminded, was also partly motivated by Juno's
desire to help her beloved Argives. We see here a pattern emerging of the
destructive nature of Juno's desire,[59] as she is made responsible for both the
Trojan War and the Punic Wars. Again, of course, we notice that war has
been personalized and desire politicized, a movement already present in
the connection between Juno and the Punic Wars.

Now that this pattern has been firmly established, the narrative moves
on to study in detail the anatomy of Juno's desire and lack of gratification.
And here we find that Juno's resentments against the Trojans are of a very
personal nature. It is injured pride and jealousy that motivate the goddess
in her hatred.[60] Both are caused by Trojan princes, namely, Paris, who
judged Venus to be more beautiful than Juno, and Ganymede, upon
whom honors were bestowed by Jupiter as a sign of his preference.[61] Her
resentments are about slights to the respect paid to her femininity: her
beauty spurned by Paris, her husband attracted erotically to Ganymede,
and her husband's philandering with Electra, the mother of Dardanus,
flaunted by Jupiter's support of Dardanus' offspring. Juno's passion is pe-
culiarly female, her resentments reflect the specific concerns of women in
the roles assigned to them in ancient culture. The link between passion
and femininity in this passage will turn out to be representative for the
text's handling of passion in general.

So far, then, the narrator has taken us inside Juno's heart and shown us
her innermost feelings, her desires and preferences, as well as her jealousy
and hatred. Until this point Juno is a subject constructed entirely by her
emotions. This is about to change. Juno is the first agent in the narrative,
an agent, moreover, whose actions profoundly influence the direction of
the narrative. The sea storm she brings about drives the Trojans off course

and causes them to land in Carthage instead of Italy. To bring all this about, Juno must act, and her visit to Aeolus, the king of the winds, from whom she solicits help for her plans, is a colorful scene, the first in the poem (*Aen.* 1.50–80). She does more than act; she also speaks. Before she goes to Aeolus, she holds a monologue that explains to us her reasons for her subsequent actions (37–49). All this, the monologue, her feelings, her actions, are triggered by a glimpse Juno catches of the Trojans, who are in good spirits as they set sail from Sicily:[62]

vix e conspectu Siculae telluris in altum
vela dabant laeti et spumas salis aere ruebant

(*Aen.* 1.34–35)

[They were hardly out of sight from Sicily and cheerfully set sail in the direction of the open sea, stirring sea foam with the bronze of their prows.]

It is this glimpse that activates all her old resentments against the Trojans and stirs her immediate wrath. Juno's gaze is the first gaze of a fictional character in the story, and the reader shares this gaze.

This is, then, an important moment for the poem's handling of the reader's gaze, as well. With our discussion about *phantasia* in mind, it does not surprise us that Juno's gaze at her enemies in high spirits causes an immediate emotional disturbance. Ancient thinking about the self saw the gaze as an entryway to the soul, and the dangers of certain images for one's emotional equilibrium are vividly described by Lucretius. The narrator establishes Juno's mind as fertile ground for such emotional disturbance by laying out her desires and resentments at the start. Such a predisposition, disturbed by an image of this sort, leads Juno directly to emotional chaos.

So far Juno's gaze and her emotions are paradigmatic of ancient theories of subjectivity. But does the reader share Juno's feelings as well as her gaze? Assuming our ancient reader is Roman, it is unlikely that he would have the same emotional reaction to seeing the Trojans in good spirits as Juno does. Juno has been established as an enemy of the Trojans and of nascent Rome, so we would expect a Roman reader to experience a certain distance to Juno's reactions.

The text, however, does not leave the work of distancing from Juno's feelings to the reader. Yet another textual strategy accomplishes this distancing of the reader's reaction from Juno's. After describing Juno's feelings about the Trojans and before the reader shares Juno's gaze at their departure from Sicily, the narrator shifts his focus from Juno to the Trojans and their sufferings at the hands of Juno:

> *His accensa super iactatos aequore toto*
> *Troas, reliquias Danaum atque immitis Achilli*
> *arcebat longe Latio, multosque per annos*
> *errabant acti fatis maria omnia circum.*
>
> (*Aen.* 1.29–32)

[Being angry about this in addition to the rest she kept the Trojans—what the Greeks and harsh Achilles had spared—far from Latium, and for many years they wandered across all the seas, tossed about by fate.]

After experiencing Juno's feelings, the reader is now led to consider the fate of the Trojans as exiles in search of a new home. This new perspective is likely to evoke the reader's sympathy for the Trojans, especially if as a Roman such a reader was already predisposed to feel for their fate because of his sense of kinship with these legendary ancestors.

In the next line the narrator reinforces this perspective by asserting his own voice in support of this sympathy with the Trojans. This is how he formulates his sentiments:

> *Tantae molis erat Romanam condere gentem.*
>
> (*Aen.* 1.33)

[So great was the toil involved in founding the Roman nation.]

This authorial comment structures the passage, separating the description of Juno's more general disposition toward the Trojans from the arousal of her more immediate wrath at the sight of her enemies' good fortune. Although the reader gets to know Juno's feelings and her perspective intimately, the narrator takes care to pull the reader out of this perspective at the very moment when he motivates her passion with the image that stirs it up. The distance he accomplishes by this device allows the reader to see the process of how Juno's wrath is aroused without being implicated in it. Although the reader shares Juno's gaze, he also sees that gaze from a distance. Thus, Juno's gaze becomes itself a spectacle. The entire scene depicting Juno's feelings, her gaze, and her actions becomes a spectacle for the reader's gaze.

The language in which the narrator couches his remark is indicative of the means by which the narrator accomplishes these effects. His appeal to *Romana gens* shows that the gaze established in these lines is that of a Roman reader. This identification is important to the kind of self the text establishes. In chapter 8 I will look at the nature of the group identity implied in this term. I will argue that it is an inclusive rather than a more narrowly ethnic identity, and hence comparable to the modern concept of nationhood.

But like modern nationhood, the Roman identity constructed in the *Aeneid* is still a type of group identity that allows for the possibility of exclusion. Presumably not only Romans read the *Aeneid,* and reading the *Aeneid* would not necessarily have turned the reader into identifying himself as Roman. Surely a Greek reading the *Aeneid* would have a different perspective on the opening scene of the poem than the one I have just outlined. A Greek would inevitably be distanced from the sympathies evoked for the Trojans and the Roman nation by the references to Juno's allegiance to the Greeks and to the Greeks as the Trojans' opponents in the Trojan War. After all, Achilles, the archetypal Greek hero, is referred to here as *immitis,* harsh, certainly not the most flattering reference imaginable to the hero of the *Iliad.*

But although such divergent readers' perspectives surely existed, it seems to me that the text itself does not make room for them. The narrator sighs for the toils involved in founding Rome. He sympathizes with the Trojans' plight, and he depicts Juno as a cosmic force opposed to fate because of resentments associated with her womanhood.[63] The text merges the perspective of Juno with that of Troy's and Rome's opponents, and thereby implicitly links their perspectives to that of Juno's archetypal female passion. The connection between ethnic identity and gender identity is a theme that we will observe in several other places in the poem again. But before I turn to this connection in chapter 6, I want to concentrate in the following chapter more explicitly on the link between gender and the emotions. Our discussion of the gendering of gazes and spectacles in the present chapter has already shown that the emotions play an integral part in this gendering. In the following chapter I will focus on the connection of gender and the emotions in other contexts.

PART 3

GENDER
AND
ETHNICITY

CHAPTER 5

Gendered Emotions

The previous two chapters have explored how the *Aeneid* establishes a gendered—and male—subject position for the reader through approximation of his gaze with the gaze of Aeneas and his differentiation from other characters represented more visually in the manner of a tragic spectacle. With this framework in mind, the last four chapters are concerned with the kind of identity the poem constructs for the reader by means of identification with and differentiation from these characters. We have already seen that this identity is constructed as male. In this chapter I will explore how gender is a determining factor in the poem's presentation of a character's emotional life.

In other words, it is not only the visual and tragic representation of some female characters that genders the reader's subject position as male; the poem also differentiates between male and female characters in the way they experience emotions and in the way their emotions define them as characters. We will see not only that female figures are portrayed as more passionate and less able to control their emotions than male characters, but that emotion is built into the female characters almost as a condition of their femininity. Several female characters' emotions, as I will show, are represented in the image of a wound: Juno, Dido, Lavinia, and Eriphyle. As subjects female characters are seen as wounded, damaged, or unstable, not because they are rendered so by outside experiences, but because woundedness is an integral part of the poem's construction of female subjectivity. Furthermore, contrasting the effects Allecto has on Amata and Turnus in book 7 will show that even when frenzy is imposed on two characters alike, gender determines the means by which frenzy is instilled in a character and the way in which the character reacts to being driven to frenzy by an outside force.

In the course of this discussion it will emerge that the femininity of some characters, as well as the representation of their emotional lives, is interlinked with the characters' ethnicities. A closer analysis of this link between gender and ethnicity in some female characters is the subject of chapters 6 and 7. As gendered and ethnic others, some female characters define the reader's Roman identity by opposition. The reader's identity, then, is constructed not only in terms of gender but also in terms of ethnicity. The last chapter explores this Roman identity further by observing the representations of other ethnic groups who are contrasted with those Trojans and Romans in the poem to which the Roman reader may feel the closest sense of identification or kinship.

MALE AND FEMALE FRENZY

In chapters 3 and 4 we observed that the subjectivities of Aeneas and Dido are constructed differently, as either spectacle or spectator in a visual scenario. We have also seen that the emotions are an integral part of Dido's identity as a spectacle, while Aeneas is constructed more through his gaze. The kinds of emotion Aeneas experiences as a spectator are also different from the kinds of emotion Dido experiences as a spectacle: Dido's emotion is passion, the passion of love driven to frenzy. Below I will argue that Dido's passion so fully absorbs her identity that its disappointment is the cause of her death in a very direct sense. Our discussion of the experience of tragedy suggests that Dido's passion is the passion of a tragic figure. Aeneas, on the other hand, on certain occasions, such as when viewing the temple of Juno or the shield Vulcan made for him, or surveying Carthage as it is being built, experiences the elation and joy attributed by ancient critics to the epic reading experience or the experience of the sublime. In terms of emotion, then, Dido and Aeneas often differ along the lines of literary genre, but their emotions are also sometimes conceived in the poem as belonging to different sides of the line between tragic spectator and spectacle. This means that to a certain extent Aeneas' emotions are qualitatively so differently conceived from those of Dido that comparison in terms of gender seems relevant only insofar as there is a gender distinction between the spectator and the spectacle.

Amata and Turnus, on the other hand, are ideal for comparing male and female emotions, because they both experience frenzy, or a passionate desire for war, and the source of their passion is identical: in book 7 both are imbued with frenzy by Allecto, who turns them into passionate and frenzied adversaries of Aeneas at the behest of Juno. Yet the means by which Allecto attempts her conversions are different, and the reactions of the two to Allecto's influence are different, too. The two scenes of Allecto's visits to Amata and Turnus are set up with such symmetry that comparison is unavoidable. In the previous chapter I discussed Allecto's conversion of Amata in terms of its visual qualities. Comparison of this scene with the conversion of Turnus brings out several features that suggest that the frenzy each of them experiences is gendered.

Juno sends Allecto to Latium after the Trojans have already established relations of hospitality and friendship with the Latins. A Trojan delegation had come to bring gifts to Latinus and to ask for a friendly reception of the Trojans in Latium. Latinus, in turn, not only welcomed them but offered his daughter Lavinia to Aeneas in marriage (7.152–285). At this point Juno arrives on the scene and declares her determination to destroy these beginnings of friendly relations between the natives and the Trojan colonists. When Juno commands Allecto to cause strife between them, Allecto goes to Amata and Turnus to instill in them a passionate desire for war with the Trojans and then creates a pretext for them to precipitate conflict (286–518).

Allecto first visits Amata in Latium. We find out that even before her arrival Amata had been brooding with anger and worry over the arrival of the Trojans and the consequences it would have on the marriage she had planned between Lavinia and Turnus:

> *Exim Gorgoneis Allecto infecta venenis*
> *principio Latium et Laurentis tecta tyranni*
> *celsa petit, tacitumque obsedit limen Amatae,*
> *quam super adventu Teucrum Turnique hymenaeis*
> *femineae ardentem curaeque iraeque coquebant.*
>
> (*Aen.* 7.341–45)

[Then Allecto with her demonic poisons first went to Latium and the palace of King Latinus and sat down silently on the threshold of Amata, who was incensed by the arrival of the Trojans and the marriage of Turnus and was seething with a woman's worry and anger.]

The very first information we get about Amata is that she is already in the grip of passions and that her anger and fear is directed at the Trojans, that is, at precisely the people against whom Allecto is commissioned to incite her passions. The language of the passage explicitly draws attention to both the nature and the intensity of her passions: the phrase *curaeque iraeque* is clear, brief and poignant, linking the two passions with the markedly poetic and epic *-que . . . -que,* the Latin adaptation of a characteristically Homeric connector, for emphasis. Line 345 as a whole is artfully constructed to highlight Amata's state of mind as seething with passion: the phrase *curaeque iraeque* is circled by *ardentem* and *coquebant,* two terms indicating her agitation. Lastly, the first word of the line, *femineae,* marks her passion as characteristically female.

There is practically nothing left for Allecto to do. She need not wrestle with an unwilling victim of forcefully imposed frenzy. What Allecto *does* can more or less be read as merely a metaphoric visualization of a preexisting passion: After quietly settling down on Amata's threshold, she takes a snake from her hair and hurls it at Amata (346–47). The snake imperceptibly glides down Amata's body and infects her mind with Allecto's poison (349–51). Then it turns into a gold necklace that remains on Amata's throat as a visible symbol of her frenzy (351–53). The stated goal of this divine intervention is to get Amata to cause uproar at the palace (348). This Amata immediately sets in motion. She approaches Latinus to dissuade him from giving Lavinia to Aeneas in marriage; when that fails she causes uproar among the women of all Latium, taking Lavinia to the mountains and gathering women around her to perform Bacchic rites in protest of the planned marriage (354–405).

When Allecto sees what she has effected in Amata, she moves on to Ardea to visit Turnus. She finds him sleeping quietly—a marked contrast to Amata's state of mind at Allecto's arrival (413–14). Allecto adopts a different tactic to infect Turnus with her frenzy: she takes on the shape of an old priestess of Juno and appears to Turnus in his sleep. As old Calybe she addresses Turnus in a speech in which she tries to incite his anger at Latinus and the Trojans for dissolving his own engagement to Lavinia and to rouse him to war against them (415–34). But Turnus' reaction seems to surprise Allecto. He replies condescendingly to her, saying that he already knows what is happening and that he has faith that Juno will not desert him. He tells her not to try to stir up fear in him and that the reason she herself is afraid is her great age, which has weakened her understanding.

Then he delivers the final insult: he tells her to mind her own business, look after the temple, and not to meddle in war, which is the concern of men (435–44).

Turnus is not a willing victim of Allecto. Not only does he put up a fight before Allecto finally vanquishes him, but his attitude to her is calm and confident. He does not admit to or show any signs of anger or fear against the Trojans. He recognizes that Allecto wants to incite his fear, but he shows himself unaffected by it. Moreover, he sees the fear she wants to stir in him as already existing in her and ascribes it to her weakness as an old woman. His imperious command to concern herself only with her work as priestess and to leave the affairs of state to men shows him asserting himself over her as a man and a prince who need not bow before her greater age or the authority she claims to have as a priestess of Juno, commissioned by the goddess to rouse him to war.

Allecto's rage erupts at Turnus' words, and she turns back into her own horrifying shape. This finally vanquishes Turnus. It is at this point that he becomes afraid (446–47: *at iuveni oranti subitus tremor occupat artus, / deriguere oculi*). And yet, he still struggles against her, even in his fear of this monstrous apparition: he hesitates and wants to say more, but he is ultimately powerless against Allecto's divine fury (449–50: *cunctantem et quaerentem dicere plura / reppulit*). She assumes a most horrifying pose and addresses Turnus, citing his insults to her in indignation and mockery and telling him exactly who she is (a Fury) and what her real business is (she brings war and death) (446–55). Then follows a description of Turnus as he wakes up from his sleep, sweating from fear. He is finally Allecto's instrument: he raves in his anger and his desire for war (458–62) and immediately takes steps to declare war (467–74).

The contrast between Amata's reception of Allecto's intervention and that of Turnus could not be more marked. While Amata is fertile ground for Allecto's anger, Turnus is calm and confident. He does not yield to Calybe's persuasion to enter into her fears and instead mocks and belittles her for them. He struggles against Allecto to the last, even when she has shown herself in her true form. In Turnus, Allecto has a real opponent to deal with. His resistance to her influence requires her to subject him by all the force at her disposal.

But her tactic does not change at the moment she encounters resistance. From the beginning, Allecto approaches the task of subjecting Turnus to her influence in a manner radically different from the one she had in approaching Amata. When faced with the already agitated Amata, she herself is calm, as the *tacitum* in line 343 suggests.[1] But in approaching a calmly sleeping Turnus, Allecto takes on the shape of an agitated woman and speaks to him in a manner that reflects the agitation she wishes to incite. Numerous imperatives, one closely following upon the other in a staccato rhythm, without connectives between them, give her words an urgent and agitated tone:

> *I nunc, ingratis offer te, inrise, periclis;*
> *Tyrrhenas, i, sterne acies, tege pace Latinos.*
>
> . . . .
>
> *quare age et armari pubem portisque moveri*
> *laetus in arva para, et Phrygios qui flumine pulchro*
> *consedere duces pictasque exure carinas.*
>
> (*Aen.* 7.425–26, 429–31)

[Go now, devote yourself to unwelcome dangers, you who have been reviled; go, rout the Etruscan ranks, protect the Latins with peace . . . Therefore come now and eagerly prepare for the young men to be armed and moved from the gates into the fields, and attack the Trojan leaders, who have settled by our beautiful river, and their painted ships with fire.]

Her words call to mind another woman in the throes of passion: the short, staccato imperatives of Dido's angry reply to Aeneas have the same agitated tone as Calybe's here, when Dido tells Aeneas to go and look for Italy amidst the stormy sea and seek his promised kingdom among the waves (*Aen.* 4.381: *I, sequere Italiam ventis, pete regna per undas*). But like Aeneas, Turnus does not respond in kind and remains calm. In response Allecto shows all the fury she is capable of, the fury that is her nature, and only then does Turnus submit, but not even then does he do so easily.

In her encounter with Turnus Allecto stays agitated throughout, the only difference between her agitation as Calybe and her fury as Allecto being the intensity of her passion. Allecto's approach to infecting Turnus with her frenzy differs from the method she adopted with Amata because there is nothing in Turnus on which Allecto can build, no seed of anger or desire for war she can intensify. A violent onslaught of her full force is necessary to bring about what seems to be a complete change in Turnus' state of mind. Turnus' initial dismissal of Calybe on the grounds that she is a weak old woman affected by fears and meddling in affairs properly looked after by men indicates that even when Turnus is faced with a goddess he considers the frenzy she wishes to incite as contrary to his masculine identity. A gender difference operates even between the mortal Turnus and the goddess Allecto. Not only Turnus and Amata, then, differ in their disposition to be affected by Allecto's frenzy, but even Allecto herself contrasts with Turnus in terms of passion. Thus, when Amata's anger is called womanly it not only reflects on her womanhood but suggests that Turnus' frenzy is intrinsically opposed to his masculine identity. Frenzy, then, is female, and it is no wonder that Juno and Allecto, the divine agents of frenzy, are female, too. But this is not all. The following sections explore to what extent female identity in the *Aeneid* is always affected by frenzy at its core.

JUNO'S WOUND

We have observed in the previous chapter that the wound Eriphyle shows to Aeneas in the Underworld most likely symbolizes love, since she dwells with Dido and other heroines in the *Lugentes Campi,* a place reserved for those who died of love. The wound as a visual and even visible symbol recurs in several other female characters. Juno, the first of them, is of particular importance, because in one respect, that of spectacle and the gaze, she can be read as a paradigm of female subjectivity in the poem. With regard to the representation of the emotions in the image of the wound, Juno will again emerge as a paradigm of female subjectivity. Discussion of the proem in the previous chapter has shown that Juno's hatred of the Trojans is peculiarly female, resulting from her jealousy of Jupiter's Trojan paramours and the slight to her beauty at the judgment of Paris. Her hatred, then, is caused by slights to her femininity, and it is her suffering from these slights that the poem associates with the image of the wound from the very beginning.

In the proem the narrator asks the Muse to explain the reasons for Juno's persecution of the Trojans. He couches this question in the language of an inner wound:

> *Musa, mihi causas memora, quo <u>numine laeso</u>*
> *Quidve <u>dolens</u> regina deum tot volvere casus*
> *Insignem pietate virum, tot adire labores*
> *Impulerit.*
>
> (*Aen.* 1.8–11)

[Muse, tell me the reasons: What was the <u>wound to her divinity?</u> Or what did the queen of the gods <u>suffer,</u> that she forced a man outstanding in his piety to endure so many misfortunes, to undergo so many toils?]

The same image of the wound is employed a few lines later, when Juno's anger is aroused by the sight of the Trojans' happy departure from Sicily before the sea storm. This time the language is particularly interesting, because the wound is described in a phrase that occurs in only three places in the poem: *sub pectore vulnus.* The phrase is once used for Juno's inner wound, and later on it is used twice for Dido, once to describe the inner wound of her love for Aeneas, and once for the actual wound she inflicts on herself with Aeneas' sword when she kills herself. Let us look at the first of these passages in greater detail:

> *Vix e conspectu Siculae telluris in altum*
> *Vela dabant laeti et spumas salis aere ruebant,*
> *Cum Iuno aeternum servans <u>sub pectore vulnus</u>*
> *Haec secum:*
>
> > (*Aen.* 1.34–37)

[They were hardly out of sight from Sicily and cheerfully set sail in the direction of the open sea, stirring sea foam with the bronze of their prows, when Juno, nursing the eternal <u>wound in her breast,</u> said this to herself:]

The positioning of this phrase right between Juno's gaze at the Trojans and her first speech gives it a special significance. We have seen the importance of the gaze in ancient thinking about the self. The following speech of Juno is the first speech of any character in the poem. It is therefore the first time a figure is characterized by her own voice.[2] We have already seen in the context of rhetoric that a person's voice was a central concern in the formation and training of the ancient self. It is the orator's voice that can exert an influence over the audience by invoking mental images.[3] We have also seen that the main component that makes up the subjectivity of Helenus is his voice. Thus, the phrase *sub pectore vulnus,* which encapsulates Juno's emotional state, is sandwiched between two major determinants of selfhood in ancient thinking about the self. Its repetition in the context of

Dido's passion lends it additional significance. In the present passage, the phrase introduces Juno's speech, and the nature of that speech gives us a more detailed understanding of Juno's wound. Therefore, we should briefly survey its implications for the characterization of Juno before we look at the other occurrences of the phrase *sub pectore vulnus*.

In this speech Juno expresses her frustration at not being able to keep the Trojans away from Italy.[4] Again, her frustrated desire in this respect is linked to jealousy, this time her envy of Minerva, who was allowed to vent her wrath at the Greeks by destroying their fleet in a sea storm.[5] Her inability to exact vengeance on the Trojans is exacerbated by her sense of injured pride, because as sister and wife of Jupiter, she says, she ought to be granted the same privileges of vengeance as Minerva. The violence of her first speech thus mirrors the violence of her emotions, which are summarized in the image of the wound and the phrase *sub pectore vulnus*. Juno goes on to effect a similarly destructive measure against Aeneas. The violence of the sea storm she orders Aeolus to bring about not only is a worthy match for Minerva's vengeance on the Greek fleet, but also perfectly matches the violence of her own emotions.[6] Thus, Juno's characterization here is quite overdetermined: the violence of her voice is reinforced by the violence her actions bring about. Both are designated as emerging from her violent passion.[7]

But this is not the only passage in which the wrath of Juno—or, to put it another way, her desire—determines the plot. Just as at the beginning of the epic she incites Aeolus to unleash his storm winds to drown Aeneas in a sea storm so that, driven off course, the Trojans land in Carthage; likewise in book 7 Juno orders Allecto to spread war in Italy between the Trojans and the Italians. Thus, the ultimate source of most of the violence that occurs in the narrative of the *Aeneid* is Juno.[8] The violence of Juno's emotions and her hatred of Aeneas throughout the epic are obvious not only in her actions but also in her speeches. The proem of the *Aeneid* marks her wrath as a central theme:

> *multum ille et terris iactatus et alto*
> *vi superum, <u>saevae memorem Iunonis ob iram,</u>*
> *multa quoque et bello passus, dum conderet urbem*
>
> (*Aen.* 1.3–5)

[He was much thrown about on land and sea, by the will of the gods, <u>because of the mindful wrath of cruel Juno</u>; and he suffered much in war, as well, until he founded the city.]

Book 7, even more than book 1, depicts Juno's wrath as the origin of all violence in the second half of the epic. The pattern, observed in book 1, of Juno's violent speech followed by her initiation of violent action is repeated in this book. The quality of her wrath, however, has become even more demonic.[9] In book 1 she was still motivated by her love of Carthage as well as her hatred of Aeneas and Rome. When she proposes to Venus a marriage between Aeneas and Dido, she does so because she sees this as an opportunity to promote the cause of her favorite city, Carthage.[10] Seeing that her efforts at influencing fate in favor of Carthage have failed, she now turns to the forces of the Underworld to satisfy her feeling of hate:

flectere si nequeo superos, Acheronta movebo

(*Aen.* 7.312)

[If I cannot bend the gods to my will, I will set in motion the forces of the Underworld.]

This time Juno acts through Allecto. While the instruments of her actions vary, her voice and her desire retain their violent quality throughout the epic. One thing has changed, however: the Juno of book 7 no longer harbors any hopes of achieving her own desires. Instead of influencing fate, her aim is now to interfere with it in whatever way is possible. She concentrates her efforts on destructiveness, and the demonic means she employs reflect that purely destructive agenda.

Juno's voice and desire can be understood as an instance of female subjectivity as it is constructed in the *Aeneid*.[11] In this respect Juno is comparable to other figures in the *Aeneid*, most notably Dido, Amata, and Andromache. As we will shortly see, the text links Juno's wound of passion explicitly with that of Dido. But although other female characters' passions are described with the same imagery of the wound as that of Juno, there is a difference between her and the mortal figures. The difference lies in the effects of her passion. While the mortal characters' metaphorical wounds will turn out to imply the fragility of the female subject, we have just seen that Juno's wound implies rather the destructiveness of her passion.

DIDO'S WOUNDS OF PASSION

As I have mentioned above, the phrase *sub pectore vulnus,* which described Juno's passion as a wound, occurs twice again in the Dido story.[12] The first refers to the metaphorical would of Dido's love, while the second refers to the real death wound Dido inflicts upon herself. Exploring the imagery of passion as a wound and its implications in this new context will give us further insight into the link between passion and femininity in the poem. Early on in *Aeneid* 4, when Dido has given way to her love for Aeneas, she is compared to a mortally wounded deer:

> *est mollis flamma medullas*
> *interea et* <u>*tacitum vivit sub pectore vulnus.*</u>
> *uritur infelix Dido totaque vagatur*
> *urbe furens, qualis coniecta cerva sagitta,*
> *quam procul incautam nemora inter Cresia fixit*
> *pastor agens telis liquitque volatile ferrum*
> *nescius: illa fuga silvas saltusque peragrat*
> *Dictaeos; haeret lateri letalis harundo.*
>
> (Aen. 4.66–73)

[In the meantime the flame eats away the soft marrow inside her very bones, and <u>a silent wound lives beneath her breast.</u> Unhappy Dido burns and wanders across the entire city in frenzy, like a hind shot with an arrow; a hunting shepherd pierced the unsuspecting animal from afar in the woods of Crete: he himself is unaware of it and leaves the flying shaft behind: but she wanders the woods and glens of Dicte in her flight, while the deadly weapon hangs from her side.]

Already we are alerted to the inevitably fatal outcome of Dido's passion. We cannot avoid linking Dido's love wound to the fatal wound of the simile, and this link is validated in retrospect by a later passage in which Dido's real death wound is referred to by the same phrase as her love wound earlier (689: *infixum stridit sub pectore vulnus*). The topography of the love wound coincides with that of the death wound. Since the love wound is called fatal, we may even say that it is Dido's metaphorical love wound itself that kills her. The death wound she inflicts on herself with the sword is a concretization of that earlier wound. Thus Dido literally dies from love; she falls victim to her own emotions.[13]

This interpretation of Dido's death as a love death is confirmed by the space she occupies in the Underworld in *Aeneid* 6. Together with several other mythical females, Dido inhabits the Fields of Mourning (*Lugentes Campi*), the place for those who died from love:

Nec procul hinc partem fusi monstrantur in omnem
Lugentes Campi; sic illos nomine dicunt.
hic, quos durus amor crudeli tabe peredit,
secreti celant calles et myrtea circum
silva tegit; curae non ipsa in morte relinquunt.
his Phaedram Procrinque locis maestamque Eriphylen
crudelis nati monstrantem vulnera cernit,
Euadnenque et Pasiphaen; his Laodamia
it comes et iuvenis quondam, nunc femina, Caeneus
rursus et in veterem fato revoluta figuram.
inter quas Phoenissa recens a vulnere Dido
errabat silva in magna.

(Aen. 6.440–51)

[Not far from here, stretching in every direction, are shown the
Fields of Mourning, thus do they call them by name. Here, solitary
paths hide those whom harsh love has destroyed with its cruel illness,
and a myrtle forest all round shields them; their cares do not leave
them even in death. In this region he sees Phaedra and Procris and
sad Eriphyle who is displaying the wounds inflicted by her cruel son,
and Euadne and Pasiphae; with them walks Laodamia as a compan-
ion, and Caeneus who was once a young man and is now a woman,
changed back again by fate into her old form. Among them in the
great forest wandered Phoenician Dido with her wound still fresh.]

Scholars who interpret Dido as heroic and tragic often argue that Dido
commits suicide to redeem her lost honor and to atone for her broken
oath of fidelity to Sychaeus.[14] However, the present passage and the ex-
plicit link the text draws between Dido's love wound and her death wound
lead us to question such a tragic interpretation of Dido's death.[15] Further-
more, the tragic interpretation of Dido's death ignores numerous refer-
ences throughout book 4 that link Dido's death to her frustrated love for
Aeneas. We have already seen that Dido's love is called fatal right from the
beginning, even before she becomes Aeneas' lover (4.73). Both Dido and
the narrator continuously draw attention to the inevitably fatal outcome
of her passion.

After Dido and Aeneas have become lovers, the narrator calls the day of
the hunt the cause of her death (4.169–70: *ille dies primus leti primusque
malorum / causa fuit*).[16] In her quarrel with Aeneas, Dido refers to herself

as "about to die" (4.308: *moritura* and 4.323: *moribunda*). After this dia-logue, when Dido sends Anna to Aeneas to ask for a delay of the Trojans' departure, the narrator calls her *moritura,* while she herself in her message to Aeneas seems to promise him her death as a reward for granting her the delay.[17] When Aeneas does not comply, Dido desires death (4.451: *mortem orat*). Her wish becomes a resolution after a series of bad omens and night-mares (4.475: *decrevit . . . mori*). Giving directions to Anna for preparing a pyre, she asks her to put her marriage bed on the pyre and says that she perished on it (4.496–97: *lectumque iugalem / quo perii super imponas*). Since Dido pretends to her sister that the pyre is for a love charm, Anna may think that Dido speaks metaphorically, but the reader who has supe-rior knowledge of Dido's feelings must view her statement in a different light. This becomes even more evident when we hear that Dido decorates the pyre with funeral wreaths (4.506–7).

It is then all the more strange that in the following scene Dido should ponder her future course of action and appear only at that point to de-cide on suicide as one of several options (4.522–52).[18] It is in this mono-logue, which she speaks during a sleepless night, that she associates her resolution to commit suicide (547) with the broken oath of fidelity she had sworn to Sychaeus (552). But the connection she draws between her suicide and her broken promise is not nearly as straightforward as a tragic or heroic interpretation of her death would warrant. The lines bridging the two ideas are notoriously difficult to interpret and by no means facilitate the notion that there is a causal connection between her suicide and her broken oath.[19] After this monologue, references to her coming death continue much as before. She refers to herself as "about to die" (4.604) and "dying Elissa" (4.610), and Mercury says she is "certain to die" (4.564) in a warning he gives to Aeneas not to postpone his de-parture. Thus, while Dido's monologue with its decision to commit sui-cide seems to suggest a tragic heroine pondering her options and decid-ing on a course of action in the manner of a tragic *anagnorisis,*[20] the rest of the narrative constructs Dido's death as the inevitable result of her passion.

Even the manner in which Dido stages her suicide is dominated by her love: the funeral pyre she orders to be erected is to be loaded with Ae-neas' weapons, his clothes, an image of Aeneas, and the bed Dido shared with him.[21] Lying on this bed, she speaks her last words. She addresses Aeneas' clothes,[22] asking them to receive her soul in death and free her from her pain:

dulces exuviae, dum fata deusque sinebat,
accipite hanc animam meque his exsolvite curis.

(Aen. 4.651–52)

[Sweet belongings of Aeneas, so dear while God and the Fates allowed it, receive my soul and release me from my sufferings.]

Then she kills herself with Aeneas' sword.[23] That Dido surrounds herself with articles associated with Aeneas in the moment of her death suggests that she seeks to be united with her former lover in death.[24] Indeed, the presence of a wax image of Aeneas on her own funeral pyre is enough to suggest such a wish on Dido's part. Not only in Greco-Roman antiquity but in many traditional societies people attribute to wax images of real persons the magical power to convey to their living counterparts all the misfortunes that befall them.[25] Thus, if Dido burns Aeneas' image along with herself, she may well think that it will mean Aeneas' death as well. Moreover, Dido's abode in the Underworld is populated by two other women whose deaths suggest similar wishes for union in death, namely Euadne and Laodamia.[26] Both women jump into a funeral pyre in an attempt to be united with their husbands in death. While Euadne jumps into her husband's funeral pyre, Laodamia jumps into the flames that consume an effigy of her dead husband.[27] Dido's death has an additional dimension: her suicide with Aeneas' sword carries overtones of a sexual union with the lost lover, since the weapons of men are often used in poetry as a metaphor for the phallus.[28] However, Dido's quest for union with Aeneas is futile, as we see in book 6. The language of her death wound makes this explicit, since it is the same language as that of her love wound: *sub pectore vulnus.*[29] Rather than linking her to Aeneas, this language separates her from him forever, because it is the language of love as ungratified desire. Thus Dido's love death emblematizes the failure of a life and death dominated by passion.

The language of Dido's love/death wound links her to Juno, as we have seen above. Like Dido, Juno desires what she cannot have, namely, the victory of Carthage over Rome. This connection conveys the destructiveness of female passion, since both Dido's and Juno's ungratified passion are made responsible for the Punic Wars in the text. Since Dido is mortal, however, she can convey the fragility of the female subject, as well. Looking back to the *Lugentes Campi,* we may observe that the list of inhabitants mentioned by name consists only of women. Does this, then, suggest that only women can die from love? A few gender ambiguities in the passage leave this question open to debate,[30] but emphasis is certainly given in the passage to the love-deaths of women. The instability of the female subject is shown not only in Dido's behavior and speeches throughout book 4, where she often shows radical changes of mood and tone, but also in Mercury's infamous warning to Aeneas: *Varium et mutabile semper femina* (*Aen.* 4.569f.: Woman is ever a fickle thing, likely to change).[31]

Dido's instability as a female subject has negative consequences for her role as leader of her people, and that not only by virtue of her death. From the beginning, love renders her forgetful of her duties as a queen and founding mother:[32]

> *non coeptae adsurgunt turres, non arma iuventus*
> *exercet portusve aut propugnacula bello*
> *tuta parant; pendent opera interrupta minaeque*
> *murorum ingentes aequataque machina caelo.*
>
> (*Aen.* 4.86–89)

[Her towers, just begun, no longer rise, the young men no longer train in arms, no longer work on ports or ramparts for safety against war; the building activities are broken off, idle stand the battlements of huge walls and cranes reaching up to the sky.]

Her city mourns her death in a manner that is compared to the effects of the sack and destruction of Carthage or Tyre:

> *it clamor ad alta*
> *atria; concussam bacchatur Fama per urbem.*
> *lamentis gemituque et femineo ululatu*
> *tecta fremunt, resonat magnis plangoribus aether,*
> *non aliter, quam si immissis ruat hostibus omnis*
> *Karthago aut antiqua Tyros, flammaeque furentes*
> *culmina perque hominum volvantur perque deorum.*
>
> (*Aen.* 4.665–71)

[The cries reached the high roofs of the palace; in a wild frenzy, Rumor rushed through a city shaken to its core. The house rang with laments, groans, and the wailing of women, the sky resounded with loud mourning, as though the entire city of Carthage or ancient Tyre were tumbling down at the onset of enemies, and wild flames were rolling over the roofs of men and gods.]

Anna formulates the same notion, when she tells the dying Dido that her death means the death of her sister, her people, her ancestors and her city, as well.[33] Thus, Dido's passion is not only accompanied by a lack of *pietas,* but it actually destroys the constituent elements of what her *pietas* could be directed at. Furthermore, in her curse monologue, Dido also expresses the desire to destroy Aeneas along with all the constituent elements of his *pietas.* Compared to Aeneas, Dido is a failure as a founding figure and as a rival model of leadership, because of the fragility and instability of her identity.

Let us look at the breakdown of Dido's identity as queen in her last monologue:

> *dulces exuviae, dum fata deusque sinebat,*
> *accipite hanc animam meque his exsolvite curis.*
> *vixi et quem dederat cursum Fortuna peregi,*
> *et nunc magna mei sub terras ibit imago.*
> *urbem praeclaram statui, mea moenia vidi,*
> *ulta virum poenas inimico a fratre recepi,*
> *felix, heu nimium felix, si litora tantum*
> *numquam Dardaniae tetigissent nostra carinae.*
>
> (Aen. 4.651–58)

[Sweet belongings of Aeneas, so dear while God and the Fates allowed it, receive my soul and release me from my sufferings. I have lived and traversed the course Fortune had given me, and now my great shade will go beneath the earth. I founded a famous city, I saw my city walls, I avenged my husband and punished my brother who was my enemy. I was happy, oh all too happy, if only Trojan ships had never reached our shores.]

The speech starts out with her wish to merge with Aeneas in death. Then she moves on to a more dignified tone, listing her life's achievements in the manner of a statesman. However, the last two lines mark a return to the persona of the female lover. The breakdown of her public persona is marked by allusions to the lament of Catullus' Ariadne and Silenus' lament for Pasiphae's passion in the *Eclogues:*[34]

> *Iuppiter omnipotens, utinam ne tempore primo*
> *Gnosia Cecropiae tetigissent litora puppes.*
>
> (Cat. 64.171–72)

[Almighty Jove, would that Athenian ships had never reached the
shores of Crete in the first place.]

et fortunatam, si numquam armenta fuissent,
Pasiphaen nivei solatur amore iuvenci.
a, virgo infelix, quae te dementia cepit!

(Verg. *Ecl.* 6.45–47)

[And he comforts Pasiphae in her love for the white bull, Pasiphae
who would have been fortunate, if cattle had never existed. O un-
happy maiden, what insanity took hold of you!]

This last line of the *Eclogues* passage is alluded to in another speech of
Dido, again at a point where it marks the breakdown of her public persona:

Quid loquor? aut ubi sum? quae mentem insania mutat?[35]
infelix Dido, nunc te facta impia tangunt?

(*Aen.* 4.595–96)

[What am I saying? Where am I? What insanity is turning my mind?
Unhappy Dido, do impious deeds now reach your mind?]

The allusion to Pasiphae is in no way accidental. Pasiphae is one of the in-
habitants of the *Lugentes Campi.*[36] The Dido episode is in many ways
evocative of the mythical descendants of the Sun god: Circe,[37] Medea,
Phaedra, Ariadne, Pasiphae. Dido's genealogy is even reinvented to reflect
the mythological relationship with these women. Vergil changes the tradi-
tion and calls her father Belus, the Latinized version of the Phoenician sun
god, Baal, who was identified by the Greeks and Romans with Helios/Sol.[38]
Dido is similar to most of these figures, especially as an example of female
passion; but another trait is common to all of them, namely, that they
transgress the patriarchal order in some way, by betraying a husband (Phae-
dra, Pasiphae, Dido) or a father (Ariadne, Medea), or simply by being an
unattached woman in a position of power (Circe, Dido.).[39]
   Dido's literary kinship to the descendants of the Sun god renders her
emblematic for a certain kind of female subjectivity, the kind that is first
and foremost constructed around passion. But the *Aeneid* narrative reaches
beyond the female daughters of Helios to depict female characters gener-
ally as such passionate subjects. Apart from Juno, whom I have discussed
above, there are most notably Amata and Andromache, who in different

ways exemplify the pattern of female subjects as dominated by passion. As Amata's suicide shows, her identity is fragile in the same way that Dido's is. Andromache is somewhat different in that her identity as Hector's widow seems to be so dominant as to eclipse the facts of her present life. In that sense it might seem wrong to speak of her identity as fragile.[40] On the other hand, Andromache seems to need a complete re-creation of her past around her in order to function as a recognizable signifier in the narrative. Seen in that light, her own identity by itself must be rather weak and indeterminate.

But Dido is special because she is in charge of Carthage. Consequently, her fragility has political meaning as well. Seen in this light, the story of Dido's love is almost certainly a reflection on the role Cleopatra played in world politics before Actium. If women are fragile as subjects because of passion, then a woman in a position of power is not only undesirable but dangerous. In that sense Dido's depiction has overtones of ethnic identity, as well. The polarization of East and West in pre-Augustan political discourse plays into Dido's literary makeup in several complex ways, which are the subject of chapter 7.

LAVINIA'S WOUND

Let me close this section with a brief look at another character whose subjectivity is represented in the image of a wound. Paradoxically, Lavinia has not much of an inner life. The one and only time we hear anything about her feelings is when she blushes.[41] At the beginning of book 12 the reader witnesses a council of war at the palace of Latinus, at which Turnus, Latinus, and Amata discuss how to proceed. Amata beseeches Turnus not to return to war with the Trojans and vows that she will die if he dies in battle, since she cannot bear to have Aeneas as her son-in-law. It is at this point that Lavinia blushes, and in describing her blush the narrator uses a simile with an ominous literary ancestry:

> *accepit vocem lacrimis Lavinia matris*
> *flagrantis perfusa genas, cui plurimus ignem*
> *subiecit rubor et calefacta per ora cucurrit.*
> *Indum sanguineo veluti violaverat ostro*
> *si quis ebur, aut mixta rubent ubi lilia multa*
> *alba rosa, talis virgo dabat ore colores.*

(*Aen.* 12.64–69)

[Lavinia heard her mother's words. Her face bathed in hot tears, she blushed violently: her cheeks were burning and color spread over her face. As when someone has stained Indian ivory with blood-red purple, or when white lilies are paired with roses to add a reddish hue, such colors you could see on the maiden's face.]

The image of purple-stained ivory is supremely apt as a comparison for a blushing maiden such as Lavinia, contrasting the whiteness of her skin with the redness of her blush and thus visualizing both her beauty and her maidenly timidity. But the simile is also an allusion to a very different context. At the beginning of *Iliad* 4, when Pandarus breaks the truce by shooting an arrow at Menelaus, Menelaus' wound is compared to the same image as Lavinia's blush, namely ivory stained with purple (*Il.* 4.141–45). Again the image seems appropriate, contrasting Menelaus' white skin with the blood emanating from his wound.

What is less clear is why a description of a maiden's blush should allude to a Homeric hero's battle wound. But the connection between the blush and the wound is made even in the simile itself, which refers to the staining of ivory with the verb *violaverat* (12.67), a word that has primarily the connotation of wounding, and only metaphorically (and rarely) that of dyeing.[42] After the preceding discussion of Dido and Juno as wounded subjects, it is easier to account for the allusion, because the allusion characterizes Lavinia as a wounded subject in the only moment when she is a subject with a hint of feelings, although we are still puzzled as to the nature of her feelings.[43]

As in the cases of Juno and Dido, the wound of Lavinia is a metaphorical one, a visualization of her feelings. By looking at the imagery of the wounds of Juno, Dido, and Lavinia, we have explored how the *Aeneid* represents passion itself as a spectacle, in Juno's and Lavinia's case purely by means of metaphor and simile, and in the case of Dido by turning a metaphorical wound of love into an actual death wound. Like the necklace of Amata that represents the madness Allecto has instilled in her, the wounds of the figures discussed here are examples of representing passion as something visible, a spectacle to be looked at.

We have also seen that female subjectivity in the *Aeneid* generally seems to involve an element of damage, be it expressed in the fragility of mortal women's identities or in the destructiveness of Juno. Beyond that blush and the hint it contains of Lavinia's fragile identity, we have not much of a subject at all in Lavinia.[44] There is only the merest hint of her desires in her enigmatic blush, which might express feelings for the valor of Turnus but might equally be a reaction to the thought of being Aeneas' bride or to her mother's misdirected passion. In terms of selfhood Lavinia is a cipher, all we have been able to tease out so far is that her selfhood is akin to other examples of female subjectivity, because the image of Menelaus' Homeric wound links her feelings to those of Dido and Juno.

Nevertheless, Lavinia is an important figure for the narrative. Her main significance, however, is in her name and its nexus to Latin identity, which will be explored in the next chapter. Thus the gender differentiations considered in this chapter have an impact on the formation of the reader's identity in ethnic terms as well. In the depiction of Juno, the narrator addresses himself to a specifically Roman reader. Dido's depiction as an ineffectual leader because of her passion recalls the foreignness of Cleopatra and the excess of passion associated with her. Lavinia by her very name invokes Lavinium and the Latin race. Even Andromache fits into this picture, because it is precisely the attachment to Troy that forms the center of her emotionality. So we have repeatedly seen that the construction of subjectivity has larger political meaning. In the following I will look more closely at the link between gender identity and ethnic identity in the poem.

CHAPTER 6

Gendered Ethnicity

In chapter 4 we have analyzed how female characters are represented as spectacles for the reader's gaze, which has the effect of distancing the reader from the experiences and emotions of these figures. By only vicariously experiencing their emotions, the reader experiences *catharsis*. Such *catharsis* functions to purge the reader of the dangers depicted in these spectacles. Additionally, it invites the reader to differentiate his own subjectivity from the fictional characters portrayed in this way. In the course of this analysis we have observed in several female characters that the depiction of passion was linked to the notion of gender. By differentiating himself from Dido and Juno, the reader will not only purge himself of their dangerous passions, but also define his own identity in opposition to them in terms of gender. This renders the reader's vantage point in the poem male (even though actual ancient readers certainly included women), in opposition to Dido and Juno.

But notions of ethnicity are also implicated in the reader's self-definition vis-à-vis Dido and Juno. There is much emphasis on Juno's preference for Carthage and Greece, especially at the beginning of the poem. The proem draws attention to the future enmity of Rome and Carthage. In this chapter I will examine the ethnic dimension of Dido and the link between gender and ethnicity in other female characters, such as Lavinia and Creusa. By reading Dido as an ethnic other, the reader's identity is defined by opposition. The nature of the reader's identity, his Romanness itself, is the subject of a subsequent chapter. The purpose of the present chapter is to locate in the text of the *Aeneid* those ethnic others who are opposed to the reader's Romanness in terms of both gender and ethnicity. Characters who embody otherness in both of these categories are especially powerful in forming the reader's sense of what it means to be Roman.

The link between gender and ethnicity in these figures often involves another such link, that between passion and ethnicity. This second link deserves more attention, because two ways of defining identity come together here, the personal one in which the self is defined by its constituent elements, such as its gaze, its emotions, and its voice, and the communal one in which the individual self is defined as part of a group and by its role or standing within that group, be it a nation, a tribe, or the body of citizens of a city-state, groups which themselves in turn are defined by their opposition to other such groups. While the link of passion to ethnicity combines these two modes of defining the self in the *Aeneid,* the link between gender and ethnicity is a combination of two communal modes of defining identity. Nevertheless, this link, too, implicates the personal mode of defining identity, because ethnic others are figured as female here because of their passion and because the link itself introduces the possibility of erotic narrative into stories about colonization and imperialist conquest, as we will shortly see. It is therefore worth exploring how deeply the link between gender and ethnicity is inscribed in the poem's conceptions of these two categories of identity. In order to do so, I want to return to some of the characters discussed in the previous chapter and look at the way ethnicity is implicated in their description. Let me begin with Lavinia, the woman whose name is also the name of Aeneas' future city.

LAVINIA AS CITY

Lavinia's silence and the lack of description concerned with her emotional life stand in stark contrast to the significance Lavinia has in the poem on the level of the structure of the epic narrative.[1] Lavinia is in a sense the signifier that frames the whole epic. If we look for something that links the proem of the *Aeneid* to its final scene, it would have to be Lavinia. The second line of the poem spells out her name, or so we might think, until we have to realize that what is referred to here is not the woman but the land Aeneas will colonize:

Arma virumque cano Troiae qui primus ab oris
Italiam fato profugus Laviniaque venit
litora

(*Aen.* 1.1–3)

[I sing of arms and the man who was first to come from the shores of Troy to Italy, exiled by fate, and to the shores of <u>Lavinium</u>.]

Lavinia is also the last female character referred to in the epic (*Aen.* 12.937: "*tua est Lavinia coniunx*"). It is not a coincidence that the word *Lavinia* is used in this way at the beginning and end of the poem. While it is the city and land of Lavinium that is referred to by this name in the first half of the epic,[2] in the second half the name refers only to the woman, the bride of Aeneas.[3] Thus, there is a movement in the narrative from promised land to flesh-and-blood woman. What is the relationship between land and woman? Aeneas says that it is Lavinia who gives the name to the city:

> *urbique dabit Lavinia nomen*
>
> (*Aen.* 12.194)

[Lavinia will give her name to the city.]

Thus, Aeneas makes the founding gesture of naming the city, a move universally associated with the male.[4] But the following passages show that the name *Lavinium* has been fixed for the land even before Aeneas hears about the woman Lavinia. Jupiter calls the city by this name when he promises Venus that the fate of Aeneas will be accomplished despite Juno's destructive efforts:

> *Parce metu, Cytherea, manent immota tuorum*
> *fata tibi: cernes urbem et promissa <u>Lavini</u>*
> *moenia*
>
> (*Aen.* 1.257–59)

[Do not fear, Cytherea, the fate of your people remains unchanged; you will see the city and the promised walls of <u>Lavinium</u>.]

Finding that Aeneas lingers in Carthage, Jupiter again calls the promised land by this name when he sends Mercury down to earth to call Aeneas back to his duties:

> *quid struit? aut qua spe inimica in gente moratur*
> *nec prolem Ausoniam et <u>Lavinia</u> respicit arva?*
> *naviget! haec summa est, hic nostri nuntius esto.*
>
> (*Aen.* 4.235–37)

[What is he planning? What hope keeps him lingering among a hostile people, and neglecting his Italian descendants and the fields of <u>Lavinium</u>? He must sail! No need to say more. Let this be my message.]

Aeneas remains ignorant of the name of both the land and the bride, until he meets the Sibyl at Cumae. She reveals the name of the promised land to him:

> *o tandem magnis pelagi defuncte periclis*
> *(sed terrae graviora manent), in regna <u>Lavini</u>*
> *Dardanidae venient*
>
> (Aen. 6.83–85)

[Aeneas, finally you are rid of the great dangers of the sea, but greater perils remain for you on land. The descendants of Dardanus will come to the realms of <u>Lavinium</u>]

But the Sibyl does not name Aeneas' future bride, even though she speaks of her. She only refers to her as "a wife who will give rise to great misfortune (6.93: *coniunx causa mali tanti*), just as Creusa had spoken only of Aeneas' future royal wife:

> *regnumque et regia coniunx*
> *parta tibi*
>
> (Aen. 2.783–84)

[A kingdom and a royal wife are in store for you.]

None of the other prophecies Aeneas receives, including those of Apollo, the Penates, Celaeno, and Helenus in book 3, even mentions his future marriage.

The story of the second half of the *Aeneid* makes it clear that woman and city are a unit that can be attained only in combination by Aeneas. Since the Lavinian land precedes the woman Lavinia in the text and in the sequence of the story line, it also becomes clear that the land is not named for the woman, as Aeneas says. Narratologically speaking it seems rather as if the woman is named after the land. Certainly the text suggests that Lavinia is linked to Lavinium by name as well as by their function in the story.

☙ CREUSA

This equation of city or land with woman is quite common. The female allegories of Persia and Greece in Atossa's dream in Aeschylus' *Persae* are one example for this connection. But we need not look so far for parallel conceptualizations of gender. Another character in the *Aeneid* can be understood in terms of the connection of woman and city. Aeneas loses Creusa, his first wife and mother of Ascanius, at the same time he loses his old city Troy.[5] The manner of Creusa's disappearance is noteworthy in this context. When Aeneas realizes that Creusa is no longer with him, he goes in search of her. But he finds her neither alive nor dead. Instead, he encounters her ghost, who tells him that the gods have decreed that she cannot leave Troy together with him. She promises him "a kingdom and a royal wife" (*Aen.* 2.783: *regnum et regia coniunx*) in his new home, Hesperia, and says that a goddess detains her in the land of Troy:

sed me magna deum genetrix his detinet oris
(Aen. 2.788)

[But the Great Mother of the gods detains me on these shores.]

The Great Mother of the gods of whom Creusa speaks is the goddess known in Rome as *Magna Mater*, otherwise called Cybele. Her sacred stone was transferred to Rome in an official ceremony by the Roman state in 204 BC. The introduction of this deity into the Roman pantheon is usually read as asserting Rome's link to Asia Minor through its Trojan origins. Thus, if Creusa is kept in Troy by Cybele, we may read the goddess as closely linked to the city in which she detains Creusa. We may even say that Creusa is kept in Troy by the land itself. The same image of Cybele emerges in the pageant of heroes in book 6, where she is envisioned both as mother of the gods and as goddess of the Phrygian cities, wearing a crown of towers:

> *qualis Berecyntia mater*
> *invehitur curru Phrygias turrita per urbes*
> *laeta deum partu, centum complexa nepotes,*
> *omnis caelicolas, omnis supera alta tenentis.*
(Aen. 6.784–87)

[As the Berecynthian Mother with her turret crown drives on her chariot through the Phrygian cities, happy in her offspring of gods, embracing a hundred children, all of them citizens of heaven, all dwelling up high.]

While this image of Creusa detained in Troy by the goddess of Troy is by itself an intriguing parallel to the functioning of Lavinia, there are other factors that underscore the connection between the two characters. Structurally, the story of Creusa is an inversion of the story of Lavinia. Aeneas loses Creusa and Troy to gain Lavinia and Lavinium. That Creusa's name is as colorless as that of Lavinia works in support of this structural mirroring: Creusa means queen or princess.[6] Finally, Creusa shares with Lavinia another significant feature, her silence. Creusa speaks only when she is no longer Aeneas' living wife. Both Creusa and Lavinia are colorless as characters for a good reason: they are connected to the land they represent and serve to communicate the will of the gods to the major characters. Creusa does not really die, but before she is whisked off by Cybele, she becomes the mouthpiece of the will of the gods, telling Aeneas to seek a new home and wife. Indeed, a wife announcing to her husband that he is destined for another wife rather than telling him that he will miss her is truly a colorless character.

Lavinia, too, communicates the will of the gods, despite her silence. But in her case the communication of the will of the gods takes a form that renders Lavinia even more passive, even less of an agent involved in such a communication. In a religious ceremony Lavinia's hair seems to catch fire. Regarding this vision as a portent, Latinus is prompted by it to consult the oracle of Faunus to learn its meaning.[7] Thus the gods use Lavinia's body, or rather Latinus' vision of her body, as a vehicle for communicating their will to Latinus, but agency in this communication is entirely in the hands of the gods and Latinus.

Roman foundation myths predating the *Aeneid* provide a remarkable parallel to the pattern observed above. Before the story of Romulus was canonized, the woman Rhome featured in various accounts as the eponymous heroine of Rome. Indeed, there was a confusing variety of versions explaining the name of Rome and the city's foundation.[8] In the beginning of his *Life of Romulus* Plutarch gives us an account of the alternative versions that were known to him. Beside Romulus and Rhome he names two other male eponymous heroes, Rhomos and Rhomanos. Thus there would seem to be no rule about the gender of the person giving the name to the city, were it not for an interesting distinction between the male name givers and Rhome: while Rhomos, Rhomanos, and Romulus function both as city founders and eponymous heroes, Rhome only gives her name to the city without being considered its founder. Rhome's genealogy varies in the different stories Plutarch lists, but she is consistently connected to the male founder or founders of the city either by marriage or descent: she is the wife of Aeneas, Latinus, or Ascanius in some accounts, the mother of Romulus in another. Thus, the pattern of naming a city after a woman is quite distinct from the alternative story type, in which it is the founder himself who gives his name to the city. In either case the founder of the city is male. In this respect the foundation myths recounted by Plutarch conform with the gender pattern observed above for the foundation of Lavinium in the *Aeneid*. Rhome and Lavinia give their names to the cities, but the cities are founded by Aeneas, Ascanius, or Romulus.

✄ THE ETHNIC OTHER EROTICIZED

Another conclusion we can draw from this material is that Roman foundation stories often involve an erotic link between founder and city, as it is the case in the story of Lavinia. The Roman legend of the rape of the Sabine women follows the same pattern.[9] This accords with colonial narratives in archaic Greek poetry, in which the colonized land is often represented as a woman and the act of colonization or city foundation as marriage or rape.[10] Ethnic difference between colonizer and colonized or city founder and woman-as-land is a nascent theme here, but it becomes more important later on in antiquity. The ethnic otherness of Lavinia vis-à-vis Aeneas, and of the Sabine women vis-à-vis the Romans, may not seem dramatic, especially since the Trojans at the end of the *Aeneid* are decreed to cease being Trojans, and the Sabines are a neighboring tribe living in the same small territory as the Romans; but in both these cases, their ethnicity is an issue in their stories: Lavinia's name links her to the city to be founded, and the Sabine women are known in legend only by this ethnic designation.

Indeed, the erotic link of conqueror and conquered or of colonizer and colonized in imperialist and colonial discourse is very common, and by no means confined to antiquity. The American continent is often feminized and eroticized in colonial discourse,[11] perhaps most famously today in the story of Pocahontas, the native American woman who married an English colonist in 1614.[12] Indeed, in his 1930 verse collection *The Bridge*, which explores a kind of American mythology, the American poet H. Crane included her, together with other historical and legendary characters, as a national symbol and called her the "mythological nature-symbol chosen to represent the physical body of the continent."[13]

David Quint has explored this eroticized link between gender and ethnicity in the epic heroines of the Western tradition. He sees seductive Oriental heroines in Western epic, such as Tasso's Armida, Ariosto's Angelica, and Milton's Eve, as the direct literary descendants of a long and august line of ancient epic heroines with similar Eastern attributes: Apollonius' Medea, Vergil's Dido, and Lucan's Cleopatra.[14] It seems likely that Vergil's Dido was the most powerful influence on later epic poets in creating such figures. In the following I will explore the use of Punic ethnicity in the Dido narrative as a means of representing Carthage, an ethnic other vis-à-vis Rome, and as a woman in love.

ঙ PUNIC DIDO

Dido is the character most beloved by ancient and modern readers in the entire epic. Although the Romans had their prejudices about the Carthaginian character—they sometimes called them perfidious, cunning, and cruel, even long after the Carthaginians had ceased to be a political threat to anyone—these prejudices seem not to have affected Vergil's portrayal of Dido. These stereotypes seem to have no place in a figure as sympathetic and attractive as Dido, one of the most appealing characters in ancient literature, a most powerful portrayal of love, integrity, despair, and vulnerability. Nevertheless, that a Carthaginian queen is a protagonist even in an Augustan epic should give us pause for thought. What are the implications of such a construct? Had the Romans overcome their fear of the long-defeated enemy so fully that they could imagine the foundress of Carthage as a wholly sympathetic figure with feelings just like their own? Or does the prominence of Dido in the *Aeneid* bear witness to the continued function Carthage still played in Vergil's time of providing the Romans with an Other against which to define themselves? Most modern readers of the *Aeneid* are inclined to agree with the first possibility more than with the second. And there is no denying that the first statement is true. But the two statements are not mutually exclusive. A case can be made for the second statement, as well, and it is a case that opens up new perspectives on the understanding of the *Aeneid* as well as on the attitudes and mentalities of readers in imperial Rome and the ways in which their sense of self was constructed.

In the following I will outline how the portrayal of Dido resonates with

ethnic stereotypes the Romans had about Carthaginians. This argument
has been made before by N. Horsfall (1973–74), but it has not been received
favorably by many scholars.[15] To say that Dido is characterized with Punic
stereotypes is for many readers unpersuasive, because it runs counter to
the very sympathetic portrayal she receives in the *Aeneid*. The presence of
ethnic stereotypes, on the other hand, implies an unsympathetic reading
of Dido. Horsfall suggested that the Punic stereotypes in Vergil's Dido
were resonances of a more unsympathetic portrayal of Dido in Naevius.
Although I agree with Horsfall's observations about Punic stereotypes in
Vergil's Dido, I do not think that it is necessary to argue either that Vergil
intended these Punic resonances to imply a hateful or derogatory inter-
pretation of Dido, or that he imported into his characterization the influ-
ence of another poet's derogatory depiction of Dido. After all, he could be
evoking the stereotypes to be held in mind along with the sympathetic
portrayal, so creating a more complex character.

Indeed, it will become clear further below that Vergil's Punic charac-
terization of Dido is absorbed so fully into his portrayal of her as an aban-
doned lover that what might be seen as her Punic traits are also always mo-
tivated by her lover's persona. In this sense Dido's identity as a woman in
love is inextricably intertwined with her ethnic identity. It is this link be-
tween gender, passion, and ethnicity in Dido that I am interested in here.
As a woman and a Carthaginian, Dido embodies otherness in a double
sense against which Aeneas' identity (and the reader's) can be defined. As
we have seen in previous chapters, such an Other is not necessarily un-
sympathetic. Understanding Dido's suffering as a tragic spectacle for the
reader's gaze has helped us to see our sympathy for and identification with
her as a cathartic experience in the Aristotelian sense. This sympathy and
identification does not cease after the first reading of the Dido episode,
but is reactivated with every reading. It is a form of identification that al-
lows the reader to differentiate himself from the tragic figure by opposi-
tion to her, despite his identification with her. An ethnic characterization
of such a tragic figure humanizes and allows identification with the ethnic
other on the one hand; on the other hand, Dido's different ethnicity fa-
cilitates the reader's differentiation from her as a tragic figure, thus allow-
ing the reader's sympathy for her to be experienced as sympathy for some-
one distinct from himself and therefore cathartic. In other words, Dido's
Punic traits support the distancing effect between the reader and the char-
acter represented as a tragic spectacle.

For these reasons it is not my intention to replace one interpretation of

Dido (as sympathetic and moving)[16] with another (as conforming to ethnic stereotypes), but rather to add another dimension to our understanding of one of the most complex and most fascinating characters of Western literature. The project of the present section is to read the Dido episode within the specific cultural context of Roman perceptions of Punicness. When Vergil's text is viewed side by side with contemporaneous evidence about stereotypes and prejudices of the Romans against their former enemies, we derive the benefit of an additional dimension to our understanding of the *Aeneid.* As founding figures, Dido and Aeneas stand for their cities and empires, but they also represent rival models of leadership. Because Horsfall's observations about Dido's Punic traits have not met with general acceptance, it is necessary to take this issue up again and reposition the arguments that support a Punic characterization of Dido in a framework that clarifies the intimate connection between Dido's persona as a sympathetic heroine and her Punic persona.

Ralph Hexter has argued that Sidonian Dido is the only Dido we do not see in the *Aeneid.*[17] His interest lies in the impossibility of representing the Other without appropriating it. That Dido is an abandoned woman in the *Aeneid* and does not resemble more closely the powerful and dangerous female lovers of Near Eastern epics is for Hexter a sign of the extent to which Dido has been appropriated and tamed by the Roman epic tradition. In this sense we certainly do not encounter Sidonian Dido in the *Aeneid.* But other scholars have argued that Dido is the only Carthaginian in Latin literature who is not portrayed in accordance with Roman stereotypes of the Carthaginians.[18] This view I believe to be a misconception. We will see that Dido's Punic characterization in the *Aeneid* is hard to detect because it is blended with her lover's persona. All the hallmarks of the Punic character, *Punica fides,* cunning and cruelty,[19] qualities that the Romans ascribed to their Punic enemies throughout the literary sources, are motivated in Dido by her love for Aeneas. Nevertheless, Dido's ethnicity cannot be overlooked, because—even outside the Dido episode—there are several places in the epic that draw attention to the importance of Carthage for the history of Rome.[20]

ᴥᴥ CARTHAGE IN THE *AENEID*

In this section I will review those passages in the *Aeneid* in which the Punic Wars are invoked as a decisive moment in Roman history. These passages suggest that Carthage plays a defining role in the *Aeneid*'s conception of

Roman identity. It has been argued, however, that the absence of the Carthage theme in other passages is equally noteworthy, suggesting that the importance of Carthage to the *Aeneid* should not be overestimated.[21] Most significant among these omissions are Jupiter's prophecy in book 1 and the shield of Aeneas in book 8, both of which are concerned with important events of Roman history.[22] I will consider both the presences and significant absences of the Carthage theme. I will argue that the Carthage theme is not treated as one historical event among others in the *Aeneid,* but that it attains mythical status and cosmic significance. Its presence in some places of the poem gives it poetic structure, while significant absences in passages about Roman history underline that the Carthage theme belongs in the mythical and cosmic plane of the narrative, rather than its historical plane.

Being one of the key causes for Juno's opposition to fate, the Carthage theme appears in scenes of cosmic significance, such as the proem and the council of gods in book 10, where Juno's opposition to fate comes to a crisis. The following passage from the beginning of the epic shows that Carthage and Rome are set up in opposition to each other as rivals for imperial power over the whole world, one favored by Juno, the other sanctioned by fate:

> *Urbs antiqua fuit (Tyrii tenuere coloni)*
> *Karthago, Italiam contra Tiberinaque longe*
> *ostia, dives opum studiisque asperrima belli;*
> *quam Juno fertur terris magis omnibus unam*
> *posthabita coluisse Samo; hic illius arma,*
> *hic currus fuit, hoc regnum dea gentibus esse,*
> *si qua fata sinant, iam tum tenditque fovetque.*
> *Progeniem sed enim Troiano a sanguine duci*
> *audierat, Tyrias olim quae verteret arces;*
> *hinc populum late regem belloque superbum*
> *venturum excidio Libyae: sic volvere Parcas.*
>
> (*Aen.* 1.12–22)

[There was an ancient city, a Tyrian colony, called Carthage, situated opposite Italy and the mouth of the Tiber, at a great distance, rich in wealth and very fierce in the pursuits of war. They say that Juno loved this city more than any other place, even more than Samos. Here were her weapons, here her chariot. That this city was to be the capital of nations, if only the Fates should allow it, was even then the goddess' ambition and cherished desire. But she had heard that descendants from Trojan blood were one day to overturn the Tyrian citadels; from there a nation was to come to the destruction of Libya, a kingly people superior to them in war; thus the Parcae had ordained.]

Juno's anxiety about the ultimate defeat of Carthage is one of the motivating factors that lead her to try to prevent Aeneas from fulfilling his destiny, as can be seen in the very next line:

id metuens veterisque memor Saturnia belli

(Aen. 1.23)

[The daughter of Saturn feared this and remembered the old war . . .]

Her love of Carthage is as much a factor in her hatred for the Trojans as is the following reference to the Trojan War and the enumeration of her reasons for siding with the Greeks there. At the end of book 6 the victorious Roman generals of the Punic Wars are pointed out to Aeneas by Anchises at the end of the parade of heroes. The Scipios (*Aen.* 6.840), Q. Fabius Maximus Cunctator (*Aen.* 6.845f.), and Marcellus (*Aen.* 6.855–58) are among the last Anchises names before he goes on to lament the death of young Marcellus, the descendant of the hero of the Punic Wars, who was Augustus' son-in-law and designated successor.

It can be no coincidence that the first half of the *Aeneid* is framed by references to Rome's rivalry with Carthage. It is therefore not surprising to find that in the very middle of the second half of the epic, at the beginning of book 10, the Punic Wars are discussed by Jupiter in a council of the gods on Olympus. He disapproves of the wars in Latium and says that the time will come when Rome will justly engage in warfare, namely, with Carthage:

adveniet iustum pugnae, ne arcessite, tempus,
cum fera Karthago Romanis arcibus olim
exitium magnum atque Alpis immittet apertas:
tum certare odiis, tum res rapuisse licebit.

(Aen. 10.11–14)

[There will be a proper time, do not hasten it, when fierce Carthage will one day bring great ruin upon the citadels of Rome, opening up

pathways through the Alps: then it will be right to fight with enmity
and to pillage everything.]

Venus responds to him by blaming Juno for trying to undo Aeneas' destiny.
She begs Jupiter to let her at least save Ascanius from Juno's destructive ac-
tions, because she fears that Aeneas will not escape from her wrath, that
there will be no Rome, and that Carthage will conquer Italy:

> *magna dicione iubeto*
> *Kathago premat Ausoniam: nihil urbibus inde*
> *obstabit Tyriis.*
>
> (Aen. 10.53–55)

[Give orders to let Carthage subjugate Italy with its great dominion:
nothing will then stand in the way of the Tyrian cities.]

The pervading sense of all these passages is that both the fate of Aeneas and
the power of the Roman Empire in Vergil's time are inextricably linked with
Rome's rivalry with Carthage in the Punic Wars. The marked positions
these passages occupy in the epic emphasize the importance of this theme
for Vergil's founding myth of Rome. Appearing in the proem in book 1, at
the end of the parade of heroes which closes book 6, and at the beginning
of book 10 in the council of gods, the Carthage theme thus frames the first
half of the poem and reappears at the center of the poem's second half.
Moreover, in the Dido episode the Carthage theme dominates the mythical
plane of the narrative for the first four books and is particularly significant
for the Aeneas story as a whole. Thus, if we add the Dido narrative to the
other appearances of the Carthage theme in the *Aeneid,* it becomes quite
clear that Carthage holds a central position in the ideological framework of
the *Aeneid.*

But what about the absence of the Carthage theme in Jupiter's prophecy
and in the shield of Aeneas? It has been argued that Jupiter's prophecy does
contain an oblique reference to the Punic Wars. When Jupiter promises
Venus that Juno will be reconciled to the Romans (*Aen.* 1.279–82), some see
this as a reference to the placation rituals the Romans performed for Juno
during the Second Punic War.[23] It has also been suggested that the dramatic
situation of Jupiter's prophecy as a speech of consolation to Venus may have
contributed to the choice of historical themes addressed there.[24] I would
add to these observations that any direct reference to Rome's hostilities

with Carthage at this point in the narrative would anticipate the outcome of the subsequent Dido narrative, which unfolds in the way that it does only because Venus is meddling with Dido solely with the intention of helping Aeneas. Were Venus to know definitely about future hostilities between Rome and Carthage, would she allow Aeneas to meet Dido and get entangled in a love affair? And for that matter, what would be the point of telling the Dido story as an *aition* for Rome's hostilities with Carthage if the outcome was clear in the beginning?

The absence of the Carthage theme on the shield of Aeneas has also been explained in terms of dramatic purpose. It has been suggested that not depicting the defeat of Carthage on the shield may serve the purpose of ensuring that knowledge of this historical event would be kept from Juno as long as possible, and its depiction on the shield might circulate this knowledge, which could then reach Juno and incite her anger against the Romans anew.[25] Another reason for the absence of the Carthage theme on the shield may have to do with the mythical status and cosmic significance the Carthage theme has in the *Aeneid* as a whole. Including the Carthage theme in a series of other events of Roman history may be seen as putting it back into the historical plane of narrative, putting it on a par with other wars and conflicts, and hence as distracting from the cosmic and mythical role Carthage plays in the *Aeneid*. Be that as it may, I do not think that, given the prominent role Carthage plays in other significant parts of the poem, it is possible to claim that its absence on the shield or in Jupiter's prophecy diminishes its significance to the poem as a whole.

The prominent role of Carthage in the *Aeneid* might or might not surprise us, depending on our point of view. Seen from the perspective of the Roman literary tradition, we would expect a Roman epic to deal with Carthage, if only to pay tribute to the epic poets of Vergil's past—Ennius and Naevius—whose epics must have been burnt into Vergil's memory just as they were burnt into Horace's (and just as Vergil's epic would later be burnt into the minds of Romans throughout the empire). But would such tribute to the old poets warrant the prominent place Vergil gave to Carthage in his epic at a time when that enemy was long defeated? With the perspective of the political situation of Augustan Rome, we have more reason to be surprised at the emphasis on the Punic Wars in the epic.[26] But instead of minimizing the role Carthage plays in the *Aeneid,* it is worth investigating what place the Punic Wars occupied in the historical imagination of Vergil's contemporaries.

CARTHAGE IN FIRST-CENTURY BC LITERATURE

In the *Rhetorica ad Herennium* and in Cicero's *de inventione* several topics for rhetorical exercises are taken from the context of the Punic Wars.[27] These two rhetorical handbooks reflect the place of Carthage in the consciousness of the Roman elite as the mighty opponent of Rome's glorious past. Though not central, the Punic Wars are nevertheless a presence in these works, whose readers are expected to be familiar with the events of this period of Roman history. Whether Carthage should be destroyed or given back to the Carthaginians, whether Roman armies should be sent to Macedonia against Philip or kept in Italy to fight against Hannibal, these are the topics envisaged for rhetorical exercises in the two handbooks.[28] By practicing their oratorical skills on topics relevant to their famous ancestors, the Romans of the first century BC found their own identity within the matrix of Roman history, often focused through Rome's rivalry with Carthage.

A similar picture emerges from Cicero's speeches, where he frequently refers to events of the Punic Wars.[29] Such gestures to the history of the Punic Wars again underscore that the Romans of the first century BC are accustomed to perceiving their own experiences within the frame of reference of the deeds of their ancestors vis-à-vis Carthage. In his philosophical writings, too, Cicero often uses historical examples from the Punic Wars to illustrate his moral teachings.[30] Cicero's works are filled with his nostalgic veneration of the Roman heroes from the time of the Punic Wars, in particular Scipio Africanus, the statesman, general, and cultural leader, and Cato Maior, the man who urged the Romans to destroy Carthage.[31]

Another body of literature that shows the point I argue here is the historiography of Sallust. In his proems Sallust links Rome's victory over Carthage with the beginning of its moral decline.[32] His nostalgia for the past is motivated by the perception that Rome is no longer true to itself, but along with *virtus, iustitia,* and *concordia,* he longs for an enemy, because Rome is true to itself only when it is at war with Carthage.[33]

Even closer in time and genre to Vergil, the works of Horace abound with references to Rome's wars with Carthage.[34] Of particular interest is Horace's use of Carthage in a poem about Cleopatra. The ninth epode, which celebrates Octavian's victory over Antony and Cleopatra, draws a parallel between the contemporary Eastern enemy and Carthage (Hor.

epod. 9.25). The same comparison is drawn by Propertius in a poem about Cleopatra (Prop. 3.11.59). But comparison with contemporary enemies is by no means the only use Carthage is put to by the poets. More typical of Horace's references to Carthage is perhaps his Regulus Ode (Hor. *carm.* 3.5), in which Carthage is used as a backdrop for putting Roman virtues, such as that of Regulus, on display.

Viewed against this backdrop, Vergil's characterization of Dido becomes crucial to the worldview of the epic as a whole. In order to understand more fully the way in which Vergil characterizes his Carthaginian queen, let me review how Vergil's contemporaries perceived Punicness. In the extant Roman literature of the first century BC, stereotypes of the Punic character included cunning, untrustworthiness, and cruelty.[35] Untrustworthiness in particular, often referred to as *Punica fides,* was seen as a characteristic of the Carthaginians. For Cicero, the Carthaginians were *foedifragi,*[36] *fraudulenti et mendaces.*[37] Their presumed cruelty manifested itself for the Romans in their practices of human sacrifice as well as in the events of the Punic Wars.[38] The figure of Hannibal had become a catalyst in the Roman imagination for the Punic character. For Cicero as well as for Livy, Hannibal was cruel, cunning, and treacherous.[39] This is not to say that this is the only light in which the Romans saw Hannibal. Cicero himself could praise Hannibal, Livy acknowledged the Carthaginian's greatness, and Nepos devoted a very positive biography to him.[40] But except for the case of Nepos, praise of Hannibal or the Carthaginians in the literature of the first century BC is always mixed with doses of stereotyping and ethnic prejudice. It is probable that a Roman reader will have come to the *Aeneid* with certain expectations and prejudices about Punicness, and we should be alert to evidence of this in the text. Coming from this survey of Roman attitudes to Punicness, the traits we (as typical Roman readers) would expect to find in Dido are *perfidia, calliditas,* and *crudelitas.* Let us now go through the Dido narrative in order, just as a reader would "discover" Dido, and pay attention to any signs of these traits.[41]

STEREOTYPES OF CARTHAGE AND CARTHAGINIANS IN THE *AENEID*

Before we encounter Dido, the city of Carthage is characterized briefly in the *Aeneid's* proem, in a passage we have already looked at in the previous pages:

Urbs antiqua fuit (Tyrii tenuere coloni)
Karthago, Italiam contra Tiberinaque longe
ostia, <u>dives opum studiisque asperrima belli</u>

(Aen. 1.12–14)

[There was an old city, Carthage (Tyrian settlers lived there), a long way opposite Italy and the mouth of the Tiber, <u>rich in wealth and stern in the pursuits of war.</u>]

Here we are introduced to Carthage as a city opposite to Italy and the mouth of the Tiber. This geographical opposition between Carthage and Rome encapsulates the antagonistic relationship between the two cities as rivals for world dominion, as is clear from the following lines where Juno's plans for Carthaginian world domination are laid out, as well as her knowledge that fate has destined Rome for that role (*Aen.* 1.15–22). But even before this rivalry between the two cities is spelled out, Carthage is characterized as rich and ferocious in the pursuits of war (1.14: *dives opum studiisque asperrima belli*). In this first encounter we have with Carthage, in a prominent place of the narrative, the proem, we are led to conceptualize Carthage in opposition to Rome, while the narrator singles out the city's wealth and its martial violence as its two chief characteristics. We will shortly see that these two characteristics resonate deeply with other elements of the Dido story, such as Dido's wealth, the presence of gold in the story of her flight from Tyre, and the ferocity with which the Carthaginians greet a contingent of the shipwrecked Trojans.

Our first encounter with Dido occurs after Jupiter's prophecy in book 1. In order to ensure a friendly welcome for Aeneas in Carthage, he sends Mercury to earth, who transforms both Dido and her subjects:

Haec ait et Maia genitum demittit ab alto,
ut terrae utque novae pateant Karthaginis arces
hospitio Teucris, ne fati nescia Dido
finibus arceret. volat ille per aëra magnum
remigio alarum ac Libyae citus adstitit oris.
et iam iussa facit, ponuntque ferocia Poeni
corda volente deo; in primis regina quietum
accipit in Teucros animum mentemque benignam.

(Aen. 1.297–304)

[Thus he spoke, and he sent Mercury down from heaven, in order that the lands and new citadel of Carthage might welcome the Trojans hospitably, lest Dido, unaware of fate, bar them from her territory. He sailed through the great expanse of the sky with wings for oars and soon alighted on the shores of Libya. He fulfilled his commands, and the Carthaginians let go of the fierceness in their hearts at the will of the god; above all the queen took on a gentle and benevolent mind toward the Trojans.]

Before we can discuss the implications of Jupiter's action here, we need to address the more general question of how divine interventions ought to be interpreted in Vergilian epic. In this passage the Carthaginians are described as having *ferocia corda,* and Dido takes on *quietum animum* and *mentem benignam.* How radical is the transformation accomplished by Mercury's intervention? Clearly the passage articulates a change of the Carthaginian people from having *ferocia corda* to being hospitable. Vergil does not portray Dido herself negatively here, but she, too, is transformed by the gods' intervention, and among the qualities she acquires is benevolence toward the Trojans. Scholars often assume that divine interventions such as the present one do not radically change a human character in an epic narrative, but rather provide an added motivation for characteristics already intrinsic to the human figure.[42] Equipped with this view, we would be led to interpret the present passage as an indication that the Carthaginians are an essentially hospitable people whose hospitality is highlighted and enhanced by Jupiter's intervention. The passage, however, does not easily fit into this mold, because we have little evidence of Dido's character previous to the lines quoted, unless we are willing to extract indirect evidence about her from what the narrator says about Carthage in the proem as being rich and warlike. Furthermore, in a later passage the Trojan Ilioneus describes the Carthaginians as behaving quite savagely toward him and his companions. This passage has an important impact on the interpretation of our present divine intervention and will be discussed below in more detail.

As to what scholars have felt about the divine intervention, Feeney has put forward a convincing argument.[43] He shows that in seeing divine interventions as tropes for human motivation in epic narratives, scholars impose standards of psychological realism on ancient epic that properly belong to the novel of the nineteenth century, but not to ancient epic narratives themselves. The distortions inherent in such realistic readings become clear in cases where divine interventions extend over a long narrative sequence. For instance, Juno's intervention in *Aeneid* 10 (where she creates a double of Aeneas to spirit Turnus away from the battlefield) and in *Aeneid* 12 (where she sends Turnus' sister Iuturna to the battlefield to help Turnus escape his inevitable death) have been interpreted as tropes for Turnus' fear.[44] But in light of the length and vividness of these passages it seems somewhat strained to take Juno's interventions as emblems for psychological characterization. Following Feeney, I suggest that we should take the divine level of the narrative action in this and other passages as seriously as the human level. If we do so, we are forced to see the intervening gods as agents with motivations much like the human characters of the narrative. Jupiter, for instance, seems to think it necessary to make the Carthaginians hospitable. Why?

In this context it may be useful to consider the Dido narrative side by side with the Nausikaa story of the *Odyssey*, since parallels between the two narratives abound: Both Aeneas and Odysseus come to a foreign shore after shipwreck; both are received hospitably by the inhabitants of the foreign region after some divine intervention has smoothed the way; both are shrouded in a protective cloud by their divine patronesses, and both have their beauty enhanced by them to appear to more advantage before their female hosts.[45] With reference to the factor of divine intervention, however, the differences between the two narratives are telling. While the Jupiter of the *Aeneid* has to ensure a hospitable reception for Aeneas in Carthage, Athena's interventions in the Nausikaa story are more subtle. She appears to Nausikaa in a dream, prompting her to go out and wash her and her family's clothes. At this point Athena does not specifically alert Nausikaa that she will meet a stranger, or direct her how to meet him.[46] Later, when Nausikaa sees a disheveled Odysseus for the first time, Athena intervenes again, and it is this intervention that is most comparable to the one Jupiter orders Mercury to perform on the Carthaginians in the *Aeneid*. Afraid of Odysseus' disheveled appearance, Nausikaa's companions run away from the stranger, while Nausikaa alone remains to face him. She does so at the prompting of Athena, who "put courage in her heart and took the fear away from her limbs":

τῇ γὰρ Ἀθήνη
θάρσος ἐνὶ φρεσὶ θῆκε καὶ ἐκ δέος εἵλετο γυίων

(*Od.* 6.139–40)

[For Athena put courage in her heart and took fear from her limbs]

Athena's intervention here concerns Nausikaa's fear and her courage. It does not directly influence her disposition to act hospitably toward the stranger before her. Granted, unlike Dido, Nausikaa can reassure herself and her companions that the land of the Phaeacians is safe from enemy attacks (*Od.* 6.199–205). Later in the story Dido justifies the Carthaginians' initially hostile reception of the Trojans by referring to her more unstable strategic position in her defense.

> *res dura et regni novitas me talia cogunt*
> *moliri et late finis custode tueri*
>
> (*Aen.* 1.563–64)

[My difficult situation and the recent foundation of my kingdom force me to undertake such measures and to protect my borders far and wide with guards.]

This defense implies that fear prevented Dido and the Carthaginians from acting hospitably. But when Jupiter sends Mercury down to the Carthaginians to ensure a hospitable reception for the Trojans, his conceren is not to remove the Carthaginians' fears. He does not put courage into their hearts to help them act hospitably, as Athena does for Nausikaa. Rather, his intervention is aimed at removing the Carthaginians' *ferocia corda,* their fierce hearts. This is quite the opposite. Dido is affected in the same way. It is not the removal of fear and the addition of courage that Jupiter effects in her, but the addition of benevolence toward the Trojans and acquiescence to their arrival (1.303–4: *quietum / accipit in Teucros animum mentemque benignam*). This language resonates well with our first encounter with Carthage in the proem, where the city had been described as fierce in the pursuits of war (14: *studiisque asperrima belli*). If the Carthaginians now lay down their ferocity at Jupiter's prompting and Dido takes on acquiescent and benevolent feelings toward the Trojans, it is in response to the ferocity which was described as the Carthaginians' characteristic trait at the beginning of the poem.

The idea that without divine intervention Dido might not extend guest friendship to the shipwrecked Trojans suggests that Dido and her people are not conceived as part of the civilized human community of epic discourse.[47] There are several parallel situations in the *Aeneid* in which divine intervention is not necessary to ensure *hospitium* for Aeneas. It is perhaps not entirely fair to compare this scene with Andromache's reception of Aeneas in book 3, because Andromache recognizes Aeneas immediately as her kinsman, while Dido has no previous ties to the Trojans, but the situations of these two female hosts of Aeneas are nevertheless somewhat similar. Both women preside over newly founded cities in foreign and potentially hostile territory, which means that both have reason to be careful about receiving strangers. The text invites the reader to draw such comparisons to the Dido narrative during the later Andromache episode, and the echoes of Dido's potential hostility resonate more strongly when seen side by side with the more voluntarily hospitable hosts of the subsequent narrative. More than Andromache, both Latinus in book 7 and Euander in book 8 provide parallels to Dido of hosts who receive Aeneas hospitably without the need for divine intervention, as in Dido's case, and without knowing him previously, as in Andromache's case.[48] In this way they mirror Eumaeus, Nausikaa and the Phaeacians, Menelaus and Nestor, the good hosts of the *Odyssey*. In the *Odyssey* a lack or a distorted use of *xenia* is the characteristic of all uncivilized and dangerous opponents of Odysseus: Polyphemus, Circe, Calypso, the Suitors, the Laestrygonians. To be sure, Dido does not fall into that category, at least not before she falls in love with Aeneas, but we must remember that the text draws attention right from the beginning to Dido's hospitality as the result of divine intervention rather than of her own will.

The very next scene gives us a different perspective on Dido. While Aeneas explores the territory where he is shipwrecked, Venus meets him in the disguise of a huntress and tells him about Dido's fate:

Punica regna vides, Tyrios et Agenoris urbem;
sed fines Libyci, genus intractabile bello.
imperium Dido Tyria regit urbe profecta,
germanum fugiens. longa est iniuria, longae
ambages; sed summa sequar fastigia rerum.
huic coniunx Sychaeus erat, ditissimus auri
Phoenicum et magno miserae dilectus amore,
cui pater intactam dederat primisque iugarat
ominibus. sed regna Tyri germanus habebat
Pygmalion, scelere ante alios immanior omnis.
quos inter medius venit furor. ille Sychaeum
impius ante aras atque auri caecus amore
clam ferro incautum superat, securus amorum
germanae; factumque diu celavit et aegram
multa malus simulans vana spe lusit amantem.
ipsa sed in somnis inhumati venit imago
coniugis; ora modis attollens pallida miris
crudelis aras traiectaque pectora ferro

nudavit, caecumque domus scelus omne retexit.
tum celerare fugam patriaque excedere suadet
auxiliumque viae veteris tellure recludit
thesauros, ignotum argenti pondus et auri.
his commota fugam Dido sociosque parabat.
conveniunt, quibus aut odium crudele tyranni
aut metus acer erat; navis, quae forte paratae,
corripiunt onerantque auro; portantur avari
Pygmalionis opes pelago; dux femina facti.
devenere locos, ubi nunc ingentia cernis
moenia surgentemque novae Karthaginis arcem,
mercatique solum, facti de nomine Byrsam,
taurino quantum possent circumdare tergo.

(Aen. 1.338–68)

[What you see is a Phoenician kingdom, people from Tyre and a city
of Agenor; but the land is Libya, a race unconquerable in war. Dido
is their queen. She came from Tyre, fleeing her brother. The story of
the injustices she suffered is long and complicated, but I will tell you
the most important points of her story in sequence. Her husband
was Sychaeus, the man richest in gold among the Phoenicians. He
was cherished by his unfortunate wife with a great love. Her father
had given her to him in marriage when she was a virgin and had
joined them with the rites of her first marriage ceremony. But the
ruler of Tyre was her brother Pygmalion, the greatest villain of all.
Mad strife came between these two men. Blinded with greed for
gold, Pygmalion treacherously killed the unsuspecting Sychaeus. He
stabbed him impiously before the altars with his sword and cared
not for his sister's love; for a long time he concealed the crime and
villainously deceived her with many lies and vain hope, while she
was sick with care. But in her sleep the shade of her unburied hus-
band appeared to her; he lifted up his face, which was strangely pale,
and laid bare to her his chest, pierced with steel, and the altars, the
site of his cruel death, and revealed the whole villainy concealed in-
side the house. Then he urged her to hasten to escape and leave the
country, and to aid her journey he told her about a treasure long
buried in the ground, untold riches of silver and gold. Moved by this
vision Dido prepared her flight and gathered companions. Those
with a fierce hatred or violent fear of the tyrant gathered around her;
they took ships which by chance were ready to sail and loaded them

with gold; the wealth of greedy Pygmalion was carried off by sea; a woman was the leader of this enterprise. They came to the region where you now see the huge city walls and the rising citadel of new Carthage, and bought a land called Byrsa, "the hide," so called because they bought as much land as could be enclosed by an oxhide.]

While the story of the death of her husband, her flight from Tyre, and the foundation of Carthage provides a strikingly close parallel to Aeneas' fate, there are also some subtle differences to be observed. The presence of gold as a driving factor of many of the events in her story stands in stark contrast to its complete absence from Aeneas' subsequent narrative about his fate. Dido's husband is said to be the richest Tyrian with respect to gold (343); her brother Pygmalion kills Sychaeus out of blind love of gold (349); when her dead husband visits her in a dream and tells her to flee from Tyre, he reveals to her a hidden treasure of silver and gold (358–59); gold is the only possession Dido and her companions take along to their new home (363–64); finally, the Phoenicians buy land in Libya (367).[49] Aeneas, on the other hand, says that all he took with him from Troy are his *Penates,* along with his companions, his pietas, and his glory:

sum pius Aeneas, raptos qui ex hoste Penatis
classe veho mecum, fama super aethera notus.
Italiam quaero patriam et genus ab Iove summo
(*Aen.* 1.378–80)

[I am faithful Aeneas; I bring with me on my fleet the Penates that I have saved from the enemy; my fame reaches the heavens. I seek Italy as my fatherland, and I trace my ancestry to Jupiter.]

Later, in book 7, we will see how Aeneas establishes a guest-friendship with Latinus. Rather than purchasing land from him, Aeneas uses gift exchange to establish friendly relations, and he is in turn offered not only land for his new city, but also Lavinia's hand in marriage.[50] This economic mode of gift exchange is significant, because it carries with it the notion of a lost world of heroes, of which Aeneas clearly is a part. He always uses gift exchange and hospitality as a means to establishing relations. He never buys. Even though the money economy was well established in Vergil's time, there seems to be something distasteful in the fact that Dido buys. In Homer, too, the Phoenicians engage in trade.[51] But in Homer it is quite clearly an insult to be called a businessman, as an episode of Odysseus' stay among the Phaeacians shows: When Odysseus declines to compete in the games, Euryalus provokes him by saying that he is probably a trader, not an athlete or warrior.[52] By portraying Aeneas as engaging in the economic mode of the Homeric heroes, Vergil creates an image of the lost purity of Rome's origins, in which Dido does not participate, both because divine intervention is necessary to ensure her hospitality and because she emblematizes an economic mode that is tainted by the shameless measurability of capital.

The difficulties Dido has with the economic mode of the Homeric heroes is illustrated by her relationship to the Libyan king, Iarbas, from whom she buys the land for her city. As a woman, Dido cannot engage in relations of hospitality with Iarbas, because Iarbas envisages a different way of establishing relations with her: marriage.[53] That would make Dido the object of the exchange, however. She refuses his offer and lives in continuous fear of the instability of her position.[54] Both *hospitium* and marriage are systems of exchange between men, while women participate in the exchange as objects. Thus, buying land becomes for Dido an alternative to the established modes of exchange that constitute society in epic discourse, an alternative that is necessary because the Homeric system of hospitality and gift exchange does not provide for the eventuality of female agents.

But let me return to Venus' narrative of Dido's life. Venus is at pains to portray Dido's fate in a manner that allows Aeneas to draw parallels to his own life,[55] thus avoiding the characterization of her protagonist according to the well-known stereotypes. She only alludes to a story that, had it been narrated in more detail, would have shown Dido's cunning side to Aeneas. Servius tells us that when Iarbas sold Dido land for the foundation of her city, it was to be as much as can be encompassed by a bull's hide. Dido cut up the hide in narrow strips and acquired a territory much larger than Iarbas had been led to expect.[56] This trick is absent from Venus' story, and indeed from the *Aeneid* as a whole, but the story is hinted at in Venus' account. At the end of her report about Dido's fate, she mentions Byrsa as the name of the territory Dido purchased from Iarbas and says that it is called so after the bull's hide with which it was measured. Servius calls Dido cunning when he reports the trick associated with the name *Byrsa* and says that Vergil alludes to Dido's trick by using the word *circumdare,* rather than *tegere,* in line 368 and by saying that Dido's territory was called Byrsa "after her deed" (1.367: *facti de nomine Byrsam*). The effect of Venus' oblique reference to Dido's cunning trick is twofold. While she leaves Aeneas in the dark about Dido's savvy business spirit, she presents to the reader a Dido whose characterization here is in line with Punic stereotypes and with her other references to Dido's wealth and businesslike transactions.

There is one other character in Venus' narrative who bears witness to the continuing presence of Punic stereotypes even in this epic. Though technically a Phoenician rather than a Carthaginian, Dido's brother Pygmalion is portrayed in the same terms as the Carthaginians. In murdering Dido's husband, Pygmalion is characterized as cruel, cunning, and even treacherous to his sister. He cunningly kills Sychaeus and hides the deed from Dido,[57] his deed is described as a betrayal of his obligations to his sister,[58] and Dido's companions flee from his cruelty as a tyrant.[59] Thus, Pygmalion fully conforms to Roman stereotypes about the Carthaginians. What is more, Pygmalion kills Sychaeus *"impius ante aras,"* an image that recalls Pyrrhus' murder of Priam at his altar. Although at first reading we realize this parallel—a parallel between Greek and Punic cruelty and impiety—only when we come to book 2, Aeneas must realize it at this point, when he hears Dido's story from Venus, and so do all readers already familiar with the poem.

The next time we encounter Dido, we see her through Aeneas' eyes as she approaches Juno's temple and proceeds to fulfill the duties of a queen.[60] The picture we get of her is quite favorable, until a group of Aeneas' companions, who were separated from him in the sea storm, approach Dido and complain to her about the outrageous treatment they have suffered at the hands of the Carthaginians:[61]

> *o regina, novam cui condere Iuppiter urbem*
> *iustitiaque dedit gentis frenare superbas,*
> *Troes te miseri, ventis maria omnia vecti,*
> *oramus: prohibe infandos a navibus ignis,*
> *parce pio generi et propius res aspice nostras.*
>
> (*Aen.* 1.522–26)

[O queen whom Jupiter has permitted to found a city and to hold in check haughty nations with your justice, we, the unhappy Trojans who have been driven across all seas by the winds, beg you: keep our ships safe from your accursed fires, spare our god-fearing nation and turn your attention more closely to our lot.]

Ilioneus relates that his ships are in danger of being set on fire and that the Trojans were even denied the hospitality of the shore by the Carthaginians. Later on in the speech he calls them barbarian and inhuman:

quod genus hoc hominum? quaeve hunc tam barbara morem
permittit patria? hospitio prohibemur harenae;
bella cient primaque vetant consistere terra.
si genus humanum et mortalia temnitis arma,
at sperate deos memores fandi atque nefandi.

(Aen. 1.539–43)

[What kind of people are you? What kind of nation is so uncivilized as to allow such behavior? We were barred from the hospitality of the shore; your people waged war on us and forbade us to set foot even on the very border of your land. If you hold the human race and the weapons of mortals in contempt, all the same, be aware that the gods are mindful of right and wrong.]

This disturbing picture of Carthage is followed by Dido's very generous offer of hospitality. But why such contrasting images?[62] One reason for Vergil to create these stark contrasts within the behavior of the Carthaginians is to suggest that Jupiter's intervention transforms the Carthaginians quite radically and should not be seen as an allegorical description of Dido's hospitality. On the contrary, divine intervention is necessary, because of their own accord Vergil's Carthaginians do not participate in the economy of *hospitium,* and indeed violate the most basic conventions of the civilized world. In the present scene the contrast seems to be organized around the hospitable and generous behavior of Dido as opposed to the more barbarous actions of her people. But Jupiter's intervention paints a different picture. He sends Mercury to Carthage to ensure that the city be hospitable to the Trojans and that Dido not bar them from her land (*Aen.* 1.298–300: *ut terrae utque novae pateant Karthaginis arces / hospitio Teucris, ne fati nescia Dido / finibus arceret*). Jupiter does not distinguish between Dido and her people. His intervention is aimed at both. Seen in the light of this previous passage, the contrast between Dido and her people in the scene with Ilioneus is not one of queen versus subjects, but a temporal contrast. The narrative of Ilioneus represents the actions of the Carthaginians previous to Jupiter's intervention. The result of this intervention is illustrated by Dido's generosity.[63]

The next scene shows that Venus doesn't even trust in the effectiveness of one divine intervention. Her worries are motivated by yet another manifestation of ethnic stereotyping: she fears *domum ambiguam Tyriosque bilinguis,*[64] that is, a lack of trustworthiness, or *Punica fides,* and cunning on the part of the Carthaginians and Dido. Therefore, she initiates a second divine intervention to ensure her son's safety and sends Cupid to Dido in order to make her fall in love. From this point onward Dido is portrayed as a lover, and it becomes more difficult to disentangle her lover's persona from the persona of the Carthaginian, but I think it will become clear that many of her actions in book 4 cannot be explained solely with reference to the lover's discourse.

ɞ A CARTHAGINIAN WOMAN IN LOVE

Dido's opening dialogue with her sister Anna provides an example for such blending of the lover and the Carthaginian.[65] Here Dido tells Anna about her love for Aeneas, but then she binds herself by oath to remain faithful to her dead husband:

> *sed mihi vel tellus optem prius ima dehiscat*
> *vel pater omnipotens adigat me fulmine ad umbras,*
> *pallentis umbras Erebi noctemque profundam,*
> *ante, Pudor, quam te violo aut tua iura resolvo.*
> *ille meos, primus qui me sibi iunxit, amores*
> *abstulit; ille habeat secum servetque sepulchro.*
>
> (*Aen.* 4.24–29)

[But let me wish that the depths of the earth split open to swallow me or that the almighty father drive me down to the shades and the deep night of the Underworld before I forsake you, Modesty, or stray from your laws. He who was first joined to me has carried off all my love; let him keep it with him and guard it in his grave.]

Anna encourages her to give way to her love, points out to her the political advantages for Carthage of such a union with Aeneas, and advises Dido to cunningly delay Aeneas' departure until the end of winter:

> *quam tu urbem, soror, hanc cernes, quae surgere regna*
> *coniugio tali! Teucrum comitantibus armis,*

Punica se quantis attollet gloria rebus!
tu modo posce deos veniam, sacrisque litatis
indulge hospitio causasque innecte morandi,
dum pelago desaevit hiems et aquosus Orion,
quassataeque rates, dum non tractabile caelum.

(*Aen.* 4.47–53)

[What a city will you see this one become, what a kingdom will you see rising with such a marriage! With what great deeds will Punic glory soar when the arms of the Trojans are by your side! Do but ask pardon from the gods, and once you have propitiated them with offerings, devote yourself to hospitality and contrive reasons for a protracted stay, while winter and watery Orion rage at sea, while the ships are in disrepair, while the weather is unmanageable.]

These arguments instantly cause Dido to abandon her oath of fidelity and her *pudor:*

His dictis incensum animum inflammavit amore
spemque dedit dubiae menti solvitque pudorem.

(*Aen.* 4.54–55)

[With these words Anna fanned the flames of love kindled in Dido's heart; she gave hope to her sister's wavering mind and broke the hold of her conscience.]

Thus, the two sisters are subtly portrayed as Carthaginians, Dido in terms of *Punica fides* and Anna as cunning, despite the fact that at first glance the conversation seems natural and sympathetic enough. Notice that Dido swears the oath of fidelity to Sychaeus only now that she loves Aeneas. It seems to be the sole narrative function of the oath that it is immediately broken by Dido.[66]

Later on in the narrative, when Dido finds out that Aeneas is preparing to leave her, she accuses him of betrayal,[67] of breaking his marriage vows,[68] of deceitfully trying to conceal his departure,[69] and of cruelty.[70] In short, she accuses him of behaving like a Carthaginian:[71]

Dissimulare etiam sperasti, perfide, tantum
posse nefas tacitusque mea decedere terra?
nec te noster amor nec te data dextera quondam[72]

nec moritura tenet crudeli funere Dido?
quin etiam hiberno moliris sidere classem
et mediis properas Aquilonibus ire per altum,
crudelis? quid? si non arva aliena domosque
ignotas peteres, et Troia antiqua maneret,
Troia per undosum peteretur classibus aequor?

(Aen. 4.305–13)

[You traitor, you hoped you could even conceal such an enormous act of betrayal and leave my country without a word, didn't you? And our love or the promise you once gave me doesn't hold you back, or the prospect that Dido might die a horrible death? You even get the fleet under way in the winter season and hasten to go to sea when the north winds are at their worst? You are cruel. What? If you did not seek a foreign land and an unknown home, and if old Troy still stood, would you go off to Troy with your fleet when the sea is stormy?]

This dialogue has often been compared to Medea's dialogue with Jason in Euripides' play. Yet, the difference between the two texts is as striking as the obviously present allusion. While Medea justly accuses Jason of breaking his marital vows, Dido's claim to marriage with Aeneas is far more problematic. Dido's union with Aeneas is a sexual union in a cave. Although it is sanctioned by Juno, the goddess of marriage, who presides over it, and although the narrator describes the presence of Juno and the forest nymphs in the language of a marriage ceremony (*Aen.* 4.166–68, see Austin (1955) on lines 166ff.), there is no formal ceremony in the midst of the community, as there is in Medea's wedding.[73] Medea's wedding is performed in society, while Dido's takes place in the wild, with Juno and the nymphs of the cave as the only wedding guests.[74] While Dido claims in her confrontation with Aeneas that their union is a marriage, the narrator suggests earlier on that she herself is aware that it is not. Commenting on the events of the hunt and the cave, he says that Dido "calls her union a marriage and covers her guilt with this label" (*Aen.* 4.172: *coniugium vocat, hoc praetexit nomine culpam*).[75]

Aeneas replies to Dido's accusations by saying that he never entered into a marital union.[76] Shifting the terms of the discussion, Aeneas picks up on Dido's appeal to his obligations as her *hospes*[77] and acknowledges his gratitude for her hospitality:

> *ego te, quae plurima fando*
> *enumerare vales, numquam, regina, negabo*
> *promeritam, nec me meminisse pigebit Elissae,*
> *dum memor ipse mei, dum spiritus hos regit artus.*
>
> (Aen. 4.333–36)

[I will never deny, queen, that you have earned my gratitude for all the kindesses to me that you can ever list in words, and I will never tire of remembering Elissa, as long as I can remember my own self, as long as life animates these limbs.]

Then he appeals to the similarity of her fate with his and her obligations as queen toward her own newly founded city, in an attempt to reconcile her to his departure:

> *si te Karthaginis arces*
> *Phoenissam Libycaeque aspectus detinet urbis*
> *quae tandem Ausonia Teucros considere terra*
> *invidia est? et nos fas extera quaerere regna.*
>
> (Aen. 4.347–50)

[You are Phoenician, and yet the citadel of Carthage and the view of the Libyan city detains you here; why be envious if the Trojans settle on Italian soil at last? It is the gods' will that we, too, seek a kingdom in foreign lands.]

This plea does not reach her, because her lover's identity has long obliterated her role as queen.[78] Thus, love leaves her unable to participate in the relationship of *hospitium.* Her appeals to Aeneas' obligations as her *hospes* show that her expectations from this relationship of *hospitium* are distorted. What Dido wants from Aeneas is not a relationship of hospitality, but one of marriage. Marriage would bind Aeneas to her more closely and impose the obligations on him that she thinks he ought to feel as her guest. In her anguish Dido does not understand that as her guest Aeneas has discharged all his obligations to her and cannot be represented as having broken his promises.

It is, of course, also not quite fair of Aeneas to represent his relationship with her as merely one of hospitality. They were lovers and he has acted as her husband while he was there, taking over the supervision of building activities, as we find out when Mercury comes to Carthage to meet Aeneas (*Aen.* 4.260–61). Neither marriage nor *hospitium,* their relationship is something in between the two, more than a simple matter of guest and host, but less than marriage. But there is no established code of obligations for such a relationship, at least not within the world of heroic epic. Their conflict, then, lies in their different expectations of the other's obligations to them. These, in turn, result from their different (and equally inadequate) interpretations of their relationship as either marriage or hospitality, because both Dido and Aeneas can envisage their relationship only within these frames of reference.

The difficulty Dido has here with the concept of hospitality reminds us of her earlier difficulties with establishing friendly relations with Iarbas. Back then, it was Iarbas who wanted marriage instead of hospitality, now it is Dido. But the common thread of both episodes is that Dido's womanhood makes it difficult for her to act as an independent agent in the systems of hospitality and exchange that create civilized society in epic discourse. While her refusal to marry Iarbas forces her to engage in an economic mode more mercantile than that established in the world of Homeric heroes, her desire to be married to Aeneas carries within it the seeds of her hatred for Rome, and Carthage's subsequent struggles to overthrow Aeneas' descendants. Thus, Dido's womanhood is linked by the narrative to features that represent her as typically Carthaginian, to her mercantile interactions with Iarbas, and to her enmity against Rome.

When Dido responds to Aeneas, her anger carries her away and induces her to wish for a terrible fate for Aeneas.[79] The cruelty of her remarks goes beyond the anger of a disappointed lover, but resonates with the stereotype of Carthaginian cruelty. The disappointed female lovers of ancient literature provide few parallels to Dido's vengefulness.[80] No Ariadne or Calypso, not even Phaedra and Medea, reach the heights of cruelty that characterize Dido's fantasies of revenge. It is at this point especially that we must try to separate the different strands of Vergil's characterization of Dido. Disappointment is natural and to be expected for her, but let us hear where Dido's disappointment leads her:

spero equidem mediis, si quid pia numina possunt,
supplicia hausurum scopulis et nomine Dido
saepe vocaturum. sequar atris ignibus absens
et, cum frigida mors anima seduxerit artus,
omnibus umbra locis adero. dabis, improbe, poenas.
audiam et haec Manis veniet mihi fama sub imos.

(*Aen.* 4.382–87)

[I hope that, if the righteous will of the gods has any power, you will drink your punishment amidst the rocks of the sea and often call upon Dido by name. I will pursue you with black fire from afar and, when cold death has separated body from soul, I will be with you everywhere as a shade. You will pay the penalty, you scoundrel. I will hear of it, and the report of your fate will come to me far down among the shades.]

Within the pool of ancient narratives of abandoned female lovers, Dido's situation is most comparable to that of Calypso and Circe, yet both of these Homeric females end up helping Odysseus with his departure from their realms. Dido's anger and desire for revenge find some precedents in the narratives about Phaedra and Medea, and her words in the present dialogue are well within the range of things these other two women might say. But Dido's later monologues go beyond even the vengefulness of a Medea, as we will see shortly. For now, let us note that within the spectrum of abandoned female lovers, Vergil's Dido occupies a position of extreme vengefulness right from the beginning, a feature that blends well with the subtle hints of her Punic characterization elsewhere throughout the episode. Thus, when she accuses Aeneas of being cruel, treacherous, and cunning,[81] we should be cautious in taking this as a fair evaluation of Aeneas' character, since these are the standard traits of a Punic character, and it is Dido, not Aeneas, who qualifies for at least one of these traits in this very dialogue. Dido's fantasies of revenge in this speech are cruel and therefore suggest a Punic characterization. That Dido sees Aeneas' wrongdoing toward her in terms of a Punic character may well be seen as reflecting back on herself. In the subsequent scenes Dido shows herself as cunning and treacherous as well as cruel. It makes sense that she would view Aeneas' flaws within the same frame of reference.

From this point on Dido is preparing to commit suicide.[82] Even in these last scenes Vergil depicts her both as lover and as Carthaginian. When Dido asks Anna to erect a pyre for her, she deceives her sister with respect to the purpose of the pyre, telling her that it is for a love charm that might bring Aeneas back to her.[83] Later Dido deceives her nurse in a similar fashion.[84] Anna finds out the truth only when it is too late, and then she, too, accuses Dido of betrayal.[85] Similarly, Dido blames herself for having betrayed her dead husband.[86] Again, the same accusation of untrustworthiness and cunning comes from Mercury, who warns Aeneas to leave Carthage quickly, because Dido might plot something dreadful.[87]

Finally, Dido's curse monologue shows the most obvious connection between Dido and the Punic Wars.[88] But not only the last section is significant, where Dido prays for an avenger and for eternal hatred between Carthage and Aeneas' descendants. Even earlier on in the speech, her rage brings Dido to indulge in excessively cruel fantasies of revenge:

> non arma expedient totaque ex urbe sequentur,
> diripientque rates alii navalibus? ite,
> ferte citi flammas, date tela, impellite remos!
> quid loquor? aut ubi sum? quae mentem insania mutat?
> infelix Dido, nunc te facta impia tangunt?
> tum decuit, cum sceptra dabas. en dextra fidesque,
> quem secum patrios aiunt portare penatis,
> quem subiisse umeris confectum aetate parentem!
> non potui abreptum divellere corpus et undis
> spargere? non socios, non ipsum absumere ferro
> Ascanium patriisque epulandum ponere mensis?
> verum anceps pugnae fuerat fortuna. fuisset:
> quem metui moritura? faces in castra tulissem
> implessemque foros flammis natumque patremque
> cum genere extinxem, memet super ipsa dedissem.
>
> (Aen. 4.592–606)

[Won't they get their weapons ready and pursue them from all over the city, and others launch ships from the docks? Go, bring fire quickly, bring weapons, set your oars in motion! What am I saying? Where am I? What insanity is overturning my mind? Unhappy Dido, are you repenting of impious deeds now? Better to have done it then, when you gave him your scepter. Just look at his promises and his honor now. And they say he is carrying with him the household gods of his forefathers, and that he carried on his shoulders his father, crippled with old age! Could not I have seized him, torn his body to pieces and scattered them on the waves? Or killed his companions or Ascanius himself with the sword and served them at his father's table to eat? But the outcome of the fight would have been uncertain. Even so, whom did I fear, I who will die soon? I should have brought firebrands into their encampment and filled their ships with flames; I should have killed the son and the father together with the entire race and collapsed on top.]

Her desire for immediate war with the Trojans is followed by her wish to tear Aeneas to pieces and throw him into the sea, to kill his companions and Ascanius, and to serve Ascanius to his father for dinner. Then she wishes she had set fire to his camp, thus killing father, son, and the whole Trojan race. Dido's revenge fantasies evoke the stories of several figures from Greek myth, among them Medea, who killed and cut up her brother, throwing pieces of his body into the sea to slow down her father's pursuit of the Argonauts, and Atreus who killed Thyestes' sons and served them to their father for dinner. But Dido's fantasies do not remain within this frame of reference. They reach a different plane when she aims her intentions at Aeneas' family, his whole community, and even his descendants. Not only does she wish she had destroyed Aeneas' people when she had the chance, but she also curses Aeneas, wishing for a war for him in Latium and wishing for eternal hatred between his descendants and hers:[89]

> *si tangere portus*
> *infandum caput ac terris adnare necesse est,*
> *et sic fata Iovis poscunt, hic terminus haeret,*
> *at bello audacis populi vexatus et armis,*
> *finibus extorris, complexu avulsus Iuli*
> *auxilium imploret videatque indigna suorum*
> *funera; nec, cum se sub leges pacis iniquae*
> *tradiderit, regno aut optata luce fruatur,*
> *sed cadat ante diem mediaque inhumatus harena.*
> *haec precor, hanc vocem extremam cum sanguine fundo.*
> *tum vos, o Tyrii, stirpem et genus omne futurum*
> *exercete odiis, cinerique haec mittite nostro*
> *munera. nullus amor populis nec foedera sunto.*
> *exoriare aliquis nostris ex ossibus ultor*
> *qui face Dardanios ferroque sequare colonos,*
> *nunc, olim, quocumque dabunt se tempore vires.*
> *litora litoribus contraria, fluctibus undas*
> *imprecor, arma armis: pugnent ipsique nepotesque.*
>
> (*Aen.* 4.612–29)

[If his damnable person must reach port and shore, and the fates of Jupiter demand it, and this outcome is fixed, then at least let him be tormented by war and the arms of a bold people, and, driven from his land and torn from the embrace of Iulus, let him beg for help and witness the cruel deaths of his people; and once he has submitted to the terms of an unjust peace, do not let him enjoy his kingdom or the life he has hoped for, but let him die prematurely and lie unburied in the sand. This is my prayer; I pour forth these last words together with my blood. Tyrians, vent your hatred on this race and all their descendants to come; bring me this as an offering to my ashes. Let there be no love nor treaties between the nations. Arise from my bones, you who will avenge me, and pursue the Trojan settlers with fire and sword, now, someday, whenever there is strength for it. Let shores be opposed to shores, seas to seas, I pray, arms to arms: let them and their descendants be locked in battle.]

It is this historical dimension that puts Dido's dangerousness ahead even of Medea's. No other disappointed lover of mythology has the force of reaching down into the recorded history of the Romans of Vergil's time and exacting vengeance for her thwarted desire on their direct ancestors. As a queen Dido has an advantage over other vengeful heroines even of Medea's caliber, because only a queen can turn her personal disappointments into affairs of historical dimensions. The resonance of Dido's cruelty in this speech is heightened when she invokes her avenger, a clear reference to Hannibal, whose cruelty was proverbial even in Vergil's time.[90] Characterizing herself as cruel by the cruelty of her own words and linking herself to Hannibal, the embodiment of the Carthaginian threat and of the Carthaginian character in Vergil's time, Dido differentiates herself from other abandoned female lovers in myth and is approximated to the stereotype of Punic cruelty. Dido's cruelty in this speech—as her cunning, betrayal, and cruelty elsewhere—is subtly mingled with her characterization as an abandoned lover to suggest that her actions are motivated not only by her passion and her womanhood, but also by her ethnic identity. The mythical figure who is made responsible for the Punic Wars in this narrative is given a Carthaginian characterization. Thus, Dido is doubly a signifier for her city. As the woman associated with the foundation of Carthage, Dido is a stand-in for the city itself, being identified with it to the point that her death is compared to that of the city.[91] But Dido also embodies the character traits associated with the Carthaginians.

WOMAN AS THE ETHNIC OTHER

What emerges when looking at Dido from the angle of ethnicity is that it is precisely her womanhood that both causes and obscures the traces of ethnic characterization. Partly this is because in her portrayal Punic traits are elided with her characterization as an abandoned heroine in love. Dido

is at times depicted as cruel, cunning, and treachereous—traits tradition-
ally attributed to the Carthaginians—but in her these traits are motivated
by her unhappy love. Dido's broken oath to her husband, the cruelty of
her revenge fantasies in response to Aeneas' departure, her cunning in de-
ceiving everyone as to the purpose of her funeral pyre, all these can be read
as the traits of a woman in love as well as those of a Carthaginian. Thus,
the double motivation for Dido's actions obscures her Punic characteriza-
tion, as well as merges ethnicity and gender as the causes of the excesses of
passion. As an etiology of the Punic Wars, the story of Dido uses the per-
sonal passions of a woman to explain the historical conflict between na-
tions. Public and private, history and desire, are mingled. What we have
here is perhaps the most spectacular example of the theme of eroticizing
the ethnic other: by conceptualizing the ethnic other as a gendered other
as well, Roman imperialist discourse figures the conquest of foreign terri-
tories as an amatory, rather than a military, theme. Dido's womanhood
and her love overshadow her ethnic otherness without leaving it behind
entirely. She is the ethnic other eroticized.

Another link of gender and ethnicity in the Dido story, which is moti-
vated by eroticization, has to do with the economic mode with which Dido
and Carthage are associated in the poem. As we have seen, Dido is associ-
ated with a mercantile economic mode unfitted for the heroic world of
epic. She is forced into this economic mode in her relations with King Iar-
bas, whose notions of *hospitium* and marriage do not allow him to accept
Dido as an equal with whom independent relations can be established. It
is her womanhood and the possibility of marriage that prevent her from
participating in the economic mode of the Homeric heroes. Hence, the
eroticization of Carthage in the figure of Dido allows the *Aeneid* to articu-
late Rome's enmity with Carthage as a story about thwarted love, as well as
to project onto Carthage an economic mode that was everyday reality for
the readers of the *Aeneid,* but that nevertheless did not figure in the ideal-
ized world of heroic gift-exchange and hospitality exemplified elsewhere in
the poem.

ᴥ§ IMPERIALIST CONQUEST AS AMATORY CONQUEST

The story of Dido also provides an etiology for Rome's ultimate possession
of Carthage, as I will now show. When Dido first encounters the Trojans,
she extends a generous offer of hospitality to them, telling them that the
city she is erecting is theirs (*Aen.* 1.573: *urbem quam statuo vestra est*). The

ambiguity of Dido's words has been remarked upon by scholars before. For Dido to tell the Trojans that her city is theirs fits not only the immediate context of her offer of hospitality to Ilioneus, but it also fits Vergil's contemporary situation: Carthage had been conquered and sacked by the Romans over a century previously, and it is now being rebuilt as a Roman colony of the same name under Augustus.[92] Even at this early stage in the narrative, Dido offers her possessions to the Trojans, prompted by the hospitality instilled in her by divine intervention.

The second divine intervention of Venus and Cupid, causing Dido to fall in love with Aeneas and to seek marriage with him, has a similar effect. When the love-stricken Dido offers herself to Aeneas during a thunderstorm on the day of the hunt, she offers her city to Aeneas along with herself, not only because the longed-for marital union would involve such a shared possession of Dido's assets, but also—and more importantly—because Dido is identified with her city by the text in a manner that renders the individual woman a sign for her community, as we have seen in the previous section. A case in point is the simile that compares Dido's death to the sack of Carthage in book 4. Here, as well as in other contexts in ancient culture, women are explicitly interpreted as signs standing in for the material possessions they are associated with. For instance, in Artemidorus' dreambook female figures in men's sexual dreams are often interpreted as signifiers for the dreamer's social status or future luck.[93]

Let us pause for a moment and look at this other cultural context to see if anything can be gained from it for the interpretation of our story. One of Artemidorus' sexual dreams has a narrative with striking similarities to the Dido story. Artemidorus tells us that it brings luck to dream of sleeping with a rich, single woman, because a woman gives not only her body but also all that belongs to her, her possessions.[94] The relevance of this otherwise unrelated text lies in the testimony it gives us of ancient conceptualizations of women and their relationship to property. The dream and the literary narrative have a common cast of characters: the rich, single woman and the man she sleeps with. Both narratives treat the woman as a stand-in for her possessions. What Artemidorus adds for us is the interpretation of the sexual union between the lovers. If it was possible for the ancients to understand the significance of a sexual dream in the light that Artemidorus would have them see it, a literary narrative might have a similar resonance with them. Seen in this light, if Dido gives herself to Aeneas, she also gives her possessions to him.

The gifts Aeneas has from Dido in later books can be better understood in this context.[95] Dido did not give these gifts to Aeneas in a context of gift exchange, because the gift exchange associated with the rites of hospitality would be expected to take place either at the arrival or departure of the guest. Aeneas presented gifts to Dido at his arrival, but we hear nothing of counter-gifts from Dido at that time.[96] At the time of Aeneas' departure, Dido was so furious at Aeneas for leaving that it is unreasonable to assume that we are to imagine a scene of gift exchange at parting that is merely omitted in the narrative. Nevertheless, Aeneas has carried with him to Italy several articles that are marked as Dido's possessions. They can, of course, be explained as the gifts of a lover who fancies herself a wife. Indeed, the robes from Dido that Aeneas uses to cover Pallas' body in book 11 are described much like the robes he himself wore at Mercury's arrival in Carthage—gifts from Dido that she herself wove with purple and gold.[97] But there is more to it than that. Like the rich, single woman in Artemidorus' sexual dream, Dido offered her possessions to Aeneas in the act of offering herself to him. This is also the way Juno (*Aen.* 4.90–104) and Iarbas (*Aen.* 4.214) see the situation at Carthage when Aeneas is there, although their views are not represented as accurate descriptions of Dido and Aeneas' relationship. Nevertheless, what suggests itself here is that Carthage was a possession of Rome even before Rome was founded, because as Dido's possession, it was given to Aeneas even then.

The text thus provides us with a double etiology of Rome's possession of Carthage. As a generous host Dido offers her city to the Trojans, then as a lover she offers it to Aeneas again. The gifts Aeneas still has from Dido in Italy are thus the faint echo of a promise the text implicitly makes about the future appropriation of Carthage by Rome. They hold the promise of closure to the longing glances Aeneas cast on the rising city of Carthage at his first sight of it, for they are tokens of his possession of Dido and all that belongs to her.

That Aeneas had found joy in looking at Carthage and at the pictures on Juno's temple there would seem irreconcilable with an interpretation of Vergil's Carthage as embodying the traits of Rome's former enemy. But the double function of the Dido story as both an etiology of Rome's enmity with Carthage and one of Rome's possession of it is felt precisely in those early scenes of Aeneas' first view of the city. His longing for possession of such a city is at odds with the underlying sense that the rising city is Aeneas' descendants' future enemy, just as his conviction that the temple pictures convey the Carthaginians' compassion for his plight stands in contrast to the other possible interpretation of these pictures as a monument to Juno's victory over the Trojans—and hence evidence for the Carthaginians' potential hostility to the hero. The tension between these two levels of meaning in the text accomplishes two characterizations at once: Carthage is potentially hostile from the beginning of its interactions with Rome, while Rome's ancestor adopts the position of one who has nothing to fear, refusing to see signs of hostility—the position of a victor and one in which the Romans liked to portray themselves, never starting wars by themselves, but only being provoked into them.

The narrator prepares us for these polarized characterizations of Carthaginians and Romans as enemies and victors, which are accomplished in these early scenes, when he tells us of Juno's doomed desire for Carthaginian world domination (*Aen.* 1.12ff.).[98] Even there we already find the inferior position of Carthage against Rome expressed in the image of a woman's unattainable longing. The same image is repeated in the story of Dido's unattainable desire for marriage with Aeneas. The distribution of power between Aeneas and Dido as lovers perfectly matches the power imbalance between the cities they represent: one conquering and strong, the other vanquished and weak. This eroticization of the vanquished enemy finds its immediate political relevance in Augustus' recent conflict with Antony and Cleopatra. We will therefore assess the Dido episode again later on from this slightly different angle to glean from it another conceptualization of ethnic and gendered otherness embodied in Dido.

DEFINING ROMAN IDENTITY THROUGH GENDERED ETHNICITY

We have seen that both Dido and Lavinia are represened in the *Aeneid* as ethnic others erotically linked to Aeneas. Furthermore, both Dido and Lavinia represent their respective communities as objects of the Romans' territorial acquisitions. Indeed, the story of Lavinia provides a foil for Dido's story, because here categories confused in Dido's story due to her role as queen are set straight. In the stories of both Dido and Lavinia, we encounter two modes of exchange (marriage, *hospitium*) that establish relations between natives and newcomers in foreign territories. But in Dido's story, these modes of exchange are confused and rendered ineffectual, because in Dido the object of the exchange threatened to collapse with its agent. In the story of Lavinia, on the other hand, woman and city are a unit that can be attained only in combination by Aeneas. Latinus offers both to him on the Trojans' arrival in Latium. His gesture is one of hospitality, as well as an offer of political alliance cemented by marriage. Here woman remains the object of exchange in a system of relationships between men.

Despite these differences in the logic of their narratives, Dido and Lavinia have the common function of defining Aeneas. Because gender and ethnicity are intertwined in these figures, Aeneas' masculinity in juxtaposition to Dido and Lavinia also causes him to be defined ethnically by opposition. Representing Carthage as an imperialist acquisition, Dido defines Aeneas as Roman in the domain of Rome's empire. Lavinia, whose Latinness is inscribed in her and her father's name, defines Aeneas as Roman and as colonist, in opposition to Rome's neighbors, the Latins. Indeed, the ethnic characterization of Aeneas is more of a cipher, a blank space onto which Roman national identity is projected through his interactions with various ethnic others. This is possible because Aeneas leaves behind him his Trojan identity when he decides to follow the commands of fate that direct him to found a new city elsewhere. This loss of his earlier identity is enacted in his loss of Creusa and Troy in book 2, and later on in his encounter with Andromache in book 3, whose overdetermined Trojanness is another example of the link between gender, ethnicity, and passion.[99]

The use of gender and passion is key to Aeneas' role as bearer of Roman identity. In the story of Andromache these two categories of identity are employed to differentiate Trojan ethnic from Roman national identity. The poem presents in Aeneas and Andromache two alternative modes of attachment to the Trojan past. When Aeneas comes to Epirus and sees Andromache, she is surrounded by a re-creation of her Trojan past. The first glimpse Aeneas catches of her is emblematic: she is pouring a libation at Hector's tomb. Living in a replica of Troy and still grieving for Hector, Andromache's identity is determined entirely by her past. Although she is now the wife of Helenus, in her words and deeds she represents herself only as Hector's widow. Her attachment to the Trojan past is so strong that it overshadows all other aspects of her identity, such as her new marriage, her new home, and the fact that she has founded a colony abroad, just as Aeneas will.

This strong attachment to Troy has its counterpart in Aeneas. When he takes leave of Dido, he tells her that if he could choose his fate, he would have remained in Troy and rebuilt it (4.340–44). Rebuilding Troy is just what Helenus and Andromache were allowed to do (3.497–99). Aeneas' parting speech to them shows that he envies them their ability to indulge their nostalgic attachment to Troy (3.493–505). But Aeneas is forced to give up the mode of life that defines Andromache. In Aeneas the Trojan past must make way for the Roman future. Aeneas and Andromache thus differ widely in their attachment to the Trojan past. While Andromache remains Trojan even in exile, Aeneas continues to be defined by the destiny he follows. When he takes leave of Andromache, he also takes leave of her way of life and her way of defining her identity within the matrix of the Trojan past. This makes him free to become something yet to be defined, the founder of a city and a nation not yet born.

You may object that this distinction between Aeneas' and Andromache's attachment to Troy is not related to gender, since Helenus, too, lives in *parva Troia*. But while Andromache speaks only of the Trojan past, Helenus occupies most narrative space with his prophecies of Aeneas' future. The passion of her attachment to the past is not mirrored in Helenus, either, who shows none of her tearfulness at seeing Aeneas and his companions. The contrast Helenus provides for Andromache is the same as the distinction between her and Aeneas: in both cases, Andromache's attachment to the Trojan past is contrasted with male figures whose identities are determined by the future. Andromache's function in the narrative, then, is to articulate more precisely the kind of choice Aeneas makes in leaving Troy behind to follow destiny. It is as though Andromache is a second Aeneas, the kind of person he would have been, had he gotten his wish. Although Aeneas is still a Trojan, he leaves behind him Andromache's overdetermined Trojanness. This makes him free to become a signifier in the poem onto which Roman national identity is projected. It is this quality of Aeneas as a cipher, a blank space that can be defined by strongly articulated contrasting figures, that makes Aeneas particularly suited as the *Aeneid*'s ultimate signifier of Roman identity. While assembling a picture of Aeneas through his opposition to others, the reader is free to imagine his own version of the Romanness supposedly embodied in Aeneas. Few determinants are given by the text, many of them negative in nature: Aeneas is not like Andromache, not like Dido, not like Lavinia.

CHAPTER 7

Cleopatra and the Politics of Gendered Ethnicity

In the previous chapter I outlined how Roman identity in the *Aeneid* is defined by juxtaposing Aeneas to a series of female figures whose ethnicity is intertwined with their womanhood and sometimes even with their emotional life. The discursive strategy that links gender and ethnicity in these figures is also operative in Roman representations of Cleopatra. In fact, Cleopatra probably contributed greatly to restructuring Roman belief systems with regard to ethnicity and gender and the relationship between them. In Augustan representations of the battle of Actium, Cleopatra's womanhood was exploited along with the fact that she was queen of Egypt in order to suggest the foreignness of Antony's forces. Depicting Cleopatra meant articulating both the anomaly she represented as a woman with political power, as well as her orientalism. As a result, Roman political discourse defined Romanness against the backdrop of its own representation of a real-life powerful foreign woman.

In a way, these Augustan representations of Cleopatra form the birth of the Western discourse of orientalism. Cleopatra not only helped shape the discursive structures that articulated the ancient self, but also helped lay the foundations for a discourse the Western world employed in various guises throughout history to define itself.[1] The *Aeneid* played a pivotal role in giving such weight to Roman representations of Cleopatra. Not only does it represent the battle of Actium, but I will show in this chapter that Vergil's Dido owes much to both the real and the Roman discursive Cleopatra.

Hence, the link between gender and ethnicity that we have observed in the *Aeneid* (and especially in the Dido episode) as an integral part of the poem's articulation of Romanness and of the self must be understood within the politics of gender and ethnicity in the Augustan discourse about Cleopatra.

I use the term *discourse* deliberately here to avoid a problem surrounding Augustan representations of Cleopatra. As we will see, the most articulate of these representations are found in poetry, and the picture that emerges from these poetic accounts is in some aspects so uniform and at the same time so unhistorical that it suggests dependence from a preexisting discourse such as an official party line or political propaganda.[2] There are two problems with approaching the texts in this way. The first problem with this approach is that most evidence for such propaganda comes precisely from the poems that are assumed to reflect or respond to the propaganda. The second problem is that a distanced, critical poetic response to propaganda is the only interpretation of these poems that prevents modern critics from condemning them as embarrassingly opportunistic, politically reprehensible, and therefore bad poetry.

As a partial solution to these two problems we should forgo the search for propaganda in these poems and instead view them as part of a public Roman discourse about Cleopatra. The Augustan poets who wrote about Cleopatra surely did so within the context of public opinions of society at large about the current political situation, but there is no need to assume that they wrote either under coercion or in opposition to it. Whatever their intentions, or indeed those of Augustus and other political leaders, may have been, the poets present us with a rich, varied, and at times contradictory tapestry of images of Cleopatra and opinions about her. This poetic discourse about Cleopatra can be useful in gaining a better understanding of the ideological underpinnings of Vergil's representation of Dido.

The most potent use of the discursive Cleopatra in the *Aeneid* is found in the Dido episode, but it is also the most complicated. Therefore, before I explore how Dido participates in Roman discourse about Cleopatra, I will review some of the most important aspects of that discursive Cleopatra in the *Aeneid* and in other Augustan poets.

VERGIL'S ACTIUM

Vergil's Actium is a founding text for the Western discourse of orientalism.[3] The text of Vergil's Actium polarizes the two opponents in the battle into representations of West and East.[4] It does so without regard for the historical distortions inherent in such an enterprise. The historical distortions are particularly apparent in the depiction of Antony's forces:

> *hinc ope barbarica variisque Antonius armis,*
> *victor ab Aurorae populis et litore rubro,*
> *Aegyptum virisque Orientis et ultima secum*
> *Bactra vehit, sequiturque (nefas) Aegyptia coniunx.*
>
> (*Aen.* 8.685–88)

[On this side is Antony with his outlandish force and weapons of all kinds, the victor over the nations of the Dawn and the shore of the Read Sea. He brings with him Egypt and the forces of the Orient and remote Bactra, and in his train follows (unspeakable crime!) his Egyptian wife.]

That Antony was a Roman general and rival of Octavian both as heir to Caesar and for the leadership of the Roman Empire is hardly recognizable any more in the orientalization of his entourage here. Vergil has him accompanied by barbarian forces and strange weapons (685: *ope barbarica variisque . . . armis*).[5] His soldiers here are Egyptian, Oriental, and even Bactrian, the last a blatant inaccuracy, because the Persian Bactra was never subject to a Roman general, not even Antony.[6] The oriental nature of Antony's armies is stressed with two expressions, *Aurorae populis* and *viris Orientis,* both of which are vague enough to suggest a vast army drawn from the entire East, known and unknown territories alike. The ethnic makeup of this oriental army is later specified when Antony's soldiers flee from the battle in terror of Apollo's intervention on Octavian's behalf:

> *omnis eo terrore Aegyptus et Indi,*
> *omnis Arabs, omnes vertebant terga Sabaei.*
>
> (*Aen.* 8.705–6)

[All the Egyptians and Indians, all Arabs and Sabaeans, took flight at this terrifying sight.]

The idea that Antony's forces were comprised of Egyptians, Indians, Arabians, and Sabaeans has little or no basis in historical fact, but it has a powerful impact on the ideological polarization of the two enemies represented here. We may expect Egyptians to have served under Cleopatra, but Indians?[7] While Vergil's account of Actium is at pains to assert the ethnic otherness of Antony's forces, this representation does not correspond to other ancient accounts of Antony's forces at Actium, such as that of Plutarch.[8] Modern historians of Actium disagree even more forcefully with Vergil's image, arguing that Antony's forces consisted mainly of Italians.[9]

The otherness of Antony's legions further manifests itself in Cleopatra, who is called Antony's Egyptian wife (688) and who is depicted with the sistrum, a ritual attribute of Isis (696: *regina in mediis patrio vocat agmina sistro*). Here, too, otherness is stressed in national terms, which in turn have a defining force for the Romanness constructed in this passage. Not only does Octavian face the forces of the East, but these forces are led by a national Other, an Egyptian queen who is endowed with the attribute of an Eastern goddess of whom she is a priestess.[10]

The polarization of Octavian's and Antony's forces is completed on a third level. The gods championing the two sides are clearly differentiated in a manner unprecedented in ancient epic:

> *omnigenumque deum monstra et latrator Anubis*
> *contra Neptunum et Venerem contraque Minervam*
> *tela tenent.*
>
> (*Aen.* 8.698–700)

[All kinds of monstrous gods, among them barking Anubis, hold their weapons ready against Neptune, Venus, and Minerva.]

At Actium the gods favoring Octavian's side (Neptune, Venus, Minerva, and, mentioned further below in line 704, Apollo) are drawn from the standard Greco-Roman pantheon, while Antony's gods are monsters with strange shapes who bark. In other words, they are Egyptian gods such as the theriomorphic dog god Anubis. By opposing two different pantheons in an epic battle scene, Vergil introduces a new element into the well-established epic topos of the battle of gods. In Homer's *Iliad* the Greeks and Trojans shared the same Olympian pantheon, from which the gods favoring each side were drawn. Vergil followed this tradition in his depiction of the battle of gods over Troy in book 2 (608–18). At Actium, however, he handles the situation differently. That the two sides in this battle don't even share the same gods only emphasizes the gulf Vergil establishes between them. Considering that Antony was as Roman as Octavian and that Cleopatra was a Hellenistic queen of Greek descent, it would have been easy to fit the battle of gods at Actium into the traditional mold. Since

Antony fashioned himself as a new Dionysus in the East in the manner of the Hellenistic kings, while Cleopatra encouraged her identification with Isis and Aphrodite, a battle between Apollo and Dionysus would have been a possible alternative for the Actium scene on Aeneas' shield.[11] The decision to oppose instead a Greco-Roman pantheon to an Egyptian one is highly significant. It articulates the profound otherness of Octavian's enemies in ethnic and national terms, an articulation that is overdetermined precisely because it has to overcome the taint of civil strife inherent in a battle between two Roman generals.

AUGUSTAN LITERARY DISCOURSES ABOUT CLEOPATRA

The Vergilian account of Actium must be seen in the context especially of four roughly contemporaneous poems about Cleopatra or the battle of Actium: Horace's ninth epode, his Cleopatra ode (*carm.* 1.37), and Propertius' poems 3.11 and 4.6. Both of Horace's poems and Propertius' poem 3.11 were published before the *Aeneid* and could therefore have influenced Vergil's depiction of Cleopatra and perhaps Dido. Propertius' poem 4.6 postdates the *Aeneid* by a few years but shares several elements of the discourse about Actium and Cleopatra established in the other poems. Additionally, the fragmentary *Carmen de bello Actiaco,* whose authorship and dating is uncertain, depicts Cleopatra and Actium in ways that recall both the discursive Cleopatras of Vergil, Horace, and Propertius, and Vergil's Dido.[12] In the following discussion of Augustan discursive Cleopatras, I will include this fragmentary poem, because it is the only other epic depiction of Cleopatra before Lucan's and therefore an important point of comparison, especially for both Vergil's Cleopatra and his Dido. But the poem is almost certainly later than the other accounts discussed here (it has been dated as late as the Neronian period), and its depiction of Cleopatra probably owed much to Vergil's Dido, in addition to its probable literary debt to the earlier poems' Cleopatras.[13]

Both of Horace's Cleopatra poems start out as sympotic exhortations to celebrate Octavian's victory at Actium. The epode represents three images of Cleopatra, who, however, is never referred to by name. First we encounter a Roman soldier enslaved by her, who carries his weapons at the behest of Cleopatra and her eunuchs (Hor. *epod.* 9.11–14). Then our gaze is directed to the next image, a mosquito net, referred to as shameful, which is set up amid a military camp (Hor. *epod.* 9.15–16). The poem provides us with an intratextual reaction to this image in the next lines. We hear that a contingent of equestrian soldiers from Gaul who previously belonged to Antony's army switched their allegiance to Octavian's side at the sight of the mosquito net (Hor. *epod.* 9.17–18). This mosquito net is a symbol of Cleopatra—it is associated with her in a Propertian poem, as well[14]—and its being pitched in a military camp causes the disgust and defection of the Gallic soldiers because the image expresses that female rule is at odds with Roman military decorum. This point was already made in the first image of the poem, the soldier obeying Cleopatra, and it is reiterated here. The last image relevant to Cleopatra in this poem is of the flight of Octavian's enemies from the battle of Actium (Hor. *epod.* 9.27–32).

Several aspects of these images from the ninth epode recur in the other three Cleopatra poems listed above. Horace's ode 1.37 explores Cleopatra's flight from the battle of Actium (Hor. *carm.* 1.37.14–21) and then her suicide (Hor. *carm.* 1.37.22–32). Propertius' Cleopatra elegy 3.11 puts Cleopatra into the context of amatory poetry. Here Cleopatra is introduced as an example of the familiar amatory theme of a man's enslavement to a woman.[15] As in Horace's epode, so here, too, Cleopatra is depicted as subjugating Romans to her rule (Prop. 3.11.32). As in Vergil's depiction of Actium, so here Cleopatra is associated with a barking Anubis (3.11.41) and with the *sistrum* (43). And again as in the Horatian epode, the *conopium,* or mosquito net, is used as a stand-in for the Egyptian queen (3.11.45). The motif of Cleopatra's flight from the battle of Actium, familiar to us already from Vergil and both of Horace's poems, also occurs here (3.11.51 and 69), as does the motif of her suicide (3.11.53–54), which we have already observed in Vergil and in Horace's ode.

Prop. 4.6 tells the story of the battle of Actium as the *aition* for the erection of the temple of Palatine Apollo (4.6.11 and 67). This elegy also associates images with Cleopatra that are already familiar to us from the other texts. The outrage at a woman's role in a Roman military context, familiar from Horace's epode and Prop. 3.11, is expressed succinctly in the image of a javelin in a woman's hand, an image Propertius proceeds to call scandalous (Prop. 4.6.22: *pilaque feminea turpiter apta manu*). Again we find the motifs of Cleopatra's flight from battle (4.6.63) and her suicide (4.6.64). But the central theme in this version of Actium is Apollo's support of Octavian (4.6.27–57), a motif we also find in Vergil.

The extant fragments of the *Carmen de bello Actiaco* indicate that this poem's depiction of Cleopatra was much more detailed than those of the other poems I have just discussed. One fragment contains what seems to be a speech addressed to Cleopatra (col. iii), another a speech of Cleopatra (col. iv); two fragments deal with her suicide plans (cols. v to vii) and two with Octavian's pursuit of Cleopatra after the battle (cols. vii and viii). In its larger scope and epic narrative mode this treatment of Cleopatra was probably more comparable to Vergil's depiction of Dido than to the Augustan poets' discursive Cleopatras.

The fragments show this poem's Cleopatra to share several features with both Vergil's Dido and the earlier poetic depictions of Cleopatra. The anomaly of her engagement in the public sphere as a woman is acknowledged in the speech addressed to her, in which her interlocutor seems to exalt her fame and glory over those of other women and even men of the past (col. iii, 1.25–26). In her own speech she seems to participate in the polarization of Octavian and Antony into representatives of West and East when she speaks of Antony as dying for the glory of her nation and as conquering Persia for Egypt (col. iv, 1.32–33). A corresponding polarization is found in a subsequent fragment in which Octavian is said to be accompanied by part of the senate and his fatherland when he reaches Alexandria in pursuit of Cleopatra (col. vii, 1.58–60).

The poem recalls the eroticized depictions of her political alliance with Antony from earlier Cleopatra poems when Cleopatra calls Antony her "husband" (col. iv, 1.31: *coniunx*), thus repeating the motif of the unsuitable marriage already present in Vergil's account of Actium and the theme of the amatory enslavement of Antony to Cleopatra. The motif of Cleopatra's responsibility for the war is present in the speech addressed to her where she is called "the greatest cause of the war" (col. iii, 1.24: *causa fores tu maxima belli*). In this motif she fits into a pattern (which I will discuss further below) that the *Aeneid* establishes of locating responsibility for each of the poem's wars in one woman, Helen for the Trojan War, Lavinia for the wars in Italy, Dido for the Punic Wars, and Cleopatra for the battle of Actium. Lastly, the *Carmen de bello Actiaco* dramatized Octavian's pursuit of Antony and Cleopatra to Alexandria after the battle of Actium and Cleopatra's suicide. One fragment speaks about Octavian's arrival and siege of Alexandria (col. vii, 1.58–60). Two longer fragments are concerned with Cleopatra's plans for her suicide. The longest continuous fragment contains a fairly lengthy tableau of different forms of suicide Cleopatra seems to try out on criminals (col. v and vi). A subsequent fragment shows her wavering between different forms of suicide for herself (col. vii, 1.55–57).

From the five poems I have just discussed, together with Vergil's account of Actium, the following picture of Cleopatra emerges: her role as queen is targeted repeatedly as an anomaly inconsistent with the poets' sense of propriety and decorum. She is associated with Eastern excess (drunkenness and greed for power),[16] luxury (the mosquito net in Horace and Propertius, her riches in Vergil), and depravity (sexual depravity in Prop. 3.11.30 and 39).[17] Her political alliance with Antony must be understood as an instance of the amatory enslavement of men by women. Her flight from the battle of Actium shows her cowardice and irresponsibility, while her suicide is sometimes seen as a redeeming feature in her story.[18]

This outline of the main features of the Augustan discursive Cleopatra will provide us with a road map for the following exploration of the Dido episode as a fictional elaboration of Cleopatra's political threat to Rome.

✎§ CLEOPATRA IN DIDO

Several problems presented to the Roman worldview by the political entity Cleopatra are worked out in the Dido episode. The first of these is the idea of female rule. Although there is little in the character of Dido as a queen that resembles ancient depictions of Cleopatra, there is a series of literary allusions that link Dido to threatening images of female rule. What is more, these images occur when we first encounter Dido. The narrative sequence from the Trojans' landing on the shore of Africa and through Aeneas' stag hunt bears resemblance to Odysseus' arrival at Circe's island.[19] Then, when Aeneas sees the temple images while awaiting Dido's arrival, the last image his gaze rests on is that depicting Penthesilea. From this image of Penthesilea the reader is guided to a glimpse of Dido as she arrives at the temple. There follows the famous simile in which Dido is compared to Diana:

> *ducit Amazonidum lunatis agmina peltis*
> *Penthesilea furens mediisque in milibus ardet,*
> *aurea subnectens exsertae cingula mammae*
> *bellatrix, audetque viris concurrere virgo.*
> *Haec dum Dardanio Aeneae miranda videntur,*
> *dum stupet obtutuque haeret defixus in uno,*
> *regina ad templum, forma pulcherrima Dido,*
> *incessit magna iuvenum stipante caterva.*
> *qualis in Eurotae ripis aut per iuga Cynthi*
> *exercet Diana choros, quam mille secutae*
> *hinc atque hinc glomerantur Oreades; illa pharetram*

fert umero gradiensque deas supereminet omnis
(Latonae tacitum pertemptant gaudia pectus):
talis erat Dido, talem se laeta ferebat
per medios, instans operi regnisque futuris.

(*Aen.* 1.490–504)

[Fierce Penthesilea leads the host of the Amazons with crescent shields. She rages in the midst of the hosts, as she fastens her golden girdle under her naked breast. A female warrior she is, and, though a young woman, she dares to enter into battle with men. While Trojan Aeneas marveled at these images, while he was stunned and remained transfixed by this one sight, queen Dido, most beautiful in appearance, approached the temple with a great crowd of young men around her. As when at the banks of Eurotas or on the ridges of Mount Cynthus Diana leads the dance, and a thousand mountain nymphs follow her, crowding around her from here and there; but she, carrying the quiver on her shoulder, towers over all the goddesses as she strides along (and joy courses through Latona's silent heart): such was Dido, so did she walk happily in their midst, intent on the work at hand and her future kingdom.]

The transition from the fierce Amazon queen to the Carthaginian queen is accomplished with an image of a queenly Diana who leads her nymphs in a dance.[20] Unlike the literary predecessors of this Diana simile that accomplish a characterization for Homer's Nausikaa and Apollonius' Medea as nubile virgins, the Vergilian simile instead stresses the regal aspect of Diana, which is particularly appropriate for Dido.[21] With its reference to Diana's hunting attire it also accomplishes a closer link between the warlike Amazon queen Penthesilea and the queen Dido whose city, the reader is explicitly told several times, is warlike.[22] In fact, a later scene that shows Dido in hunting attire recalls both the Penthesilea and the Diana of the present passage: there she has a quiver just like Diana (*Aen.* 4.138), and the description of her attire (4.139: *aurea purpuream subnectit fibula vestem*) alludes to that of Penthesilea (*Aen.* 1.492: *aurea subnectens exsertae cingula mammae*). The text makes another connection between Dido and Penthesilea when it draws attention to the two queens' intrusion into a male domain: Penthesilea the woman dares to fight with men (*Aen.* 1.493: *audetque viris concurrere virgo*), and Dido is said—with less overt attention to the unusual nature of the situation—to give laws to men (*Aen.* 1.507: *iura dabat legesque viris*).

Circe and Penthesilea are thus the images associated with Dido at her first entrance onto the narrative stage. These figures are, of course, representative for ancient attitudes to female rule and female autonomy. Ancient thought consistently associates female rule with danger and chaos, a world upside-down. That Vergil invokes these images when he introduces his heroine to his readers is significant. Rather than presenting a new version of what female rule could be like, the *Aeneid* participates in a discourse about female rule well established in antiquity, which was employed forcefully against Cleopatra. Significantly, Propertius explicitly compares Cleopatra to Penthesilea, Omphale, and Semiramis in a move very similar to the one made in our Vergilian passage.[23] We may conclude that the problem of female rule presented to the Roman worldview by Cleopatra is addressed in the Dido episode in terms that reassert well established attitudes about women's roles in ancient societies.

In most ancient myths female rule is located geographically at the margins of the known world. Semiramis is the remotest autonomous queen in this discourse, but Penthesilea and Omphale, too, belong to the realms of the East, being located in Asia Minor rather than Greece. It is therefore not surprising to see Dido and Cleopatra associated with the discourse of orientalism. Female rule and orientalism intersect in these two figures to create powerful images of the Other against which Romanness is defined.

Thus both figures are represented in terms of Eastern luxury. Dido has many traits of Eastern excess usually associated with Cleopatra. Her palace is decorated luxuriously with silver, gold, and purple in preparation for the banquet she holds for the Trojans (*Aen.* 1.637–42). Throughout the last part of book 1 references abound to the luxurious furnishings of Dido's palace.[24] I have already discussed the visuality of the scene in which the splendor of Dido's preparations is displayed to great effect at her guests' arrival (*Aen.* 1.697–700), as well as the visual effect of a later scene from the banquet in which an abundance of light turns night into day (*Aen.* 1.726–27). A passage from Plutarch's *Life of Antony* about Cleopatra's first encounter with Antony bears a striking resemblance to this *Aeneid* scene:

Πολλὰ δὲ καὶ παρ᾽ αὐτοῦ καὶ παρὰ τῶν φίλων δεχομένη γράμματα καλούντων, οὕτω κατεφρόνησε καὶ κατεγέλασε τοῦ ἀνδρὸς ὥστε πλεῖν ἀνὰ τὴν Κύδνον ποταμὸν ἐν πορθμείῳ χρυσοπρύμνῳ, τῶν μὲν ἱστίων ἁλουργῶν ἐκπεπετασμένων, τῆς δὲ εἰρεσίας ἀργυραῖς κώπαις ἀναφερομένης πρὸς αὐλὸν ἅμα σύριγξι καὶ κιθάραις συνηρμοσμένον. αὐτὴ δὲ κατέκειτο μὲν ὑπὸ σκιάδι χρυσοπάστῳ

κεκοσμημένη γραφικῶς ὥσπερ Ἀφροδίτη, παῖδες δὲ τοῖς γρα-
φικοῖς Ἔρωσιν εἰκασμένοι παρ᾽ ἑκάτερον ἑστῶτες ἐρρίπιζον.
ὁμοίως δὲ καὶ θεραπαινίδες αἱ καλλιστεύουσαι Νηρηΐδων ἔχουσαι
καὶ χαρίτων στολάς, αἱ μὲν πρὸς οἴαξιν, αἱ δὲ πρὸς κάλοις ἦσαν.
(Plut. *Ant.* 26)

[Though she received many letters of summons both from Antony
himself and from his friends, she so despised and laughed the man
to scorn as to sail up the river Cydnus in a barge with gilded poop,
its sails spread purple, its rowers urging it on with silver oars to the
sound of the flute blended with pipes and lutes. She herself reclined
beneath a canopy spangled with gold, adorned like Venus in a paint-
ing, while boys like Loves in paintings stood on either side and
fanned her. Likewise also the fairest of her serving-maidens, attired
like Nereïds and Graces, were stationed, some at the rudder-sweeps,
and others at the reefing-ropes.][25]

Like Dido, Cleopatra actively sets the stage for her encounter with Antony,
arranging herself as the centerpiece of an elaborate scene that resembles a
painting and is calculated for its effect on the onlooker. Silver, gold, purple,
and an abundance of servants are elements of Cleopatra's spectacle as much
as of Dido's. Later on in this passage Plutarch tells of Cleopatra's banquet as
something beyond description, but points out the abundance of lights as
the most memorable thing about it (Plut. *Ant.* 26). The sequence of images
in these two texts is thus completely parallel: in both passages the queens re-
ceive their future lovers with spectacular displays of themselves amidst their
luxurious surroundings; this is followed by banquets during which a multi-
tude of lights again shows off the splendor of the queens' preparations.

Later in the Dido narrative there are more references to her luxurious
lifestyle. On the day of the hunt Dido and her horse are decorated with
much gold and purple.[26] At Mercury's arrival in Carthage, Aeneas is sim-
ilarly attired with a jeweled sword and a purple and gold cloak, gifts from
Dido.[27] Lastly, the report of *Fama* about Dido's love affair with Aeneas
that reaches Iarbas' ears alleges not only that the two lovers spend their
winter in oblivion of their duties and in passion, but also in luxury.[28]
Again parallels to Antony and Cleopatra are apparent. The image of Ae-
neas in Eastern attire, building the city of Carthage, recalls an Antony cor-
rupted by Cleopatra's influence, who rules from Alexandria rather than
Rome. It also resonates with Vergil's own representation of Antony at the
head of an Eastern army at Actium.

I began my discussion of Cleopatra parallels in the Dido story with the proposition that the Dido story works out problems presented to the Roman worldview by Cleopatra. We have seen that one of them, female rule, has been associated with the discourse of orientalism in the case of both Vergil's Dido and many literary representations of Cleopatra. Another problem that is worked out in the Dido episode is the political alliance of Cleopatra with Antony. Ancient literary representations of Cleopatra as well as the Dido episode worked out this problem by fashioning a love story in which the foreign queen entangles a heroic male in a love affair that presents a threat to Roman power. If Aeneas had stayed in Carthage, would Rome have been founded? Equally, if Antony had won the battle of Actium, would the Romans have been ruled from Alexandria by a woman? When Mercury calls Aeneas *uxorius* (*Aen.* 4.266), it is an accusation close to the one Dio has Octavian bring against Antony on the eve of Actium: he calls him γυναικὶ δουλεύων (Dio 50.26.5).

Finally, Cleopatra's departure from the battle of Actium had since Vergil been represented as a flight and as evidence of women's ultimate unsuitability for positions of military and political power.[29] This, too, finds a reflection in the Dido episode, which is at pains to stress Dido's irresponsibility as a queen once she has fallen in love with Aeneas. I have already argued that literary allusions to Catullus' Ariadne in her later monologues show the obliteration of her regal role by her lover's persona. But this process begins much earlier. Early on in book 4 we are told that the constructions at Carthage have come to a halt because of Dido's love (*Aen.* 4.86–89). *Fama* later calls both Dido and Aeneas *regnorum immemores* (*Aen.* 4.194). The charge is confirmed when Jupiter turns his eyes to Carthage in response to Iarbas' prayer and sees Dido and Aeneas forgetful of their better reputation (221: *oblitos famae melioris amantis*). When Mercury is sent down to Aeneas to rouse him to depart, it is Aeneas, no longer Dido, who supervises the construction activity at Carthage (*Aen.* 4.260). When Dido confronts Aeneas about his preparations for departure, he tries to make her understand his responsibilities by appealing to hers:

> *si te Karthaginis arces*
> *Phoenissam Libycaeque aspectus detinet urbis,*
> *quae tandem Ausonia Teucros considere terra*
> *invidia est? et nos fas extera quaerere regna.*
>
> (*Aen.* 4.347–50)

[You are Phoenician, and yet the citadel of Carthage and the view of the Libyan city detains you here; why be envious if the Trojans settle on Italian soil at last? It is the gods' will that we, too, seek a kingdom in foreign lands.]

Dido does not respond to this appeal, because her lover's persona has long obliterated her role as queen. Her suicide is her ultimate abandonment of this role. Not only does her death mean the death of her city, as the simile in her death scene suggests, but her sister explicitly formulates this interpretation when she finds the dying Dido on her pyre:

> *exstinxti te meque, soror, populumque patresque*
> *Sidonios urbemque tuam.*
>
> (*Aen.* 4.682–83)

[Sister, you have killed yourself and me, your people, your Tyrian fathers and your city.]

The irresponsibility of the two queens as rulers corresponds to the responsibility ascribed to them by the text for causing wars. Dido's curse monologue makes her responsible for the Punic Wars, interpreting them as an act of vengeance for her abandonment by Aeneas. Similarly, Vergil's Actium subtly confers responsibility for the war on the Egyptian side when he portrays the Egyptian gods as the first to raise their arms against their opponents (*Aen.* 8.698–700), a move that fits well with Octavian's declaration of war on Cleopatra, rather than Antony, because this declaration of war also confers responsibility for the war on Cleopatra.[30] Both Dido and Cleopatra fit into a larger pattern in the epic that consistently associates specific women with the causes of wars.[31] The mother of all such women, metaphorically speaking, is, of course, Helen, who is blamed for the Trojan War in the *Aeneid* as she had been in Greek tragedy.[32] The last figure to conform to this pattern is Lavinia, who is compared to Helen several times and is explicitly called the cause of the war between Trojans and Italians. In *Aen.* 6.93–94 the Sibyl prophesies wars in Latium for Aeneas, the cause of which, she says, will again be a foreign bride, meaning Lavinia and comparing her to Helen (*causa mali tanti coniunx iterum hospita Teucris / externique iterum thalami*). Later, in book 7 Amata compares her daughter to Helen as well (*Aen.* 7.359–64). In book 11 Lavinia is again called *causa mali tanti* (*Aen.* 11.479–80), repeating the phrase used by the

Sibyl in book 6. What is more, the war in Latium is also part of Dido's curse (*Aen.* 4.615–20). Thus, the wars that occupy one half of the epic's narrative space have two women as their cause, while Dido, the most prominent female character of the poem, has the double function as cause for both the Punic Wars and the war in Latium.

The *Aeneid* thus introduces four wars into its narrative, for each of which it casts a female figure bearing the burden of causing the war. These four women also share the motif of their false marriages. In the case of Helen, her false marriage to Paris is mentioned at a particularly ominous moment: Aeneas chooses Helen's robes as gifts for Dido, robes which Helen had brought from Greece when she came to Troy with Paris to seek a forbidden marriage (*Aen.* 1.651: *inconcessosque hymenaeos*). The problematic nature of Dido's marriage to Aeneas emerges from a comment the narrator makes after the cave scene: he says that Dido no longer considers her relationship with Aeneas a secret love affair and that she calls it a marriage; but the narrator comments that marriage is just a name that serves her to cover up for what the narrator calls a guilty transgression (*Aen.* 4.171–72: *nec iam furtivum Dido meditatur amorem: / coniugium vocat, hoc praetexit nomine culpam*). The narrator also comments on Cleopatra's marriage to Antony when he exclaims "*nefas*" before calling her his Egyptian wife (*Aen.* 8.688). Finally, it is precisely the legitimacy of Turnus' and Aeneas' claims on Lavinia's hand that cause the conflict between Trojans and Italians in the second half of the epic.

By linking Cleopatra and Dido with Helen and Lavinia the *Aeneid* integrates these autonomous queens into a more male-centered belief system in which women operate as symbols of a conflict between men or as scapegoats for such conflicts rather than as agents in it. Wyke has drawn attention to the uneasy position Cleopatra occupied within the validating discourses of Roman imperialism surrounding Actium.[33] Although female figures were part of such discourses, Cleopatra fit uneasily into them, because women usually functioned as abstractions in them (personifications such as Gaul depicted as a grieving woman on Roman coins issued after Caesar's conquest of Gaul), rather than being an enemy a Roman general would have been proud to have defeated.[34] This might in part explain why Cleopatra as a specific female opponent disappeared so quickly from such discourses, and why Horace depicted her death as heroic and unwomanly in his Cleopatra Ode.[35]

The figure of Dido occupies an intermediate position between Cleopatra, the problematic female signifier and actual contemporary female opponent of Rome, and the more traditional female characters Lavinia and Helen, who fit more easily into established belief systems about women's roles in society. Vergil projects Cleopatra, the specific female opponent of Rome, onto Dido, the mythical representative of Carthage. Dido represents Carthage in the *Aeneid* much as Lavinia stands for Lavinium or Creusa and Andromache stand for Troy. But unlike Lavinia, Creusa, and Andromache, Dido represents an enemy city. And like Cleopatra, Dido enters the Roman discourse of imperialism as the representative of the vanquished, the Other, the East. If Cleopatra was a problematic signifier in Roman discursive systems, it was in part because her presence in such discourses potentially evoked the rivaling discourses that served to validate Cleopatra's own position of power, her own propaganda, and her representation of herself.[36] By projecting the problematic signifier Cleopatra onto the fictional Dido, the evocation of these rival discourses was circumvented, because Dido has no voice of her own. Despite Dido's eloquence, we must remember that Dido's voice is a Roman creation.

Said says that one of the fundamental components of the discourse of orientalism is the power and the prerogative of the West to articulate the East.[37] In Dido the *Aeneid* has created a particularly powerful signifier in the discourse of orientalism. Cleopatra, the autonomous African queen who rivaled Octavian's political power, has been transformed here into an abandoned Eastern heroine. Augustan discourse has tamed the East as it has incorporated it. Said has observed that one of the most important functions orientalism has served in more recent European history was as "an aspect of both imperialism and colonialism."[38] Representing the Orient in the nineteenth century in France and England was part of an ideology that accommodated both imperialist acquisition of foreign territories and the definition of a group identity in nationalist terms. So, for instance, the famous orientalist Renan also wrote an influential essay about nationhood.[39] Vergil's orientalism is also connected to imperialism: the oriental images of Cleopatra and Dido are both connected to vanquished territories now in Rome's possession. They are etiologies of Rome's rightful possession of Carthage and Egypt, just as they reassert established patterns of power distribution between the sexes. What is more, the Romans of the Augustan period articulated their conception of Romanness using orientalism (Cleopatra, Dido), Punicness, and Greekness to define themselves. Thus Vergil's images of gendered ethnicity also contribute to the formation of a notion of Roman national identity.

Although the use of gendered ethnicity to define Roman identity involves excluding others so radically different as to be the opposite of Romanness, the extent of this radical exclusion is in fact very limited. Choosing Dido as such a defining Other is a brilliant stroke, because Carthage was an enemy long overcome, and the enmity invoked in the poem had lost its immediacy. The representation of Cleopatra's Eastern entourage as such a defining Other is equally elegant, because the very fact of its exaggeration and distortedness renders it a discursive signifier without referents in the outside world; that is, the actual troops following Antony were so different from the poetic images of Indians, Bactrians, and dog-headed gods that the depiction of such others did not in fact exclude many of those who belonged to the losing side.

Dido's relationship with Cleopatra thus can show us the delicate negotiations at work in Vergil's poetry, where the perplexing realities of the last phase of the civil war were transformed into a compelling narrative that could articulate a new identity for a unified and pacified empire. Cleopatra's womanhood and her orientalism were such powerful symbols of otherness for the Romans of the Augustan period precisely because, as a major player in the last phase of the civil war, her defeat meant the end of the civil wars, and therefore her otherness in gender and ethnic terms could also cast the times of the civil wars as an otherness removed from *pax Augusta*. Yet narratives of Cleopatra herself would inevitably recall these times. Projecting Cleopatra's gendered and ethnic otherness on Dido, on the other hand, allowed Vergil to define Roman identity in the *Aeneid* not so much against the backdrop of the civil wars but by gesturing toward Rome's conflict with Carthage, a time the Romans of the first century BC often invoked as representing the true nature of what was best about the Romans, as I have discussed above.

In this sense, Dido is a tamed Cleopatra. By that I mean that the Dido narrative transformed a political opponent into a symbol of territory newly incorporated into the empire. As Dido in her own right articulates Rome's possession of Carthage, so she also articulates its possession of the East, and especially Egypt, in her function as a reflection of Cleopatra. We have seen that this transformation of a woman into a symbol of land involves eroticization. Indeed, it is the eroticization of land and the eroticization of a political opponent that incorporates the otherness of both into Roman imperial discourse. Cleopatra's transformation into Dido accomplished this amatory taming. But we have also seen in the previous chapter that Dido herself still presented an anomaly, because her womanhood is at odds with her political power, thus confusing systems of exchange such as hospitality and marriage within epic discourse. We have seen that Lavinia serves to rectify the confusions Dido causes in these systems of exchange by setting straight the balance of power between the sexes. Thus, it seems that the real threat Cleopatra presented to Rome ideologically, the aspect of her discursive makeup that was most in need of taming, was not her ethnic otherness but the anomaly she represented as a single woman in a position of supreme power.

Through her transformation into Dido, Cleopatra's impact on the Western discourse of Orientalism has been formidable. Renaissance epics such as Tasso's *Gerusalemme Liberata,* Ariosto's *Orlando Furioso,* and Milton's *Paradise Lost* above all owe their Armidas, Angelicas, and Eves to Dido. With such an array of literary embodiments of the eroticized ethnic other as precedents and models, later female symbols of colonial territory such as Pocahontas may have inherited some of the potency of their symbolism from Cleopatra, as well. It is, then, the very power of the *Aeneid* and its articulation of Roman identity through gendered ethnicity that has kept Cleopatra's power alive, as a signifier of female power and ethnic otherness.[40]

CHAPTER 8

Romanitas

ETHNICITY: ESSENTIALISM OR DISCURSIVITY?

In the previous two chapters I explored the role of gendered and ethnic otherness in defining Roman identity. I now want to put these considerations into the context of other forms of defining Roman identity in the *Aeneid.* I see three major forms of defining ethnic identity operating in the *Aeneid:* first through genealogy and ancestry, second with the use of ethnic stereotypes, and third by means of gender differentiation. In the case of Dido we have seen that her Punicness is expressed by ethnic stereotypes, but that gender differentiation also plays a major role in her juxtaposition with Aeneas. Andromache and Lavinia, on the other hand, acquire meaning in their juxtaposition to Aeneas solely through gender differentiation. There is no trace of ethnic stereotyping in the portrayal of these two figures. Their ethnic otherness thus is a result entirely of their womanhood.

The interdependence of ethnicity and gender in the construction of these figures draws attention to the discursive constructedness of both categories as they are conceptualized in the *Aeneid.* By intertwining gender and ethnicity in the ways I have explored above, the *Aeneid* calls into question the notion of ethnic essentialism, the idea that there is one and only one way of being Punic, Greek, Italian, or Trojan. In several other instances, ethnic essentialism is similarly called into question by different textual strategies. Ethnic stereotyping of a group is at times juxtaposed with portraits of these people that are entirely at odds with such stereotyping. Dido is an obvious example. Her Punicness is concealed in her lover's persona. Despite that Punicness she welcomes the Trojans to Carthage in the warmest terms and declares that she will make no distinction between them and her own people (*Aen.* 1.574: *Tros Tyriusque mihi nullo discrimine agetur*). Her suffering and suicide evoke every reader's pity, sympathy, and compassion.

The portrayal of the Trojans themselves is equally indeterminate: Eastern stereotypes are attributed to them as Trojans, but this kind of ethnic characterization of the Trojans as Easterners is apparent only in the taunts of enemies. When the Nubian king Iarbas complains to Jupiter of Dido's liaison with Aeneas, he describes Aeneas as:

> *ille Paris cum semiviro comitatu*
> *Maeonia mentum mitra crinemque madentem*
> *subnexus*
>
> (Aen. 4.215–17)

[That Paris with his troop of half-men, an Eastern turban fastened around his chin and oily hair]

The image invoked is clearly a stereotype of the Easterner with strange attire (*Maeonia . . . mitra*)[1] and foreign grooming (*mentum . . . crinemque madentem subnexus*). The use of *Maeonia* as ethnic designation of the Trojans is telling: it does not really matter, Iarbas seems to say, whether you are dealing with Phrygians, Lydians, Maeonians, or Trojans; they are all the same. Maeonian, imprecise as the term is for the Trojans, invokes all the alien associations of the Easterner. Iarbas calls into question the manliness of these Eastern intruders (*semiviro comitatu*) and glosses Aeneas as a Paris, the worst kind of Homeric hero to choose, as far as manliness is concerned.

The same stereotypes reappear later when the Italian Numanus Remulus taunts the Trojans.

> *Vobis picta croco et fulgenti murice vestis,*
> *Desidiae cordi, iuvat indulgere choreis,*
> *Et tunicae manicas et habent redimicula mitrae.*
> *O vere Phrygiae, neque enim Phryges, ite per alta*
> *Dindyma, ubi adsuetis biforem dat tibia cantum.*
> *Tympana vos buxusque vocat Berecyntia Matris*
> *Idaeae; sinite arma viris et cedite ferro.*
>
> (Aen. 9.614–20)[2]

[You wear clothes dyed with saffron and bright purple, idleness is what you love, you take pleasure in dancing, your tunics have long sleeves and your turbans have long ribbons. Indeed, you Phrygian women, not even Phrygian men; go back to the heights of Mount Dindyma, where the double flute sounds its music for those accustomed to it. The drums and the boxwood pipe of the Great Mothers call you; leave weapons to men and withdraw from the sword.]

For Iarbas, the Trojans are only half-men (*semiviro*), whereas for Numanus they are actually women (*Phrygiae*). Like Iarbas, Numanus invokes the *mitra* as a stand-in for all the foreignness of Eastern costume. Numanus' ethnic designation for the Trojans, Phrygians, is turned into an insult by adding the element of gender. It is their exotic attire and their dancing, he suggests, that turns Phrygians into women. The linking of ethnic stereotypes with gender differentiation takes its crudest form in this slur. Whether Numanus accurately portrays the Trojans he is facing is questionable, as we will shortly see, but one element hits home: Numanus links the Trojans' attire and dancing to the worship of Cybele, whose priests at Rome probably would have fit Numanus' description precisely. Although the priests of Cybele at Rome were always Phrygians, the Romans did adopt the cult at Rome as a gesture that affirmed their kinship with this region of Asia Minor on the basis of their Trojan origins.

Turnus, too, reviles the Trojans as being only half-men, in this prayer:

> da sternere corpus
> loricamque manu valida lacerare revulsam
> semiviri Phrygis et foedare in pulvere crinis
> vibratos calido ferro murraque madentis.
>
> (*Aen.* 12.97–100)

[Grant me to strike down his body and to tear open and mangle with strong hand the breastplate of this Phrygian half-man, and to soil with sands his hair curled with hot iron and dripping with myrrh.]

The picture he draws of Aeneas as wearing his hair in the Eastern fashion accords precisely with Iarbas' portrait. The problem with these portrayals of the Trojans is that Aeneas and his crew never exhibit such characteristics. Descriptions of Aeneas' appearance in the *Aeneid* are so unspecific that by poem's end we have no idea even about the color or length of his hair.³ A typical example of this indeterminacy is the description of Aeneas as he first appears to Dido (*Aen.* 1.588–93). Aeneas is handsome, so handsome that Dido is stunned. His appearance is enhanced by his mother, who sheds beauty over him. But despite the simile that enlarges on Aeneas' appearance at that moment, the description is entirely unspecific. Another example of this is found in the scene of the hunt at Carthage, discussed above.⁴ There we are given to understand that Aeneas is very good-looking, in fact that he looks like Apollo. But specifics are not forthcoming. In contrast to the description of Dido in this scene, Aeneas remains a visual cipher. The only time the narrator describes Aeneas' appearance is when Mercury comes to call him away from Carthage. At that point he is attired like an Eastern monarch, in robes given to him by Dido.

> *Atque illi stellatus iaspide fulva*
> *ensis erat Tyrioque ardebat murice laena*
> *demissa ex umeris, dives quae munera Dido*
> *fecerat, et tenui telas discreverat auro.*
>
> (*Aen.* 4.261–64)

[He wore a sword studded with red jasper, the cloak that hung from his shoulders was bright purple; Dido had given him these things and had woven fine gold threads into its fabric.]

Are we to imagine that this kind of appearance is unusual for him, or is this what he looks like at other times as well? A definite answer to this question is impossible, but the effect of the scene is greater if we picture Aeneas' appearance at Carthage as substantially changed. That still does not give us any idea of his looks at other times.

The indeterminacy of Aeneas' appearance is useful for the function I have argued he fulfills in the poem as a figure of identification for the reader. By being vague about what Aeneas looks like, Vergil allows a wide range of different readers to identify with him. While visual description is reserved for other figures, Aeneas is not seen; he sees, like the reader. The characteristics of Aeneas that are described in the poem are largely moral or at times emotional: he is brave, dutiful, heroic, and sometimes angry, sad or happy. If being Roman means being a bit like Vergil's Aeneas, then any one ethnicity is not a requisite or an obstacle to being Roman.

However, the poem does not relegate the Eastern appearance of the

Trojans entirely to the realm of hostile fictions. Just when readers are convinced that the taunts of Iarbas and Numanus Remulus have no basis in reality, we encounter a Trojan who exactly fits that description, in the priest pursued by Camilla just before her death.

> *Forte sacer Cybelo Chloreus olimque sacerdos*
> *insignis longe Phrygiis fulgebat in armis*
> *spumantemque agitabat equum, quem pellis aënis*
> *in plumam squamis auro conserta tegebat.*
> *ipse peregrina ferrugine clarus et ostro*
> *spicula torquebat Lycio Gortynia cornu;*
> *aureus ex umeris erat arcus et aurea vati*
> *cassida; tum croceam chlamydemque sinusque crepantis*
> *carbaseos fulvo in nodum collegerat auro*
> *pictus acu tunicas et barbara tegmina crurum.*
>
> (*Aen.* 11.768–77)

[It so happened that Chloreus, who was once a priest sacred to Mount Cybelus, drew her attention because of the splendor of his Phrygian arms; he spurred on his horse, which was foaming at the mouth; it was covered by a coat of bronze scales laid featherwise and buckled with gold. He himself was gleaming with colors of exotic rusty red and purple, and the arrows he shot from his Lycian bow were from Crete; the bow that hung from his shoulders was golden, and golden the priest's helmet; then he had gathered his saffron cloak with its rustling linen folds into a knot with a tawny gold brooch, and his tunic and foreign trousers were embroidered with needlework.]

As a priest of Cybele, Chloreus instantly evokes his Eastern identity, summoning up in ancient Roman readers' minds the exotic appearance of the priests of Cybele familiar to them from everyday experience. The foreignness of Chloreus' appearance is signaled with several ethnic designations: Phrygian (769), Lycian (773), Cretan (773). Costly materials like gold, bronze, and purple and saffron dyes enhance the Eastern associations of this description. The style of his clothing, too, marks him explicitly as Eastern: Phrygians were depicted in both Greek and Roman literature and art as wearing trousers.[5] As if this were not obvious enough already, the adjectives *peregrina* (772) and *barbara* (777) are added to items of his attire to spell out his foreignness.

One such depiction of a Trojan according to Eastern stereotypes does not imply that we are to imagine all Trojans to look like this. But it does give some degree of validity to such stereotypes. Dido's Punicness functions in much the same way. While her actions and her words can be explained without any reference to Punic stereotypes, they do conform to them to a certain extent. Thus, the notion of ethnic essentialism is explored here not simply with the result of negating it. To be sure, the text destabilizes any simplistic version the reader may have previously had of ethnic essentialism. But the notion of ethnic differences is not abandoned entirely; it still forms part of the poem's ideological framework, at the same time as the discursive nature of ethnicity is laid open.

The portrayal of the Greeks is particularly interesting in this respect.[6] There are good Greeks and bad Greeks in the poem: the good ones, like Evander, Hercules, or even Diomedes, as noble as the Trojans themselves, the bad ones brutal like Neoptolemus, or deceitful like Sinon. Indeed, analysis of the negative portrayals of Greeks in the *Aeneid* with attention to ethnic stereotypes renders a startling discovery: the characteristics attributed to the bad Greeks are exactly the same as the ones attributed to the Carthaginians. Sinon's cunning and untrustworthiness and Neoptolemus' cruelty mirror Venus' fear of *Tyrios bilinguis* and the cruelty of Dido's brother Pygmalion, who had killed her husband, Sychaeus. Such convergence of ethnic stereotypes again underscores the arbitrary nature of these stereotypes and the main function they serve as parameters for the definition of Roman identity by opposition with ethnic others. The following section will explore these stereotypes of the Greeks, as we find them in the poem.

ETHNIC STEREOTYPES OF THE GREEKS IN THE *AENEID*

In book 1 the Greeks appear as favorites of Juno together with the Carthaginians. Samos is mentioned as one of Juno's favorite cities along with Carthage (*Aen.* 1.16), and the causes of her continued hostility to Troy are discussed along with her earlier support of the Greeks during the Trojan War (*Aen.* 1.23–28). The proem thus links the Greeks with the Carthaginians as Others who have to be seen in terms of their enmity to the Trojans and Aeneas. Juno, the goddess who presides over the forces opposed to Rome, is also the goddess linked most closely to the Greeks. Later on in the same book, her temple at Carthage is covered with images of victorious Greeks triumphing over their Trojan opponents (*Aen.* 1.456–93).

Then, in book 2, Aeneas tells Dido how his mother Venus showed to him the battle of the gods raging over Troy (*Aen.* 2.608–18). Here again, Juno is among the deities championing the Greeks.

Book 2 is generally full of unfavorable portraits of the Greeks, and that quite understandably so, for it is, after all, Aeneas who is speaking here about the destruction of his beloved home by the Greeks.[7] The figures that stand out in this book are the treacherous Sinon, who takes advantage of the Trojans' trust and thereby brings about the sack of the city (*Aen.* 2.57–198);[8] Helen, whose presence in the midst of Troy's destruction rouses Aeneas to a quite indecorous fit of anger, which is checked only by the intervention of his divine mother (*Aen.* 2.567–603); and Achilles' son Neoptolemus, whose brutality is shown in a long sequence of scenes in which he murders first Priam's sons and then Priam himself (*Aen.* 2.469–558).

Book 2 especially is rich in characterization of the Greeks as a people. Greek cunning is referred to twice directly as an ethnic characteristic in the expression *ars Pelasga* (105 and 152). It is again implied in Laocoon's speech, when he warns the Trojans not to take the wooden horse into the city. He asks whether they think any gifts of the Greeks do not involve tricks and then reminds them of Odysseus, whose cunning was so proverbial that his name alone evoked his cunning (*Aen.* 2.43–44: *ulla putatis / dona carere dolis Danaum? sic notus Ulixes?*). Then he ends by advising the Trojans not to extend their trust, for the Greeks must be feared even when they bring gifts (*Aen.* 2.48–49: *equo ne credite, Teucri. / quidquid id est, timeo Danaos et dona ferentis*).[9]

The language of untrustworthiness and cunning is pervasive to the narrative about Sinon and the Trojan Horse as a whole. The Greeks pretend that they decide to sail home (*Aen.* 2.17: *simulant*), and then they secretly hide warriors in the wooden horse (*Aen.* 2.18: *furtim*); the wooden horse is referred to several times as a trick (*Aen.* 2.44, 196: *dolus*) and an ambush (*Aen.* 2.36, 65, 195: *insidiae*). Sinon is described as cunning (*Aen.* 2.62: *versare dolos,* 2.152: *dolis instructus*), as deceptive (*Aen.* 2.107: *ficto pectore,* 2.196: *lacrimis coactis*), and as treacherous (*Aen.* 2.195: *periurique arte Sinonis*). Lastly, when Sinon opens the wooden horse inside the city at night, he does so furtively (*Aen.* 2.258: *furtim*).

Several points are important to notice in this characterization of the Greeks. First, the Greeks are here characterized as cunning, treacherous, and untrustworthy, a stereotype already familiar from the discourse about the Carthaginians.[10] Secondly, this characterization of the Greeks indirectly characterizes the Trojans as the opposite of the Greeks: where the

Greeks are untrustworthy, the Trojans trust Sinon, perhaps even too much. Aeneas makes the point that the Trojans could not be conquered by the valor of Achilles and Diomedes but were conquered by a trick and by the false tears of Sinon (*Aen.* 2.196–98: *captique dolis lacrimisque coactis / quos neque Tydides nec Larisaeus Achilles, / non anni domuere decem, non mille carinae*). While this observation may imply that the Trojans are a bit too credulous, it also clearly implies that they were too brave and strong to be conquered in honest, open combat.[11]

The guilelessness of the Trojans, which contributes to the final destruction of their city, is a trait we have already observed in Aeneas. When he sees the images on Juno's temple, he refuses to see hostility in them and instead sees compassion for human suffering. The scenes of Trojan trust in books 1 and 2 point to one another. Indeed, it is the same quality of trust in the world that leads to the destruction of Troy as well as enables Aeneas to draw strength from what he sees around him.

The story of Achaemenides in book 3 provides a parallel situation to the Sinon story in which the Trojans' guilelessness does not have the same disastrous consequences (*Aen.* 3.588–691).[12] Achaemenides, a companion of Odysseus, was left behind on the Cyclops' island, and when the Trojans reach the shores of this island, he asks them to rescue him from there. Although they recognize him as a Greek, the Trojans trust Achaemenides and take him with them, just as they had trusted and shown mercy to Sinon. This time their trust is rewarded, because Achaemenides is able to warn them about the danger awaiting them on this island. At Achaemenides' advice, the Trojans immediately leave the island and escape the approaching Cyclops. They thus avoid the fate Odysseus and his companions endured in Polyphemus' cave.

The story of Achaemenides thus confirms a characteristic trait of the Trojans, their trust, while at the same time showing that it is a noble trait. Similarly, Aeneas' claim in book 2 that the Trojans were too brave and strong to be conquered by the valor of Achilles and Diomedes is also confirmed later on. When Turnus sends an embassy to Diomedes to ask his assistance against his old Trojan enemies (*Aen.* 8.9–17), Diomedes refuses (*Aen.* 11.243–95).[13] He recounts the misfortunes that have befallen the Greeks after the sack of Troy and calls them penalties for the crimes they committed at Troy (*Aen.* 11.258). Then he says that if the Trojans had had two more heroes like Aeneas, they would have come to Greece and conquered it rather than being conquered themselves (*Aen.* 11.285–87). The valor of the Trojans is thus confirmed by one of the most valorous of their former enemies.

Diomedes' account of his companions' fate links up with another passage in which the misfortunes of the Greeks after the sack of Troy are thematized: When Juno resolves at the beginning of the epic to inflict a sea storm on the Trojans, she justifies her plan by comparing it with Minerva's punishment of the Greeks for the offense committed by Ajax against her (*Aen.* 1.39–45). Minerva had sent a sea storm to the Greek fleet, because Ajax had violated Cassandra in her temple (*Aen.* 2.403–4 and 6.840). Diomedes supplements this story by telling what happened to Menelaus, Odysseus, Neoptolemus, Agamemnon, and himself. But he conceives of the Greeks' offence more broadly than Juno. For him, it was the war itself that the Greeks waged with Troy that caused their punishment (*Aen.* 11.255, 257–58: *quicumque Iliacos ferro <u>violavimus</u> agros / (. . .) infanda per orbem / <u>supplicia</u> et <u>scelerum poenas expendimus</u> omnes*).

The historical relevance of the offenses of the Greeks during the Trojan War is spelled out by Anchises in the parade of heroes. There he hails the souls of Mummius, who sacked Corinth, and the Aemilius Paullus, who conquered Perseus of Macedon, in recompense, he says, for the sack of Troy and the violation of Minerva's temple:

> *ille triumphata Capitolia ad alta Corintho*
> *victor aget currum caesis insignis Achivis.*
> *eruet ille Argos Agamemnoniasque Mycenas*
> *ipsumque Aeaciden, genus armipotentis Achilli,*
> *ultus avos Troiae templa et temerata Minervae.*
>
> (*Aen.* 6.836–40)

[That man will triumph over Corinth and drive his chariot to the heights of the Capitol as victor, famous for slaying the Achaeans. That one will overthrow Argos and Agamemnon's Mycenae, and the descendant of Aeacus himself, the seed of mighty Achilles; he will avenge our Trojan forefathers and the defiled temple of Minerva.]

The image evoked here is focused entirely on the mythical plane.[14] The historical figures and events, the sack of Corinth by Mummius in 146 BC and the victory of Aemilius Paullus over Perseus in 168 BC, are conflated into one act of vengeance for the destruction of Troy by the Greeks. Rome's conquest of Greece is here turned into a justified response to Greek aggression. When Rome conquers, it is in response to an offense committed against it, and Greece offended by sacking Troy.

I have already remarked that the portrayal of the Greeks in book 2 as

cunning and treacherous recalls Roman stereotypes about the Carthagini-
ans. But Punic cruelty, another ethnic stereotype the Romans had about
the Carthaginians, is also mirrored in the depiction of the Greeks in book
2. We need only think of Neoptolemus, who pursues Priam's son Polites,
until the latter collapses dead in front of his father (*Aen.* 2.526–32). Hav-
ing to witness his own son's death, Priam is roused to scold Neoptolemus
by comparing him to his more humane father, Achilles, who at least had
the decency to return Hector's body to his aged father (*Aen.* 2.533–46).
Neoptolemus is unmoved by Priam's words or by the spear he had hurled
against him. Not only does he kill Priam in a pool of his son's blood, but,
before he does, he mocks him by telling him to complain about him to
Achilles personally in the Underworld (*Aen.* 2.547–58).[15]

A similar picture emerges when we look at the Greeks' use of gift ex-
change in book 2. We have seen that Dido is excluded from the economic
modes of epic discourse, when she is represented as buying land in Libya
instead of receiving it by gift exchange, as Aeneas does later on in Latium.
Here in book 2 the Greeks are also shown to be problematic users of the
heroic modes of economy established in epic discourse. Several times in
this book the Trojan Horse is referred to as a gift, and each time Greek
gifts are called problematic or suspicious in general (*Aen.* 2.36–37: *pelago
Danaum insidias suspectaque dona* / *praecipitare iubent; Aen.* 2.44–45: *ulla
putatis* / *dona carere dolis Danaum?; Aen.* 2.49: *quidquid id est, timeo
Danaos et dona ferentis*). Although the Trojan Horse was not an offering of
gift exchange to the Trojans, not even overtly, but a pretended offering to
Minerva (*Aen.* 2.183–94), the Trojans speak about it as though it were a gift
to them. By representing the Trojan Horse as an item of gift exchange,
Aeneas, the narrator in this book, succeeds in representing the Greeks as
using gift exchange in a perverted manner. This is significant, because gift
exchange in the *Aeneid* and elsewhere in epic discourse is used to distin-
guish civilized societies from uncivilized ones.

This picture is counteracted by figures such as Euander in the second
half of the poem, who equals the Trojans in their correct use of gift ex-
change. There is thus a fundamental ambivalence surrounding the Greeks
in the poem.[16] They can be characterized as Others on the order of ene-
mies such as the Carthaginians, but they can also be conceived as equals
and allies of the Trojans. Even the figure of Diomedes ends up in the lat-
ter group, when he sends back Turnus' offerings of gifts (which were in-
tended to establish an alliance between Turnus and Diomedes) and sug-
gests the gifts be given to Aeneas instead so as to establish an alliance with

him (*Aen.* II.281–82: <u>*munera*</u> *quae patriis ad me portatis ab oris / vertite ad Aenean*). While Euander uses gift exchange to establish an alliance with Aeneas, Diomedes refuses to receive gifts from Aeneas' enemy. Both Greeks use gift exchange correctly and in the service of peace with Aeneas.

There is one more intriguing instance of a Greek who violates the heroic modes of economy established in epic discourse. In the pictures on Juno's temple in Carthage, Achilles is shown selling Hector's body back to this father, Priam, for gold (*Aen.* 1.483–84: *ter circum Iliacos raptaverat Hectora muros / exanimumque* <u>*auro*</u> *corpus* <u>*vendebat*</u> *Achilles*).[17] It is the language of buying and selling that stands out in epic discourse as an anomaly. Achilles sells Hector's body, *vendebat,* just as we saw Dido buying land in Carthage (*Aen.* 1.367: *mercati*). But unlike Dido, Achilles uses the body of his most celebrated and noblest enemy as an object of barter. This is both cruel and savage. Achilles uses the money economy here as a way of degrading and humiliating his opponent. Vergil's tableau of Achilles and the dead Hector is a distortion of the *Iliad* scene from which it is drawn. Although Achilles also receives a ransom for Hector's body in the *Iliad,* the ransom he receives in the Greek poem plays a far less important role than the relationship between Achilles and Priam that develops during Priam's visit in the Greek camp.[18] This developing relationship between Achilles and Priam in the *Iliad* scene puts the exchange of Hector's body for ransom in the context of the economic mode of gift exchange well endorsed in epic discourse, while Vergil's tableau puts its emphasis on the crudely disembedded exchange of body for gold. The greatest hero of Greek mythology is shown as engaging in a degraded form of exchange. With one word suggesting the money economy, the emblem of Homeric heroism has been moved as far away from the *Aeneid*'s world of Homeric gift exchange as could possibly be done.

The poem's ambivalent depiction of the Greeks is of the same order as that of Dido and the Trojans. Ethnic stereotypes of the Greeks are counteracted by the depiction of Greeks like Anius, Achaemenides, Euander, and Diomedes, hence drawing attention to the discursive nature of these stereotypes. The resemblance between stereotypes about Greeks and those about Carthaginians contributes further to suggesting their arbitrariness and their main function as defining Roman identity by contrast. But in figures such as Sinon, Neoptolemus, and even Achilles the stereotypes are validated to a considerable degree, with the consequence that the notion of ethnic essentialism is not eradicated by the destabilizing strategies of the text.

☙ GENEALOGY AND THE SEARCH FOR ORIGINS

I have mentioned that the proem of the *Aeneid* sets up an opposition be-
tween Troy and Rome on the one hand, and both Carthage and Greece on
the other. As we have seen in the previous section and in the discussion of
Dido's Punic traits, this opposition remains a defining force for Roman
identity throughout the poem. But the poem is not primarily interested in
these ethnic others for their own sake, to exalt or revile them, but precisely
as one of the tools it employs to define Roman identity. The openly
avowed purpose of the poem, as the proem suggests, is to recount the
foundation of a nation. In the proem, the narrator draws attention to this
purpose when he comments that Juno's hatred of Troy is the cause for the
troubles Aeneas had in founding *Romana gens* (*Aen.* 1.33: *tantae molis erat
Romanam condere gentem*), that is, she is the cause for the narrative of the
poem.

This interest in the foundation of the Roman nation, although grand
enough to be worthy of the epic genre, is nevertheless not shared by any
other extant ancient epics. Much as the Homeric poems may have served
the Greeks as a cultural icon that encapsulated a certain idea of what it
means to be Greek, they themselves do not directly reflect on Greekness
as such, nor do they give an account of the origins of the Greeks. The
Aeneid, on the other hand, does reflect on the meaning of Romanness, as
well as recounts Rome's origin.

This focus is established in the proem not only through reference to the
foundation of *Romana gens.* The proem also claims to account for the
foundation of *genus Latinum* with its narrative. The origin of *genus Lat-
inum,* the narrator says, must be traced to Aeneas' arrival in Latium, the
foundation of his city, and the introduction of his gods to his new home:

> *Arma virumque cano, Troiae qui primus ab oris*
> *Italiam fato profugus Laviniaque venit*
> *litora, multum ille et terris iactatus et alto*
> *vi superum, saevae memorem Iunonis ob iram,*
> *multa quoque et bello passus, dum conderet urbem*
> *inferretque deos Latio; genus unde Latinum*
> *Albanique patres atque altae moenia Romae.*
>
> (*Aen.* 1.1–7)

[I sing of arms and the man who was first to come from the shores
of Troy to Italy, exiled by fate, and to the shores of Lavinium. He was

much thrown about on land and sea, by the will of the gods, because of the mindful wrath of cruel Juno; and he suffered much in war, as well, until he founded the city and brought his gods to Latium; this is the origin of the Latin race, of the forefathers of Alba Longa and of the city walls of high Rome.]

It is the story of Aeneas, the narrator claims, his sufferings and his arrival in Italy from which the Latin race derives its origin. This claim is especially interesting in the light of my earlier remarks about the discursive constructedness of ethnic identity in the poem, because the poem later contradicts the proem's claim. The people of Latium are called *Latini* throughout books 7 to 12, not only by the narrator, but also by mortal and immortal characters alike, among them King Latinus himself, Amata, Turnus, and Aeneas.[19] Indeed, Latinus' name itself suggests that *genus Latinum* predates Aeneas' arrival in Latium, the point of time designated by the proem as the origin of the Latin race. Moreover, when Juno requests from Jupiter in book 12 that the people of Latium not become Trojans and that the name Troy be abandoned, she calls the name *Latini* an old name (823: *ne vetus indigenas nomen mutare Latinos <iubeas>*).

But the proem's claim is not simply wrong. In one sense the story of the *Aeneid* does constitute the origin of *genus Latinum*. Jupiter promises Juno he will grant her wish not to change the old name of the *Latini*, but his language suggests that the people who will descend from the intermarriages of Trojans and Latins will not simply be a continuation of the old Latin race, but rather an entirely new people: they will be called *Latini*, he says (*Aen.* 12.837: *faciam omnis . . . Latinos*), but he goes on to say that from the mingling of Trojans and Latins will rise a nation yet to be born (*Aen.* 12.838: *hinc genus Ausonio mixtum . . . sanguine surget*), and he locates the origin of this nation, the proem's *genus Latinum*, at the joining of the two peoples into one.

By both fulfilling and not fulfilling the proem's promise of recounting the origin of the Latin race, the poem draws attention to the discursive constructedness of that origin. Just when we think we have located the source from which *genus Latinum* sprang, it eludes us again. The same ambiguity about locating origins is found elsewhere in the poem. I have already discussed Aeneas' false claim that he will name his city for his bride Lavinia (*Aen.* 12.194). We have seen in chapter 6 that this naming gesture is an illusion, because Aeneas knows the name of his future city long before he knows the name of his future bride. Latinus makes a similarly misleading naming gesture. He is said to have named his people *Laurentes* for a lau-rel tree he had consecrated to Apollo (*Aen.* 7.59–63). But only a few lines earlier, Latinus' own mother, Marica, is referred to as a Laurentine nymph (*Aen.* 7.47), and later on Latinus' grandfather Picus, his father's father, is also called *Laurens* (*Aen.* 171).[20] On both sides of his family tree, Latinus is Laurentine long before he names his people so. Hence, upon closer ex-amination, the etiological tales promised or recounted in the *Aeneid* turn out to problematize the notion of a fixed ethnic origin, rather than to sta-bilize it.

Nevertheless, the poem's preoccupation with the origins of Rome con-tinues to show itself. The origins of individual Roman families, for in-stance, are referred to several times, especially in book 5, where we find out about the descent of the Memmii, the Sergii, the Cluentii, and the Atii.[21] These examples show that genealogy and ancestry play an important role in the definition of Roman identity along with ethnic differentiation. In the frequent use of words like *gens* and *genus,* the poem continuously draws attention to issues of ethnicity. This is particularly apparent in the second half of the poem, where the terms used to designate the ethnicities of the various Italians are often very specific but also are often used in an ambiguous fashion, as we have seen above, or even in an almost mislead-ing manner. So the Rutulian Turnus is called a Laurentine in *Aen.* 7.650, an odd designation for Turnus if, as the text suggests, the *Laurentes* are the people ruled by Latinus, while the Rutulians are not subject to Latinus.[22]

Most of the pivotal moments of the plot are marked by references to ethnicity, a fact that should alert us to the poem's focus on ethnic defini-tions. So in the story of Dido, Rome's enmity with Carthage is the result of her love for Aeneas, a passion inspired in her by Venus and Cupid on account of Venus' fear for Aeneas' safety among a people stereotypically considered untrustworthy. Dido becomes the abandoned lover she has come to emblematize in Western literature because at a crucial moment in Aeneas' story Venus was afraid of *Tyrios bilinguis* (*Aen.* 1.661), of Punic untrustworthiness.

Similarly, book 2 of the *Aeneid* tells the sack of Troy as the result of the duplicity of Sinon, a duplicity the Trojan priest Laocoon warns the Tro-jans about when he cautions them from taking the Trojan Horse into the city. Laocoon does not see this duplicity as specific to Sinon, but rather as typically Greek. Could any gifts of the Greeks, he asks, ever be without duplicity (*Aen.* 2.43–44: *ulla putatis / dona carere dolis Danaum*)? The point is driven home by several stabs at the stereotype of Greek duplicity.

Do you still not know Odysseus, Laocoon asks (*Aen.* 2.44: *sic notus Ulixes?*). Laocoon closes his appeal by urging that he fears the Greeks in every situation, even when they bear gifts (*Aen.* 2.49: *quidquid id est, timeo Danaos et dona ferentes*). It is the stereotype of Greek duplicity from which Laocoon's warning derives much of its force. His appeal to the Trojans makes use of the assumption that he shares with them a common conviction that Greek identity is inextricably bound up with the character trait of untrustworthiness.

Ethnicity is also a central point of contention in the conflict between Aeneas and Turnus in the second half of the poem. Latinus offers Lavinia's hand in marriage to Aeneas in spite of Amata's wish to marry her to Turnus, because an oracle from his father, Faunus, had commanded Latinus to seek *externa conubia*:

> *ne pete conubiis natam sociare Latinis,*
> *o mea progenies, thalamis neu crede paratis;*
> *externi venient generi, qui sanguine nostrum*
> *nomen in astra ferant, quorumque a stirpe nepotes*
> *omnia sub pedibus, qua sol utrumque recurrens*
> *aspicit Oceanum, vertique regique videbunt.*
>
> (*Aen.* 7.96–101)

[Do not seek to join your daughter in a Latin marriage, my son, nor put your trust in the weeding that has been prepared; a foreign son-in-law will come to raise our name to the stars through his blood; descendants from this stock will see everything at their feet, wherever the sun looks upon the ocean as it traverses its course from East to West, overturned and ruled.]

The language of Faunus' oracle is replete with references to ethnic identity. The marriage Latinus is to avoid is a Latin marriage. Instead, he is to seek a foreigner for a son-in-law, and the benefit derived from this marriage will be glory for *nostrum nomen* and world domination for their descendants. The ethnic identity of the son-in-law, it is suggested, will determine the glory and power of Latinus' people. What is more, the means by which the foreigner will confer these benefits on the Latins is his blood, the admixture of a bodily fluid that will mark his descendants as his descendants and hence determine their ethnic identity.

When Aeneas arrives in Latium and sends an embassy to Latinus, bearing gifts and seeking a welcoming reception and peaceful relations, Latinus concludes that Aeneas is the foreigner Faunus had promised him (*Aen.* 7.255–56) as a son-in-law, and he offers him Lavinia's hand in marriage on the basis of Aeneas' foreignness (*Aen.* 7.270). But when Amata finds out about this, she makes a case that Turnus, too, can be considered an *externus*. She argues that everyone not under Latinus' dominion is an *externus*, and that moreover Turnus has Inachus and Acrisius among his ancestors and hence should be regarded as Greek by descent (*Aen.* 7.367–72). Her appeal has no effect on Latinus, but it does show that ethnic identity is a contested field for the characters of the poem, that Turnus' ethnicity is both debatable and debated.

It is ironic that Amata omits using an argument against Aeneas that is brought up between Latinus and the Trojans. At their first meeting, Latinus and the Trojan embassors mention Aeneas' descent from Dardanus, who came from Italy originally (*Aen.* 7.206–7 and 240). By invoking Aeneas' Italian ancestry, both Latinus and the Trojans implicitly destabilize the claim that Aeneas is a foreigner and hence fit to marry Lavinia, because in one sense Aeneas is an Ur-Italian. I will discuss the context of Vergil's genealogical claim about Dardanus below. For the purposes of the present discussion we should note that the ancestries of Aeneas and Turnus leave room for differing interpretations of the two characters' ethnic identities. Nevertheless, it is by means of ancestry that the poem's characters make claims and draw conclusions about ethnicity at another key moment of the poem.

Amata's argument in favor of Turnus shows how ancestry and ethnic identity can be manipulated or at least variously interpreted to suit individual purposes. Again the *Aeneid* calls into question the notion of ethnic essentialism. But in this example, even more than in its use of gendered ethnicity and its virtual equation of bad Greeks with Punic stereotypes, the *Aeneid* seems almost consciously to draw attention to the artificiality involved in its own definition of Roman identity. Aeneas' ancestry, on the other hand, is handled in a somewhat different manner. The *Aeneid* does not allow Amata to use Aeneas' descent from Italian Dardanus as an argument against his foreignness. Aeneas' Italian descent thus does not enter into a field of contestation within the poem; it is affirmed rather than questioned. This is especially interesting, because, as we will see further on, outside the *Aeneid* Dardanus' ethnicity was subject to debate, both before and during Vergil's time. Here the poem seems to function as stabilizing and legitimizing one version of the myth, and with it one version of Roman identity, over others.

At the heart of the poem's definition of Roman identity through Rome's Trojan origin is the connection established in the poem between Troy and Rome. Again we can observe contradictory textual strategies at work in the conceptualization of this connection. The poem often conflates Troy and Rome, while at other times drawing a sharp distinction. In the proem, for instance, Troy is constantly conflated with Rome. This conflation is achieved in the narrative movement of the first seven lines of the poem, which begin with Aeneas' origin and departure from Troy (*Aen.* 1.1: *Troiae . . . ab oris*) and end with Rome as the end result of a series of foundations (*Aen.* 1.6–7: *genus unde Latinum . . . atque altae moenia Romae*). Afterward, the two are conflated when the Romans are referred to as the offspring of Trojan blood (*Aen.* 1.19: *progeniem . . . Troiano a sanguine duci*) and when Juno's persecution of Aeneas' Trojan host is followed by the conclusion: *tantae molis erat Romanam condere gentem* (*Aen.* 1.33). Yet, when Aeneas visits Andromache in *parva Troia* in book 3, the distinction between the two is one between the excessive attachment to the Trojan past on one side, and obliteration of that identity in favor of following destiny on the other. Hence, for Aeneas to become a signifier of Roman identity, he must be differentiated from his Trojan past.

What is important to notice in the poem's treatment of Troy vis-à-vis Rome is not so much the fact that Rome is seen as descended from Troy, a notion well established at that time, but that an effort is made here to establish the nature of that connection. Given the fact that the Romans had adopted to Trojan legend at least since the third century BC, one might assume that all conceptual work on establishing the connection had been done, and that a narrative about the connection had been canonized. But this was not the case.[23] The continuing malleability of the legend emerges not only from the *Aeneid*'s concern with this theme. The *Aeneid* shares this interest in the origins of the Roman people with the works of several of Vergil's contemporaries.

GENEALOGY IN FIRST-CENTURY BC ROME

At the end of the republic and the beginning of the Augustan period, a genre of genealogical writing sprang up. Much of the information we have on these works comes from Servius' commentary on the *Aeneid*. We know that Caesar's funeral oration for his aunt Julia, held in 69 BC, was concerned with the descent of the Julian family from Aeneas.[24] Varro, Messalla, Hyginus, and Atticus are known to have written monographs on the genealogies of Roman families and their descent from Trojan ancestors.[25] Furthermore, we know that Varro's research in this area extended even further. He is known to have written a work with the title *de gente populi Romani,* which probably dealt with concerns very close to the subject matter of the *Aeneid.*[26] The aristocracy of the period was intensely interested in positioning itself in a framework of historical and mythical descent, thereby articulating their own perception of their identities vis-à-vis their Roman and Italian peers, as well as their Greek and other subjects.

In the *Academica* Cicero says this about Varro's interests:

> *nam nos in nostra urbe peregrinantis errantisque tamquam hospites tui libri quasi domum reduxerunt, ut possemus aliquando <u>qui et ubi essemus agnoscere</u>.*   (1.iii.9)

> [For we were strangers in our own city and wandering around like guests, and your books have brought us home, so to speak, so that we could at last <u>understand who and where we are</u>.]

Varro's research, says Cicero, has allowed the Romans to understand who they are. The proliferation of genealogical writing in this period suggests a hunger for self-definition among the Romans. In this context it is interesting to find that the Greeks had no genre of technical writing per se that was devoted to genealogy, in the same way as the Romans at the end of the republic.[27] The Romans' interest in defining themselves as Roman finds no direct counterpart among the Greeks precisely beause the Greeks were the ones from whom the Romans wanted to differentiate themselves. Both Greeks and Romans saw Greek identity as culturally dominant and as defining the civilized world of the Mediterranean, to the exclusion of almost all other Mediterranean cultures. Not to be Greek and still to be civilized, that is what required the intellectual work of genealogical research to establish a separate Roman identity. This intellectual work found its most powerful and most beautiful articulation in the *Aeneid.*

But the *Aeneid*'s version of Roman identity was not the only one articulated at the time. Dionysius of Halicarnassus argued in his *Roman Antiquities* that Rome is ultimately a Greek city. His arguments are at odds with the position the *Aeneid* takes in this matter, where Rome is founded by descendants of Trojans, who themselves are descended from Italian ancestors; both authors make the Romans' ethnicity ultimately dependent on the ethnicity and provenance of a minor mythological figure: Dardanus.

✒ DARDANUS AND THE ETHNIC ORIGINS OF TROY

The adoption of the Trojan legend as a foundation story for Rome allowed the Romans to connect themselves culturally with the Greek world by claiming common descent from the heroes of Greek myth. But descent from Trojans also involved claiming an ethnic connection with the East. The problems with such a claim are well illustrated in the *Aeneid,* as we have already seen. Such associations with stereotypes about the East of course run counter to the Romans' ideas about themselves and their use of Rome's Trojan origins as providing them with a heroic pedigree equal to their Greek imperial subjects.[28] One way of deflecting such associations was to give the Trojans themselves a genealogy that set them apart from the Easterners that surrounded them in Asia Minor. Over-subtle and inconsequential as such a strategy may seem to us today, this is precisely what scholars in the first century BC did to establish a more acceptable ethnic identity for the Romans within the framework of the Trojan legend.

The precise nature of that identity, however, was still subject to debate. Vergil entered that debate. In the proem of the *Aeneid* he ascribes an ethnicity to the Trojans by using an ethnic designation that is both enigmatic and learned, but that already encapsulates his position: *genus invisum.* That is how the Juno of the *Aeneid* sees the Trojans. The use of *genus* in this expression indicates that this is an ethnic designation for the Trojans, based on descent. But of what kind? Juno's hate, as the commentators tell us (see Serv. *ad Aen.* 1.28), is a hidden reference to Juno's jealousy of Electra, one of Jupiter's mistresses and the mother of Dardanus. The logic of the expression conforms with other definitions of ethnicity in the *Aeneid:* the Trojans are here defined as a race (*genus*) by their descent from Jupiter, and especially from his hated mistress Electra. It is the ethnic manipulation of this minor mythical character that allows for a subtle debate among the Romans and their contemporaries in the first century BC about the ultimate nature of the Romans' ethnic identity. The two authors who most fully attest to us this debate are Vergil and Dionysius of Halicarnassus, but Dionysius' side of the debate was also taken by Varro.

Here is what I take to be at issue in this debate. When Vergil and Dionysius give us their respective accounts of the origins of Rome, they agree on the, by their time well-established, story of Rome's Trojan origins, the foundation of Lavinium by Aeneas, and the subsequent foundation of Rome by Aeneas' descendant Romulus. The issue under debate between the two authors is the ethnic origin of the Trojans themselves. Both authors go to some lengths in establishing their respective versions of the story, which gives us an idea of the importance attached to this issue at the time. Pivotal to the question is the ethnic identity of Dardanus and his mother, Electra, whom Vergil sees as Italian, while Dionysius and Varro claim them to be Arcadian and hence Greek.[29]

Vergil's enigmatic *genus invisum* is fully elaborated in book 3, where Aeneas is told to return to the ancient home of the Trojans (94–98). Anchises first supposes this to be Crete. Indeed, Servius tells us that there were people who saw the Trojans as descendants of a Cretan Dardanus, which means that these people disagreed not only with Vergil but also with Dionysius and Varro in the debate about the ethnicity of the Trojans. In the *Aeneid,* the Trojans at last realize that their ancient home is Italy, and their journey becomes a *nostos.* But the oldest traditions about Dardanus and Electra associate them with Thrace, and those same traditions have Aeneas make another kind of *nostos,* having him settle in Thrace and dying there.[30] And then there were those, again according to Servius, who saw the Trojans as simply Trojan and who situated Electra's and Dardanus' homeland in the Troad. We don't know whether this opinion was held contemporaneously with Vergil, Varro, and Dionysius, but there were those at that time who saw the Trojan legend as unconnected to Rome, Italy, and Greece in another way: Strabo thought that Aeneas never traveled to Italy and died in the Troad, a view that was supported by the best mythographic evidence imaginable, a passage from the *Iliad,* which states that Aeneas was to rule among the Trojans.[31]

The fact that the Romans and Greeks of the first century BC spent time and energy on establishing the remote and obscure ancestry of the Trojans bears witness to the relevance of this subject to the Romans, and their interest in establishing their ethnic identity. The significance of establishing these respective ancestries for the Trojans is fairly clear, at least for the versions of Vergil and Dionysius. As a Greek, Dionysius had an interest in seeing the Roman imperial masters as Greeks, thus lessening the ignominy for the Greeks of being imperial subjects of non-Greeks. Vergil, on the other hand, was more interested in assimilating Roman and Italian identity; hence, for him the ultimate origins of Rome lay in Italy. For Vergil, Rome was emphatically not Greek.

This assertion of difference from the Greeks lies at the very heart of Roman identity as a historical and cultural phenomenon. Erich Gruen has shown in a series of studies that the Romans sought to assert their identity as difference from the Greeks in various ways as they gained supremacy in

the Mediterranean from the third century BC onward.[32] The adoption of
the Trojan legend itself can be seen as an articulation of this difference. By
articulating Roman identity both politically and culturally, the Romans in
some sense invented the concept of nationhood. Greek identity was, after
all, a cultural, not a political, identity.[33] A Roman, by contrast, was mem-
ber of a political as well as a cultural community, as are Americans, Ger-
mans, or Italians today. It was in the cultural, as well as the ethnic, sense
that Dionysius of Halicarnassus could designate Rome as a Greek city.
Vergil, on the other hand, made a significant gesture by articulating differ-
ence even on the subtle level of mythological ancestry. Thus, Vergil fuses
the political and cultural aspects of Roman identity with an ethnic com-
ponent through mythological ancestry.

This fusion of political, cultural, and ethnic identity comes very close
to the modern concept of nationhood. The application of this term to
Rome, however, is not unproblematic. Below I will explore some of the
difficulties in doing so, but first I want to bring the issue of Roman iden-
tity back to the *Aeneid* and consider some passages in which the terms
Roma and *Romanus* are used. I have argued above that the poem articu-
lates Roman identity by differentiating the reader's subject position from
the ethnic identities of some characters of the poem. Approaching the
question from a different angle, the way the poem uses the terms for
"Rome" and "Romans" in themselves can help us understand whether
Roman identity was conceived in the poem as an ethnic or a national
identity, that is, whether it was an ethnically restricted category or a more
inclusive one. Close attention to these terms in their context will reveal
that it is conceived differently from other ethnic terms.

ROMANS IN THE *AENEID*

I have already discussed the use of the term *Roman* in the proem of the
Aeneid and have shown how it proclaims that the *Aeneid* as a whole is a
chapter in the story of the foundation of the Roman nation. I have also
discussed the poem's references to the origins of individual Roman fami-
lies and its conflation of Rome with Troy. Apart from these contexts, the
terms *Rome* and *Roman* in the *Aeneid* occur most frequently in prophecies
and other passages that anticipate Rome's future.[34] But there are a few oc-
currences of these terms outside these prophecies and proleptic passages.
They are used in three distinct contexts: first, in etiological accounts of
Roman cultural practices such as the *ludus Troiae* (*Aen.* 5.601) and the

Gates of War (*Aen.* 7.603); secondly, in an apostrophe the narrator addresses to Nisus and Euryalus after his account of their deaths in battle (*Aen.* 9.449); and lastly in two epithets applied to Aeneas and Ascanius (*Aen.* 12.166, 168).

These passages are important for our understanding of Roman identity in the *Aeneid* because they connect the notion of Rome more intimately with the narrated world of the poem, a world in which Rome is not yet in existence. Although all these instances are found in authorial comments on the narrative rather than part of the narrative proper, they intrude more directly into the narrative than the proleptic passages. In this way they provide a bridge between the world of Aeneas and the world of Vergil's Rome, which in the poem can only feature as prophesied future.

How does Vergil use the notion of Rome/Romanness in these passages? I will argue that these passages serve to establish the concept of Romanness as an inclusive category, able to supersede the more narrowly ethnic categories that abound in the poem, such as Latins or Rutulians. While continuing to suggest that Romanness involves descent from Aeneas, that is, a group limited by blood and genealogy, it opens up the concept of Romanness in such a way that descent from Aeneas can be understood as symbolic rather than literal.

There are two ways in which this inclusiveness is signaled. The first is poetic ambivalence in the usage of the term. In book 9 Vergil comments on the deaths of Nisus and Euryalus, addressing his characters and promising them eternal fame (446–49):

> *Fortunati ambo! Si quid mea carmina possunt,*
> *Nulla dies umquam memori vos eximet aevo,*
> *Dum <u>domus Aeneae</u> Capitoli immobile saxum*
> *Accolet imperiumque <u>pater Romanus</u> habebit.*

> [Happy pair! If there is any power in my poetry, you will never be forgotten as long as the <u>house of Aeneas</u> stands on the unshaken rock of the Capitol and the <u>Father of Rome</u> holds power.]

What is meant by *domus Aeneae* and *pater Romanus*? Taken literally, Vergil would be saying that Nisus and Euryalus will be famous as long as the *gens Iulia* exists, because they specifically claimed descent from Aeneas. But does it make sense for Vergil to say this? Most people, I think, would agree in taking *domus Aeneae* to have a broader meaning here, designating Romans in general ("they will have fame as long as there are Romans"). The term is so vague that it seems almost inevitable to interpret descent from Aeneas symbolically here, as synonymous with "Roman."

Pater Romanus is even more vague. Is it the emperor? Jupiter? The senate?[35] All the term really suggests is this: Nisus and Euryalus will be famous as long as there is a Roman father figure who guarantees the continued existence of certain values and beliefs, by holding the power of *imperium*. Romanness, then, is associated here with adherence to certain values (honoring martial valor and self-sacrificing love) and the maintenance of these values by means of a paternal hierarchy of power. Descent does not matter in this use of the term *Romanus,* because Romanness is here conceived as a cultural identity that can be acquired. It depends on acculturation to a system of beliefs and values. The point of the vagueness in these terms, then, is to broaden them so as to achieve greater inclusiveness. Deciding on one *Pater Romanus* (the emperor, a god) robs the passage of its true rhetorical force, which consists exactly in its vagueness.

There are other passages in which the poem advances the idea that Romanness is a cultural construct, an identity that can be learned. The two etiological passages designate as Roman certain cultural practices that are described in detail. The first of these is the *ludus Troiae* in *Aen.* 5.545–603. The following passage explains the ritual as an ancestral tradition handed down from the Trojans to the Latins and from them to the Romans:

> *Hunc morem cursus atque haec certamina primus*
> *Ascanius, Longam muris cum cingeret Albam,*
> *Rettulit et Priscos <u>docuit</u> celebrare <u>Latinos</u>,*
> *Quo puer ipse modo, secum quo Troia pubes;*
> *<u>Albani docuere</u> suos; hinc maxima porro*
> *Accepit <u>Roma</u> et <u>patrium</u> servavit <u>honorem</u>;*
> *Troiaque nunc pueri, Troianum dicitur agmen.*
>
> (*Aen.* 5.596–602)

[As Ascanius and the Trojan youths performed then, just so did he revive the performance when he built the walls of Alba Longa, and he <u>taught it</u> to the <u>Latins</u>. The <u>Albans taught</u> it to their children; from this great <u>Rome</u> learned the practice and kept it as an <u>ancestral custom</u>; the boys are now called Troia and the troop Trojan.]

The *ludus Troiae* is described as *patrius honor,* that is, a custom learned from the forefathers. The element of teaching is emphasized (598, 600), as is the connection with Ascanius. Hence the *ludus Troiae* conveys to its audience a sense of Romanness both as a reference to Rome's mythical ancestry and as a teachable cultural practice. The practice is handed down from an ancestor (Ascanius) to his subjects who are Latins (598), or more specifically Albans (600). Latins here become Roman by learning, even though they are not literally descended from the ancestors whose customs they adopt. The teachability of this cultural practice turns Ascanius into a symbolic ancestor.

The other ritual described in the poem as handed down to the Romans from their ancestors is the practice of opening the Gates of War:

<u>Mos</u> erat Hesperio in Latio, quem protinus urbes
Albanae coluere sacrum, nunc maxima rerum
<u>Roma</u> colit . . .

. . . .
<u>hoc</u> et tum Aeneadis indicere bella Latinus
<u>more</u> iubebatur.

(Aen. 7.601–3, 616–17)

[There was a <u>custom</u> in Hesperian Latium which later the Alban cities held sacred, and now <u>Rome</u>, the greatest of cities, observes it, too . . . <u>by this custom</u> Latinus was bidden to declare war on the Trojans.]

The Roman custom of opening the Gates of War in the temple of Janus in times of military conflict, we learn in this passage, is older even than Rome itself. Again the observance of a cultural practice at Rome is connected to the ancestors, this time the native Italian, specifically the Latin ancestors of the Romans. By placing the origin of this custom in Latium and deriving it from the Latin people, the poem signals that Romanness is an aggregate of practices from various different cultures, some Trojan, some Latin. Hence, Romanness becomes a broader category than Latin or Trojan identity, but not only this: it also becomes a category that is qualitatively different from the others, because it is based on cultural practice rather than ancestry.

While these practices in themselves do not confer Romanness on every onlooker, they are spectacles that build community simply because one has to be physically present to see them. By representing these spectacles in literary discourse, the *Aeneid* renders them portable: no longer is it necessary to be physically present in Rome to "see" the spectacles. Readers can share these cultural practices vicariously, and the written spectacle still conveys a sense of community built on cultural practices, that is, learned and learnable behavior, rather than descent ("this is the sort of thing we Romans do, we open the gates of the temple of Janus to indicate we are at war, this is what makes us Roman").

On the other hand, some passages suggest that specific forms of Romanness, primarily belonging to a particular Roman *gens,* are determined by descent. In several places the term *Romanus* occurs when the origin of a Roman *gens* is traced back to characters appearing in the poem. At those moments in the poem, Romanness may seem a narrow category: you have to belong to a Roman *gens* to be Roman. But such forms of Romanness, although they seem to limit the concept of literal descent in the sense of bloodline, acquire a different meaning when we read them together with passages that use the term in a more inclusive way.

This becomes clear when we look at a passage in which Aeneas is given as an epithet the designation "ancestor of the Romans" (12.166: *Romanae stirpis origo*). This is the only time Aeneas is called so, although it would have been possible to call him so in other places of the poem. Moreover, two lines later Ascanius is called "the second hope of Rome" (12.168: *magnae spes altera Romae*). Again, this is the only time Ascanius bears an epithet containing the word *Rome.* The significance of these epithets lies in the place they occupy in the poem. Only at the end of the poem, in the last book, is Aeneas ever called the ancestor of the Romans. The cumulative weight of the passages I have discussed above has made it clear that Romanness is an inclusive concept. Hence, in this passage descent from Aeneas is symbolic rather than literal.

Roman identity in the *Aeneid,* then, is symbolically expressed as descent from Aeneas. As such Vergil's treatment of Roman identity reflects the dramatic changes the concept underwent during the first century BC. The granting of citizenship to all Italians after the Social War, and to an unprecedented number of communities outside Italy under Augustus, expanded not only the Roman citizen body, but the very notion of who was a Roman and what it meant to be Roman. Growing from a face-to-face community to an empire, Romans continually had to change their conception of Roman identity. A face-to-face community can rely on visual familiarity of its members to conceptualize their commonalities. A larger community such as the Greek *polis* needed other markers such as citizenship determined by descent. In Vergil's time, Roman identity was a far more open category, since citizenship was not dependent on descent alone. In constructing its version of Roman identity, the *Aeneid* uses the concept of the community of citizens descended from citizens (*polis* concept), but it also expands it: descent as a symbolic rather than a literal category. This is what distinguishes Romanness in the *Aeneid* from other group identities (Latins, Greeks, Carthaginians). While these are ethnic categories, dependent on descent of its members from other members, Romanness has been cut loose from descent as a necessary condition for membership in the group. In this the concept of Roman identity can best be compared to the modern concept of nationhood.

It is debatable how far it is useful for our understanding of Roman identity to make things more complicated by using terms such as *ethnicity* and *nationhood,* which introduce all kinds of modern implications that might be inappropriate for the ancient context. It is, indeed, very problematic to transpose ancient conceptions of group identity into a modern context, especially by using modern terms such as *ethnicity* and *nationhood.* But asserting this problem is not enough. When we are called upon to translate terms like *Romana gens* into English, we will have to settle on an English word for *gens* that conveys what kind of group identity is implied in *Romana gens.* Understanding the ancient concept of Roman identity, as well as the modern concepts of nationhood and ethnicity, will raise our awareness of the differences between the concepts as well as help us decide, when we have to, what term may be the most appropriate English translation for the Latin term. The following discussion of the modern concepts of nationhood and ethnicity and their applicability to ancient concepts of group identity will highlight some problems as well as suggest some connections and continuities between the ancient and modern terms.

NATIONALISM IN ANTIQUITY?

Romanam condere gentem—the toils involved in this task are, in a nutshell, the theme of Vergil's epic, as the poet himself tells us in the proem. In some sense, then, the *Aeneid* recounts the foundation of the Roman *gens.* I leave the term untranslated here intentionally, because I want to draw attention to the problematic involved in making a choice in its translation. The range of meanings of the word *gens* encompasses the very narrow concept of "clan" as well as the rather broad concept of the human race in its totality. Somewhere in between these two extremes it also translates as "race, nation, people," the sense most appropriate in the present instance.[36] But what exactly should we call the Romans? A nation? A race? In recounting Rome's origin the *Aeneid* certainly reflects on the meaning of Romanness, but how exactly should we fit the concept of *Romanitas* constructed in the poem into these modern terms? Terms, moreover, which are hotly debated, because they carry the enormous baggage of political conflicts and the disasters of recent history.[37] The Roman identity that emerges from the poem can best be compared to the modern concept of nationhood, as it strives to unite within itself various ethnic groups to form a whole unified by common language, customs, and religion.[38]

Elements such as ethnicity, language, customs, and religion are often invoked as unifying factors in the formation of nations.[39] Both ethnic identity and national identity are cultural constructs, not essences. This is why looking at their construction in the *Aeneid* is important: the poem exerted a powerful influence on broad audiences in the imperial period, articulating Romanness in discourse, adding its voice to the many competing discourses about what it meant to be Roman in the Roman Empire.

I have used the terms *ethnicity* and *nation* above, but what are the problems involved in doing so? Much work has been done in the past two decades on the concept of nationhood that helps us to understand that this notion—as we understand it today—is of a very recent vintage.[40] Rooted in the political, social, and economic changes of the late eighteenth and early nineteenth centuries, modern concepts of nationhood are inextricably linked to modern phenomena such as print capitalism and mass literacy.[41] Similarly, modern concepts of ethnicity are bound up with the specific concerns of modern society and reflect modern-day sensibilities that grew out of recent historical developments.[42] As classicists we are aware that the ancient world had a different relationship to ethnic differences than we do today.[43]

One of the difficulties in working on national identity in the ancient world lies in the view modern scholars of nationhood have of communities predating the eighteenth century AD. In their efforts to define what constitutes the modern phenomenon of nationhood, they often ignore— for the sake of their arguments—the vast diversity of community identities in societies other than the ones they focus on. Benedict Anderson bunches these earlier community identities together under two headings: religious communities such as Christendom and Islam on the one hand, and dynastic empires such as the Habsburg Empire on the other.[44] As classicists we would be hard pressed to fit either fifth-century Athens or first-century Rome into one of these molds. But the problem is not merely one of classicists finding themselves and their interests marginalized. Ignoring

the contribution of antiquity to the formation of modern notions of na-
tionhood runs the risk of missing an important component. As Anderson
points out himself, in the nineteenth century the activities of philologists
were central to the shaping of nationalism at that time. More specifically,
the rise of classical philology in Western and central Europe contributed
to awakening a national consciousness in the Greeks of the Ottoman Em-
pire, which eventually led to their 1821 uprising.[45] Anderson also tells us
that the rise of the philologies of the vernacular languages in the nine-
teenth century had a strong impact on the shaping of modern national-
ism. If this is so, then it must be of some importance that these philolo-
gies defined themselves, their methods and interests, in direct and
conscious opposition to the Classics. This leads us to ask whether modern
ideas of national consciousness were formed on the model of the national
pride embodied in the works of Greek and Roman authors. The present
chapter is therefore an attempt to contribute not only to the understand-
ing of Roman national consciousness, but also to that of nationalism more
generally.

Despite the reservations I have mentioned about recent work on na-
tionhood, it cannot be stressed too strongly how useful these studies have
been to the present project. Anderson's definition of the nation as a cul-
tural artifact and an imagined community is, indeed, ideally fitted to de-
scribe how the *Aeneid* articulates Roman identity. The element of imagi-
nation that forms so vital a part in Anderson's definition of nationhood is
indeed crucial to the construction of *Romanitas.*

Imagining that one shares beliefs with a group of other individuals fos-
ters a sense of belonging to that group, a process that lies at the heart of
the construction of group identities. For the case of national identity the
element of imagination extends also to the beliefs shared. It is character-
istic of the sentiment of nationalism that it involves a usually false belief
in the antiquity of its nation. Renan formulates this well when he says,
"Getting its history wrong is part of being a nation."[46] The project of the
Aeneid is just this: a reinvention of Rome's past that enables Romans all
over the empire to imagine a community of Romans with a shared past.
Gruen's analysis of the development of the Trojan legend bears witness to
the element of reinvention and instability involved in creating what seems
to us today a monolithic version of Rome's imagined past.[47] But even
within the monolithic version of Rome's past that is embodied in the
Aeneid and had become canonical during the imperial period, the signs of
instability and effort are hard to overlook. Bringing together within its

narrative characters of different ethnic groups and casting them as allies or opponents, the *Aeneid* wrestles with the concept of nationhood, struggling to define a common ground for inhabitants of the Roman Empire to serve as a point of identification.[48]

When we look at the *Aeneid* as a project of reinventing Rome's past, we must not forget the obstacles involved in such a project. As the Roman Empire grew rapidly, more and more of its inhabitants from diverse cultural backgrounds were granted Roman citizenship.[49] This in itself demanded a continuous adjustment of the nature in which Romanness was imagined.[50] Moreover, the tensions and power struggles within the old core of the Roman citizenry had just come to a lengthy explosion during a century of civil wars.

The *Aeneid*'s struggle for a definition of Romanness that includes all inhabitants of the Italian peninsula is most apparent in the second half of the poem where native Italians, Etruscans, and Greeks are found on both sides of a war that too patently resembles Rome's own civil wars of the recent past.[51] While the former Etruscan king Mezentius fights with Turnus, his people have joined the Trojans.[52] There is ethnic ambiguity even in many individual characters when we find out about their ancestries. Aeneas is Trojan, but his ancestor Dardanus came from Italy. Turnus is Italian, but on one side of his family tree he is descended from Greeks.[53] Many heroes on the Italian side have ancestries similar to that of Turnus.[54]

We have seen in our discussion of the Greeks and of the ambiguous Easternness of Aeneas and the Trojans that the notion of ethnic essentialism is continuously called into question in the *Aeneid*, laying open to the reader the discursive nature of ethnicity. At the same time the poem continues to use ethnicity as an indispensable category for its definition of Romanness. The reason for this ambivalent use of ethnicity is that the poem has to come to terms with the fundamental changes the concept of Roman identity was constantly undergoing while the Roman Empire expanded and, with it, the body of its citizenry.

Initially the privilege of free-born inhabitants of the city with indigenous ancestry, Roman citizenship was expanded gradually until it was extended to all freeborn inhabitants of the Roman Empire in AD 212 by the edict of Caracalla. At the beginning of this process, Rome could hardly have been called a nation. Equally, by AD 212, the community of Roman citizens was more culturally heterogeneous than most modern nations are today. But when Vergil wrote the *Aeneid,* the Roman citizen body experienced its greatest expansion by the grants of Roman citizenship to large groups of inhabitants of the Roman Empire outside of Italy.[55] At that time, imperial subjects from foreign ethnic backgrounds became Romans politically. The *Aeneid* did the cultural work of defining what Roman identity meant culturally in these changed circumstances. It is, then, the fact of empire, of the expansion of Roman territory through imperial conquest, that necessitated such cultural work of adjustment in the meaning of Roman identity. At a time when the Roman citizen body became more ethnically diverse, the *Aeneid* articulated Roman identity as a concept that allowed for ethnic diversity.

Conclusion

The project of this book has been to analyze the influence the *Aeneid* had on shaping the ancient self in the Roman imperial period, when the poem had gained an authoritative status matched only by the Homeric epics. In chapter 1 I documented the poem's monumental impact on many aspects of Roman culture and explored some cultural beliefs and practices that contributed to the poem's importance to Roman cultural identity. Looking at Augustine's rejection of his love for the *Aeneid* as a boy has alerted us to the cultural specificity of the ancient reading experience and suggested that we should be wary of uncritically eliding it to our own modern experience of reading the *Aeneid*. Quintilian and Augustine suggested that the *Aeneid* had a centrality in the education of literate Romans that is unparalleled today. Ancient modes of instruction were such that memorizing large parts of such central texts as the *Aeneid* was inevitable. It therefore figured largely in the minds of the educated as a central point of reference for further literary pursuits and more generally for readers' other cultural experiences.

Ancient rhetorical theory saw epic poems such as the *Aeneid* as holding power over their audiences because of their sublime style. The *Aeneid* specifically was also identified as a poem whose visual qualities exerted an influence over its readers. In chapter 2 I explored the various strands of ancient thinking about the power of poetry and its visual qualities over the soul. Philosophers were generally in agreement with rhetoricians in believing that poetry and the mental images it could evoke in the reader's imagination exerted an influence over the reader's emotions. While many philosophers considered poetry as dangerous to the soul and to cities because of this power, Aristotle provided a framework in which it was possible to see the emotions invoked in the reader by poetry as beneficial to the soul. The effects of the sublime qualities of epic were generally seen in ancient theory as positive, often being described as joy, elation, an increase of courage, and a greater awareness of right and wrong. I have argued that Vergil used visuality and the sublime qualities of epic in the *Aeneid* to achieve the rhetorical effects on his audience that rhetorical theory and Aristotle's theory of *catharsis* in tragedy expected to achieve: influence over the emotions of the reader, benefiting him either through the cathartic effects of experiencing tragic spectacles, or through the joy, elation, and moral benefits of the sublime reading experience.

Based on the insights gained from discussion of ancient rhetorical and philosophical theories of poetry's power over the soul, I focused in chapters 3 and 4 on the fictional relationship the *Aeneid* establishes between its readers and its fictional characters. I observed how a sequence of passages in book 1 establishes Aeneas as a spectator of various spectacles and images and draws the reader into Aeneas' view of the fictional events of the poem, aligning the reader's gaze with that of Aeneas. In chapter 4 I considered how numerous other, usually female, characters are represented in the poem as spectacles for Aeneas' and the reader's gaze. The two chapters together argue that the reader's subject position is male and often closely aligned with Aeneas, while identification with figures such as Dido, who are represented as spectacles, is more transitional, in the sense of the cathartic experience of identifying with the suffering of a tragic hero, which provides an outlet for emotions from which the reader is cleansed.

The last part of the book has considered more closely the various figures who are represented in the poem as spectacles for the reader's gaze, rather than as figures of identification similar to Aeneas, whose gaze the reader shares. In chapters 5 and 6 I have looked at these figures, whom I have identified in part 2 as Others in the sense of spectacles vis-à-vis the reader and Aeneas as spectators, in terms of their gender and ethnicity. This line of inquiry has led me in chapter 5 to conclude that the *Aeneid* genders not only the reader's subject position, but also the way it represents emotions more generally. Comparison of the reactions of Amata and Turnus to Allecto's efforts to instill frenzy in them has shown that the two characters' emotions are different before the divine intervention and that their attitude to the divine intervention, and hence to frenzy, is different, too. Gender is intertwined with the emotions here and in the various female characters whose emotions are represented in the image of the wound. In these characters emotions are represented as detrimental, but also as an integral part of their subjectivities.

In chapter 6 I have investigated the link between gender and ethnicity in various figures, but my focus has been particularly on Dido. Not only is she the most important character in the first four books apart from Aeneas and hence of great importance to the formation of the reader's subject position, but her character is also an intriguing intersection of various forms of otherness vis-à-vis Aeneas, emotionally, in terms of gender, and ethnically. Dido's Punic ethnicity is frequently overlooked or denied in scholarship, and it is therefore important to reevaluate its significance to Vergil's Dido narrative. I do not believe that the Punic traits ascribed to Dido in the *Aeneid* are intended to make her depiction derogatory. Rather, I see her Punic traits as artfully intertwined with her portrayal as an abandoned heroine in love. Differentiating her not only in terms of gender but also in terms of ethnicity from Aeneas facilitates the reader's differentiation from her as a tragic figure and hence promotes the experience of *catharsis*.

Furthermore, the representation of a conquered city and empire in the figure of a woman allows Roman imperialist discourse to represent imperialist conquest as an amatory conquest. In this the Dido story not only functions as an amatory narrative about the conquest of Carthage, but also absorbs the amatory elements and gender politics of Augustan discourses about Cleopatra and the subjection of Antony and Egypt by Octavian. Chapter 7 has explored the resonances of the Dido story with Cleopatra, who, like Dido, was conceived in Augustan poetic discourses as both a gendered and an ethnic other.

The final chapter of this book has explored the conceptualization of ethnicity in the *Aeneid* more generally, arguing that the poem draws attention to the discursive constructedness of ethnic identity. The analysis of Greek and Trojan ethnic identity in chapter 8, together with that of Punic ethnicity in chapter 6, has suggested that ethnicity is a narrow concept in the *Aeneid* that serves primarily to define Roman identity in ethnic terms by opposition to Greek, Trojan, Punic, and other ethnically different characters. By destabilizing the concept of ethnic identity through various textual strategies, the *Aeneid* undermines ethnicity as a defining category for the ancient self in favor of the concept of Roman identity. Looking at the use of the terms *Rome* and *Roman* showed that Roman identity is conceived in the poem as a much broader, more inclusive category that is not ethnically defined by literal descent from Roman ancestors. Aeneas and Ascanius are conceived as symbolic ancestors of the Romans, and Roman identity is conceived as a cultural identity that can be learned and enacted by following cultural practices such as the *ludus Troiae* in book 5 or the custom of opening the Gates of War in book 7. In its political and cultural dimensions the Roman identity of the *Aeneid* is an ethnically inclusive concept of group identity that bears most resemblance to the modern concept of nationhood. It is, however, problematic to equate Roman identity unquestioningly with the modern concept of nationhood, because modern terms like national and ethnic identity carry with them the baggage of associations with the modern contexts to which they belong. Nevertheless, reflecting on the continuities and discontinuities between ancient and modern concepts of group identities clarifies our understanding of both.

This study can be seen as only a partial explication of Roman identity in the *Aeneid*, because the scope of characters and passages considered here is limited and has led to inevitable biases in favor of some issues and omissions of others. The most glaring omission has been that of considering more Italian characters and generally of giving more attention to the second half of the poem. This focus has been a personal decision on my part and does not imply that the issues considered here have more relevance than the ones omitted. A study of Roman identity in the *Aeneid* that focuses on the parts I have neglected here would be a highly desirable addition to this study.

Notes

INTRODUCTION

1. Studies of ancient sexuality and the ancient self are often influenced by Foucault's *History of Sexuality* (Foucault [1980, 1985, 1986]), for instance: Halperin, Winkler, and Zeitlin (1990); Hallett and Skinner (1997); Larmour, Miller, and Platter (1998). In the last see esp. duBois (1998). For a discussion of Foucault's impact on Classics see Larmour, Miller, and Platter (1998, 22–23). On the ancient self see also Veyne (1987, 5–234, esp. 36–49, 68–69, 229–32, and 95–116).

2. There are, for instance, several studies of sexuality and the self in Catullus alone. A more literary focus is represented by W. Fitzgerald, *Catullan Provocations: Lyric Poetry and the Drama of Position* (Berkeley, 1995); a psychoanalytic approach by M. W. Janan, *When the Lamp Is Shattered: Desire and Narrative in Catullus* (Carbondale, 1994); and a feminist reading by M. B. Skinner, "Ego Mulier. The Construction of Male Sexuality in Catullus," *Helios* 20 (1993): 107–30.

3. See, for instance, Hall (1997), Gruen (1992), Sordi (1979).

4. Throughout this study I refer to the reader as male. I do this because the ancient sources are not interested in accounting for a separate female experience. They also always assume that readers are male. This does not mean that there were no female readers of the *Aeneid*. It does, however, mean that female readers entered the fictional world of the poem with the same gendered subject position as male readers.

5. On desire see Silverman (1983, 176): "Within the Lacanian account of subjectivity one other momentous event is linked to these others—to the inauguration of meaning, the loss of the real, the formation of the unconscious, and the entry into the symbolic—and that event is the birth of desire. Desire commences as soon as the drives are split off from the subject, consigned forever to a state of non-representation and non-fulfillment. In short, it begins with the subject's emergence into meaning. Desire has its origins not only in the alienation of the subject from its being, but in the subject's perception of its distinctness from the objects with which it earlier identified. It is thus the product of the divisions by means of which the subject is constituted, divisions which inspire in the subject

a profound sense of lack." On Lacan's notion of the symbolic order, the subject's acquisi-
tion of language as a signifying system see Silverman (1983, 166): "<Lacan> tells us that lan-
guage isolates the subject from the real, confining it forever to the realm of signification;
he indicates that the unconscious comes into existence at the moment of the subject's ac-
cess to language" and Belsey (1980, 65) (speaking of the Lacanian model of the subject):
"The unconscious is constructed in the moment of entry into the symbolic order, simul-
taneously with the construction of the subject."

6. On the gaze see Humm (1988), Kaplan (1983, 23–35) and the classic discussion of
Laura Mulvey from 1975.

7. W. R. Johnson (1976) has a penetrating and insightful discussion of the two main
schools of Vergilian criticism. See also the discussion of H.-P. Stahl (1981).

8. See Otis (1964) 41–97.

9. See Conte (1986) 164–214.

10. Putnam (1998), Barchiesi (1997), Fowler (1991).

11. Fowler (1990), (1991), (1997b).

12. Keith (2000) 111–19.

13. Feldherr (1998); see also Davidson (1991) on the gaze in Polybius' Histories.

14. Vasaly (1993).

15. See Stahl (1981, 1990), Galinsky (1988), E. Lefèvre (1989).

16. Lyne (1987) and (1989), Hexter (1990), (1992). Fowler (1990) explicitly states this
goal: "ultimately it seems to me that the strongest imperative is to preserve the challenge
of the *Aeneid*. (. . .) We can go through the *Aeneid* using switches of focalisation to remove
all moral challenge from the work, or we can go through creating problems rather than
solving them, making things more complex rather than less, confusing rather than clarify-
ing. My own preference for the latter procedure will be clear" (58).

17. See esp. Hexter (1994), Keith (2000) 8–35.

18. See T. Docherty (1983). On characterization in Vergil see Laird (1997).

CHAPTER I

1. Suet. *Gramm.* 16.

2. *Am.* 1, 15, 25; *Trist.* 2, 533–36.

3. On the Greek rhetorician Cestius Pius, imitating Vergil see Sen. Rhet. *Controv.*
7.1.27. On Arellius Fuscus see id. *Suas.* 3.4–5, 4.4–5. On Seneca discussing Vergilian imita-
tions for rhetorical instruction: *Suas.* 1.12 and on the poet Julius Montanus: Sen. Rhet. *fr.*
3 (= Donat. *Vita Vergili* 29).

4. On Pompeii see S. Ferraro (1982).

5. See Franklin (1991, 88), Kaster (1995, 257), Harris (1989, 261), Bonner (1977, 119–20,
214).

6. See Bonner (1977, 119–20). The school in question is in Rome.

7. See Kaster (1988, 45).

8. R. Cavenaile (1956). Fragments 1 to 9 are bilingual *Aeneid* passages; fragments 10 to
16 and 19, Latin *Aeneid* passages; fragments 17 and 18, passages from the *Georgics*.

9. See R. P. Hoogma (1959), and Heikki Solin, "epigrafia," in *Enc. Virg.*, vol. 2 (1985),
332–40.

10. Citroni makes a similar point about recitations and other forms of performance as
a means for reaching a broader audience than the literate elite. See M. Citroni, 1995, 21.

11. Comparetti's study of Vergil's influence in antiquity and the Middle Ages is still a

valuable source of information on the subject. Comparetti ([1885] 1997, 52, 71); see Horsfall (1995b) on *Aeneid* subjects in art. On recitations of the poem see Bonner (1977) 123–24; for the sixth century AD see Venant. Fort. *Carm.* 2.18, 7–8; 7.8, 26.

12. See G. Polara (1988). "sententiae Vergilianae," in *Enc. Virg.* 4, 772–76.

13. On recitals of epic in the first century AD see Markus (2000). On Quintilian's prescription of a virile style for epic recital see Markus (2000, 142–43) and below in this chapter.

14. Comparetti ([1885] 1997, 53–54).

15. On centos see R. Herzog, *Die Bibelepic der Lateinischen Spätantike I* (Munich, 1975; R. Lamacchia, "Dall' arte allusiva al centone," *A&R*, n.s., 3 (1958): 193–216.

16. On scholia see J. E. G. Zetzel, "On the History of Latin Scholia," *HSCPh* 79 (1975): 335–54; D. Daintree and M. Geymonat, "Scholia" in *Enc. Virg.*, vol. 4 (1988), 706–20; on Servius see Kaster (1988, 169–97).

17. On grammatical works see V. Lomanto, "Grammatici Minori," in *Enc. Virg.* 2, 788–90. On rhetorical works see L. C. Montefusco (1988). "Retori Latini Minori," *Enc. Virg.* 4, 460–62.

18. On the belief in late antiquity in Vergil as master of all areas of knowledge see W. Suerbaum, "Von den Vitae Vergilianae über die Accessus Vergiliani zum Zauberer Virgilius. Probleme, Perspectiven, Analysen," in *ANRW* 2.31.2, 1156–1262.

19. See Y. De Kisch, "Les Sortes Vergilianae dans l'histoire Auguste," *MEFRA* 82 (1970): 321–63; R. Ganszyniec, "De Sortibus Vergilianis," *Eos* 33 (1930–31) 179–86; H. A. Loane, "The Sortes Vergilianae," *CW* 21 (1928) 185–89.

20. On the social realities of Roman education see Bonner (1977). Kaster (1988) deals with the professionals of the Roman educational system. Keith (2000, 20–32) adduces the interpretation of *Aeneid* passages by Servius and Donatus as evidence for the modes of reading grammarians prescribed in reading and understanding the *Aeneid*. On the interpretive practices of the extant commentaries on Vergil see also Irvine (1994, 118–61).

21. See E. Kenney (1982, 7).

22. See Kaster (1988, 12–18). Quote from 14.

23. Comparetti ([1885] 1997); Courcelle (1984); Horsfall (1995b), Horsfall (1984); Tarrant (1997); Liversidge (1997); MacCormack (1998) on Augustine; Starr (1991) and (1992) on Donatus.

24. Kaster (1988, 24); Oros. *Adv. Pagan.* 1.81.1.

25. On education and provincial administration see D. Nellen (1977). On the Romanization of local elites see P. A. Brunt (1968). Note that recent scholarship on cultural change in the provinces of the Roman Empire has shifted its focus from the concept of Romanization, or the model of Roman ways being adopted by native populations as a one-way process, to a more interactive model that focuses on archaeological evidence for cultural change of native populations and their negotiation of native with Roman culture. See Wells (1999). On the usefulness to the empire of providing education see Bolgar (1954, 32–35); see comments on Bolgar's position in John Guillory, *Cultural Capital: The Problem of Canon Formation* (Chicago, 1993), 60–63. The idea that the Romans had a conscious policy of disseminating Latin throughout the empire goes back to Gibbon; see Farrell (2001, 2).

26. So also Farrell (2001, 7).

27. Farrell (2001, 1–8).

28. As is to be expected, Quintilian concerns himself with boys' education. Girls may have had similar training at this age, but this is not a subject that interests him.

29. For such data see the previous section.

30. See Webb (1997) and Tompkins (1980a).

31. Webb (1997, 113–14); her italics.

32. Quint. 1.11, 1 ff.; 2.10, 13; 11.34; Pliny *Epp.* 5.19, 3; *Rhet. ad Herenn.* 3.14, 24; see Bonner (1977, 224).

33. On Vergil's role in Augustine's thinking see MacCormack (1998). On Augustine as a reader of Vergil see also Stock (1996, 4, 28–31); on the *Aeneid*'s role in Augustine's *Confessions* see Bennett (1988).

34. So also O'Meara (1963, 257–58). For the influence of Vergil on Augustine see also Bennett (1988), Spence (1988, 55ff.), O'Donnell (1980, 166), Hagendahl (1967, 384–463), Marrou (1938, 18), Bassi (1930), Coffin (1923).

35. See for example Lact. *Div. Inst.* 5.10, where Aeneas' human sacrifice at the tomb of Pallas is compared to Christianity. On Lactantius' criticism of Vergil as well as Christian appropriations of Vergil see Wlosok (1983). Courcelle (1984) collects references to Vergil's writings in pagan and Christian authors.

36. Doniger O'Flaherty (1988) 37 (my italics).

37. Ovid refers to the Aeneas-Dido story as the most popular part of the *Aeneid* (*Trist.* 2.533–36). Later on, Lucian refers to the *Aeneid* as "the wanderings of Aeneas and Dido's love" (*The Dance* 46).

38. Quint. 6.ii.32–33, quoting *Aen.* 9.476, *Aen.* 11.40, *Aen.* 11.89, and *Aen.* 10.782.

39. The beginning of book 4 of the *Saturnalia* is missing. The first extant chapter of the book deals with the expression of emotion through description of outward appearance (*habitus*) in Vergil, but the chapter starts in the middle of the argument, and the speaker's identity is unclear.

40. See Meijering (1987, 14–38) on these terms. Φαντασία is discussed by Aristotle, but he does not use the term itself in his *Poetics* or his *Rhetoric*. On φαντασία in Aristotle see Modrak (1987, 81–110). In the *Poetics* Aristotle speaks of "πρὸ ὀμμάτων τίθεσθαι" (55a22–34). The term φαντασία is most prominently used in Ps.-Longinus' *On the Sublime* 15.1, where it is defined as visualization of the spoken word, but it is also extremely common in the Greek scholia generally. See Schlunk (1974, 41–42); Rispoli (1984); Lausberg (1990, 257, 3c; 811); Feeney (1991, 51–52). On εἰδωλοποιία, used since Aristotle, διατύπωσις, a term common in rhetorical handbooks, and ἐναργεία see Meijering (1987, 27–30), Lausberg (1990, 810). On *sub oculos subiectio* and *evidentia* see Quint. 9.2.40. On φαντασία see also Rosenmeyer (1986).

41. See also Scholion T on *Il.* 6.467 on the visuality of the scene between Hector, Andromache, and Astyanax. The bT-scholia (ad *Il.* 4.541) discuss another *Iliad* passage where an anonymous man is introduced as an instance of the poet creating an internal spectator of the battle scene he is describing. Commenting on the same passage, Eustathius (506.6–8) suggests that Homer is using the figure to represent the listener of the poet's performance who enjoys the spectacle of the war stories in his mind. For a discussion of these hints of intratextual audiences see I. J. F. de Jong, 1987, 58–60.

42. For the importance of the sublime in postclassical times see P. DeBolla, *The Discourse of the Sublime: Readings in History, Aesthetics and the Subject* (Oxford, 1989): S. H. Monk, *The Sublime: A Study of Critical Theories in XVIII Century England* (New York: 1935).

43. The dating of Dionysius' *Lysias* is uncertain, but it belongs to the Augustan period. *Sublimis* is also used in the present sense in Ov. *Am.* 1.15.23 and 3.1.39, which are roughly contemporaneous, although probably somewhat later.

44. Apart from Ps.-Longinus and Dionysius, the Greek terms occur in Plut. *Per.* 5 and Metrod. *Herc.* 831.8. Apart from Ovid (see above), *sublimis* and *sublimitas* occur in this sense in Quint. 1.8.5; 8.3.3, 6 and 74; 10.1.46 and 66; 11.1.3; 12.10.23 and 73. Plin. *Ep.* 1.10.5; 1.16; 4.20.3. Juv. 7.28; Mart. 9.77.3; and Fro. *Aur.* 2. 48 (114N).

45. The standard edition, which includes a commentary, is D. A. Russell, ed., 1964.

46. Aug. *Conf.* 1.13; Quint. 1.8.5.

CHAPTER 2

1. The earliest examples are Xenophanes and Theagenes of Rhegium in the sixth century BC. See Russell (1981, 19).

2. On these views see the discussion below on Strabo and the grammarians referred to by Sextus Empiricus.

3. See Plato, *Rep.* 10.605c6–7a10.

4. See Arist. *Poetics* 1449c2.

5. Vergil's literary debt to Lucretius, especially in the *Georgics,* is well known and amply documented. On Vergil's relationship with Philodemus see D. Sider (1995b, 43–44). On the Epicurean affiliations of Horace and other poets in Vergil's circle see the brief but helpful remarks by Sider (1995a, 37–38).

6. Asmis (1995, 26) calls the view that poetry is harmful one of the "fundamental tenets of Epicureanism." Epicurus himself is generally regarded as being particularly hostile to poetry, but evidence for this view is not straightforward. On reviewing the evidence, Asmis concludes that Epicurus rejected the idea that poetry can be useful for instruction, because no part of the traditional Greek education was useful as instruction on how to be happy, but that he probably welcomed it as entertainment. See E. Asmis (1995, 21). This article provides a fuller discussion of the issues addressed in my subsequent summary of the Epicurean position.

7. On love songs: *On Music* 4 col. vi 5–13 A. Neubecker (Napoli, 1986); on dirges: *On Music* 4 col. vi 13–18.

8. On Philodemus' criticism of poetry about the gods in *On Piety* see Obbink (1995b).

9. *Adv. Math.* 1.278–80.

10. The statement is taken from Philodemus' *On Poems,* book 5, ed. C. Jensen (Berlin, 1923, 33). On the attribution to Neoptolemus and Neoptolemus' theories of poetry in relation to those of Aristotle and Horace see Brink (1963, 43–150, esp. 128–29) on Neoptolemus' claim that the perfect poet must be useful as a flattening out of Aristotle's more sophisticated theory of *catharsis.*

11. See DeLacy (1948, 250–51).

12. Note, however, that DeLacy (1948) takes Strabo as a main informant for Stoic views of the effects of poems on the emotions or passions of the hearer. DeLacy discusses Strabo's evidence in the context of Stoic theories of the effects of sense perceptions of other art forms, like music and visual arts, on the emotions (249–51).

13. See DeLacy (1948, 269–70) for further references and a discussion of the evidence.

14. Williams, 1968, 31ff.

15. See Bonner (1977, 214–15) on Greek and Roman tragedy as part of reading in Roman school education. Martial pairs epic and tragedy as typical genres for the schoolmaster's work (8.3.13–16).

16. For the relationship between author and addressee in *De Rerum Natura* see also G. B. Conte (1994b).

17. Recent work on Lucretius and Epicurean poetics gives a much more nuanced account of the seeming contradiction of a poem about Epicurean philosophy. See Asmis (1995); Wigodsky (1995); Obbink (1995b); G. B. Conte (1994b).

18. On the Stoics' philosophical (as opposed to their philological) interest in poetry see Long, 1996, 44–57.

19. For epic and tragedy producing the same emotional effects see Arist. *Poetics* 1462b15; for the visuality of tragedy see ibid. 1462a9–12.

20. *Helen* 15–19.

21. On sense perceptions as part of the reasoning faculty see Long and Sedley (1987) (eds.), fragments 53G, H, M, S, 65U. On the passions and on the soul as composed entirely of reason see Long and Sedley section 65, esp. frg. 65G.

22. See Posidonius F 168 Edelstein and Kidd (L. Edelstein and I. G. Kidd, eds., *Posidonius I: The Fragments* [Cambridge, 1972]) = Galen, *De Placitis Hippocratis et Platonis* V 6.472–73 (p. 330, 6–21 DeLacy). P. DeLacy, ed., *Galeni De Placitis Hippocratis et Platonis libri I–V* (Berlin, 1978). On poetry as a cure for the irrational see A. A. Long, 1986, 220; L. Edelstein, 1966, 56–59.

23. See DeLacy (1948, 245–51).

24. I discuss this in more detail below.

CHAPTER 3

1. Juno's gaze and the reader's separation from it are discussed in chapter 4.

2. This fiction is shared by other Augustan poets. See for example Hor. *carm.* 3.1.2–4: *carmina non prius / audita, Musarum sacerdos, / virginibus puerisque canto*. See Barchiesi (1996, 12) and Feeney (1993, 55).

3. On *cano* and the voice of the narrator, see also Feeney (1991, 186) and Buchheit (1963, 13 with n. 8), which has a good bibliography on the narrator's presence and authority in the opening statements of ancient epics.

4. See Feeney (1991, 184–87) on the authority of Vergil's narrator in the *Aeneid* in contrast to the narrator in Apollonius Rhodius, who is constructed as much less knowledgeable.

5. See especially my discussion below of the bee simile.

6. See Williams (1983) on epitaphs (196ff.) and apostrophes (183ff.) in his section on the poet's voice (164ff.).

7. On the uses of the gaze and of eyes in the Vergilian corpus see Heuzé (1985, 540–79).

8. On the passive role of Aeneas in the sequence of *Aen.* 1.305–519 see Mackie (1988, 38).

9. On the visuality of the *Aeneid* in general see Johnson (1976, 75–99) and Bartsch (1998).

10. There are, of course, numerous other addressees of such speeches, e.g., Venus hearing Jupiter's prophecy in book 1, Dido hearing Aeneas' narrative of books 2 and 3, and Dido hearing Ilioneus' narrative of his crew's landing at Carthage in book 1. The latter, however, as we will see below, although addressed to Dido, also has Aeneas as an audience. Bibliography on the *ecphraseis* of the *Aeneid* abounds. The fullest and most recent contribution is Putnam (1998).

11. Segal (1981) covers some of the passages I discuss in this section, but he starts from very different premises, seeking to identify in the figure of Aeneas a multiplicity of voices similar to the poet's two voices as they are postulated by Parry (1963) and other pessimist

Vergil critics. He distinguishes between an "authorial" and a "participatory" voice of Aeneas (68), a dichotomy also postulated by Conte (1986, 175–82).

12. Only Servius and Hyginus tell us about Harpalyce. Otherwise, she is an obscure mythological figure whose claim to fame seems to depend entirely on Vergil. See Serv. ad loc. and Hyginus, *fab.* 193.

13. The image of the Spartan maiden is used without any concomitant description, as Harpalyce seems to require. It must have been quite well known to Vergil's readers that at Sparta women received physical education, which was elsewhere reserved for men. See Xen. *Lac.* 1.4; Plut. *Lyc.* 14; and Marrou (1956, 23).

14. Conventions of civilized society are often broken in myths set in Thrace. The brutal and barbaric Tereus, who raped, maimed, and imprisoned his wife's sister, is a king of Thrace (Ov. *Met.* 6.405ff.). Also, Aeneas encounters Thrace on his journey from Troy, and it is there that he is warned off from founding a city there by the shade of Polydorus, a son of Priam and ward of the Thracian king, whose greed and opportunism led him to kill Polydorus for the sake of Priam's gold (*Aen.* 3.13ff.).

15. It would be a Herculean labor to list all references in Vergilian scholarship that touch upon this topic. The most recent contribution, with further bibliography, is P. Hardie (1997). Much material can be found in the two commentaries on book 4, Pease (1935) and Austin (1955), but this represents only the tip of the iceberg. Fenik (1960) is perhaps the most focused study on the literary influence of tragedy on the *Aeneid*. See Wlosok (1976) for a good, critical discussion of the previous scholarship on this question.

16. E. L. Harrison (1972–73).

17. On the significance of hunting imagery in this scene see Lyne (1987, 194). On Venus as huntress in this scene see Dunkle (1973, 129–31).

18. Discussing the occurrence of the word *scaena* (*Aen.* 1.164) in the description of the African harbor (1.157ff.) and in the passage about Dido's dreams (*Aen.* 4.471), Harrison observes in a later article (1989) "that right from the start Vergil visualized Carthage as a stage on which a tragedy was about to be enacted" (5).

19. On this sequence and its effect on Aeneas see Hornsby (1970, 48–52). On the visuality of *Aen.* 1.418–519 see Quinn (1968, 76).

20. On the speeches of Aeneas in general see Highet (1972, 29–43, 72–81, 187–210), Feeney (1983).

21. See Bettini (1991, 197–240) on the cultural significance of bees in the Greek and Roman context: for the ancients, bees were an image of the souls of the just.

22. For *Aen.* 1.431–33 cf. *G.* 4.162–64, which varies somewhat from the *Aeneid* passage (underlined words are the same in both passages): *aliae spem gentis adultos / educunt fetus: aliae purissima mella / stipant et liquido distendunt nectare cellas. Aen.* 1.434–36 is the same as *G.* 4.167–69. See Briggs (1980), J. Griffin (1979), Lyne (1989, 7 n. 9).

23. According to *G.* 4.149–52 Jupiter gave the bees their ideal qualities as a reward for feeding him as an infant in the Dictaean Cave. Later on (*G.* 4.219ff.) the narrator refers to beliefs about the bees as having a share of divine intelligence. Starting from another *Aeneid* simile involving bees (*Aen.* 6.707–9), Bettini (1991, 198–202) has collected references to ancient popular beliefs about bees as an image of the souls of the just. This is particularly interesting, since the bee simile of *Aeneid* 6 compares to bees the souls of the dead who will be born as Aeneas' Roman descendants. Bettini's conclusions support my claim of the positive quality of the simile in *Aeneid* 1. For an opposing view on the passage see Lyne (1987), who states that "bees symbolized an ordered type of collective society in *Georgics* IV, but one which was not in all senses attractive" (7 n. 9). Lyne builds on the conclusions of

J. Griffin (1979), who interprets Vergil's description of the bees in the *Georgics* as ironic (63–65). See also Cairns (1989, 40 with n. 47) on the foundation of Carthage and the bee simile as characterizing Dido as a "good king." See Henry (1989, 189 n. 22) on the Homeric and Vergilian bee similes.

24. This passage has been discussed widely in recent scholarship. For Aeneas' subjective reading of the temple images see especially D. Clay (1988). See also R. D. Williams (1960b), Johnson (1976, 99–114), Segal (1981, 67–83), E. L. Harrison (1984), Lyne (1987, 209–10), O'Hara (1990, 35–39), Fowler (1991, 31–33), Bettini (1992, 197–200), Hexter (1992, 353ff.), Putnam (1998), Bartsch (1998).

25. *Aen.* 456–93, esp. 458, 471, 474–75, 479.

26. This parallel has also been observed by Knauer (1964, 166–67) and Du Bois (1982, 30).

27. On these parallels see Knauer (1964, 152–73), esp. 158–67.

28. On Aeneas' comment see Stanley (1965).

29. Cf. W. R. Johnson (1976, 103ff).

30. For *inanis* = "illusory" see OLD s.v. *inanis*, no. 11.

31. But see Johnson (1976, 104) for a different view: "There is nothing in the pictures to cheer Aeneas, and in fact he is not cheered. He deludes himself into feeling heartened because the realities he confronts are, literally, intolerable." So also Hexter (1992, 355): "Aeneas is a bad reader here."

32. Cf. Johnson (1976, 103).

33. For a similar interpretation of Aeneas' reaction to the images see Bettini (1992, 197–200), Klingner (1967, 396–400).

34. On the visuality of the *Aeneid* and Aeneas as spectator of it see Quinn (1968, 77–82). On its theatricality see Klingner (1967, 401–2).

35. *Aen.* 1.496–578.

36. *Aen.* 6.20–33. In 6.37 the images are called *spectacula*.

37. *Aen.* 6.703–887.

38. *Aen.* 8.626–728.

39. For a different view see Lyne (1987, 209), who argues that Aeneas "cannot (. . .) take heart" here because of his ignorance.

40. Another way of interpreting the address to the Roman would be to say that Anchises addresses Aeneas as a Roman. But even if we take it in this way, a Roman reader would still in some degree feel himself addressed by Anchises' words.

41. *Aen.* 2.567–88.

42. Austin's commentary (1964, 217–19) has a good discussion of the arguments adduced on both sides, and a bibliography of the scholarly debate surrounding the genuineness of the episode. For an account of the scholarly debate see Conte (1986, 196–207). See also see Büchner (1958, 1353–56). Goold (1970), Gransden (1985, 69–70).

43. See Austin 1964 ad loc., Williams 1972 ad loc., Conte (1986, 196–207).

44. Serv. *ad Aen.* 2.592: *turpe est viro forti contra feminam irasci.*

45. See the Servian preface (Rand 1946, 2, *Praef.*, lines 30–68). The passage is given as an example of the mode of editing followed by Varius and Tucca "*hac lege emendare, ut superflua demerent.*" This does not help us much, since the passage is not superfluous in the sense that the narrative does not need it to make sense.

46. This point is made by Leach (1999).

47. *Aen.* 6.20–33. On this passage see Du Bois (1982, 35–41), Fitzgerald (1984), Spence (1988, 38–42), Putnam (1995, 73–99), Miller (1995).

48. See also Henry (1989, 142).

49. See also ibid., 141–42.

50. On the affinities between Aeneas and Daedalus in this passage see the bibliography in Mackie (1988, 115 n. 1).

51. So also Hornsby (1970, 53).

52. For *Aen.* 4.657–58 cf. *Ecl.* 6.45–46; for *Aen.* 4.595–96 cf. *Ecl.* 6.47. For a discussion of these verbal echoes see below, chapter 4.

53. Book 5 presents a third kind of spectacle: games, the most visual and to the Roman audience most familiar spectacle, but there Aeneas is an agent, not a spectator.

54. Bettini (1992, 204–6) discusses this passage of Achilles Tatius as an important example of what he calls premonitory images. He connects it to other instances of narratives containing such images to establish precisely the kind of cultural pattern I suggest here. Bartsch (1989, 66–71) discusses the foreshadowing of events in this *ecphrasis* of Achilles Tatius in terms of reader response theory.

55. Greek text from the edition by J.-P. Garnaud (Paris, 1991); translated by J. J. Winkler, in: *Collected Ancient Greek Novels,* ed. B. P. Reardon (Berkeley, 1989).

56. Bettini (1992, 205).

57. *Aen.* 4.441–49.

58. See Bettini (1997).

CHAPTER 4

1. I have not attempted to give a complete list of instances of female subjectivity as spectacle. Other such instances include Venus, Juno, Juturna, Camilla, Allecto, the mother of Euryalus, Celaeno, and the Trojan women who burn their ships in Sicily. The most recent discussion of women in the *Aeneid* is Nugent (1999). See also Nugent (1992) on the Trojan women and Euryalus' mother.

2. On Amata see Fantham (1998).

3. On the snake iconography of the Furies in vase painting see 841–42 of H. Sarian, "Erinys," in *LIMC* 3.1 (Zurich, 1986), 825–43. One of Dido's dream images in *Aen.* 4.465–73, Orestes pursued by a Clytemnestra armed with torches and serpents in the company of the Furies, suggests that snakes were a component of the representation of the Furies on stage, as well.

4. Later on in book 7 Amata continues to put her madness on display for the reader's gaze. When she fails to dissuade Latinus from his resolve to marry Lavinia to Aeneas, she escapes with her daughter to the woods under the pretense of Bacchic rites, leading with her the matrons of Italy (7.385–405). Despite the vague and impressionistic depiction of Amata's Bacchic rites, the passage has spectacular quality in more than one way. It recalls scenes from Greek and Roman tragedy, especially Euripides' *Bacchae,* but also refers back to the Dido episode where Dido's madness is also pictured as Bacchic frenzy in a simile. Compare especially 7.376–77 (*tum vero infelix ingentibus excita monstris / immensam sine more furit lymphata per urbem*) with 4.300–302 (*saevit inops animi totamque incensa per urbem / bacchatur, qualis commotis excita sacris / Thyias*).

5. See Norden 1903, ad loc.

6. The earliest references to Eriphyle and her greed are Homer, *Od.* 11.326f.; 15.247; Soph. *Electra* 836ff. Pausanias describes a representation of the myth on the so-called chest of Cypselus in the Heraeum at Olympia, a lost artwork now commonly dated to the seventh or sixth century BC (Paus. 5.17.7f; see *LIMC* 1.1, 695: Amphiaraos 15). In archaic and

classical Greek art Eriphyle is often depicted with necklace in hand (see *LIMC* 1.1, 694 Amphiaraos 7, 8, 10, 19 for sixth-century BC vases of Eriphyle with necklace at the departure of Amphiaraos and *LIMC* 3.1, 843–46 Eriphyle I for fifth-century Attic vases of Eriphyle with necklace). The story is told in Diod. 4.65.5f; 9.41.2; Schol. *Od.* 11.326; Apollod. *Bibl.* 3.6.2.

7. On Eriphyle and Dido in the Underworld see Kraggerud (1965, 70) and Perret (1964, 249).

8. With regard to her death, Keith (2000) also discusses Dido as a spectacle for the reader's gaze (117). Keith makes the connection between the spectacular quality of female death in the *Aeneid* and the Roman taste "for spectacles like the arena" (121–22). The present discussion has a broader focus, looking at Dido's passion as a spectacle, of which her death is, of course, one part.

9. In addition to the points I made in chapter 3, mention should be made of Vergil's use of the word *scaena* in *Aen.* 1.164, to which Harrison (1989, 4–5) draws attention. Cf. ch. 3, n. 18.

10. On the banquet scene see Moles (1987, 153–54). On similarities of this scene with the banquets of Cleopatra in Lucan see Tucker (1975).

11. On the significance of light in book 1 see Otis (1964, 240f). Knight comments on the visuality of the banquet scene in his discussion of the beginning of book 2 (1967, 26). On the presence of gold in this scene see Crookes (1984).

12. Griffith (1985, 311).

13. On Cupid and Dido in this scene see the discussion of Johnson (1976, 36–45).

14. Later on in book 4 her gaze is again a spectacle expressing her inner life, e.g., in 4.362–64 (Dido rolls her eyes in anger at Aeneas) and 4.688–92 (Dido lifts her eyes to the sky in her death struggle). See Griffith (1985, 314). Williams (1983, 189) discusses another instance of Dido's gaze in book 4 when she sees the departure of the Trojans (409). The narrator addresses her at that moment, asking what she might feel at this sight. Williams recognizes a distance between the reader and Dido: They see the same thing, but the reader needs the narrator to explain Dido's reaction to the spectacle.

15. So also Farron (1980, 34).

16. My model of the reader's gaze differs from Hexter (1992, 336): "Vergil presents the figure of Dido from several perspectives not so that she thereby attains three-dimensionality but, on the contrary, in order to frustrate any attempt on the reader's part to see her as univocal and coherent. Vergil deflects the interpreter's *gaze* from this resolution-defying image to each of the multiple perspectives from which a focus would be possible, and thereby to the assumptions of the would-be interpreter" (my emphasis).

17. On Vergil's use in this passage of the passive voice as a Greek middle with retained accusative see Williams (1972) ad loc.

18. See DeWitt (1907) and (1930), Pease (1935, 5–11 and 30–47), Pöschl (1964, 141, 150, 167), Fenik (1960, 32–43, 168–77, 216–21), Camps (1969, 34–35), Hardie (1986, 269–71). Skepticism about the tragic qualities of Dido are expressed by Heinze (1928, 119) and Quinn (1963). Wlosok (1976) has a good discussion of the scholarship on this topic.

19. See especially Quinn (1968, 135ff.) and Wlosok (1976) for divisions of book 4 into acts. Harrison (1989), Moles (1984) and (1987), and Rudd (1976) discuss the Dido narrative in terms of the Aristotelian concept of *hamartia*. See also Duckworth (1957), Abel (1957–58), Harrison (1972–73), Foster (1973–74), Lefèvre (1978) and Muecke (1983). Harrison (1989) has a short bibliography (1 n. 2). Interestingly, Servius disagrees with modern critics when he refers to the "comic style" of book 4 (Serv. *ad. Aen.* 4 praef.). See Anderson (1981).

20. See Harrison (1972–73) and (1989, 11); Foster (1973–74).

21. See Williams (1971); Highet (1972, 220ff.); Foster (1973–74); Farron (1980, 38); Feeney (1983); Moles (1987, 157–58); Harrison (1989, 15–16). See also Wigodsky (1972, 93) on the influence of Roman republican drama on *Aeneid* 4. Williams (1971, 427) points out that in her reply to Aeneas in her second dialogue in the book, Dido uses words not so much to communicate, but "to satisfy her desire for venegeance." Much like her monologues, her present speech also serves to put her inner life on display.

22. See Lyne (1987) 45–49 on Dido's characterization in this part of *Aen.* 4.

23. Highet (1972, 23f) and Feeney (1983, 213) point out that in Homer dialogues with address and reply are very common, while in Vergil the ratio of monologues to dialogues decidedly tilts the other way. Note also that of the eight soliloquies Highet counts in the *Aeneid,* three are in the second half of *Aeneid* 4.

24. See also Harrison (1989, 5), Foster (1973–74, 37).

25. See pp. 97–98 and p. 103.

26. Cairns (1989, 129–50) discusses Dido in the context of the elegiac tradition, comparing her character to the elegiac lover.

27. On Juno see below in this chapter.

28. Similar scenes in Greek tragedy include Deianeira's suicide in Sophocles' *Trachiniae* and Alcestis' death in Euripides' *Alcestis.* Such allusions to tragedy again underscore the spectacular quality of the narrative. See Harrison (1989, 20).

29. See also Lyne (1987, 47–48).

30. On the colors and visuality of this passage see the discussion of Johnson (1976, 68–72).

31. See Griffith (1985), esp. 313 where he discusses the color of Dido's hair.

32. Dunkle (1973, 133–36) discusses this hunting scene in the larger context of the hunting imagery and motifs of books 1 and 4 of the *Aeneid.*

33. On the appropriateness of Dido's attire for the occasion see the remarks of Thornton (1985, 620).

34. See Griffith (1985, 314–15).

35. On the imbalance between Dido and Aeneas see Farron (1980, 34–35). Otis (1964, 265ff.) and Williams (1983, 43ff.) discuss why the focus of *Aen.* 4 is on Dido rather than Aeneas. Feeney (1983) discusses Aeneas' taciturnity in *Aen.* 4 and Aeneas' words to Dido in 4.333–61 (204–10). On the characterization of Aeneas in *Aen.* 4 see also Mackie (1988, 11–14 and 77–93).

36. On this point see also the discussion of Cairns (1989, 50).

37. See Lyne (1987, 161ff.). But Lyne (1987, 196) claims that the deer simile (*Aen.* 4.69–73) implies that Aeneas courted and pursued Dido "in the hunt of love." This idea is repeated in Lyne (1989, 77–79). The hunting shepherd who wounds the deer in the simile, however, is called *nescius:* he wounds the deer unknowingly, which strongly argues against Lyne's interpretation of the simile (my thanks go to Mark Griffith for this observation).

38. *Aen.* 1.498–502. See Pöschl (1964, 126–27). The Homeric precedent of *Od.* 6.106 is at least partly the reason for Latona's presence here. Williams (1983, 61–62) discusses the multiple correspondence of this simile with its context. Stating that Vergilian similes differ from Homeric similes in lacking nonfunctional details, Williams argues that Latona's joy at beholding Diana suggests to the reader Aeneas' joy at seeing Dido, an element otherwise unexpressed in the text. But Aeneas' relationship to Dido is so different from Latona's to Diana that I think Williams' suggestion is far-fetched. Maternal pride and incipient male desire are very different kinds of *gaudia.* See also Mackie (1988, 38–39).

39. Austin ad loc. leaves the ambiguity unsolved. But see Williams (1983, 43), Lyne (1987, 163), Cairns (1989, 50), and Harrison (1989, 21), who assert that it is Aeneas' love.

40. Williams (1983, 183) argues that they must be Aeneas' tears, because the tears correspond to the falling leaves in the tree simile in *Aen.* 4.441–46. But the narrator repeatedly refers to Dido's and Anna's words as *fletus* (437 and 439) and says that Aeneas is not moved by them. It appears therefore that the tears that fall in vain might very well be Dido's or Anna's.

41. On the allusion to Catullus 66.39 ("*Invita, o regina, tuo de vertice cessi*") see Austin (1977, 164), Wigodsky (1972, 127), Tatum (1984), Skulsky (1985), Conte (1986, 88–90). For further bibliography see Skulsky (1985, 447 n. 2).

42. Lyne (1987, 167–75 and 177–79) calls Vergil's characterization of Aeneas in his relationships with Dido and Creusa "the 'too late' phenomenon."

43. Of course, the formulation I use here runs the risk of treating Dido and Aeneas as real people, when all we can observe is the text's reticence. On the lack of characterization of Aeneas during his love affair with Dido see Lyne (1987, 161ff.) and Mackie (1988, 81ff.). See also Griffith (1985, 316).

44. So also Cairns (1989, 50): "Virgil obviously wanted to avoid suggesting that Aeneas felt love for Dido, at least until his 'love' was in the past and so no longer a threat to the fates. Once the danger has receded, however, Aeneas' rejection of temptation can be enhanced by hinting at the strength of his feelings."

45. Pöschl (1970, 158) observes a pattern of gender differentiation in the construction of subjecthood in the *Aeneid:* "Während Aeneas sich aufgeben muss, hat Dido ihr wahres Selbst in der Liebe gefunden: hier ist ein anderer Urgegensatz zwischen Mann und Frau Gestalt geworden." Pöschl is talking about essential differences between man and woman, but his observation as to the text is quite in line with my own argument.

46. See Bettini (1997), Putnam (1995, 56–59), West (1983), Grimm (1967), Otis (1964, 260–61) on this episode. See also Williams (1983, 274–75), Wiltshire (1989, 75).

47. So also Wiltshire (1989, 43).

48. The theatricality of this scene is also stressed by Bettini (1997, 13).

49. Andromache has been interpreted as a foil for Aeneas by many critics. See Bettini (1997, 30), Quint (1989, 14–31), West (1983, 259), DiCesare (1974, 67–68), Grimm (1967, passim), Saylor (1970, 26–28).

50. On Helenus see Grimm (1967, 152), Putnam (1995, 57–59). On Helenus' prophecies see O'Hara (1990, 26–34). On Helenus and Andromache as representing public and private spheres respectively see Wiltshire (1989, 111–12).

51. The best account of Vergil's Juno is by Feeney (Feeney, 1991, 129–37 and 146–51). See also Lieberg (1966), Coleman (1982, 149–53), Thornton (1976), Camps (1969, 41–50), Bailey (1935, 130–32), Buchheit (1963). For Juno as personification, e.g., Turnus' fear in book 12 see G. Williams (1983, 29–30). On Juno's motivations in book 1 and the symbolic nature of her actions see also Otis (1964, 227–29). On Juno in *Aen.* I 1.86 see also Kühn (1971, 11–17). On Vergil's gods as a literary failure see Coleman (1982, 164): "the gods of the Hellenized literary-religious tradition . . . were not capable of bearing the serious burden of causation that Vergil placed upon them. Better to have swept away all the divine personalities and replaced them with more abstract beings . . ."

52. On Carthage and its significance in the Romans' historical imagination see further my discussion in chapter 6.

53. This inside look at the emotional life of Vergil's characters has been commented on since Heinze (1928), who refers to it as Vergil's *Empfindung;* Otis refers to it as Vergil's *em-*

pathy, Conte as his *emphatheia.* On Juno's desire and her subjecthood see also Spence (1988, 22ff.).

54. Pöschl (1950, 15) also stresses Juno's desire, rather than her anger, as the driving force of the epic narrative.

55. See Feeney, who refers to the Greeks equating Hera with the Punic Tanit (1991, 116–17); Hexter (1992) and Buchheit (1963).

56. On this connection see Feeney (1991, 130–34); see also Otis (1964, 227–29); Lieberg (1966, 151–53); Buchheit (1963, 20–22).

57. On Dido's desire see my discussion below.

58. So also Knight (1967, 272–73): "There is a difficulty in seeing what the personality of Juno means, and why a goddess, honoured at Rome, should be so hostile. The answer is that Juno is fiercely *feminine.* She was not among the principal early deities of Rome, and was never one of the greatest. Rome worshipped male gods first; Rome began, because Juno acknowledged defeat" (my italics).

59. So also Pöschl (1950, 18), who calls Juno a divine symbol of the demonic forces of violence and destruction. See also Putnam (1965, 166–67 and 200–201); Johnson (1976, 13–15); Klingner (1967, 387).

60. See Putnam (1995, 32).

61. On *genus invisum* see chapter 8.

62. On the visuality of this passage see Quinn (1968, 100–101). On Vergil's use of "*laetus*" see Lyne (1989, 181–82), Henry (1989, 157–63).

63. *Aen.* 1.27–28: *iudicium Paridis spretaeque iniuria formae / et genus invisum et rapti Ganymedis honores.*

CHAPTER 5

1. Servius (ad loc.) takes *tacitum* to refer to Allecto, and most commentators follow this suggestion. See Fordyce (1977) and Williams (1973) on 7.343, but Page (1900) takes it literally with *limen* and explains that the threshold is calm because Amata nurses still her cares in silence.

2. *Aen.* 1.37–75. On this and the following speeches of Juno see Highet (1972, 161–64) and 266–67); on Juno's characterization through her voice see Lyne (1987, 49–53).

3. On the voice as another building block of the self in ancient thinking see my discussion below.

4. *Aen.* 1.36–49.

5. On Minerva see Henry (1989, 101–2).

6. On the sea storm as an expression of Juno's inner life see also Hardie (1986, 229).

7. Aside from the proem, cf. 1.36–37: "*cum Iuno aeternum servans sub pectore vulnus / haec secum*" and 1.50: "*talia flammato secum dea corde volutans.*"

8. On the development of Juno's actions throughout the epic see Della Corte (1983).

9. I cannot agree with Lieberg (1966), who sees a gradual development of Juno's feelings from hateful in book 1 to reconciled in book 12.

10. It is Venus who senses the purpose of Juno's proposal (cf. 4.105–6: "*sensit enim simulata mente locutam, / quo regnum Italiae Libycas averteret oris*").

11. For Juno and the other gods of the *Aeneid* as characters in their own right like the human characters see Feeney (1991). For a more symbolic or figurative reading of Vergil's gods see Williams (1983) and Coleman (1982).

12. Keith (2000, 112–16) has arrived at similar conclusions in her discussion of this clus-

ter of passages. On wounds in the Dido narrative see also Ferguson (1970, 61–63). Newton (1957, 38) discusses the verbal echo of the phrase *sub pectore vulnus* with reference to Dido.

13. See also Moorton (1989–90) on the assimilation of love wound and death wound in this passage.

14. See Fenik (1960, iiif.), Pöschl (1964, 119f.), Klingner (1967, 462f.), Wlosok (1976, 246–48).

15. See Moorton (1989–90, 164–66) on the Underworld scene as part of the metaphorical sequence of love and death in the Dido narrative. On the *Lugentes Campi* see Perret (1964), Kraggerud (1965), Lefèvre (1978), West (1980), Tatum (1984).

16. See Austin 1955 on *primus*.

17. See Austin 1955 on the discussion surrounding this line.

18. On Dido's hesitation here see Segal (1990).

19. See Austin 1955.

20. For this interpretation see Wlosok (1976, 246–47).

21. *Aen.* 4.494–98 and 508.

22. So Austin 1955. It could be his armor, too.

23. On this sword see Bradley (1958), Basto (1984), and Harrison (1989, 18–20).

24. So also Quinn (1968, 148).

25. On such sympathetic magic see Pinch 1994, 90–95. Bettini (1992) traces cultural patterns attached to images of the beloved in Greco-Roman antiquity. See especially Bettini (1992, 12–16) on Laodamia and her wax image of her dead husband.

26. *Aen.* 6.447. See Lyne (1987, 49) for Dido's death recalling Euadne. He suggests that Dido's death recalls the Suttee, an Indian ritual where the widow kills herself on the funeral pyre of her husband. That this ritual was known to the Romans of Vergil's time can be seen from a poem of Propertius that deals with it at length (3.13). See also Kraggerud (1965, 70), Perret (1964, 252).

27. Eur. *Suppl.* 980–1122: Euadne and Capaneus; Hyg. 104: Laodamia and Protesilaus.

28. Cf. Plaut. *Pseud.* 4.7.80 and 84, Ov. *Am.* 1.9.25f., and Prop. 1.3.16 for *arma* as phallus. The erotic connotations of the military language in this passage have been discussed by Lyne (1987, 20–23). See also Keith (2000, 104): "Female death is pervasively sexualized in Latin Epic"; Moorton (1989–90, 162–64), Gillis (1983, 49–51). For a different view of the scene see Harrison (1989, 19–20): "As for the irony of letting Dido's suicide weapon be the gift of someone who is now her enemy (. . .), that recalls Ajax's similar employment of a sword once given to him by Hector in an exchange of gifts after their inconclusive duel (Sophocles *Ajax* 815f., cf. *Il.* 6. 303ff.)."

29. *Aen.* 4.67 and 689.

30. As Dido joins Sychaeus after running from Aeneas, it is possible to consider him an inhabitant of the *Lugentes Campi* (see Hexter [1994, 18–21], following Serv. *in Aen.* 6.444). The presence of the masculine pronoun *quos* in *Aen.* 6.442 also allows for the possibility that men *and* women inhabit the *Lugentes Campi* (*hic quos durus amor* . . .). Since Sychaeus' death is recounted in book 1 as murder at the hands of Pygmalion, I prefer to take Sychaeus' presence to be motivated solely by Dido (on Sychaeus see also Dyck [1983]). Another figure to consider in this context is the gender-ambivalent Caeneus, who was once a woman, then a man, and is now, in death, once again a woman.

31. For a discussion of this line in terms of gender hierarchies and their endorsement by *Aeneid* commentators see Keith (2000, 23–26). Even Juno, though immortal, can be seen in this light, since she changes her mind when she surrenders to Jupiter and Fate in book 12—unlike Jupiter.

32. See also Cairns (1989, 43ff.).

33. *Aen.* 4.683f. See Farron (1980, 39–40), Newton (1957, 32–37).

34. The relationship of Catullus' Ariadne and Vergil's Dido has been analyzed by Oksala (1962) and Kilroy (1969). On the following verbal parallels see Oksala (1962, 187) and Kilroy (1969, 56).

35. Cf. also Latinus' breakdown and question in *Aen.* 12.37: "*Quo referor totiens? Quae mentem insania mutat?*"

36. *Aen.* 6.447.

37. For echoes of Circe in the Dido narrative see Knauer (1964, 175–80).

38. Elsewhere he is called Mutto or Mettes: Cf. Serv. *ad Aen.* 1.343; Just. 18.4.3. For the identification of Baal with Helios/Sol see Ov. *Heroid.* 1.7; Cic. *de nat. deor.* 3.16.42; Serv. *ad Aen.* 1.642 and *ad Aen.* 1.729; Dio Cass. 79.8.5; Diod. 2.9.4; Timaeus (*Fragmente der Griechischen Historiker,* ed. F. Jacoby, (Leiden 1957), 566 F 82); Herodotus 1.181f. and 3.158.

39. On the instability of the female subject in the *Aeneid* see also Keith (2000, 26).

40. See Bettini (1997), who speaks of "*an excess of identity*" in the inhabitants of *parva Troia.*

41. See Putnam (1965, 158–60); Johnson (1976, 56–58); Todd (1980); Lyne (1987, 114–22); Lyne (1989, 80–82).

42. See Lewis and Short 1879, s.v. *violo.*

43. Lyne (1987, 119–21) connects Lavinia's blush with Dido's wounds.

44. R. Heinze (1928, 460) comments on Lavinia's silence in a chapter on "simplification of the narrative" (subsection "Vereinfachung" in a chapter "Komposition"). As a minor character, he says, Lavinia cannot occupy a prominent position in the narrative, since this would distract from the main line of narrative. This argument is circular. Quinn (1968, 256 n. 2) argues that Lavinia doesn't speak because in Vergil's day young brides were used to seal political alliances with marriages. He also discusses why Lavinia blushes and suggests that she might be longing for a husband. Lyne (1989, 79–80) explains Lavinia's silence differently. He dismisses the possibility that Lavinia is silent because she doesn't have an opinion on the topic of her future husband (he finds this unlikely). Rather, Vergil silences Lavinia because her love for Turnus, the enemy of Aeneas, is a topic too sensitive to be discussed openly in epic. On Lavinia in the context of lyric discourse see Cairns (1989, 151–76).

CHAPTER 6

1. Keith (2000, 49–50) develops a similar argument about Lavinia. On Lavinia see also Woodworth (1930), Cairns (1989, 151–76). For a helpful narratological study of the effects of "focalization" of the action through silent characters see I. J. F. de Jong (1987). "Silent characters in the *Iliad,*" in J. M. Bremer and I. J. F. de Jong (eds.). *Homer: Beyond Oral Poetry. Recent Trends in Homeric Interpretation* (Amsterdam), 105–21.

2. *Aen.* 1.2.258, 270; 4.236; 6.84.

3. *Aen.* 6.764; 7.72, 314, 359; 11.479; 12.17, 64, 80, 194, 605, 937.

4. For the context of archaic Greece, similar observations have been made by Carol Dougherty (1993). See also the more general remarks of H. Cixous in *Sorties (La Jeune née,* Paris, 1975), 115f.

5. On Creusa see Hughes (1997), Gall (1993), Perkell (1981).

6. Creusa is a name applied to quite a few princesses in mythology. In Euripides' *Medea,* Creusa is the daughter of the king Creon. Thus the main characters of this play are

Jason, Medea, The King, and The Princess. In Euripides' *Ion,* Creusa is The Queen (of Athens) and mother of Ion. Again, the names convey something of the allegorical significance of the characters.

7. *Aen.* 7.71–80.

8. See Gruen (1992, 6–51), especially 11, 16.

9. See, for instance, Livy 1.ix.6–16.

10. On marriage as a cultural metaphor of the confrontation between Greeks and native populations in Greek colonial discourse see Dougherty (1993, 61–80), esp. 63f. on the figurative equation of marriage and plowing, which implies an equation of woman with land; and 65–67 on Greek city foundation narratives figuring the foundation of a city as erotic conquest (either rape or marriage). Quint (1993, 28–29), discussing the Actium scene on the shield of Aeneas, observes the equation of gender opposition with the opposition of East and West in the Augustan discourse about Cleopatra and sees this pattern repeated in other seductive oriental heroines in epic such as Angelica, Armida, and Milton's Eve.

11. See Dougherty (1993, 69), referring to Kolodny (1975, 5). On North America as "feminized landscape," controlled by an imperial, male gaze see Parker (1987, 151). Keith discusses the feminization of the land in the *Aeneid* within the Roman epic tradition, linking Mars' rape of Ilia in Ennius with her son Romulus' political mastery of the same land (2000, 44–50).

12. Pocahontas' story is told by John Smith in his 1624 account *The General History of Virginia, New England, and the Summer Isles.* The English dramatist Jonson introduces her in his 1626 comedy *The Staple of News* (II.i.). In Thackeray's *The Virginians* the character George Warrington (born in Virginia, but his parents are English aristocrats) writes a tragedy about her.

13. The quote is from a letter of Crane to Otto Kahn, dated September 12, 1927. See Hammer, L. and B. Weber, eds., 1997. *O my land, my friends: The selected letters of Hart Crane.* New York. 345. For *The Bridge* see Crane, H. 1930. *The bridge: a poem.* New York.

14. See also Quint (1993, 29).

15. See, for instance, the criticisms of Muecke (1983, 136 n. 12) and Vicenzi (1985).

16. Here I particularly refer to the interpretation of Dido as an embodiment of the ideals of *humanitas.* See especially Monti (1981, passim, esp. 18–24); Klingner (1967, 398–400); Büchner (1958, 1345); Pöschl (1964, 95); Quinn (1948, 107); Heinze (1928, 139); Klingner (1965c, 723); Clausen (1987, 26); Otis (1964, 269f.).

17. R. Hexter (1992, 360).

18. See Vicenzi (1985, 105), Burck (1943, 341). Rudd (1986, 38) comes to a similar conclusion, but his arguments are too cursory.

19. See also Horsfall (1973–74) 1, Hexter (1992, 344–46), Prandi (1979, 90–97), Burck (1943, 301–14, 319–26, 330, 333–34, 341–44).

20. See Horsfall (1973–74), Vicenzi (1985), Harrison (1984) for other discussions of the role of Carthage in the *Aeneid.*

21. Burck (1943, 338), Brisson (1969, 164), Wigodsky (1972, 29), Williams (1983, 73 and 140).

22. But note that Feeney (1984) and Horsfall (1973–74) see Jupiter's promise of Juno's reconciliation with the Romans as a reference to the placation ceremonies held in Rome during the Second Punic War.

23. Feeney (1984, 180) and Horsfall (1973–74, 3).

24. Horsfall (1973–74, 1), Harrison (1984, 103).

25. Harrison (1984, 110).

26. On the Cleopatra resonances of the Dido episode see my discussion below, chapter 7.

27. See *ad Her.* 3.2.2 and Cic. *de inv.* 1.11 and 1.17. Other references to the Punic Wars in *ad Her.*: 3.4.8; 4.13.19, 20; 4.27.37; 4.32.43; 4.33.45; 4.53.66.

28. *Ad Her.* 3.2.2; Cic. *de inv.* 1.17.

29. Cic. *Phil.* 11.9; 14.9; 5.25–27. On historical exempla in Cicero's speeches see Schoenberger (1910).

30. See, e.g., *de off.* 3.99ff. (the story of Regulus). In *De officiis* historical examples are often taken from the Punic Wars (e.g., 1.11.35; 1.12.38; 1.13.39, 40; 1.23.79; 1.26.90; 1.30.108; 1.33.121; 2.22.76; 3.1.1–4; 3.4.16; 3.11.47).

31. *Cato Maior de Senectute* and other philosophical works, e.g., *Tusculan disputations* and *De Re Publica.*

32. Cf. Sall. *Cat.* 10 and *Hist.* frg. 11, 12.

33. See also Livy's narrative of the Punic Wars, esp. the battle of Cannae.

34. *Carm.* 1.12.37–38; 2.12.2–3; 3.5.13–56; 3.6.34–36; 4.4.37–76; 4.8.16–19; *epod.* 7.5; 9.25; 16.8; *serm.* 2.1.17, 66, 72.

35. See Burck (1943), Horsfall (1973–74), Prandi (1979), Hexter (1992). Cunning and untrustworthiness: *ad Her.* 4.13.20, 4.53.66; Cic. *de inv.* 1.71; *de off.* 1.38, 108; *de har. resp.* 19; *pro Scauro* 42; Sall. *Jug.* 108.3; Livy 22.22.15, 30.24.5–12, 30.25, 21.4.9, 30.20. Cruelty: *ad Her.* 4.13.20; Cic. *Phil.* 11.9, 14.9; *de nat. deor.* 3.80; *de rep.* 3.15; *de off.* 1.38, 3.100; *Lael.* 28; Livy 21.4.9, 23.5.12; Hor. *carm.* 3.6.36, 4.4.42; Juv. 7.161.

36. *de off.* 1.38.

37. *de leg. agr.* 2.95.

38. For human sacrifice see Cic. *de rep.* 3.15.

39. Cic. *Lael.* 28; *de off.* 1.38, 108; *de div.* 1.48; *Phil.* 5.25f.; Livy 21.4.5–9.

40. Cic. *Sest.* 142; *de or.* 1.210, Livy 21.4.5–9; 22.52.6; 27.28.2.

41. Many of the points I raise in the following section are mentioned by Horsfall (1973–74), but in the light of the complexity of Dido's character and the fact that Horsfall's assessment of Dido has not been met with general acceptance, a fuller discussion of various single points is necessary to make a successful argument about Dido's association with Carthaginian stereotypes.

42. See esp. Williams (1983, 20–35), Quinn (1968, 316–20), Lyne (1987, 66–71).

43. Feeney (1991, 164–76).

44. See Williams (1983, 29–31). *Aen.* 10.645–88 and 12.138–60, 216–382, 446–680.

45. Knauer (1964, 152–56) discusses the Homeric parallels for this passage, but he does not spell out the parallels listed here. He compares Jupiter's intervention at the end of his dialogue with Venus to the dream Athena sends to Nausikaa.

46. *Od.* 6.13–43.

47. See Horsfall (1973–74, 4), Moles (1987, 153), Muecke (1983, 151–52).

48. Euander has previous ties of hospitality to Anchises (*Aen.* 8.154ff.).

49. So also Horsfall (1973–74). On gold in *Aeneid* 1 see Crookes (1984).

50. Cf. *Aen.* 7.192–285.

51. *Od.* 14, 287–98: Odysseus tells Euryalus a lying story about his wanderings, meeting a *cunning, untrustworthy, evil* Phoenician who is a *rich trader* and seafarer. See also the beginning of Herodotus' *Histories*, which are referred to by Horsfall (1973–74).

52. *Od.* 8, 159–64. On this passage see Bettini (1996, xli).

53. See *Aen.* 4.36, 211–14.

54. *Aen.* 4.36ff.

55. On these see Harrison (1989, 6).

56. Serv. *ad Aen.* 1.367. See also Justin 18.9.9; Livy 34.62.11f. Austin 1971 (ad loc.) adds that the name *Byrsa,* the Greek word for "bull's hide," was the Greek version of "the Phoenician name for the citadel of Carthage, Bosra."

57. *Aen.* 1.350–52: *clam . . . incautum, celavit, simulans . . . lusit.*

58. *Aen.* 1.350: *securus amorum germanae.*

59. *Aen.* 1.361: *odium crudele tyranni.*

60. *Aen.* 1.494–508.

61. On this speech see Monti (1981, 10–11 and 24).

62. Muecke (1983, 152) discusses Ilioneus' speech and Mercury's earlier intervention in the context of dramatic irony.

63. Divine intervention is often treated by scholars as an allegory for human motivation. Often it is possible to view it in this way, but the present passage does not fit into this mold. Significantly, Williams (1983, 17–39) does not discuss this important passage at all, although he argues at length that the gods in the epic are used as tropes (for authorial interventions, for human motivation, or for reconciling free will and determinism). Heinze (1928, 331, n.1) discusses Mercury's intervention as superfluous, because Aeneas' friendly reception in Carthage can be explained in human terms. See Otis (1964, 225–27 and 377–79), Thornton (1976), Feeney (1991, 129–87).

64. *Aen.* 1.661. On Venus' evaluation of the Tyrians see also Horsfall (1973–74, 5). Foster (1973–74) argues that Venus has motives for causing Dido's downfall other than the ones stated here. He sees the royal house of Tyre as having offended Venus and therefore being persecuted by her in the manner of the house of Atreus.

65. On this dialogue and Anna's role in Dido's story see Moles (1987, 154–55), Harrison (1989, 11–13), Foster (1973–74, 35–36), Daviault (1991, 185–86). Horsfall (1973–74) lacks a discussion of this dialogue in light of Punic stereotypes, and I have not found another such discussion elsewhere. Note that the speech addressed to Cleopatra in the *Carmen de bello Actiaco* (col. iii ed. Courtney) bears a certain resemblance to Anna's speech here.

66. Harrison (1989, 12) stresses the grave consequences of breaking vows "in the context of Roman epic, where sanctions of Roman religion operate."

67. *Aen.* 4.305, 366, 373.

68. *Aen.* 4.307, 316, 324.

69. *Aen.* 4.305f.

70. *Aen.* 4.308, 311.

71. Horsfall (1973–74, 5–6) discusses Dido's accusations against Aeneas and Dido's own duplicity and treachery in the context of Roman stereotypes about Carthaginians.

72. On Dido's appeal to the right hand of Aeneas "as a claim on *fides*" see Monti (1981, 1–8).

73. Apoll. Rh. *Arg.* 4.1111ff. See especially Feeney's discussion of this question in 1983, who also lists previous scholarship.

74. *Aen.* 4.165–68.

75. For a discussion of the issue of Dido's marriage to Aeneas and for bibliography on this question see Cairns (1989, 46–49). According to Moles (1987, 155–59), lines 221, 338–39, and 550–51 of book 4 confirm that Dido is not married to Aeneas. It may be of interest to consider Ovid's assessment of the question who calls Dido's affair with Aeneas "*non legitimo foedere iunctus amor*" (*Trist.* 2.536).

76. *Aen.* 4.338f.

77. *Aen.* 4.317, 323. On Aeneas' reply to Dido see also Monti (1981, 42–44). On Aeneas as *hospes* see Gibson (1999).

78. So also Pöschl (1964, 47).

79. *Aen.* 4.382–87.

80. See Heinze (1928, 136f. with note 2) on curses of disappointed lovers. See also Pease (1935, ad 586, 590, and 629) and Clausen (1987, 53).

81. Cruelty: 4.308, 311; betrayal: 4.305, 366, 373; breaking of marriage vows: 4.307, 316, 324; deceit: 4.305–6.

82. Cf. *Aen.* 4.451.

83. *Aen.* 4.476–98.

84. *Aen.* 4.634–40.

85. *Aen.* 4.675: *me fraude petebas?*

86. *Aen.* 4.552: *non servata fides cineri promissa Sychaeo.*

87. *Aen.* 4.563: *illa dolos dirumque nefas in pectore versat.*

88. *Aen.* 4.590–629.

89. On this curse see Murgia (1987, 52–54), who shows that all of Dido's wishes articulated in this curse come true, although not always in the manner she intended.

90. Cic. *Lael.* 28; Livy 21.4.9; Hor. *carm.* 3.6.361, 4.4.42; Juv. 7.161.

91. See my discussion above and Farron (1980, 39–40), Hardie (1986, 282–84), Newton (1957, 32–37).

92. See Horsfall (1973–74) 129, Fraenkel (1954) 157f. These overtones of Rome's sack of Carthage resurface again in one of Dido's later speeches, in which she asks Anna to beg Aeneas to delay his departure. In this speech Dido calls Aeneas *hostem superbum* (4.424) and herself *victam* (434).

93. Artemid. 1.78.

94. Artemid. 1.78: "To have sexual intercourse with a woman with whom one is familiar and on intimate terms . . . is auspicious for him, whenever the woman is well-to-do. At all events, the man will derive some profit . . . . For it is quite natural that a woman who freely gives her body to someone would also give her possessions to him" (tr. R. J. White [1975], *The Interpretation of Dreams: Oneirocritica by Artemidorus* [Park Ridge]). See Foucault's famous discussion of sexual hierarchies in Artemidorus in Foucault (1986, 4–36).

95. *Aen.* 9.266 (Ascanius offers a bowl from Dido to Nisus for his bravery); 11.72–75 (Aeneas covers Pallas' body with robes he had from Dido). On these see Murgia (1987, 53), who sees Dido's gifts in the later books as reminders of Dido's curse monologue. Farron (1980, 36–37) sees them as a reminder of Dido's love for Aeneas. See also Baker (1980, 140–41).

96. *Aen.* 1.647–55, 709, 714.

97. Compare *Aen.* 4.262–64 (*Tyrioque ardebat murice laena / demissa ex umeris, dives quae munera Dido / fecerat, et tenui telas discreverat auro*) with *Aen.* 11.72–75 (*tum geminas vestis auroque ostroque rigentis / extulit Aeneas, quas illi laeta laborum / ipsa suis quondam manibus Sidonia Dido / fecerat et tenui telas discreverat auro*).

98. Note that Juno, too, is cast as an amatory loser in the proem, where her fierce hatred of the Trojans is partially motivated by her jealousy of Jupiter's mistress Electra, the mother of Trojan Dardanus (expressed in the phrase *genus invisum* in *Aen.* 1.28), and of Jupiter's boy lover, the Trojan Ganymede. Her anger at Paris' judgment of the three goddesses' beauty contest is closely related to this theme, again showing her as losing in a contest of attractiveness (*Aen.* 1.27).

99. Note also that the Trojan women who burn the ships in book 5 are similarly overdetermined in their Trojan identity. See Nugent (1992).

CHAPTER 7

1. Hamer (1993) has demonstrated the potency of the image of Cleopatra at various points of time in Western culture.

2. For a discussion of the issues involved see the most recent and fullest account of the problem by Gurval (1995). On Hor. *epod.* 9 see 137ff., on Prop. 3.11 see 191ff., on Prop. 4.6 see 249ff. It has been argued by some that these poems uncritically reflect an Augustan party line on Cleopatra as a political enemy, by others that they represent the poets' more complicated—and more distanced—poetic responses to the political themes of their poems. Gurval also discusses nonliterary evidence for the use of Actium in Augustan propaganda, such as Octavian's triple triumph, the so-called Actian arch, the evidence of coinage, and the significance of the Augustan temple of Apollo on the Palatine.

3. Perhaps it is even more so than Aeschylus' *Persae* and Euripides' *Bacchae,* the ancient texts Said (1978) uses in his classic on the topic to argue his point about the workings of that discourse.

4. So also Gurval (1995, 262–63), Quint (1993, 23–27), Wyke (1992, 106–8), Syme (1939, 297). See also Binder (1971, 213–70), Toll (1997, 45–50). Other discussions of the shield of Aeneas include Hardie (1986, 97–110, 336–76), Gabelmann (1986), West (1975–76), Poduska (1970), Rowland (1968), Griffith (1967–68), Becker (1964).

5. The expression *ope barbarica* is usually taken to refer to the riches of the Orient. I see another meaning of *ops,* military force, contained in it as well.

6. See Plut. *Ant.* 55.1–2 and Dio 50.1.2–3 for Antony's Eastern conquests. Toll (1997, 45–50) discusses the misrepresentations in the passage as an intentional and systematic feature of the Vergilian narrative: "The enemies on the shield have a foreignness whose facticity could best be expressed as a misrepresentation precisely because it was not a set fact, but naturally plastic and alterable" (48).

7. India is a set ingredient of many of Vergil's catalogs of exotic places, often associated with the luxury products it exports to Rome, such as ivory and ebony. See *Georg.* 1.57; 2.116, 122, 138, 172; 4.293, 425; *Aen.* 6.794; 7.605; 8.705; 12.67. That Vergil locates the source of the Nile in India suggests that he really means Ethiopia by that name (*Georg.* 4.293). On this geographical confusion see Meyer (1961, 20–21, 27–29) and Norden (1899, 470–72). It is interesting that in *Georg.* 1.57 Vergil pairs Indians with Sabaeans, as in the present passage, but there he explicitly names them for the luxury products that they produce (India sends ivory, Saba incense). In *Aen.* 7.605–6 Vergil pairs the Indians with the Arabs and the lands of Dawn (*Aurora*) as opponents of the Romans when he relates the ancient custom of opening the gates of the temple of Janus.

8. For a list of Antony's allies see Plut. *Ant.* 61.

9. See Tarn (1932), 81. See also Becher (1966, 48). Carter (1970), whose book on Actium is still the standard work, does not even bother with this question any more. Similarly, the most recent literary studies on Vergil's Actium (Hardie [1986, 97–110], Quint [1993, 21–31], Gurval [1995, 234–47]) do not address them either.

10. Quint (1993, 21–31) discusses the East-West polarizations in this passage at length.

11. According to Dio 50.5.3 Antony and Cleopatra posed for portraits, he as Osiris or Dionysus, she as Selene or Isis. In 50.25.4 Dio tells us that Antony took the titles of Osiris or Dionysus and venerated Cleopatra as Isis or Selene. On Cleopatra as Aphrodite see Plut. *Ant.* 26. See also Becher (1966, 17 n. 2 and 25). See Zanker (1987, 52–61 and 65–73) on the iconography of Antony's side.

12. I cite the *Carmen de bello Actiaco* from Courtney (1993).

13. The poem has been variously ascribed in Rabirius or Cornelius Severus. On the dating see Courtney (1993, 334) and Benario (1983, 1657 with n. 12).

14. Prop. 3.11.45.

15. The amatory theme of a man's enslavement to a woman is stated in the beginning of the poem, 3.11.1–4. Cleopatra is the culminating *exemplum* in a long list of powerful women from Greek myth.

16. Her drunkenness (literal or figurative): Hor. *carm.* 1.37.12 and 14, Prop. 3.11.56. Her greed for power: Hor. *carm.* 1.37.6–12, Prop. 3.11.31–32 and 41–46.

17. The suicide experiments Cleopatra conducts in the *Carmen de bello Actiaco* may also be read as depravity (cols. v and vi).

18. It is positive in Hor. *carm.* 1.37, but not so in Prop. 3.11.53–56. In the *Carmen de bello Actiaco* the description of her suicide experiments does not suggest a positive interpretation (cols. v and vi).

19. Knauer (1964, 175–80), Johnson (1976, 32–36).

20. So also Pöschl (1964, 115–27).

21. On the Diana simile see also Austin 1971 ad loc., Otis (1964, 70–76), West (1969, 43–44), Hornsby (1970, 89–90), Dunkle (1973, 131–32), Rieks (1981, 1034–38), Briggs (1981, 965), Thornton (1985).

22. *Aen.* 1.14 (Carthage is called *studiis asperrima belli*) and *Aen.* 1.442–45 (the horse's head that the Carthaginians dug out in a grove and which Juno told them was a sign of their success in war).

23. Prop. 3.11.13–26.

24. References to gold in the palace furnishings: *Aen.* 1.698: *aurea sponda;* 726: *laquearibus aureis;* 728–29: *gravem gemmis auroque / pateram;* 739: *pleno auro;* 740–41: *cithara aurata.* See Crookes (1984). References to opulent lounging furniture: 1.697: *aulaeis superbis;* 698: *aurea sponda;* 700: *strato ostro;* 708: *toris pictis.* See Moles (1987, 153).

25. Tr. Bernadotte Perrin in id. (ed.) (1988). *Plutarch's Lives,* vol. 9 (*Demetrius and Antony, Pyrrhus and Caius Marius*). (Cambridge).

26. *Aen.* 4.134–35: *ostroque insignis et auro / stat sonipes;* 138–39: *cui pharetra ex auro, crines nodantur in aurum / aurea purpuream subnectit fibula vestem.* See my discussion above and Thornton (1985).

27. *Aen.* 4.261–64: *atque illi stellatus iaspide fulva / ensis erat Tyrioque ardebat murice laena /demissa ex umeris, dives quae munera Dido / fecerat, et tenui telas discreverat auro.*

28. *Aen.* 4.193–94: *nunc hiemem inter se luxu, quam longa, fovere / regnorum immemores turpique cupidine captos.*

29. Cleopatra's flight from the battle of Actium is a motif in several poems about her from the Augustan period. See my discussion above.

30. Note also that Cleopatra is called *causa . . . maxima belli* in the *Carmen de bello Actiaco* (col. iii, l. 24 Courtney).

31. This idea is also discussed in Keith (2000, 67–78). Keith observes a "relentless displacement of responsibility for murderous conflict between men onto the transgressive figure of the militant woman in the *Aeneid*" (78).

32. See *Aen.* 2.567–88, esp. 573: *Troiae et patriae communis Erinys.*

33. Wyke (1992, 126).

34. See Wyke (1992, 121–22).

35. Hor. *carm.* 1.37.21–23: *generosius / perire quaerens nec muliebriter / expavit ensem.*

36. On Cleopatra's validating discursive strategies see Wyke (1992, 100–103) and Hamer (1993, 7–18).

37. Said (1978, 57): "It is Europe that articulates the Orient; this articulation is the prerogative, not of a puppet master, but of a genuine creator, whose life-giving power represents, animates, constitutes the otherwise silent and dangerous space beyond familiar boundaries." See also Said (1978, 20–21): "Orientalism is premised upon exteriority, that is, on the fact that the Orientalist, poet or scholar, makes the Orient speak. . . . What he says and writes, by virtue of the fact that it is said or written, is meant to indicate that the Orientalist is outside the Orient, both as an existential and as a moral fact. The principal product of this exteriority is of course representation: as early as Aeschylus' play *The Persians* the Orient is transformed from a very far distant and often threatening Otherness into figures that are relatively familiar (in Aeschylus' case, grieving Asiatic women). The dramatic immediacy of representation in the Persians obscures the fact that the audience is watching a highly artificial enactment of what a non-Oriental has made into a symbol for the whole Orient."

38. Said (1978, 123).

39. On Renan's importance to academic orientalism see Said (1978, 130–48). On his thought about nationhood see Renan (1990), originally published in 1939 and discussed in chapter 8 below.

40. But see Keith (2000, 78), who sees "the unprecedented visibility of upper class Roman women in the political upheaval of the decade after Caesar's assassination" as a stronger influence on the association of women with war in the *Aeneid* than Cleopatra.

CHAPTER 8

1. On the associations of the *mitra* see esp. the discussion of Dickie (1985).

2. On this speech see Horsfall (1971) and Dickie (1985).

3. See Griffith (1985). Descriptions of Aeneas' appearance are found in 1.588–93; 2.721–24; 4.4, 11, (83–85), 141–50, 215–27, 280; 7.152–68; 10.565–70; 12.97–100, 312, 699–703, 938–39. His armor is described in 2.671–72; 3.466–69; 4.261–64, 646–47; 7.447–49, 617–731; 10.270–75, 638–40; 12.167, 430–34, 441–42, 887–88, 919–24.

4. See chapter 4.

5. See Page 1900 ad loc. And *LIMC* s.v. Aineias.

6. On the Greeks in the *Aeneid* see Papaioannou (1998). The cultural context of Vergil's portrayal of the Greeks can be explored by reading Crawford (1978), who discusses Roman attitudes to the Greeks and Greek attitudes to Rome in the first century BC. On the use of ethnic stereotypes about Greeks and Carthaginians in Cicero's oratory see Vasaly (1993, 191–243). On the Romans' ethnic stereotypes more generally see Balsdon (1979, 30–76).

7. On book 2 see Gransden (1985).

8. On this episode see Lynch (1980), Gransden (1985, 62–66), Hexter (1990).

9. Lynch (1980) discusses the speeches of Laocoon and Sinon in terms of Roman rhetorical styles. He sees Laocoon linked "to a pristine form of Romanness and Sinon to a decadent form of Greekness" (118).

10. On this see my discussion in chapter 6.

11. Gransden (1985) observes that pre-Vergilian ancient traditions concerning the fall of Troy must have depicted the Trojans as silly (61).

12. On the Achaemenides episode see Römisch (1976), Ramminger (1991, with further bibliography 53, n. 1), Putnam (1995, 61–64), Khan (1998).

13. On Diomedes in Vergil see Grummond (1967).

14. So also Williams (1964, 204), who discusses these lines in conjunction with the sub-

sequent passage *Aen.* 6.847–53, in which the unnamed Greeks and their achievements (*excudent alii spirantia mollius aera, / credo equidem, vivos ducent de marmore vultus, / orabunt causas melius, caelique meatus / describent radio et surgentia sidera dicent*) are contrasted with the Roman arts of empire (*tu regere imperio populos, Romane memento* . . .).

15. Gransden (1985, 68) summarizes the effect of these scenes similarly: "All these scenes, cumulating in the death of Priam himself, slain at his own altar, mutilated like Hector and Deiphobus, add up to an indictment of Greek sacrilege and depravity."

16. For this view see also the remarks of Rudd (1986, 36–37).

17. On gold in *Aeneid* 1 see Crookes (1984).

18. *Il.* 24.143–676.

19. The narrator refers to them as *Latini* in *Aen.* 7.151, 160; 8.448; 9.717; 10.311, 895; 11.134, 193, 203, 229, 603, 618, 621, 745; 12.1, 240, 448, 548, 556, and 730. Latinus: *Aen.* 7.202; 11.302; Amata: *Aen.* 7.367; Turnus: *Aen.* 7.470; 12.15, 693; Aeneas: *Aen.* 8.117; 11.108.

20. See Page (1900), Fordyce (1977) ad loc. for the use of *Laurens* as more general and synonymous with *Latinus*.

21. *Aen.* 5.116–17: *genus a quo nomine Memmi;* 121: *domus Sergia;* 122–23: *genus unde tibi, Romane Cluenti;* 568: *genus unde Atii*. The descent of the gens Iulia is referred to in Jupiter's prophecy in book 1 (*Aen.* 1.288: *Iulius a magno demissum nomen Iulo*).

22. On Vergil's Latium see McKay (1970, 147–93).

23. On the adoption of the Trojan legend at Rome see especially Gruen (1992, 6–51).

24. Suet. *Iul.* 6.1.

25. Serv. *ad Aen.* 2.166 tells us that Varro wrote a *De Familiis Troianis*. In Nepos' *Life of Atticus* we learn that Atticus wrote a *liber annalis* and monographs of histories of separate families (Nep. *Att.* 18). Messala's *De Familiis* is mentioned by Pliny the Elder (*NH* 34.137). Hyginus' *De Familiis Troianis* is mentioned in Servius (*ad Aen.* 5.389). We also know of the genealogical writings of a L. Iulius Caesar (cos. 64) (Serv. *ad Aen.* 1.267). Bäumerich (1964) has collected the fragments of these and other genealogical works.

26. For an edition of the fragments see P. Fraccaro 1907, 184–97. On Varro's interests in this area see Rawson (1985, 244–45) and Dahlmann (1973).

27. The Greeks did have genealogical poetry and prose writers on genealogy such as Hekataios, Akusilaos, Pherekydes of Athens, and Hellanikos. See Haedicke 1936; Nimsch 1924. On the genealogical aspects of the Greek conceptualization of ethnic identity more generally see Hall (1997, 67–110).

28. See Gruen (1992, 6–51).

29. For Vergil's version see *Aen.* 3.163–71, where the Penates tell Aeneas in a dream that the ancient home of the Trojans promised to them by Delian Apollo as their new homeland is Italy; and *Aen.* 7.206–7 and 240, where Latinus and the Trojan embassy talk about the Trojans' descent from Dardanus who came from Italy, more specifically from Corythus in Tyrrhenian country. On Corythus see Horsfall (1973). For Dionysius' version see DH 1.61.1. For Varro see Serv. *ad Aen.* 3.167.

30. Dardanus from Thrace: Hellanikos: Schol. Apoll. Rhod. 1.916 = Jacoby FGrH 1.4.23. Aeneas settles in Thrace: DH 1.47.6, who credits Hellanikos' *Troika*. Aeneas dies in Thrace: Cephalon of Gergis, Hegesippus (DH 1.49.1).

31. Strabo 13.1.53 (C 608). Homer: *Il.* 20.302–8. Aeneas' rule among the Trojans is also mentioned in the *Homeric hymn to Aphrodite* (196–97).

32. See Gruen (1990) on the Bacchanalian affair in 186 BC (34–78), on the advent of the Magna Mater in 204 BC (5–33), and on the discovery of the tomb of Numa Pompilius in 181 BC (158–92), and Gruen (1992) on the adoption of the Trojan legend (6–51).

33. See Walbank (1951) on Greek national identity and Walbank (1972) on Roman national identity.

34. See the proem: *Aen.* 1.7, 33; the pageant of heroes: *Aen.* 6.781, 789, 810, 851, 857, 870, 876; the shield: *Aen.* 8.626, 635, 638, 654, 714; Euander at the site of Rome: *Aen.* 8.99, 313, 338, 361; and the following prophetic contexts: *Aen.* 1.234, 277, 282 (dialogue of Jupiter and Venus); 4.234, 275 (Mercury's mission to Aeneas); 10.12 (council of gods); 12.827 (reconciliation of Juno).

35. See Hardie (1994) ad loc.

36. See Lewis & Short, s.v. *gens.*

37. See Hall (1997).

38. See Gruen (1990) and (1992), Walbank (1972).

39. See Smith (1986), Hall (1997), Anderson (1983).

40. See especially Anderson (1983) and Hobsbawm (1990). The latter lists the most important studies of the recent past (4).

41. Hobsbawm (1990, 10), Anderson (1983, 46ff.).

42. See Smith (1986), Smith and Hutchinson (1996).

43. This does not mean that the Romans did not have a concept of nationhood or of ethnic differences. On Roman patriotism see Madeleine Bonjour (1975), who traces a pattern of attachment among Romans to their place of origin as well as to Rome, or what she terms *grande patrie* and *petite patrie.* This double allegiance is different from modern concepts of nationhood, but it is not surprising to find that the Romans' concept of national identity differs from its modern-day equivalents. Indeed, modern-day conceptions of nationhood differ so widely among themselves that Hobsbawm (1990), perhaps the most eminent of contemporary scholars of nationhood, is driven to the position that "agnosticism is the best initial posture of a student in this field, and so [my] book assumes no a priori definition of what constitutes a nation." (10). On ethnicity in antiquity see M. Sordi (ed.), 1979, F. Snowden, *Blacks in Antiquity* (Cambridge, 1970) and *Before Color Prejudice* (Cambridge, 1983); Sherwin-White (1967); Hall (1997).

44. Anderson (1983, 20ff.).

45. Anderson (1983, 69f.). Other examples he gives of countries where philology played a role in the rise of national consciousness include Finland and Norway.

46. Renan (1990).

47. Gruen (1992, 6–51).

48. See Rudd (1986) for a cursory survey of ethnic groups as they are represented in the *Aeneid.*

49. The most recent works on Romanization include Wells (1999), Millar (1993), Wood and Queiroga (1992), and Brunt (1990). On Roman citizenship see Sherwin-White (1973). The question of Roman citizenship in the context of the *Aeneid* is also discussed by Toll (1997).

50. Aelius Aristides' concept of Roman citizenship in the second century A.D. (in *Roman Oration* 59–71a) is much broader than even the one implied in Livy's story of Romulus' asylum and the rape of Sabine women (*AUC* 1.8–9).

51. For discussions of the treatment of different Italian ethnicities in the *Aeneid* see Horsfall (1973), Cairns (1977) and (1989, 109–28), Hahn (1984), Dickie (1985), Toll (1991) and (1997).

52. On Mezentius see Basson (1984) and Gotoff (1984), with further bibliography in Basson (1984, 68 n. 1) and Gotoff (1984, 191 n. 1). On the Etruscans in the *Aeneid* see Wilhelm (1992).

53. On Turnus' ancestry see Mackie (1991). The narrator tells us in *Aen.* 7.409–12 that Turnus' city, Ardea, was founded by Danae, the daughter of Acrisius. In *Aen.* 7.371–72 Amata argues that Turnus is descended from Inachus and Acrisius, and therefore Greek.

54. Aventinus is the son of Hercules and the local priestess Rhea (*Aen.* 7.655–69). The twins Catullus and Coras are called Argives (*Aen.* 7.670–77). The hero Halaesus is one of Agamenon's men (*Aen.* 7.723–24). Virbius is the son of Hippolytus and Aricia (*Aen.* 761–82).

55. See Sherwin-White (1973) on Caesar's grants of citizenship and Augustus' policies regulating the granting of Roman citizenship.

Bibliography

Abel, D. H. 1957–58. Medea in Dido. *CB* 34:51–53, 56.

———. 1961–62. Ariadne and Dido. *CB* 38:57–61.

Anderson, B. 1983. *Imagined Communities: Reflections on the Origin and Spread of Nationalism.* London.

Anderson, W. S. 1969. *The Art of the Aeneid.* Englewood Cliffs, NJ.

———. 1981. Servius and the "Comic Style" of *Aeneid* 4. *Arethusa* 14:115–25.

Armstrong, J. A. 1982. *Nations before Nationalism.* Chapel Hill.

Asmis, E. 1995. Epicurean Poetics. In *Philodemus and Poetry: Poetic Theory and Practice in Lucretius, Philodemus, and Horace,* ed. D. Obbink, 15–34. Oxford.

Austin, R. G., ed. 1955. *P. Vergilii Maronis Aeneidos Liber Quartus.* Oxford.

———, ed. 1964. *P. Vergilii Maronis Aeneidos Liber Secundus.* Oxford.

———, ed. 1971. *P. Vergilii Maronis Aeneidos Liber Primus.* Oxford.

———, ed. 1977. *P. Vergilii Maronis Aeneidos Liber Sextus.* Oxford.

Bailey, C. 1935. *Religion in Virgil.* Oxford.

Baker, R. 1980. *Regius Puer:* Ascanius in the *Aeneid.* In *Vindex Humanitatis: Essays in Honour of John Huntly Bishop,* ed. B. Marshall, 129–45. Armidale, Australia.

Balsdon, J. P. V. D. 1979. *Romans and Aliens.* Chapel Hill.

Barchiesi, A. 1984. *La traccia del modello: Effetti omerici nella narrazione virgiliana.* Pisa.

———. 1996. Poetry, Praise, and Patronage: Simonides in Book IV of Horace's Odes. *ClAnt* 15:5–47.

———. 1997. Ecphrasis. In *The Cambridge Companion to Virgil,* ed. C. Martindale, 271–81. Cambridge.

Bartsch, S. 1989. *Decoding the Ancient Novel: The Reader and the Role of Description in Heliodorus and Achilles Tatius.* Princeton.

———. 1998. *Ars* and the Man: The Politics of Art in Virgil's *Aeneid. CPh* 93:322–42.

Bassi, D. 1930. Sant' Agostino e Virgilio. *AIM* 6:420–31.

Basson, W. P. 1984. Vergil's Mezentius: A Pivotal Personality. *AClass* 27:57–70.

Basto, R. J. 1984. The Swords of *Aeneid* 4. *AJPh* 105:333–38.

Baswell, C. 1995. *Virgil in Medieval England: Figuring the* Aeneid *from the Twelfth Century to Chaucer.* Cambridge.

Bäumerich, H. J. 1964. Über die Bedeutung der Genealogie in der römischen Literatur. Diss. Universität Köln.

Beard, M., et al., eds. 1991. *Literacy in the Roman World.* Ann Arbor.

Becher, I. 1966. *Das Bild der Kleopatra in der griechischen und lateinischen Literatur.* Deutsche Akademie der Wissenschaften zu Berlin. Schriften der Sektion für Altertumswissenschaft, Bd. 51. Berlin.

Becker, C. 1964. Der Schild des Aeneas. *WS* 77:111–27.

Belsey, C. 1980. *Critical Practice.* London.

Benario, H. W. 1983. *The Carmen de bello Actiaco* and Early Imperial Epic. *ANRW* 2.30.3:1656–62.

Benario, J. M. 1970. Dido and Cleopatra. *Vergilius* 16:2–6.

Bennett, C. 1988. The Conversion of Vergil: The *Aeneid* in Augustine's *Confessions. REAug* 34:47–69.

Bettini, M. 1991. *Anthropology and Roman Culture.* Baltimore.

———. 1992. *Il Ritratto dell'Amante.* Turin.

———. 1996. Le orecchie di Hermes: Luoghi e simboli della comunicazione nella cultura antica. In *I signori della memoria e dell' oblio: Figure della communicazione nella cultura antica,* ed. M. Bettini, vii–lii. Florence.

———. 1997. The Ghosts of Exile: Doubles and Nostalgia in Vergil's *Parva Troia. ClAnt* 16:8–33.

Bhabha, H. K., ed. 1990. *Nation and Narration.* London.

Binder, G. 1971. *Aeneas und Augustus: Interpretationen zum 8. Buch der Aeneis.* Meisenheim am Glan.

———. 1990. Vom Mythos zur Ideologie: Rom und seine Geschichte vor und bei Vergil. In *Mythos, erzählende Weltdeutung im Spannungsfeld von Ritual, Geschichte und Rationalität,* ed. G. Binder and B. Effe, 137–61. Trier.

Block, E. 1984. *The Effects of Divine Manifestation on the Reader's Perspective in Vergil's* Aeneid. Salem, NH.

Bloomer, W. M. 1992. *Valerius Maximus and the Rhetoric of the New Nobility.* Chapel Hill.

———. 1997. *Latinity and Literary Society at Rome.* Philadelphia.

Boas, H. 1938. *Aeneas' Arrival in Latium: Observations on Legends, History, Religion, Topography, and Related Subjects in Vergil,* Aeneid *VII 1–135.* Amsterdam.

Bolgar, R. R. 1954. *The Classical Heritage and its Beneficiaries.* Cambridge.

Boyle, A. J. 1999. *Aeneid* 8: Images of Rome. *Vergil's* Aeneid: *An Interpretive Guide,* ed. C. Perkell, 148–61. Norman, OK.

Bonfanti, M. 1986. *Punto di vista e modi della narrazione nell'Eneide.* Pisa.

Bonjour, M. 1975. *Terre Natale: Etudes sur une composante affective du patriotisme romain.* Paris.

Bonner, S. F. 1977. *Education in Ancient Rome: From the Elder Cato to the Younger Pliny.* Berkeley.

Bradley, D. R. 1958. Swords at Carthage. *CPh* 53:234–36.

Braund, S. M., and C. Gill, eds. 1997. *The Passions in Roman Thought and Literature.* Cambridge.

Briggs, W. W. 1980. *Narrative and Simile from the Georgics in the* Aeneid. Leiden.

———. 1981. Virgil and the Hellenistic Epic. In *ANRW* 2.31.2:948–84.

Brink, C. O. 1963. *Horace on Poetry: Prolegomena to the Literary Epistles.* Cambridge.

Brisson, J.-P. 1969. Carthage et le *fatum:* Reflexions sur un thème de l'Énéide. In *Hommages à Marcel Renard,* ed. J. Bibauw, 1:162–73. Collection Latomus 101. Brussels.

Brunt, P. A. 1968. Romanization of the Local Ruling Classes in the Roman Empire. In *Assimilation et résistance a la culture greco-romaine dans le monde ancien,* ed. M. Pippidi, 161–73.

———. 1978. Laus Imperii. In *Imperialism in the Ancient World,* ed. P. D. A. Garnsey and C. R. Whittaker, 159–91. Cambridge.

———. 1990. *Roman Imperial Themes.* Oxford.

Buchheim, H. 1960. *Die Orientpolitik des Triumvirn M. Antonius: Ihre Voraussetzungen, Entwicklung, und Zusammenhang mit den politischen Ereignissen.* Heidelberg.

Buchheit, V. 1963. *Vergil über die Sendung Roms: Untersuchungen zum Bellum Poenicum und zur Aeneis.* Heidelberg.

———. 1990. Der frühe Vergil und Octavian. *SO* 65:53–62.

Büchner, K. 1958. P. Vergilius Maro. *RE,* VIIIA.1:1021–VIIIA.2:1486.

Burck, E. 1943. Das Bild der Karthager in der römischen Literatur. In *Rom und Karthago,* ed. J. Vogt, 297–345. Leipzig.

Cairns, F. 1977. Geography and Nationalism in the *Aeneid. LCM* 2:109–16.

———. 1989. *Virgil's Augustan Epic.* Cambridge.

Camps, W. A. 1969. *Introduction to Virgil's* Aeneid. Oxford.

Cardauns, B. 1983. *Stand und Aufgabe der Varroforschung (mit einer Bibliographie der Jahre 1935–1980).* Mainz.

Cavenaile, R. ed. 1956. *Corpus Papyrorum Latinarum* vol. 1. Wiesbaden.

Carter, J. 1970. *The Battle of Actium.* London.

Christes, J. 1979. *Sklaven und Freigelassene als Grammatiker und Philologen im antiken Rom.* Wiesbaden.

Citroni, M. 1995. *Poesia e lettori in Roma Antica.* Rome.

Clausen, W. 1987. *Virgil's* Aeneid *and the Tradition of Hellenistic Poetry.* Berkeley.

Clay, D. 1988. The Archaeology of the Temple to Juno in Carthage. *CPh* 83:195–205.

Coffin, H. C. 1923. The Influence of Vergil on St. Jerome and St. Augustine. *CW* 17:170–75.

Coleman, R. 1982. The Gods in the *Aeneid. G&R* 29:143–68.

Collard, C. 1973. Medea and Dido. *Prometheus* 1:131–52.

Comparetti, D. [1885] 1997. *Vergil in the Middle Ages.* Trans. E. F. M. Benecke. Reprint of 1966 translation with a new introduction by J. M. Ziolkowsky, Princeton.

Conte, G. B. 1986. *The Rhetoric of Imitation: Genre and Poetic Memory in Virgil and Other Latin Poets,* ed. C. P. Segal. Ithaca, NY.

———. 1994a. *Genres and Readers: Lucretius, Love Elegy, Pliny's Encyclopedia.* Baltimore.

———. 1994b. Instructions for a Sublime Reader: Form of the Text and Form of the Addressee in Lucretius's *De Rerum Natura.* In *Genres and Readers: Lucretius, Love Elegy, Pliny's Encyclopedia,* ed. G. B. Conte, 1–34. Baltimore.

Courcelle, P. 1979–80. La suivie litteraire de l'Eneide. *Annuaire du Collège de France* 80:681–93.

———. 1984. *Lecteurs païens et lecteurs chrétiens de l'Eneide.* Paris.

Courtney, E., ed. 1993. *The Fragmentary Latin Poets.* Oxford.

Cowherd, C. 1986. Dido Sacerdos. *Augustan Age* 5:17–21.

Crawford, M. H. 1978. Greek Intellectuals and the Roman Aristocracy in the First Century B. C. In *Imperialism in the Ancient World,* ed. P. D. A. Garnsey and C. R. Whittaker, 193–207. Cambridge.

Creighton, J. D., and R. J. A. Wilson, eds. 1999. *Roman Germany: Studies in Cultural Interactions. JRS* Suppl. 32. Portsmouth, RI.

Crookes, D. Z. 1984. A Note on Gold in Aen. I. *LCM* 9:14–16.

Curtius, E. R. 1953. *European Literature and the Latin Middle Ages.* Trans. W. R. Trask. Princeton.

Dahlmann, H. 1948. Vates. *Philologus* 97:337–53.

———. 1973. Varroniana. In *ANRW* 1.3:3–25.

Daviault, A. 1991. La dimension politique de la legende virgilienne d'Elissa-Didon. *CEA* 25:183–88.

Davidson, J. 1991. The Gaze in Polybius' Histories. *JRS* 81:10–24.

de Jong, I. J. F. 1987. *Narrators and Focalizers. The Presentation of the Story in the Iliad.* Amsterdam.

DeLacy, P. 1948. Stoic Views of Poetry. *AJPh* 69:241–71.

Della Corte, F. 1983. Giunone come personaggio e come dea in Virgilio. *A&R* 28.21–30.

De Witt, N. W. 1907. The Dido Episode as a Tragedy. *CJ* 2:283–88.

———. 1930. Vergil and the Tragic Drama. *CJ* 26:19–27.

Di Cesare, M. A. 1974. *The Altar and the City: a Reading of Vergil's Aeneid.* New York.

Dickie, M. 1985. The Speech of Numanus Remulus (Aen. 9. 598–620). *Papers of the Liverpool Latin Seminar* 5:165–221.

Docherty, Thomas. 1983. *Reading (Absent) Character: Towards a Theory of Characterization in Fiction.* Oxford.

Doniger O'Flaherty, W. 1988. *Other Peoples' Myths: The Cave of Echos.* (Chicago).

Dougherty, C. 1993. *The Poetics of Colonization: From City to Text in Ancient Greece.* Oxford.

Du Bois, P. 1976. The *pharmakos* of Vergil: Dido as Scapegoat. *Vergilius* 22:14–23.

———. 1982. *History, Rhetorical Description, and the Epic: From Homer to Spenser.* Cambridge.

———. 1998. The Subject in Antiquity after Foucault. In *Rethinking Sexuality: Foucault and Classical Antiquity,* ed. D. H. J. Larmour, P. A. Miller, and C. Platter, 85–103. Princeton.

Duckworth, G. E. 1957. The *Aeneid* as a Trilogy. *TAPhA* 88:1–10.

Dunkle, J. R. 1973. The Hunter and Hunting in the *Aeneid. Ramus* 2:127–42.

Dyck, A. R. 1983. Sychaeus. *Phoenix* 37:239–44.

Edelstein, L. 1966. *The Meaning of Stoicism.* Cambridge, MA.

Eliot, T. S. 1945. *What Is a Classic? An Address Delivered before the Virgil Society on the 16th of October 1944.* London.

Fantham, E. 1998. Allecto's First Victim: A Study of Vergil's Amata (*Aen.* 7.341–405 and 12.1–80). In *Vergil's Aeneid: Augustan Epic and Political Context,* ed. H.-P. Stahl, 135–53. London.

Farrell, J. A. 1990. Which *Aeneid* in Whose Nineties? *Vergilius* 36:74–80.

———. 1991. *Vergil's Georgics and the Traditions of Ancient Epic: The Art of Allusion in Literary History.* Oxford.

———. 2001. *Latin Language and Latin Culture: From Ancient to Modern Times.* Cambridge.

Farron, S. G. 1980. The Aeneas-Dido-Episode as an Attack on Aeneas' Mission and Rome. *G&R* 27:34–47.

Feeney, D. C. 1983. The Taciturnity of Aeneas. *CQ* 33:204–19.

———. 1984. The Reconciliation of Juno. *CQ* 34:179–94.

———. 1991. *The Gods in Epic: Poets and Critics of the Classical Tradition.* Oxford.

————. 1993. Horace and the Greek Lyric Poets. In *Horace 2000: A Celebration,* ed. N. Rudd, 41–63. Ann Arbor.

————. 1997. The Virgil Commentary of Servius. In *The Cambridge Companion to Virgil,* ed. C. Martindale, 73–78. Cambridge.

————. 1998. *Literature and Religion at Rome: Cultures, Contexts, and Beliefs.* Cambridge.

Feldherr, A. 1998. *Spectacle and Society in Livy's History.* Berkeley.

Fenik, B. C. 1960. The Influence of Euripides on Vergil's *Aeneid.* PhD Diss., Princeton University.

Ferguson, J. 1970. Fire and Wound: The Imagery of *Aeneid* IV 1 ff. *PVS* 10:57–63.

Ferraro, S. 1982. *La Presenza di Virgilio nei Graffiti Pompeiani.* Naples.

Finley, M. I. 1968. The Silent Women of Rome. In *Aspects of Antiquity: Discoveries and Controversies,* ed. M. I. Finley, 129–42. London.

Fitzgerald, W. 1984. Aeneas, Daedalus, and the Labyrinth. *Arethusa* 17:51–65.

Foley, H. P., ed. 1981. *Reflections of Women in Antiquity.* New York.

Fordyce, C. J., ed. 1977. *P. Vergilii Maronis Aeneidos Libri VII–VIII.* Oxford.

Foster, J. 1973–74. Some Devices of Drama in *Aeneid* 1–4. *PVS* 13:28–41.

————. 1977. Divine and Demonic Possession in the *Aeneid. LCM* 2:117–28.

Foucault, M. 1980. *The History of Sexuality.* Vol. 1, *An Introduction.* New York.

————. 1985. *The History of Sexuality.* Vol. 2, *The Use of Pleasure.* New York.

————. 1986. *The History of Sexuality.* Vol. 3, *The Care of the Self.* New York.

Fowler, D. 1990. Deviant Focalization in Vergil's *Aeneid. PCPhS* 36:42–63.

————. 1991. Narrate and Describe: The Problem of Ekphrasis. *JRS* 81:25–35.

————. 1997a. Epicurean Anger. In *The Passions in Roman Thought and Literature,* ed. S. M. Braund and C. Gill, 16–35. Cambridge.

————. 1997b. Story-Telling. In *The Cambridge Companion to Virgil,* ed. C. Martindale, 259–70. Cambridge.

Fraccaro, P., ed. 1907 *Studi Varroniani: De gente populi Romani libri IV.* Padua.

Fraenkel, E. 1954. Urbem quam statuo vestra est. *Glotta* 33:157–59.

Franklin, J. L., Jr. 1991. Literacy and the Parietal Inscriptions of Pompeii. In *Literacy in the Roman World,* ed. M. Beard et al., 77–98. Ann Arbor.

Funke, H. 1965–66. Univira. *JbAC* 8–9:183–88.

Gabelmann, H. 1986. Zur Schlussszene auf dem Schild des Aeneas (Vergil Aeneis VIII 720–728). *MDAICR* 93:281–300.

Galinsky, G. K. 1969. *Aeneas, Sicily, and Rome.* Princeton.

————. 1981. Vergil's *Romanitas* and His Adaptation of Greek Heroes. In *ANRW* 2.31.2:985–1010.

————. 1988. The Anger of Aeneas. *AJPh* 109:321–48.

————. 1996. *Augustan Culture: An Interpretive Introduction.* Princeton.

Gall, D. 1993. *Ipsius umbra Creusae: Creusa und Helena.* Stuttgart.

Genette, G. 1982. *Palimpsestes: La littérature au second degré.* Paris.

Giardina, A. 1993. *The Romans.* Chicago.

Gibson, R. K. 1999. Aeneas as *hospes* in Vergil, *Aeneid* 1 and 4. *CQ* 49:184–202.

Gill, C. 1997. Passion as Madness in Roman poetry. In *The Passions in Roman Thought and Literature,* ed. S. M. Braund and C. Gill, 213–41. Cambridge.

Gillis, D. 1983. *Eros and Death in the* Aeneid. Rome.

Glei, R. 1991. *Der Vater der Dinge: Interpretationen zur politischen, literarischen, und kulturellen Dimension des Krieges bei Vergil.* Bochum.

Goold, G. P. 1970. Servius and the Helen Episode. *HSPh* 74:101–68.

Görgemanns, H., and E. A. Schmidt, eds. 1976. *Studien zum antiken Epos*. Beiträge zur klassischen Philologie, Heft 72. Meisenheim am Glan.

Gosling, A. 1975. The Political Level of the *Aeneid*. *Akroterion* 20:42–45.

Gotoff, H. C. 1984. The Transformation of Mezentius. *TAPhA* 114:191–218.

Gould, H. E., and J. L. Whiteley, eds. 1950. *P. Vergilius Maro: Aeneid Book 12*. London.

Gransden, K. W., ed. 1976. *Virgil Aeneid Book VIII*. Cambridge.

———. 1985. The Fall of Troy. *G&R* 32:60–72.

———, ed. 1991. *Virgil Aeneid Book XI*. Cambridge.

Grassmann-Fischer, B. 1966. *Die Prodigien in Vergils Aeneis*. Munich.

Griffin, J. 1979. The Fourth *Georgic*, Virgil, and Rome. *G&R* 26:61–80.

———. 1986. *Virgil*. Oxford.

Griffith, J. G. 1967–68. Again the Shield of Aeneas (*Aeneid* VIII 625–731). *PVS* 7:54–65.

Griffith, M. 1985. What Does Aeneas Look Like? *CPh* 80:309–19.

Grimm, R. E. 1967. Aeneas and Andromache in *Aeneid* III. *AJPh* 88:151–62.

Gruen, E. S. 1990. *Studies in Greek Culture and Roman Policy*. Berkeley.

———. 1992. *Culture and National Identity in Republican Rome*. Ithaca, NY.

Grummond, W. W. de. 1967. Vergil's Diomedes. *Phoenix* 21:40–43.

Gurval, R. A. 1995. *Actium and Augustus: The Politics and Emotions of Civil War*. Ann Arbor.

Haedicke, W. 1936. Die Gedanken der Griechen über Familienherkunft und Vererbung. PhD Diss. Universität Halle.

Hagendahl, H. 1967. *Augustine and the Latin Classics*. Studia Graeca et Latina Gothoburgensia XX, 1 and 2. Göteborg.

Hahn, I. 1984. Trojanitas, Latinitas, Tuscitas, Graecitas in der Aeneis. In *Symposium Vergilianum*, Acta Univ. de Attila Joszef Nominatae, Acta Antiqua et Archaeologica, tom. 25, ed. I. Hahn, 43–74. Szeged.

Hall, E. 1989. *Inventing the Barbarian: Greek Self-Definition through Tragedy*. Oxford.

Hall, J. 1997. *Ethnic Identity in Greek Antiquity*. Cambridge.

Hallett, J. P., and M. B. Skinner, eds. 1997. *Roman Sexualities*. Princeton.

Halperin, D. M., J. J. Winkler, and F. I. Zeitlin, eds. 1990. *Before Sexuality: The Construction of Erotic Experience in the Ancient Greek World*. Princeton.

Hamer, M. 1993. *Signs of Cleopatra: History, Politics, Representaiton*. London.

Hardie, P. R. 1986. *Vergil's Aeneid: Cosmos and Imperium*. Oxford.

———. 1992. Augustan Poets and the Mutability of Rome. In *Roman Poetry and Propaganda in the Age of Augustus*, ed. A. Powell, 59–82. Bristol.

———, ed. 1994. *Virgil Aeneid Book IX*. Cambridge.

———. 1997. Virgil and Tragedy. In *The Cambridge Companion to Virgil*, ed. C. Martindale, 312–26. Cambridge.

Harris, W. V. 1989. *Ancient Literacy*. Cambridge, MA.

Harrison, E. L. 1972–73. Why Did Venus Wear Boots? Some Reflections on *Aeneid* I 314f. *PVS* 12:10–25.

———. 1984. The *Aeneid* and Carthage. In *Poetry and Politics in the Age of Augustus*, ed. T. Woodman and D. West, 95–115. Cambridge.

———. 1989. The Tragedy of Dido. *EMC* 33, n.s., 8:1–21.

Harrison, S. J., ed. 1990. *Oxford Readings in Vergil's Aeneid*. Oxford.

———, ed. 1991. *Virgil Aeneid 10*. Oxford.

Havelock, E. A. 1986. *The Muse Learns to Write: Reflections on Orality and Literacy from Antiquity to the Present*. New Haven.

Heinze, R. 1928. *Virgils Epische Technik³*. Leipzig.

Henry, E. 1989. *The Vigour of Prophecy: A Study of Virgil's* Aeneid. Carbondale, IL.

Heuzé, P. 1985. *L'image du corps dans l'oeuvre de Virgile.* Rome.

Hexter, R. 1990. What Was the Trojan Horse Made Of? Interpreting Virgil's *Aeneid. YJC* 3:109–31.

———. 1992. Sidonian Dido. In *Innovations of Antiquity,* ed. R. Hexter and D. Selden, 332–84. New York.

———. 1994. Aporia and Vergil's *Aeneid:* The Problem of Reading. Unpublished address to the classics department, University of California at Berkeley, November 9, 1994. Typescript furnished by the author (available on request to hexter@socrates.berkeley.edu).

———. 1999. Imitating Troy: A Reading of *Aeneid* 3. In *Vergil's* Aeneid: *An Interpretive Guide,* ed. C. Perkell, 64–79. Norman, OK.

Highet, G. 1972. *The Speeches in Vergil's* Aeneid. Princeton.

Hillard, T. 1992. On the Stage, behind the Curtain: Images of Politically Active Women in the Late Roman Republic. In *Stereotypes of Women in Power: Perspectives and Revisionist Views,* ed. B. Garlick, S. Dixon, and P. Allen, 37–64. New York.

Hine, H. 1987. Aeneas and the Arts (Vergil, Aeneid 6. 847–50). In *Homo Viator: Classical Essays for John Bramble,* ed. M. Whitby, 173–83. Bristol.

Hobsbawm, E. J. 1990. *Nations and Nationalism since 1780.* Cambridge.

Hoogma, R. P. 1959. Der Einfluss Vergils auf die Carmina Latina Epigraphica. Amsterdam.

Hopkins, K. 1974. Elite Mobility in the Roman Empire. In *Studies in Ancient Society,* ed. M. I. Finley, 103–20. London.

———. 1991. Conquest by Book. In *Literacy in the Roman World,* ed. M. Beard et al., 133–58. Ann Arbor.

Hornsby, R. A. 1970. *Patterns of Action in the* Aeneid: *An Interpretation of Vergil's Epic Similes.* Iowa City.

Horsfall, N. 1971. Numanus Remulus: Ethnography and Propaganda in *Aeneid* 9.598 ff. *Latomus* 30.1108–16. Reprinted in *Oxford Readings in Vergil's* Aeneid, ed. S. J. Harrison (Oxford, 1990), 305–15.

———. 1973. Corythus: The Return of Aeneas in Vergil and His Sources. *JRS* 63:68–79.

———. 1973–74. Dido in the Light of History. *PVS* 13:1–13. Reprinted in *Oxford Readings in Vergil's* Aeneid, ed. S. J. Harrison (Oxford, 1990), 127–44.

———. 1976. Virgil, History, and the Roman Tradition. *Prudentia* 8:73–89.

———. 1984. Aspects of Virgilian Influence in Roman Life. In *Atti del Convegno Mondiale Scientifico di Studi su Virgilio,* 2:47–63. Milan.

———. 1989. Aeneas the Colonist. *Vergilius* 35:8–27.

———. 1991. Externi Duces. *RFIC* 119:188–92.

———, ed. 1995a. *A Companion to the Study of Virgil.* Leiden.

———. 1995b. Virgil's Impact at Rome: The Non-literary Evidence. In *A Companion to the Study of Virgil,* ed. N. Horsfall, 249–55. Leiden.

Hughes, L. B. 1997. Vergil's Creusa and *Iliad* 6. *Mnemosyne* 50:401–23.

Humm, M. 1988. Is the Gaze Feminist? Pornography, Film, and Feminism. In *Perspectives on Pornography: Sexuality in Film and Literature,* ed. G. Day and C. Bloom, 69–82. New York.

Huß, W. 1985. *Geschichte der Karthager.* Munich.

Hutchinson, J., and A. D. Smith, eds. 1996. *Ethnicity.* Oxford.

Irvine, M. 1994. *The Making of Textual Culture: "Grammatica" and Literary Theory 350–1100.* Cambridge.

Iser, W. 1974. *The Implied Reader.* Baltimore.

Jocelyn, H. D. 1990. The Ancient Story of the Imperial Edition of the *Aeneid*. *Sileno* 16: 263–78.

Johnson, W. A. 2000. Toward a Sociology of Reading in Classical Antiquity. *AJPh* 121: 593–627.

Johnson, W. R. 1976. *Darkness Visible: A Study of Vergil's* Aeneid. Berkeley.

———. 1999. *Dis Aliter Visum:* Self-Telling and Theodicy in *Aeneid* 2. In *Vergil's* Aeneid: *An Interpretive Guide,* ed. C. Perkell, 50–63. Norman, OK.

Johnson, P. A. 1998. Juno's Anger and the Sibyl at Cumae. *Vergilius* 44:13–23.

Kallendorf, C. 1991. Recent Trends in Vergilian Scholarship. *Helios* 18:73–82.

Kaplan, E. A. 1983. *Women and Film: Both Sides of the Camera.* New York.

Kaster, R. 1988. *Guardians of Language: The Grammarian and Society in Late Antiquity.* Berkeley.

———, ed. 1995. *C. Suetonius Tranquillus De Grammaticis et Rhetoribus.* Oxford.

Keith, A. M. 2000. *Engendering Rome: Women in Latin Epic.* Cambridge.

Kenney, E. 1982. Books and Readers in the Roman World. In *Latin Literature (The Cambridge History of Classical Literature; 2),* 3–50. Cambridge.

Kerényi, K. 1944. *Töchter der Sonne.* Zurich.

Khan, H. A. 1998. Anchises, Achaemenides and Polyphemus: Character, Culture and Politics in Aeneid 3, 588f. In *Studies in Latin Literature and Roman History 9,* ed. C. Deroux, 231–66. Brussels.

Kilroy, G. 1969. The Dido Episode and the 64th Poem of Catullus. *SO* 44:48–60.

Klingner, F. 1965a. Virgil und die Römische Idee des Friedens. In *Römische Geisteswelt: Essays zur lateinischen Literatur,* ed. K. Büchner, 614–44. Munich.

———. 1965b. Rom als Idee. In *Römische Geisteswelt. Essays zur lateinischen Literatur,* ed. K. Büchner, 645–66. Munich.

———. 1965c. Humanität und humanitas. In *Römische Geisteswelt: Essays zur lateinischen Literatur,* ed. K. Büchner, 704–46. Munich.

———. 1967. *Virgil: Bucolica, Georgica, Aeneis.* Zurich.

Knauer, G. N. 1964. *Die Aeneis und Homer: Studien zur poetischen Technik Vergils mit Listen der Homerzitate in der Aeneis.* Göttingen.

Knight, W. F. J. 1944. *Roman Vergil.* London.

———. 1967. *Vergil: Epic and Anthropology.* London.

Kolodny, A. 1975. *The Lay of the Land: Metaphor as Experience and History in American Life and Letters.* Chapel Hill.

Kopff, E. C. 1977. Dido and Penelope. *Philologus* 121:244–48.

Kosthorst, A. 1934. Die Frauen- und Jünglingsgestalten in Vergils Aeneis. PhD Diss., Universität Münster.

Kragelund, P. 1976. Dream and Prediction in the *Aeneid. Opuscula Graecolatina.* Suppl. MT 7. Kopenhagen.

Kraggerud, E. 1965. Caeneus und der Heroinenkatalog, Aeneis VI 440 ff. *SO* 40:66–71.

Krevans, N. 1993. Ilia's Dream: Ennius, Virgil, and the Mythology of Seduction. *HSPh* 95:257–71.

Kühn, W. 1971. *Götterszenen bei Vergil.* Heidelberg.

Laird, A. 1997. Approaching Characterization in Virgil. In *The Cambridge Companion to Virgil,* ed. C. Martindale, 282–93. Cambridge.

Lamberton, R., and J. J. Keaney, eds. 1992. *Homer's Ancient Readers: The Hermeneutics of Greek Epic's Earliest Exegetes.* Princeton.

Larmour, D. H. J., P. A. Miller, and C. Platter, eds. 1998. *Rethinking Sexuality: Foucault and Classical Antiquity.* Princeton.

Lausberg, H. 1990. *Handbuch der literarischen Rhetorik: Eine Grundlegung der Literaturwissenschaft³.* Stuttgart.

Leach, E. W. 1999. Viewing the *Spectacula* of *Aeneid* 6. In *Vergil's* Aeneid: *An Interpretive Guide,* ed. C. Perkell, 111–27. Norman, OK.

Lefèvre, E. 1978. *Dido und Aias: Ein Beitrag zur Römischen Tragödie.* Akademie der Wissenschaften und der Literatur: Abh. der Geistes- und Sozialwissenschaften Kl. 2. Wiesbaden.

———. 1989. *Das Bildprogramm des Apollo-Tempels auf dem Palatin.* Konstanz.

Levitan, W. 1993. Give up the Beginning? Juno's Mindful Wrath (*Aen.* I 37). *LCM* 18:14.

Lewis, C. T., and C. Short. 1879. *A New Latin Dictionary.* New York. Cited as Lewis & Short.

Lieberg, G. 1966. La Dea Giunone Nell'Eneide di Virgilio. *A&R* 11:145–65.

Liversidge, M. J. H. 1997. Virgil in Art. In *The Cambridge Companion to Virgil,* ed. C. Martindale, 91–103. Cambridge.

Long, A. A. 1986. *Hellenistic Philosophy: Stoics, Epicureans, Sceptics.* London.

———. 1996. *Stoic Studies.* Cambridge.

Long, A. A., and D. N. Sedley, eds. 1987. *The Hellenistic Philosophers.* Cambridge.

Lonsdale, S. 1990. Simile and Ecphrasis in Homer and Virgil. *Vergilius* 36:7–30.

Loraux, N. 1987. *Tragic Ways of Killing a Woman.* Cambridge, MA.

Lowenstam, S. 1993. The Pictures on Juno's Temple in the *Aeneid. CW* 87:37–49.

Luce, J. V. 1963. Cleopatra as *Fatale Monstrum. CQ* 57:251–57.

Lynch, J. P. 1980. Laokoon and Sinon: Virgil. *Aeneid* 2.40–198. Reprinted in *Greece and Rome Studies: Virgil,* ed. I. McAuslan and P. Walcott (Oxford, 1990), 112–20.

Lyne, R. O. A. M. 1983. Vergil and the Politics of War. *CQ,* n.s., 33:188–203.

———. 1987. *Further Voices in Vergil's* Aeneid. Oxford.

———. 1989. *Words and the Poet: Characteristic Techniques of Style in Vergil's* Aeneid. Oxford.

MacCormack, S. 1998. *The Shadows of Poetry: Vergil in the Mind of Augustine.* Berkeley.

Mackie, C. J. 1988. *The Characterisation of Aeneas.* Edinburgh.

———. 1991. Turnus and His Ancestors. *CQ* 41:261–65.

Markus, D. 2000. Performing the Book: The Recital of Epic in First Century C.E. Rome. *CLAnt* 19:138–79.

Marrou, H. I. 1938. *Saint Augustin et la fin de la culture antique.* Paris.

———. 1956. *A History of Education in Antiquity.* London.

Martindale, C., ed. 1997. *The Cambridge Companion to Virgil.* Cambridge.

McAuslan, I., and P. Walcot, eds. 1990. *Greece and Rome Studies: Virgil.* Oxford.

McKay, A. G. 1970. *Vergil's Italy.* Greenwich, CT.

Meijering, R. 1987. *Literary and Rhetorical Theories in Greek Scholia.* Groningen.

Meyer, H. D. 1961. *Die Aussenpolitik des Augustus und die augusteische Dichtung.* Kölner historische Abhandlungen Bd. 5. Cologne.

Miles, G. 1977. Glorious Peace: The Values and Motivation of Virgil's Aeneas. *CLAnt* 9: 133–64.

———. 1999. The *Aeneid* as Foundation Story. In *Vergil's* Aeneid: *An Interpretive Guide,* ed. C. Perkell, 231–50. Norman, OK.

Millar, F. 1993. *The Roman Near East 31 BC–AD 337.* Cambridge, MA.

Miller, P. A. 1995. The Minotaur Within: Fire, the Labyrinth, and Strategies of Containment in Aeneid 5 and 6. *CPh* 90:225–40.

Modrak, D. K. W. 1987. *Aristotle: The Power of Perception.* Chicago.

Moles, J. L. 1984. Aristotle and Dido's *Hamartia. G&R* 31:48–54.

———. 1987. The Tragedy and Guilt of Dido. In *Homo Viator: Classical Essays for John Bramble,* ed. M. Whitby, 153–61. Bristol.

Monti, R. 1981. *The Dido-Episode and the* Aeneid: *Roman Social and Political Values in the Epic.* Mnemosyne Suppl. 66. Leiden.

Moorton, R. F. 1989–90. Love as Death: The Pivoting Metaphor in Virgil's Story of Dido. *CW* 83:153–66.

Morland, H. 1957. Nisus, Euryalus, und andere Namen in der Aeneis. *SO* 33:87–109.

Morwood, J. 1991. Aeneas, Augustus, and the Theme of the City. *G&R* 38:212–23.

Muecke, F. 1983. Foreshadowing and Dramatic Irony in the Story of Dido. *AJPh* 104:134–55.

Mulvey, L. 1975. Visual pleasure and narrative cinema. *Screen* 163:6–18.

Murgia, C. E. 1987. Dido's Puns. *CPh* 82:50–59.

Nellen, D. 1977. *Viri litterati: Gebildetes Beamtentum und das spätrömische Reich im Westen zwischen 284 und 395 n. Chr.* Bochum.

Newton, F. L. 1957. Recurrent Imagery in *Aeneid* IV. *TAPhA* 88:31–43.

Nimsch, S. M. 1924. Genealogie und Familientradition bei den älteren Historikern. PhD Diss., Universität Leipzig.

Norden, E. 1899. Ein Panegyricus auf Augustus in Vergils Aeneis. *RhM* 54:466–82.

———., ed. 1903. *P. Vergilius Maro: Aeneis Buch VI.* Leipzig.

Nugent, S. G. 1992. Vergil's Voice of the Women in *Aeneid* V. *Arethusa* 25:255–92.

———. 1999. The Women of the *Aeneid:* Vanishing Bodies, Lingering Voices. In *Vergil's Aeneid: An Interpretive Guide,* ed. C. Perkell, 251–70. Norman, OK.

Nutton, V. 1978. The Beneficial Ideology. In *Imperialism in the Ancient World,* ed. P. D. A. Garnsey and C. R. Whittaker, 209–21. Cambridge.

Obbink, D., ed. 1995a. *Philodemus and Poetry: Poetic Theory and Practice in Lucretius, Philodemus, and Horace.* Oxford.

———. 1995b. How to Read Poetry about the Gods. In *Philodemus and Poetry: Poetic Theory and Practice in Lucretius, Philodemus, and Horace,* ed. D. Obbink, 189–209. Oxford.

O'Donnell, J. J. 1980. Augustine's Classical Readings. *RecAug* 15:144–75.

O'Hara, J. 1990. *Death and the Optimistic Prophecy in Vergil's* Aeneid. Princeton.

Oksala, P. 1962. Das Aufblühen des römischen Epos: Berührungen zwischen der Ariadne-Episode Catulls und der Dido-Geschichte Vergils. *Arctos,* n.s., 3:167–97.

Oliensis, E. 1997. Sons and Lovers: Sexuality and Gender in Virgil's Poetry. In *The Cambridge Companion to Virgil,* ed. C. Martindale, 294–311. Cambridge.

O'Meara, J. J. 1963. Augustine the Arist and the Aeneid. In *Mélanges offerts à Mademoiselle Christine Mohrmann,* ed. L. J. Engels, H. W. F. M. Hoppenbrouwers, and A. J. Vermeulen, 252–61. Utrecht.

Otis, B. 1964. *Virgil: A Study in Civilized Poetry.* Oxford.

Page, T. E., ed. 1894. *The* Aeneid *of Virgil: Books I–VI.* London.

———, ed. 1900. *The* Aeneid *of Virgil: Books VII–XII.* London.

Papaïoannou, S. 1998. *Romanization and Greeks in Vergil's Aeneid.* Thesis (PhD) University of Texas, Austin.

Parker, P. 1987. *Literary Fat Ladies: Rhetoric, Gender, Property.* London.

Parry, A. 1963. The Two Voices of Virgil's *Aeneid. Arion* 2:66–80.

Pease, A. S., ed. 1935. *P. Vergilii Maronis Aeneidos Liber Quartus.* Cambridge, MA.

Perkell, C., ed. 1999a. *Vergil's* Aeneid: *An Interpretive Guide.* Norman, OK.

————. 1999b. *Aeneid* 1: An Epic Programme. In *Vergil's* Aeneid: *An Interpretive Guide,* ed. C. Perkell, 29–49. Norman, OK.

————. 1981. The Quality of Aeneas' Victory in the *Aeneid.* In *Reflections of Women in Antiquity,* ed. H. P. Foley, 355–71. New York.

Perret, J. 1964. Les Compagnes de Didon aux Enfers. *REL* 42:247–61.

Phillips, C. R. 1976. A Note on Vergil *Aen.* V 744. *Hermes* 104:247–49.

Pinch, G. 1994. *Magic in Ancient Egypt.* London.

Poduska, D. 1970. Ope Barbarica or Bellum Civile? *CB* 46:33–34, 46.

Pöschl, V. 1950. *Die Dichtkunst Virgils: Bild und Symbol in der Aeneis.* Wiesbaden.

————. 1970. Dido und Aeneas. In *Festschrift K. Vretska,* ed. H. Gugel and D. Ableitinger, 148–73. Heidelberg.

Prandi, L. 1979. La fides Punica e il pregiudizio anticartaginese. In *Conoscenze etniche e rapporti di convivenza nell' antichita,* ed. M. Sordi, 90–97. Milan.

Putnam, M. C. J. 1965. *The Poetry of the* Aeneid: *Four Studies in Imaginative Unity.* Cambridge, MA.

————. 1995. *Virgil's Aeneid: Interpretation and Influence.* Chapel Hill.

————. 1998. *Virgil's Epic Designs: Ekphrasis in the* Aeneid. New Haven.

Quinn, K. 1963. Virgil's Tragic Queen. In *Latin Explorations: Critical Studies in Roman Literature,* 29–53. London.

————. 1968. *Vergil's* Aeneid: *A Critical Description.* London.

Quint, D. 1989. Repetition and Ideology in the *Aeneid. MD* 23:9–54.

————. 1993. *Epic and Empire: Politics and Generic Form from Virgil to Milton.* Princeton.

Rand, E. K., et al. 1946. Servianorum in Vergilii Carmina Commentariorum editio Harvardiana. vol. 2. Lancaster.

Ramminger, J. 1991. Imitation and Allusion in the Achaemenides Scene (Vergil, Aeneid 3.588–691). *AJPh* 112.53–71.

Rawson, E. 1985. *Intellectual Life in the Late Roman Republic.* Baltimore.

Renan, E. 1990. Que est-ce qu'une nation? In *Nation and Narration,* ed. H. K. Bhabha, 8–22 (London).

Rengakos, A. 1993. Zum Griechenbild in Vergils Aeneis. *A&A* 39:112–24.

Rieks, R. 1981. Die Gleichnisse Vergils. In *ANRW* 2.31.2:1011–1110.

Rispoli, G. M. 1984. φαντασία ed ἐναργεία negli scoli all' Iliade. *Vichiana* 13:311–39.

Rochette, B. 1997. Grecs, Romains, et Barbares: A la Recherche de l'Identité Ethnique et Linguistique des Grecs et des Romains. *RBPh* 75:37–57.

Römisch, E. 1976. Die Achaemenides-Episode in Vergils *Aeneis.* In *Studien zum antiken Epos,* Beiträge zur klassischen Philologie, Heft 72, ed. H. Görgemanns and E. A. Schmidt, 208–27. Meisenheim am Glan.

Rosati, G. 1979. Punto di vista narrativo e antichi esegeti di Virgilio. *ASNP* ser. 3, 9:539–62.

Rosenmeyer, T. G. 1986. ΦΑΝΤΑΣΙΑ und Einbildungskraft: Zur Vorgeschichte eines Leitbegriffs der europäischen Ästhetik. *Poetica* 18, no. 3–4:197–248.

Rosivach, V. J. 1980. Latinus' Genealogy and the Palace of Picus (Aen. 7. 45–9, 170–91). *CQ* 30.140–52.

Rowland, R. J. 1968. Foreshadowing in Vergil *Aeneid* VIII 714–28. *Latomus* 27:832–42.

Rudd, N. 1976. Dido's *Culpa.* In *Lines of Enquiry: Studies in Latin poetry,* ed. N. Rudd, 145–66. Cambridge. *Lines of Enquiry,* 32–53. Reprinted in *Oxford Readings in Vergil's* Aeneid, ed. S. J. Harrison (Oxford, 1990), 145–66.

———. 1986. The idea of Empire in the *Aeneid*. In *Virgil in a Cultural Tradition: Essays to Celebrate the Bimillenium,* ed. R. A. Cardwell and J. Hamilton, 28–42. Nottingham.

Russell, D. A. ed. 1964. *"Longinus" on the Sublime.* Oxford.

———. 1981. *Criticism in Antiquity.* Berkeley.

Said, E. W. 1978. *Orientalism.* London.

———. 1993. *Culture and Imperialism.* New York.

Saylor, C. F. 1970. Toy Troy: The New Perspective of the Backward Glance. *Vergilius* 16: 26–28.

Schlunk, R. R. 1974. *The Homeric Scholia and the* Aeneid. Ann Arbor.

Schoenberger, H. 1910. Beispiele aus der Geschichte: Ein rhetorisches Kunstmittel in Ciceros Reden. (PhD Diss., Universität Erlangen).

Scott, K. 1929. Octavian's Propaganda and Antony's *de sua ebrietate. CPh* 24:133–41.

———. 1933. The Political Propaganda of 44–30 BC. *MAAR* 11:7–50.

Segal, C. 1981. Art and the Hero: Participation, Detachment, and Narrative Point of View in Aeneid 1. *Arethusa* 14:67–83.

———. 1990. Dido's Hesitation in *Aeneid* 4. *CW* 84:1–12.

Sherwin-White, A. N. 1967. *Racial Prejudice in Imperial Rome.* Cambridge.

———. 1973. *The Roman Citizenship.* Oxford.

Sider, D. 1995a. Epicurean Poetics: Response and Dialogue. In *Philodemus and Poetry: Poetic Theory and Practice in Lucretius, Philodemus, and Horace,* ed. D. Obbink, 35–41.

———. 1995b. The Epicurean Philosopher as Hellenistic Poet. In *Philodemus and Poetry: Poetic Theory and Practice in Lucretius, Philodemus, and Horace,* ed. D. Obbink, 42–57. Oxford.

Silverman, K. 1983. *The Subject of Semiotics.* Oxford.

Skulsky, S. 1985. *"Invitus Regina . . .":* Aeneas and the Love of Rome. *AJPh* 106:447–55.

Slavitt, D. R. 1991. *Virgil.* New Haven.

Smith, A. D. 1971. *Theories of Nationalism.* London.

———. 1986. *The Ethnic Origins of Nations.* Oxford.

——— and J. Hutchinson, eds. 1996. *Ethnicity.* Oxford.

Snowden, F. 1970. *Blacks in Antiquity.* Cambridge.

———. 1983. *Before Color Prejudice.* Cambridge.

Sordi, M. ed. 1979. *Conoscenze etniche e rapporti di convivenza nell'antichità.* Milan.

Spence, S. 1988. *Rhetorics of Reason and Desire: Vergil, Augustine, and the Troubadours.* Ithaca, NY.

———. 1999. *Varium et Mutabile:* Voices of Authority in *Aeneid 4.* In *Vergil's Aeneid: An Interpretive Guide,* ed. C. Perkell, 80–95. Norman, OK.

Stabryla, S. 1970. *Latin Tragedy in Virgil's Poetry.* Warsaw.

Stahl, H.-P. 1981. Aeneas: An "Unheroic" Hero? *Arethusa* 14:157–77.

———. 1990. The Death of Turnus: Augustan Vergil and the Political Rival. In *Between Republic and Empire: Interpretations of Augustus and His Principate,* ed. K. A. Raaflaub and M. Toher, 174–211. Berkeley.

———, ed. 1998. *Vergil's Aeneid: Augustan Epic and Political Context.* London.

Stalker, D. 1991. The Role of the Etruscans in Vergil's *Aeneid.* PhD Diss., Princeton University, Princeton.

Stanley, K. 1965. Irony and Foreshadowing in Aeneid 1.462. *AJPh* 86:267–77.

Starr, R. J. 1991. "Explaining Dido to Your Son." Tiberius Claudius Donatus on Vergil's Dido. *CJ* 87:25–34.

————. 1992. An Epic of Praise: Tiberius Claudius Donatus and Vergil's *Aeneid*. *CLAnt* 11:159–74.

Stock, B. 1996. *Augustine the Reader: Meditation, Self-Knowledge, and the Ethics of Interpretation*. Cambridge.

Suerbaum, W. 1980. Hundert Jahre Vergil-Forschung. In *ANRW* 2:31.1.3–358.

Syme, R. 1939. *The Roman Revolution*. Oxford.

Tarn, W. W. 1932. Antony's legions. *CQ* 26:75–81.

Tarrant, R. J. 1997. Aspects of Virgil's Reception in Antiquity. In *The Cambridge Companion to Virgil*, ed. C. Martindale, 56–72. Cambridge.

Tatum, J. 1984. Allusion and Interpretation in *Aen.* VI 440–476. *AJPh* 105:434–52.

Thornton, A. 1976. *The Living Universe: Gods and Men in Virgil's* Aeneid. Mnemosyne Suppl. 46. Leiden.

Thornton, M. K. 1985. The Adaptation of Homer's Artemis-Nausikaa Simile in the *Aeneid*. *Latomus* 44:615–22.

Todd, R. W. 1980. Lavinia Blushed. *Vergilius* 26:27–33.

Toll, K. 1991. The *Aeneid* as an Epic of National Identity. *Helios* 18:3–14.

————. 1997. Making Roman-ness and the *Aeneid*. *CLAnt* 16:34–56.

Tompkins, J. 1980a. The Reader in History. In *Reader-Response Criticism from Formalism to Post-Structuralism*, 201–32. Baltimore.

————. 1980b. *Reader-Response Criticism from Formalism to Post-Structuralism*. Baltimore.

Tucker, R. A. 1975. The Banquets of Dido and Cleopatra. *CB* 52:17–20.

Van Nortwick, T. 1992. *Somewhere I Have Never Travelled: The Second Self and the Hero's Journey in Ancient Epic*. Oxford

Vanotti, G. 1995. *L'altro Enea*. Rome.

Vasaly, A. 1993. *Representations: Images of the World in Ciceronian Oratory*. Berkeley.

Veyne, P., ed. 1987. *A History of Private Life: From Pagan Rome to Byzantium*. Cambridge, MA.

Vicenzi, P. 1985. Cartagine nell'Eneide. *Aevum* 59:97–106.

Walbank, F. W. 1951. The Problem of Greek Nationality. *Phoenix* 5:41–60.

————. 1972. Nationality as a Factor in Roman History. *HSPh* 76:145–68.

Wallmann, P. 1989. *Triumviri Rei Publicae Constituendae: Untersuchungen zur politischen Propaganda im zweiten Triumvirat (43–30 v. Chr.)*. Frankfurt.

Warwick, H. H. 1975. *A Vergil Concordance*. Minneapolis.

Weaver, P. R. C. 1974. Social Mobility in the Early Roman Empire: The Evidence of the Imperial Freedmen and Slaves. In *Studies in Ancient Society*, ed. M. I. Finley, 121–40. London.

Webb, R. 1997. Imagination and the Arousal of the Emotions in Greco-Roman Rhetoric. In *The Passions in Roman Thought and Literature*, ed. S. M. Braund and C. Gill, 112–27. Cambridge.

Wells, P. S. 1980. *Culture Contact and Culture Change*. Cambridge.

————. 1999. *The Barbarians Speak: How the Conquered Peoples Shaped Roman Europe*. Princeton.

West, D. 1969. Multiple-Correspondence Similes in the *Aeneid*. *JRS* 59:40–49.

West, D. A. 1975–76. Cernere erat: The Shield of Aeneas. *PVS* 15:1–7. Reprinted in *Oxford Readings in Vergil's* Aeneid, ed. S. J. Harrison (Oxford, 1990), 295–304.

West, G. S. 1975. Women in Vergil's Aeneid. PhD Diss., University of California, Los Angeles.

————. 1980. Caeneus and Dido. *TAPhA* 110:315–24.

————. 1983. Andromache and Dido. *AJPh* 104:257–67.

Whitby, M., ed. 1987. *Homo Viator: Classical Essays for John Bramble.* Bristol.

White, P. 1993. *Promised Verse: Poets in the Society of Augustan Rome.* Cambridge, MA.

Wigodsky, M. 1972. *Vergil and Early Latin Poetry.* Hermes Einzelschriften 24. Wiesbaden.

————. 1995. The Alleged Impossibility of Philosophical Poetry. In *Philodemus and Poetry: Poetic Theory and Practice in Lucretius, Philodemus, and Horace,* ed. D. Obbink, 58–68. Oxford.

Wilhelm, R. M. 1992. Dardanus, Aeneas, Augustus, and the Etruscans. In *The Two Worlds of the Poet: New Perspectives on Vergil,* ed. R. M. Wilhelm and H. Jones, 129–45.

Wilhelm, R. M., and H. Jones, eds. 1992. *The Two Worlds of the Poet: New Perspectives on Vergil.* Detroit.

Williams, G. W. 1968. *Tradition and Originality in Roman Poetry.* Oxford.

————. 1983. *Technique and Ideas in the* Aeneid. New Haven.

Williams, R. D., ed. 1960a. *P. Vergillii Maronis Aeneidos Liber Quintus.* Oxford.

————. 1960b. The Pictures on Dido's Temple (*Aeneid* I. 450–93). *CQ* n.s., 10:145–51. Reprinted in *Oxford Readings in Vergil's* Aeneid, ed. S. J. Harrison (Oxford, 1990), 37–45.

————. ed. 1962. *P. Vergilii Maronis Aeneidos Liber Tertius.* Oxford.

————. 1964. The Sixth Book of the *Aeneid.* *G&R* n.s. 11:48–63. Reprinted in *Oxford Readings in Vergil's* Aeneid, ed. S. J. Harrison (Oxford, 1990), 191–207.

————. 1971. Dido's Reply to Aeneas. In *Vergiliana: Recherches sur Virgile,* ed. H. Bardon and R. Verdiere, 422–28. Leiden.

————. ed. 1972. *The* Aeneid *of Virgil: Books 1–6 Edited with Introduction and Notes.* London.

————. ed. 1973. *The* Aeneid *of Virgil: Books 7–12 Edited with Introduction and Notes.* London.

Wiltshire, S. F. 1989. *Public and Private in Vergil's* Aeneid. Amherst, MA.

————. 1999. The Man Who Was Not There: Aeneas and Absence in *Aeneid* 9. In *Vergil's Aeneid: An Interpretive Guide,* ed. C. Perkell, 162–77. Norman, OK.

Wiseman, T. P. 1974. Legendary Genealogies in Late-Republican Rome. *G&R* 21:153–64.

Wlosok, A. 1976. Vergils Didotragödie: Ein Beitrag zum Problem des Tragischen in der Aeneis. In *Studien zum antiken Epos,* Beiträge zur klassischen Philologie Heft 72, ed. H. Görgemanns and E. A. Schmidt, 228–50. Meisenheim am Glan.

————. 1983. Zwei Beispiele frühchristlicher "Vergilrezeption": Polemik (Lact., div. inst. 5, 10) und Usurpation (Or. Const. 19–21). In *Res Humanae—Res Divinae: Kleine Schriften,* 437–59. Heidelberg.

————. 1990a. Aeneas Vindex: Ethischer Aspect und Zeitbezug. In *Res Humanae—Res Divinae: Kleine Schriften,* 419–36. Heidelberg.

————. 1990b. *Res Humanae—Res Divinae: Kleine Schriften.* Heidelberg.

Wood, M., and F. Queiroga, eds. 1992. *Current Research on the Romanization of the Western Provinces.* Oxford.

Woodworth, D. C. 1930. Lavinia: An Interpretation. *TAPhA* 61:175–94.

Wyke, M. 1992. Augustan Cleopatras: Female Power and Poetic Authority. In *Roman Poetry and Propaganda in the Age of Augustus,* ed. A. Powell, 98–140.

Zanker, P. 1987. *Augustus und die Macht der Bilder.* Munich.

Zetzel, J. E. G. 1983. Recreating the Canon: Augustan Poetry and the Alexandrian Past. *Critical Inquiry* 10:83–105.

————. 1989. Romane Memento: Justice and Judgment in *Aeneid* 6. *TAPhA* 119:263–84.

Ziolkowski, T. 1993. *Virgil and the Moderns.* Princeton.

List of Passages Cited

Index